That thing over my head in the volume 5 author photo is a temple bell. A friend and I were on a road trip when we discovered it deep in the woods. Since no one was there to see, I stuck my head inside and asked my friend to strike the bell... lo and behold! The bell wasn't very loud on the inside. The whole thing was quite educational -- or childish depending on how you view it.

—Kentaro Yabuki, 2001

Kentaro Yabuki made his manga debut with *Yamato Gensoki*, a short series about a young empress destined to unite the warring states of ancient Japan and the boy sworn to protect her. His next series, *Black Cat*, commenced serialization in the pages of *Weekly Shonen Jump* in 2000 and quickly developed a loyal fan following. *Black Cat* has also become an animated TV series, first hitting Japan's airwaves in the fall of 2005.

BLACK CAT VOL. 6
The SHONEN JUMP Manga Edition

STORY AND ART BY
KENTARO YABUKI

x

x

x

SHONEN JUMP MANGA EDITION

BLACK CAT™

ブラック・キャット

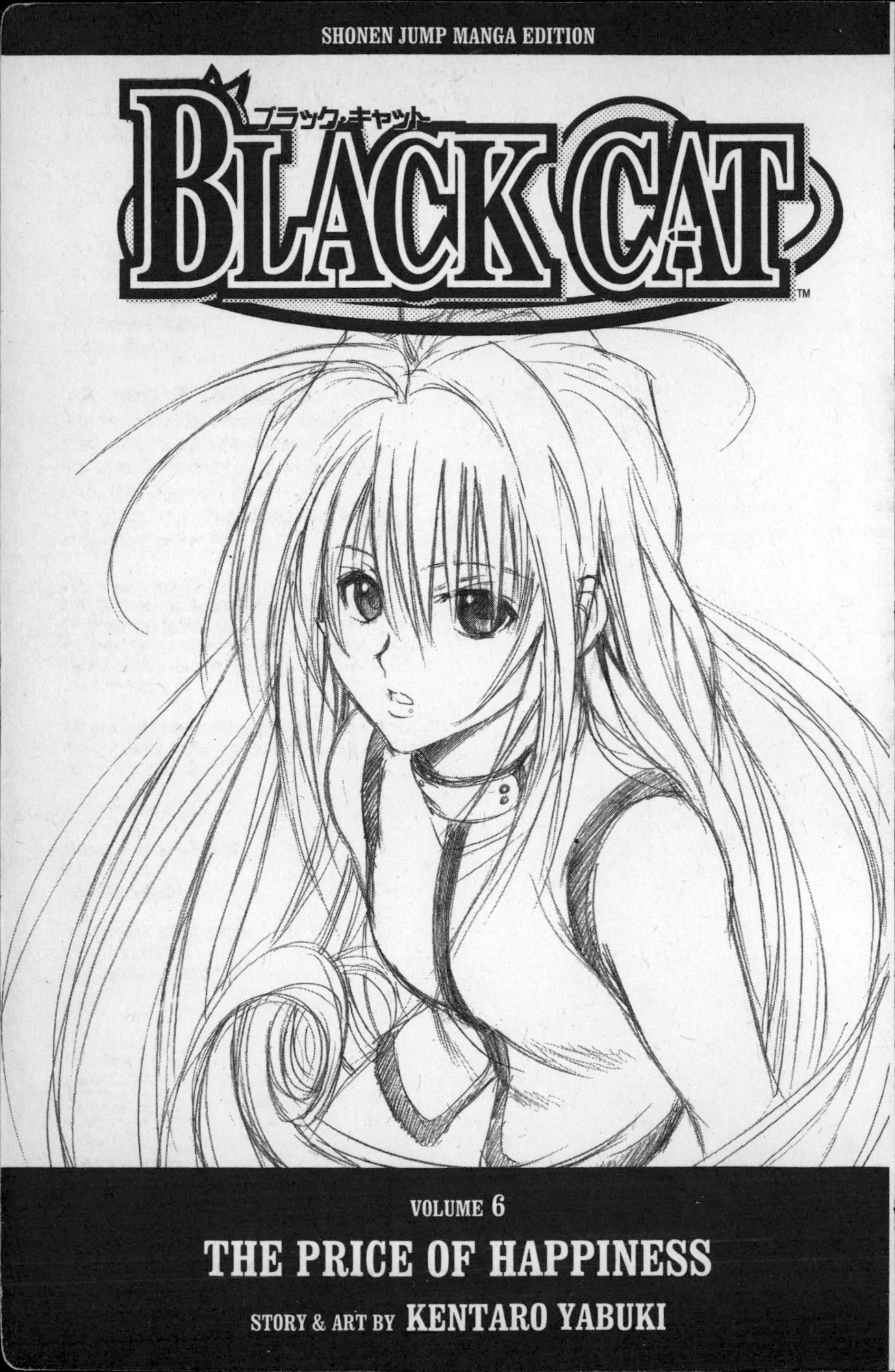

VOLUME 6

THE PRICE OF HAPPINESS

STORY & ART BY **KENTARO YABUKI**

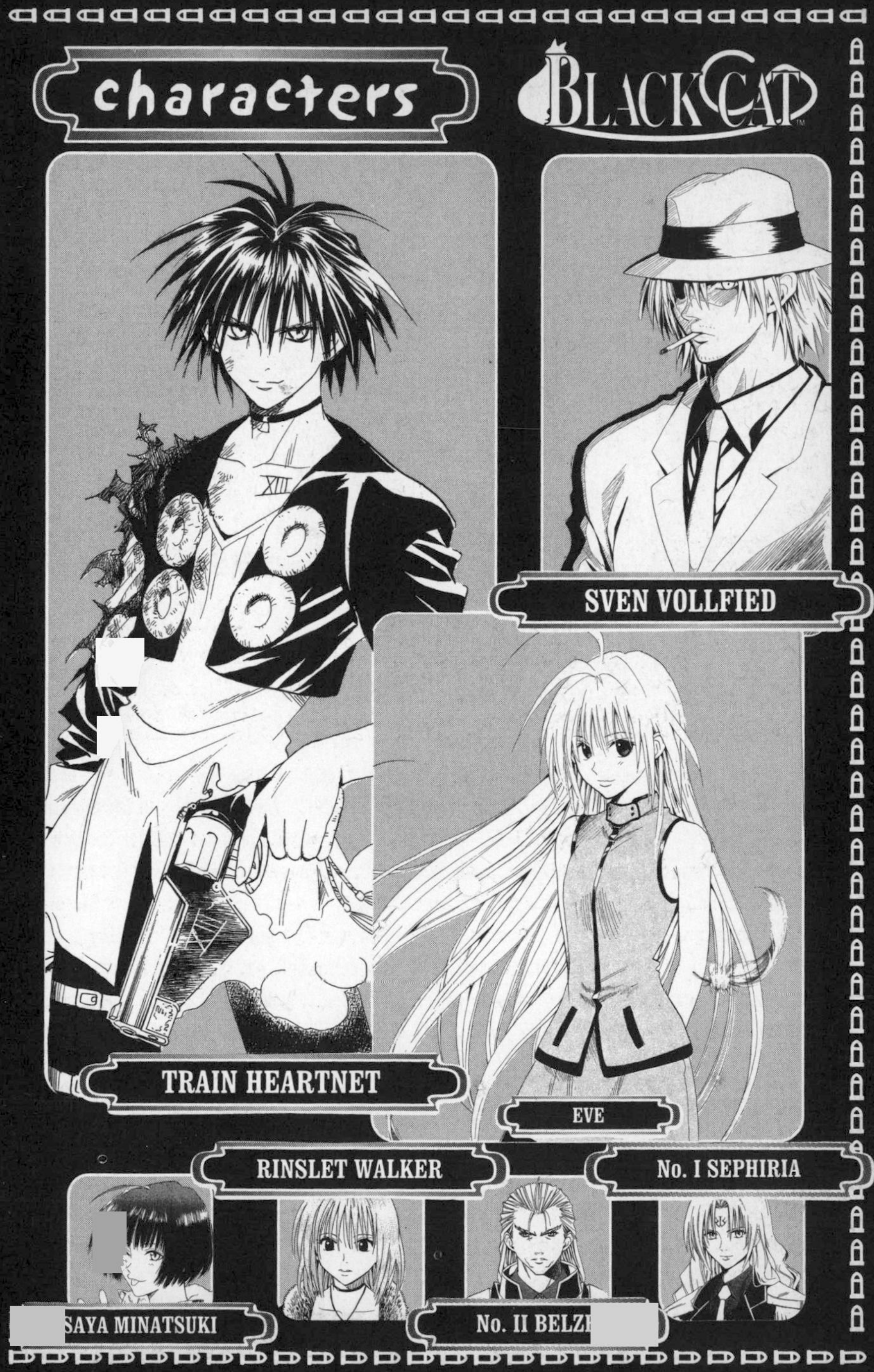
characters
BLACK CAT
SVEN VOLLFIED
TRAIN HEARTNET
EVE
No. I SEPHIRIA
RINSLET WALKER
No. II BELZ
SAYA MINATSUKI

APOSTLES of the STARS

SHIKI

LEON

ECHIDNA

DURHAM

CREED DISKENTH

DOCTOR

KYOKO

CHARDEN

MARO

A fearless "eraser" responsible for the deaths of countless powerful men, Train "Black Cat" Heartnet carries an ornate pistol called "Hades." The gun is engraved with the Roman numeral XIII, Train's agent number as an assassin for the crime syndicate Chronos, a mysterious organization that quietly controls one-third of the world's economy. Two years after his departure from Chronos, Train lives a carefree wanderer's life, working with his partner Sven as a bounty hunter ("sweeper") and pursuing Creed Diskenth, the man who murdered Train's beloved friend Saya. The two sweepers are allied with sexy thief-for-hire Rinslet Walker and Eve, a young girl (and experimental living weapon) whom they rescued from a nanotech lab.

When Train and Creed finally cross paths, Train is shocked to learn that his enemy wants to join forces in a revolution against Chronos and the world. When Train declines, a fierce battle ensues…but ends in a stalemate. Creed and his followers, the Apostles of the Stars, set their grand scheme in motion by staging a mass assassination attempt at a summit of global leaders and Chronos executives. In response, the Chronos elders summon Number I, Sephiria Arks, to lead the campaign against the Apostles. Her first move: Recruiting Train to aid the Numbers in their fight…

BLACK CAT

VOLUME 6 **THE PRICE OF HAPPINESS**

CONTENTS

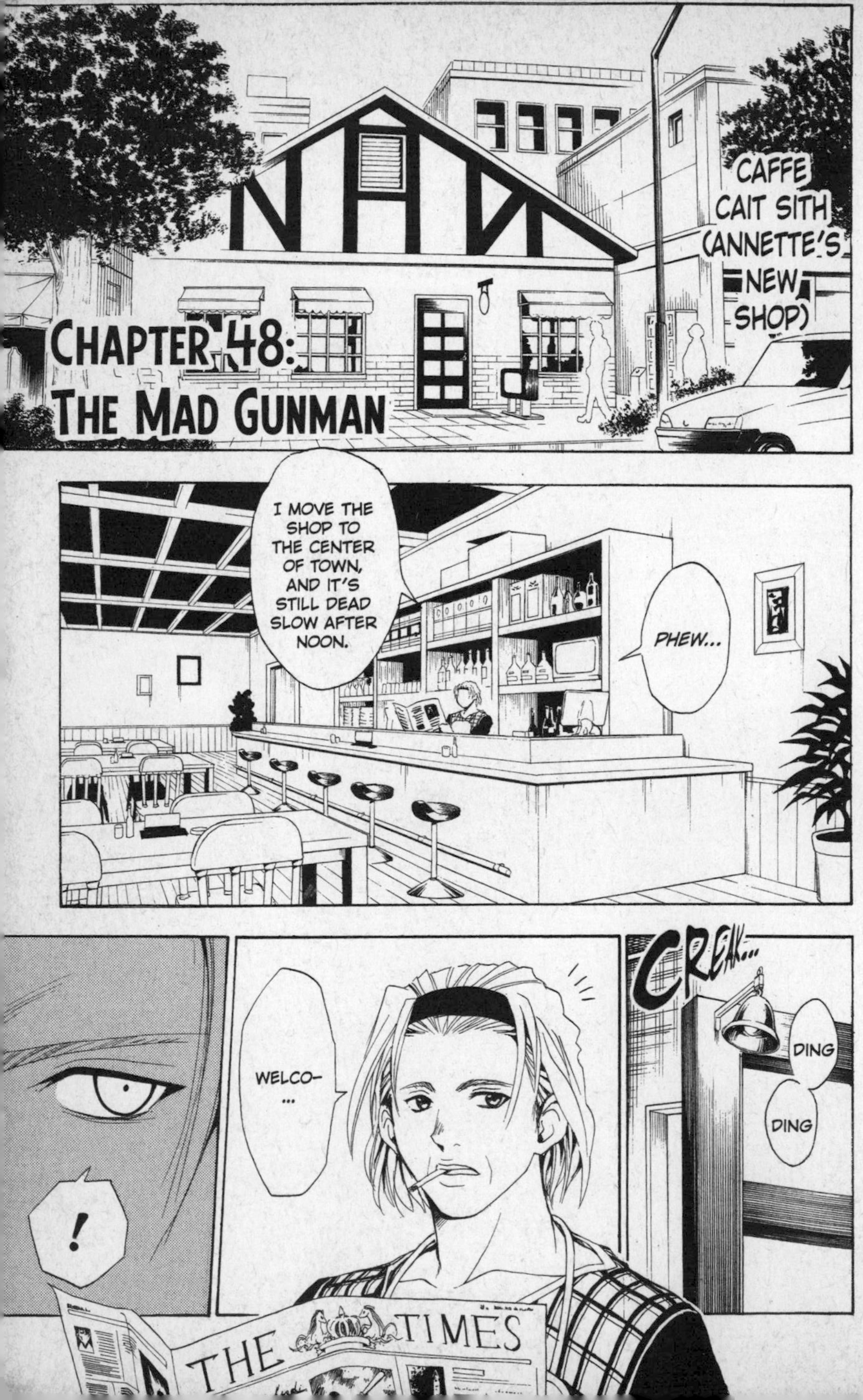
CAFFE CAIT SITH (ANNETTE'S NEW SHOP)
CHAPTER 48: THE MAD GUNMAN
PHEW...
I MOVE THE SHOP TO THE CENTER OF TOWN, AND IT'S STILL DEAD SLOW AFTER NOON.
CREAK...
DING
DING
WELCO- ...
THE TIMES
!

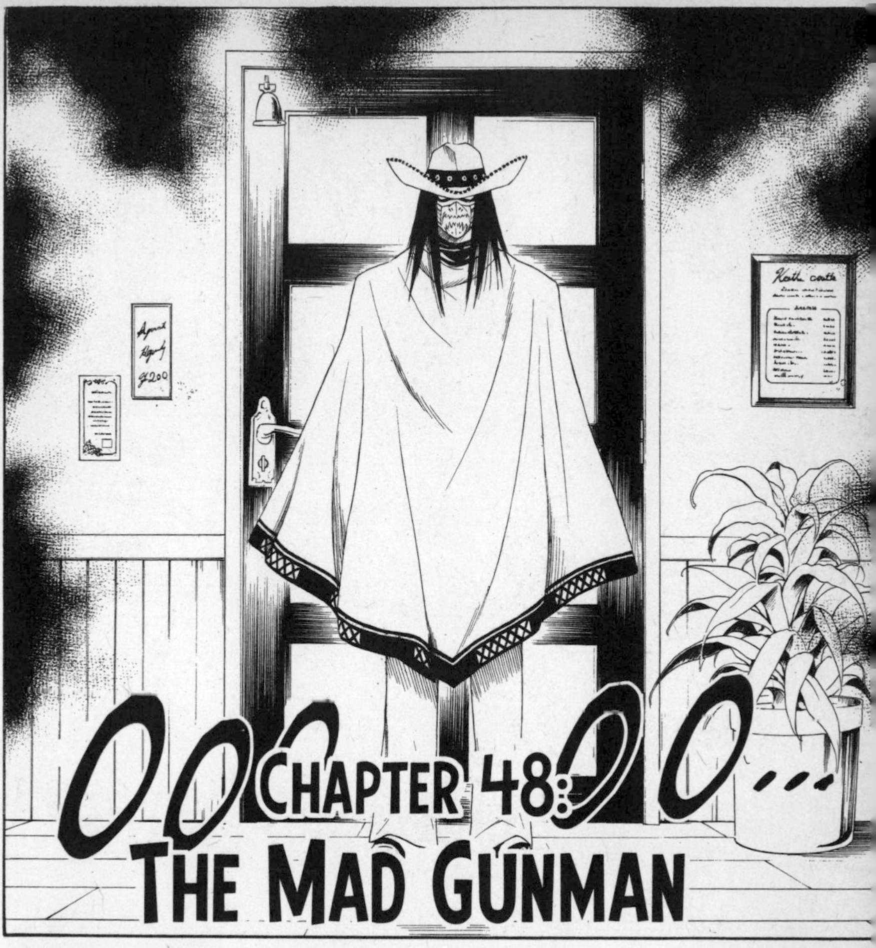
OOOO...
CHAPTER 48:
THE MAD GUNMAN

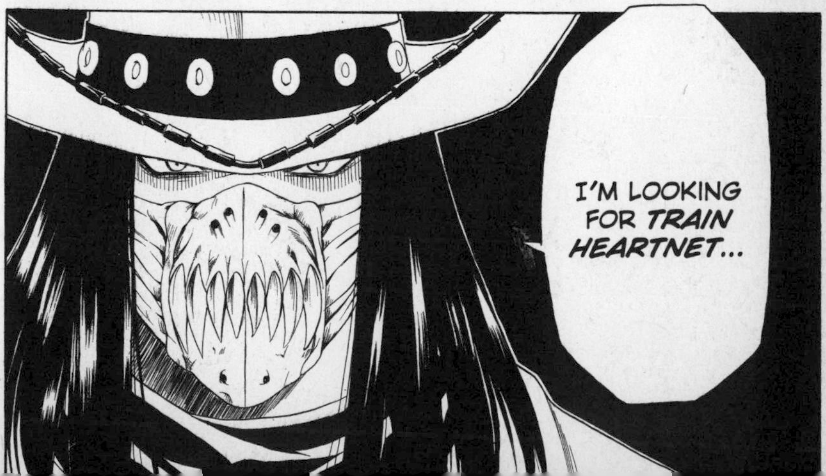
I'M LOOKING FOR TRAIN HEARTNET...

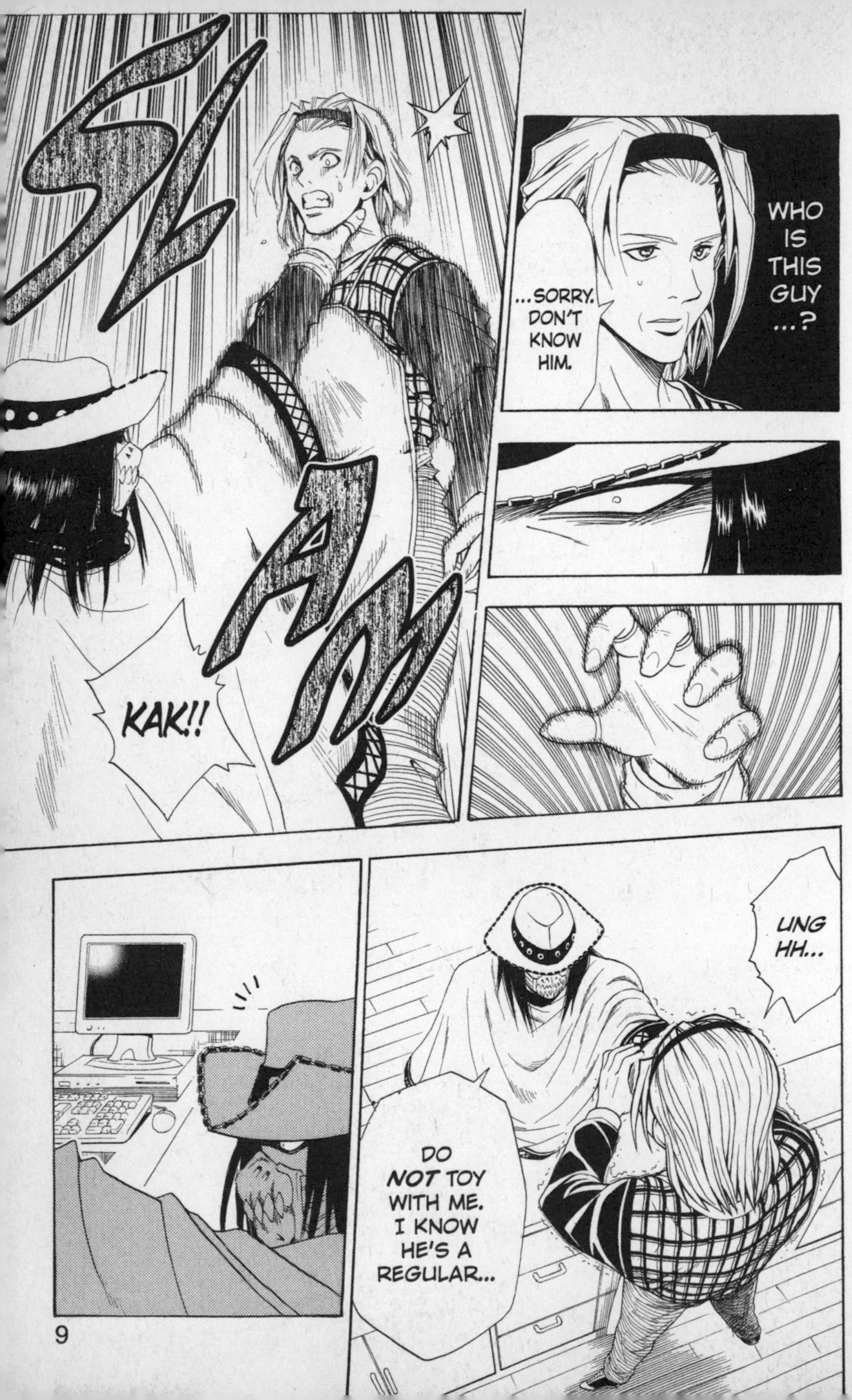
WHO IS THIS GUY...?
...SORRY. DON'T KNOW HIM.
SLAM
KAK!!
UNG HH...
DO *NOT* TOY WITH ME. I KNOW HE'S A REGULAR...

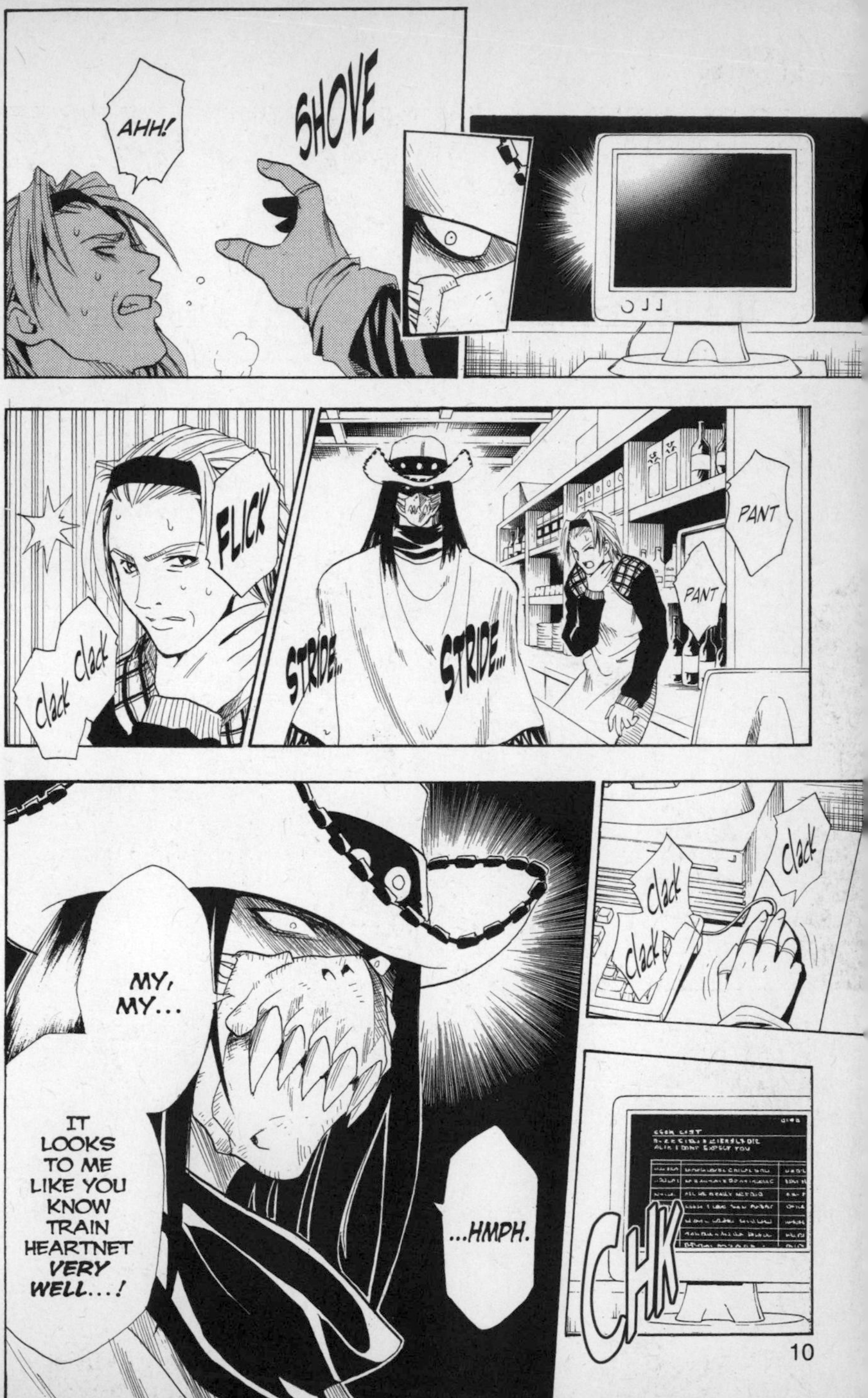
SHOVE
AHH!
PANT
PANT
STRIDE...
STRIDE...
FLICK
clack clack clack
clack
clack clack
MY, MY...
...HMPH.
IT LOOKS TO ME LIKE YOU KNOW TRAIN HEARTNET *VERY WELL*...!
CHK

READ THIS WAY

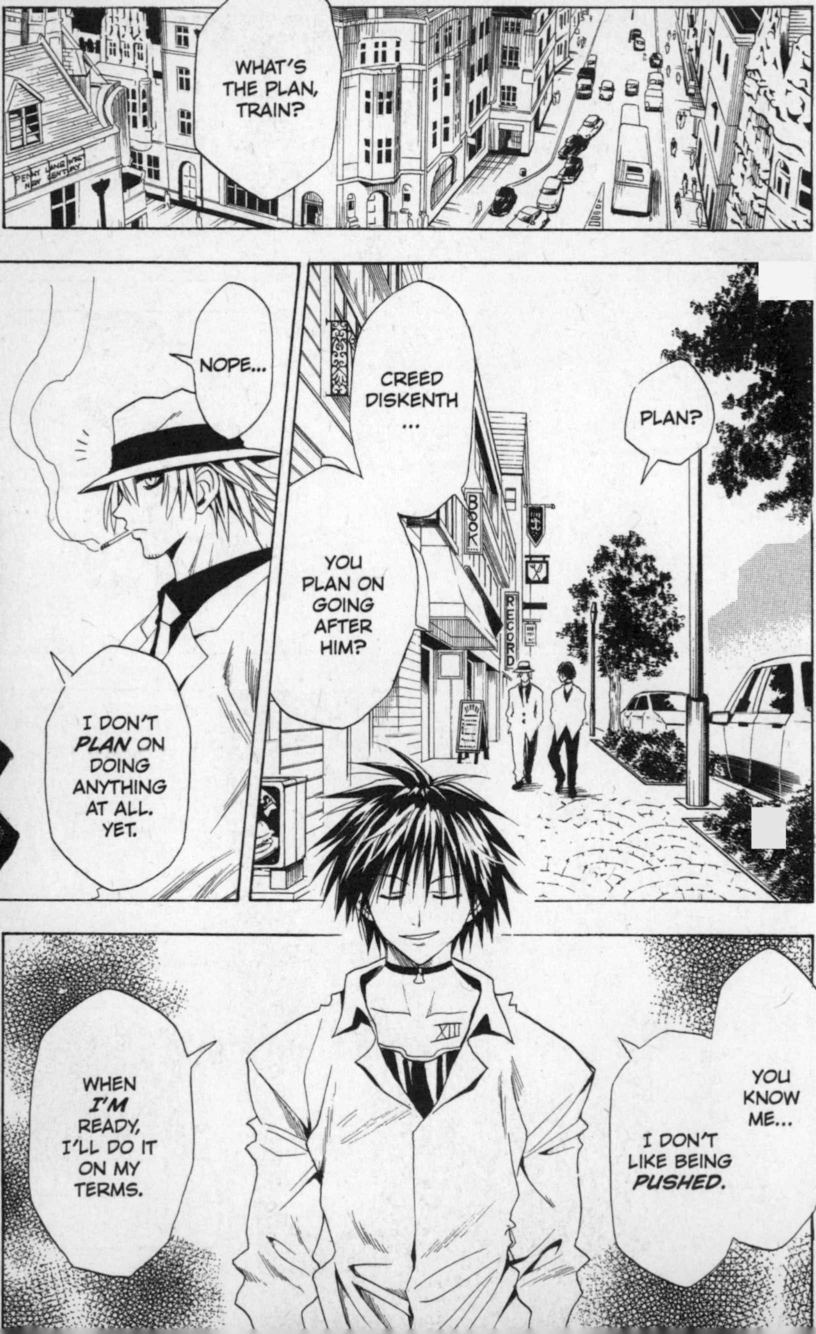
WHAT'S THE PLAN, TRAIN?
PLAN?
CREED DISKENTH ...
BOOK
RECORD
YOU PLAN ON GOING AFTER HIM?
NOPE...
I DON'T *PLAN* ON DOING ANYTHING AT ALL. YET.
YOU KNOW ME...
I DON'T LIKE BEING *PUSHED*.
WHEN *I'M* READY, I'LL DO IT ON MY TERMS.

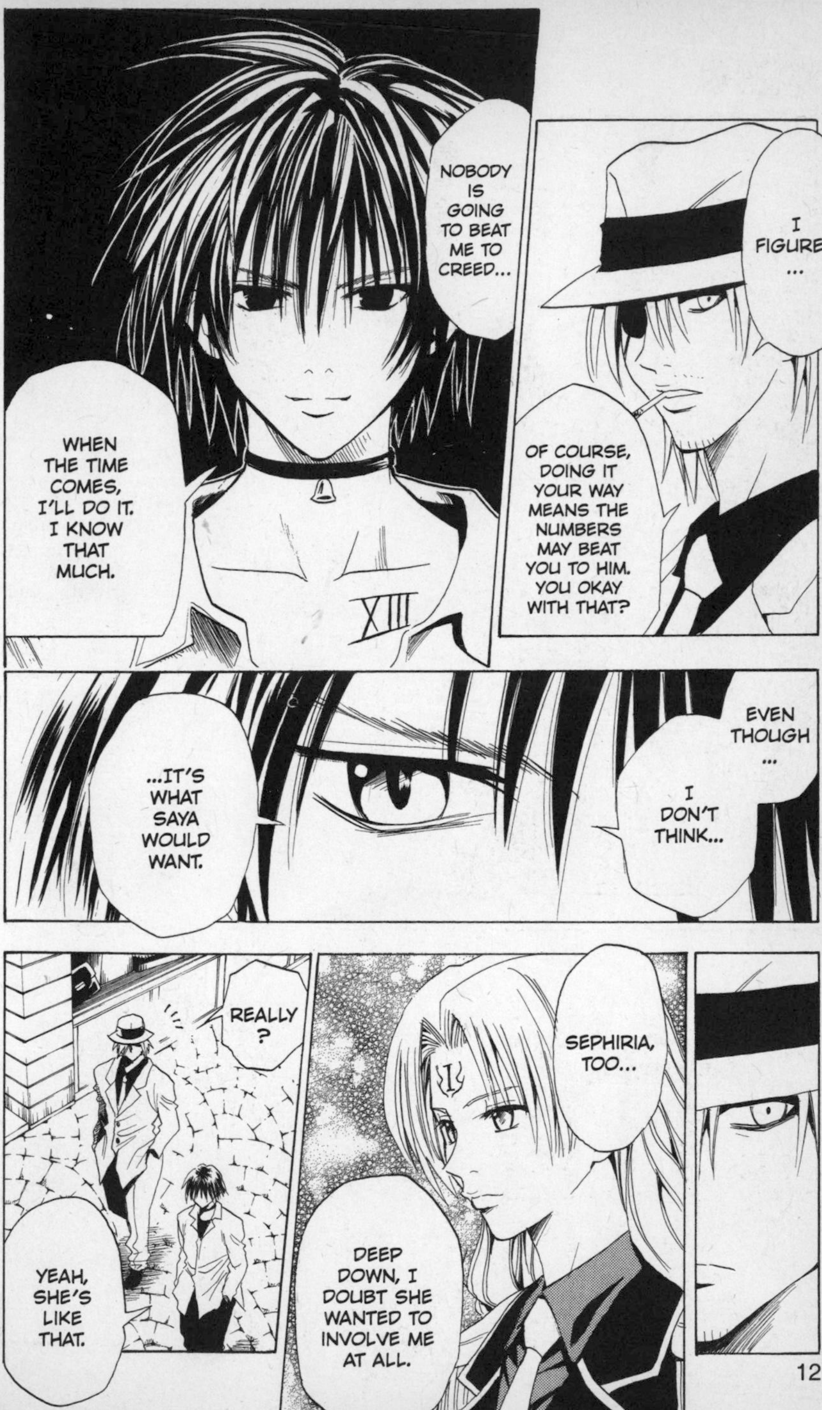
I FIGURED ...
OF COURSE, DOING IT YOUR WAY MEANS THE NUMBERS MAY BEAT YOU TO HIM. YOU OKAY WITH THAT?
NOBODY IS GOING TO BEAT ME TO CREED...
WHEN THE TIME COMES, I'LL DO IT. I KNOW THAT MUCH.
EVEN THOUGH ...
I DON'T THINK...
...IT'S WHAT SAYA WOULD WANT.
SEPHIRIA, TOO...
DEEP DOWN, I DOUBT SHE WANTED TO INVOLVE ME AT ALL.
REALLY ?
YEAH, SHE'S LIKE THAT.

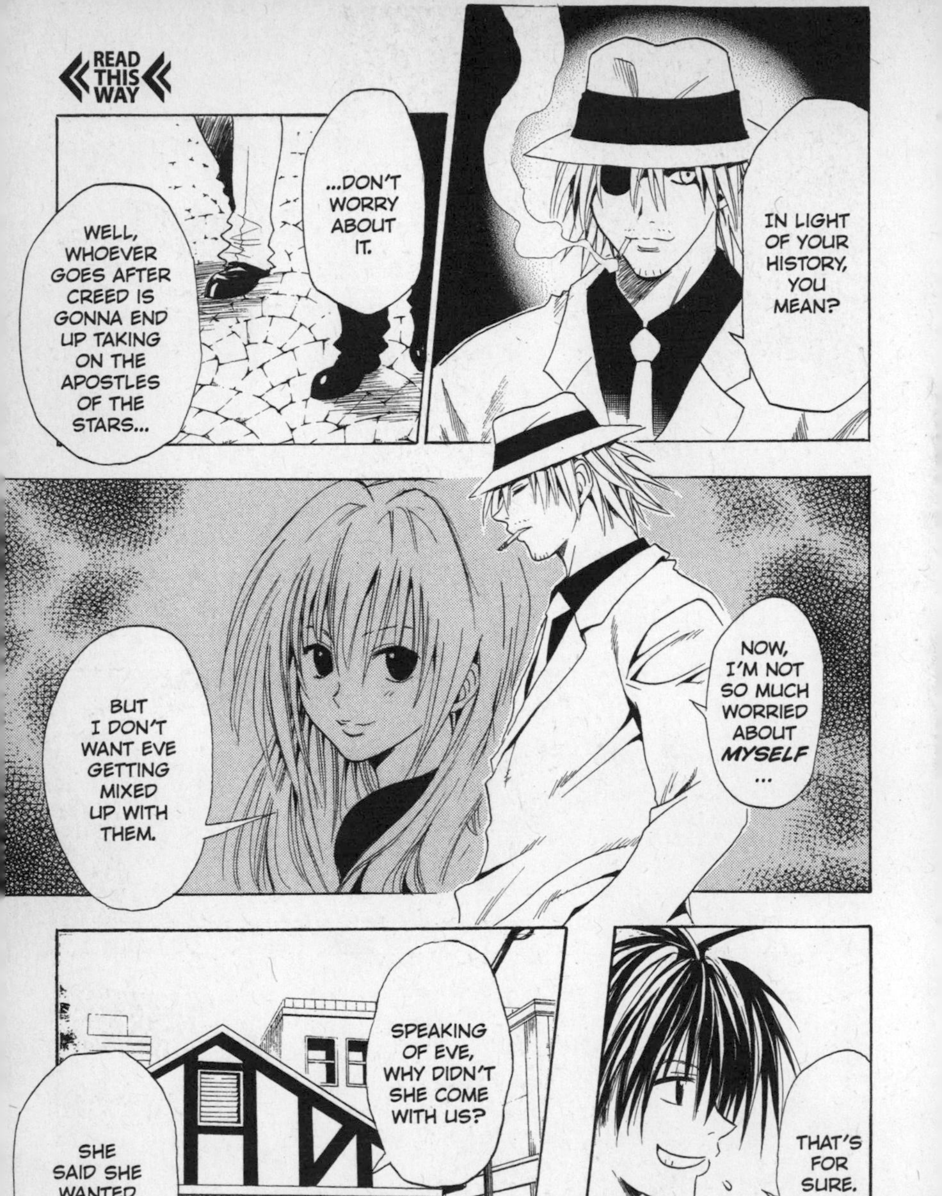
READ THIS WAY
IN LIGHT OF YOUR HISTORY, YOU MEAN?
...DON'T WORRY ABOUT IT.
WELL, WHOEVER GOES AFTER CREED IS GONNA END UP TAKING ON THE APOSTLES OF THE STARS...
NOW, I'M NOT SO MUCH WORRIED ABOUT *MYSELF* ...
BUT I DON'T WANT EVE GETTING MIXED UP WITH THEM.
THAT'S FOR SURE.
SPEAKING OF EVE, WHY DIDN'T SHE COME WITH US?
SHE SAID SHE WANTED TO READ.

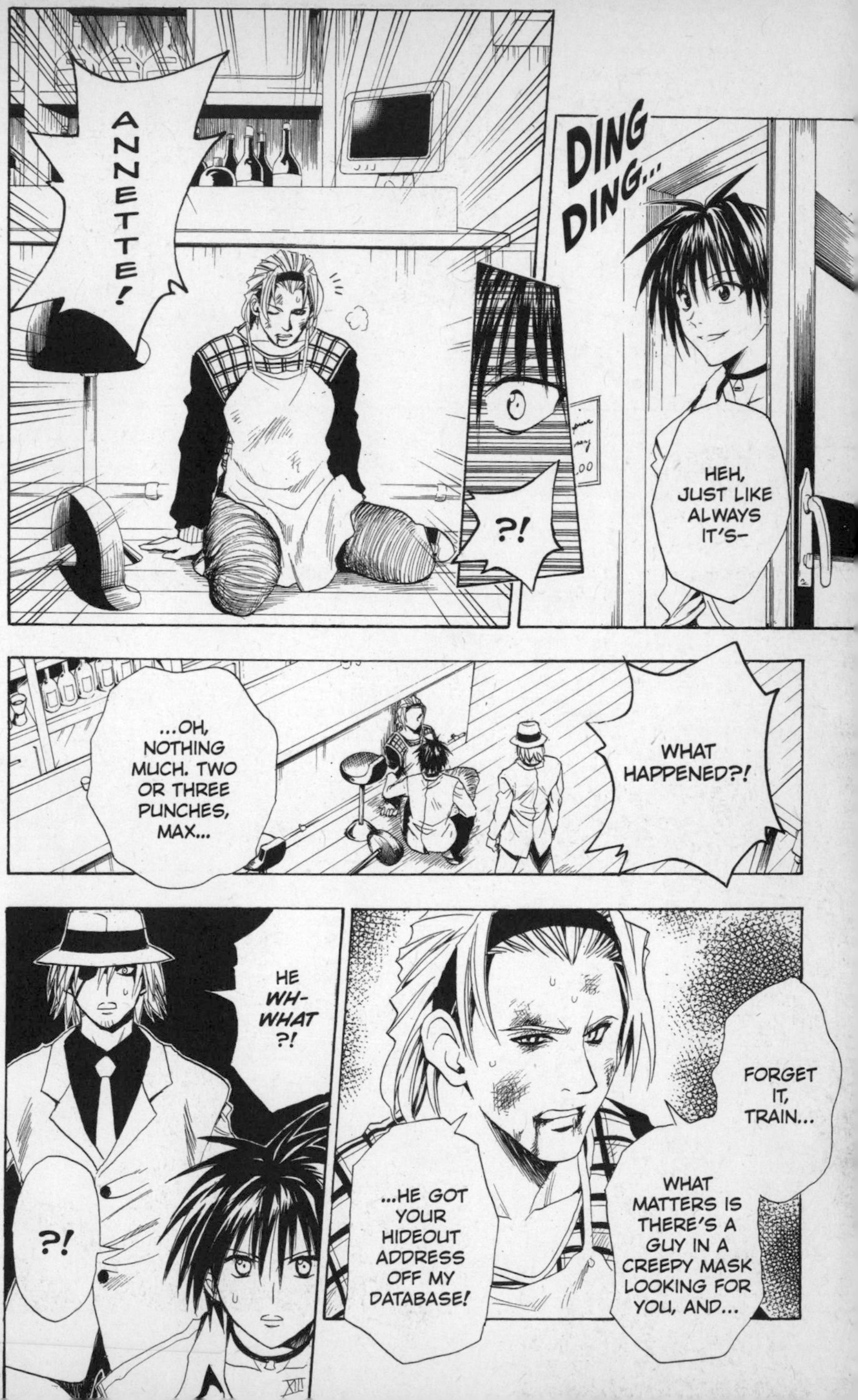
DING DING...
HEH, JUST LIKE ALWAYS IT'S–
?!
ANNETTE!
WHAT HAPPENED?!
...OH, NOTHING MUCH. TWO OR THREE PUNCHES, MAX...
FORGET IT, TRAIN...
WHAT MATTERS IS THERE'S A GUY IN A CREEPY MASK LOOKING FOR YOU, AND...
...HE GOT YOUR HIDEOUT ADDRESS OFF MY DATABASE!
HE WH-WHAT?!
?!

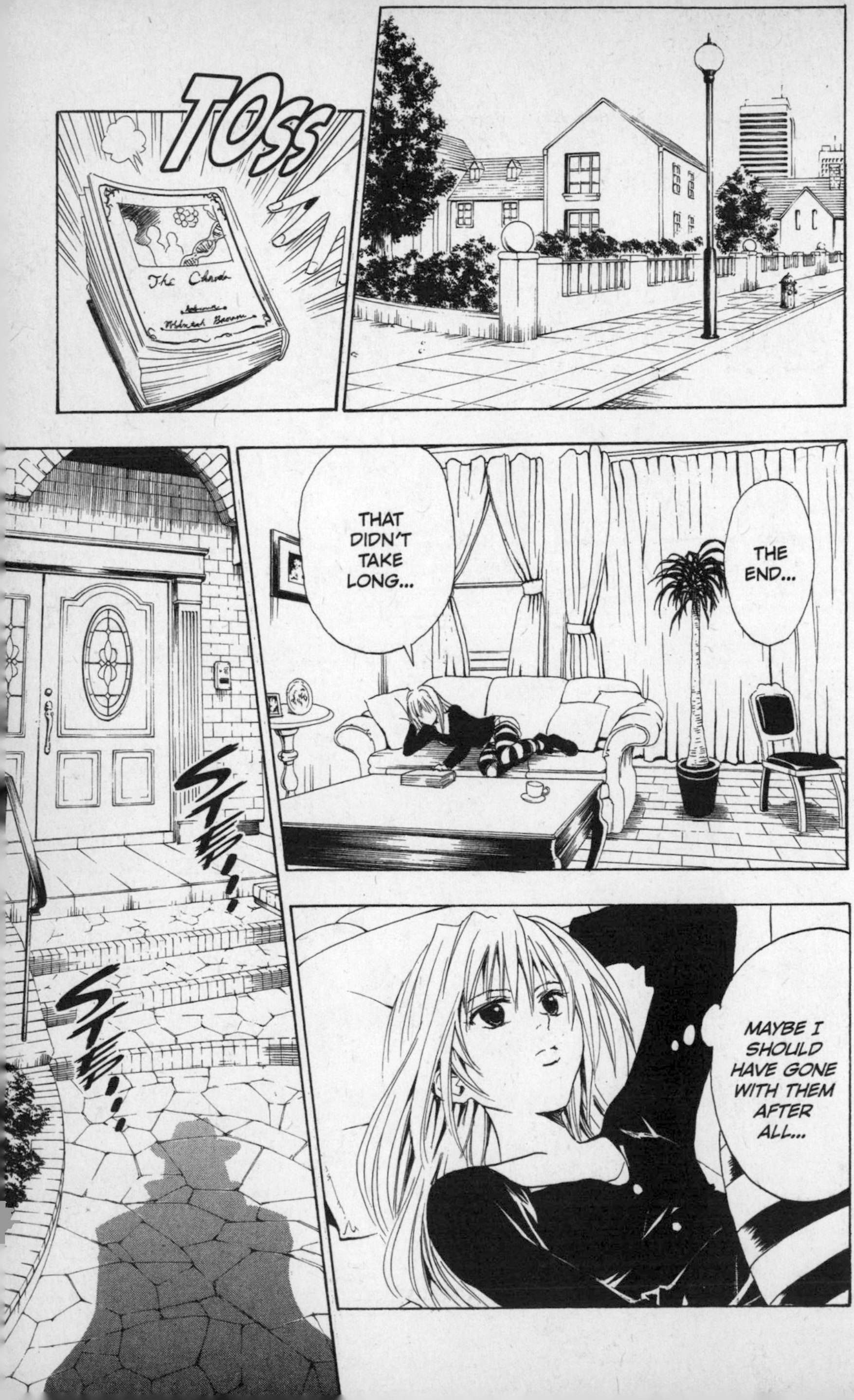
TOSS
THE END...
THAT DIDN'T TAKE LONG...
MAYBE I SHOULD HAVE GONE WITH THEM AFTER ALL...
STEP...
STEP...

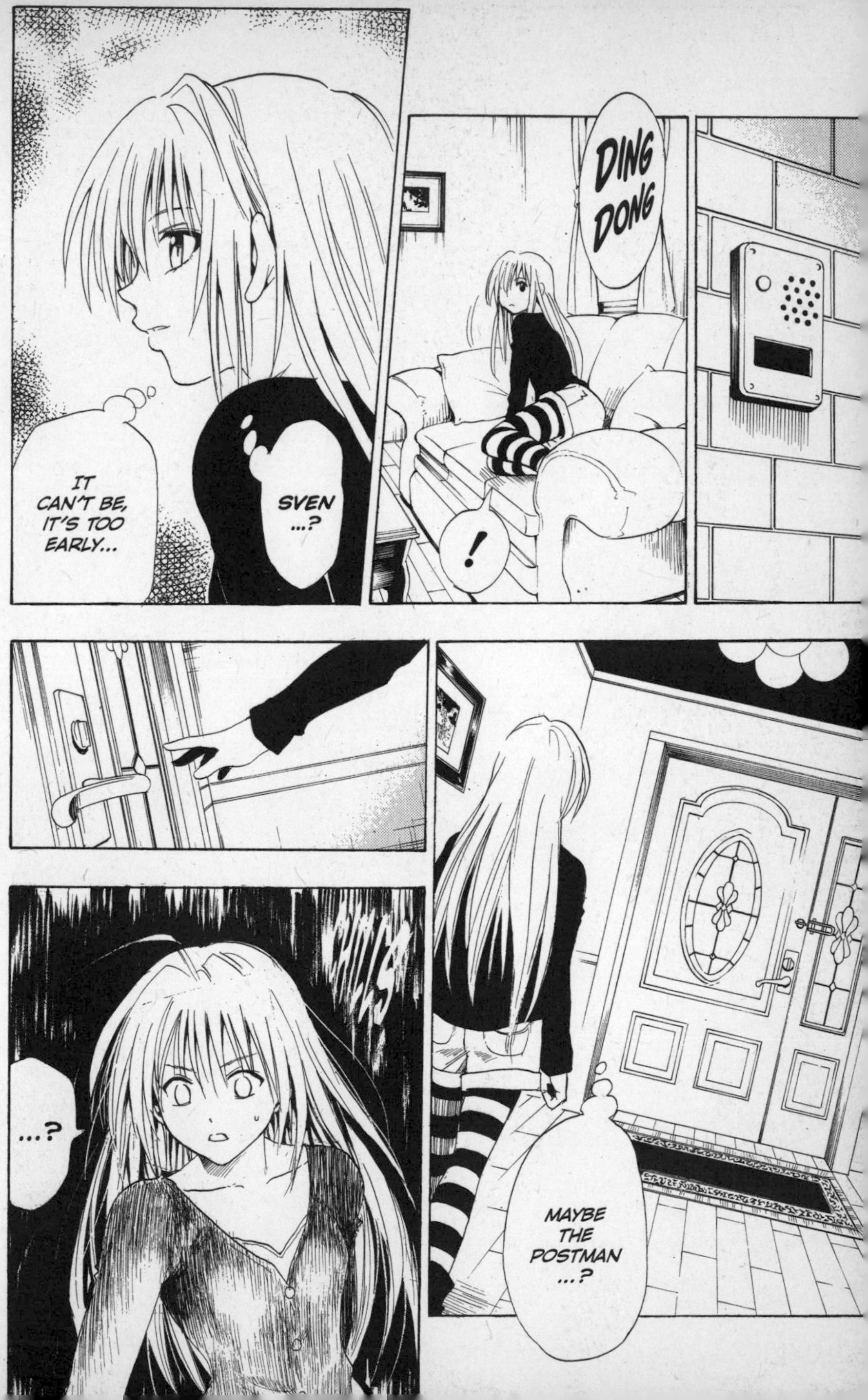
DING DONG
!
SVEN ...?
IT CAN'T BE, IT'S TOO EARLY...
MAYBE THE POSTMAN ...?
...?

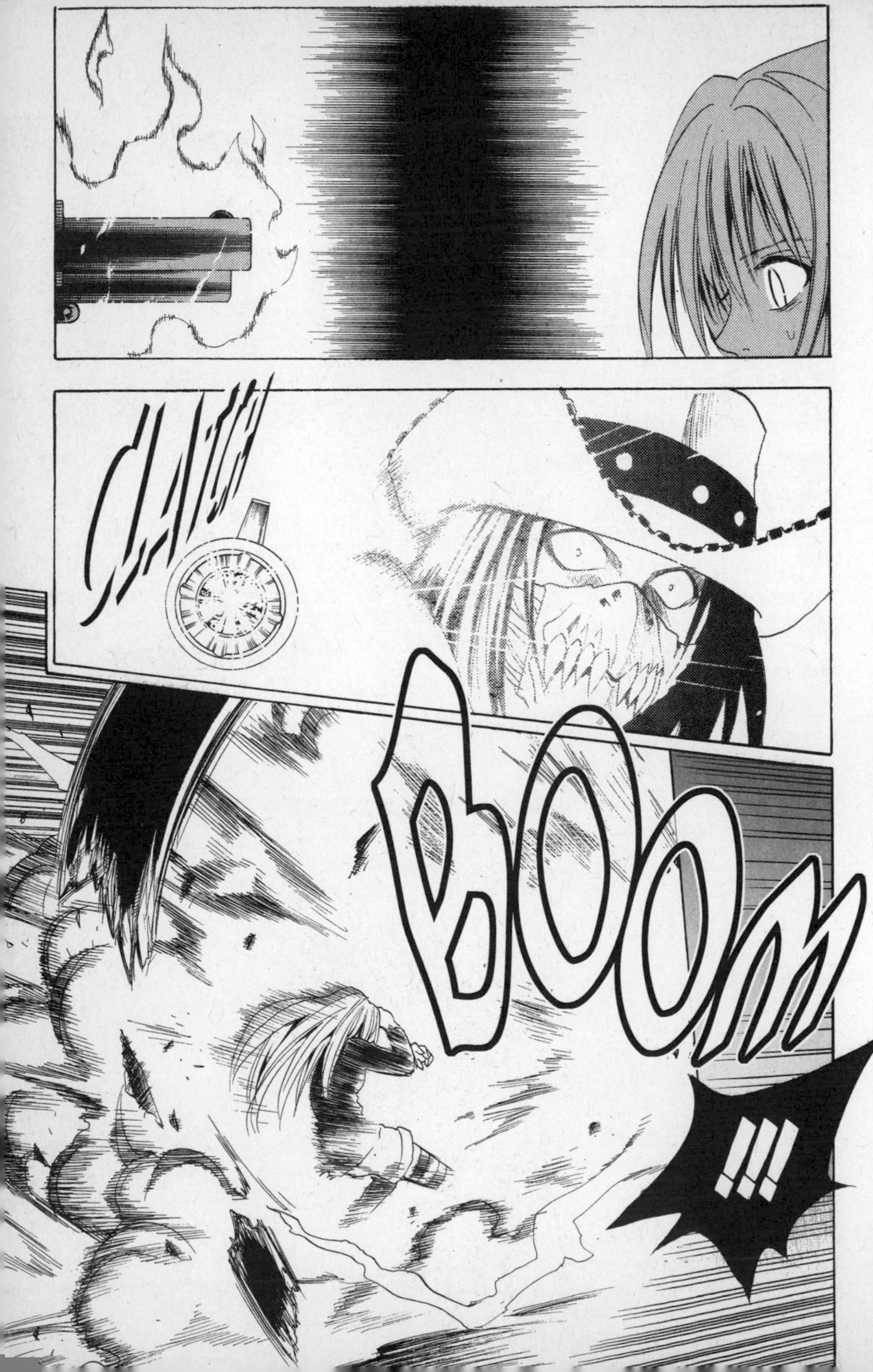
CLATCH
BOOM
!!!

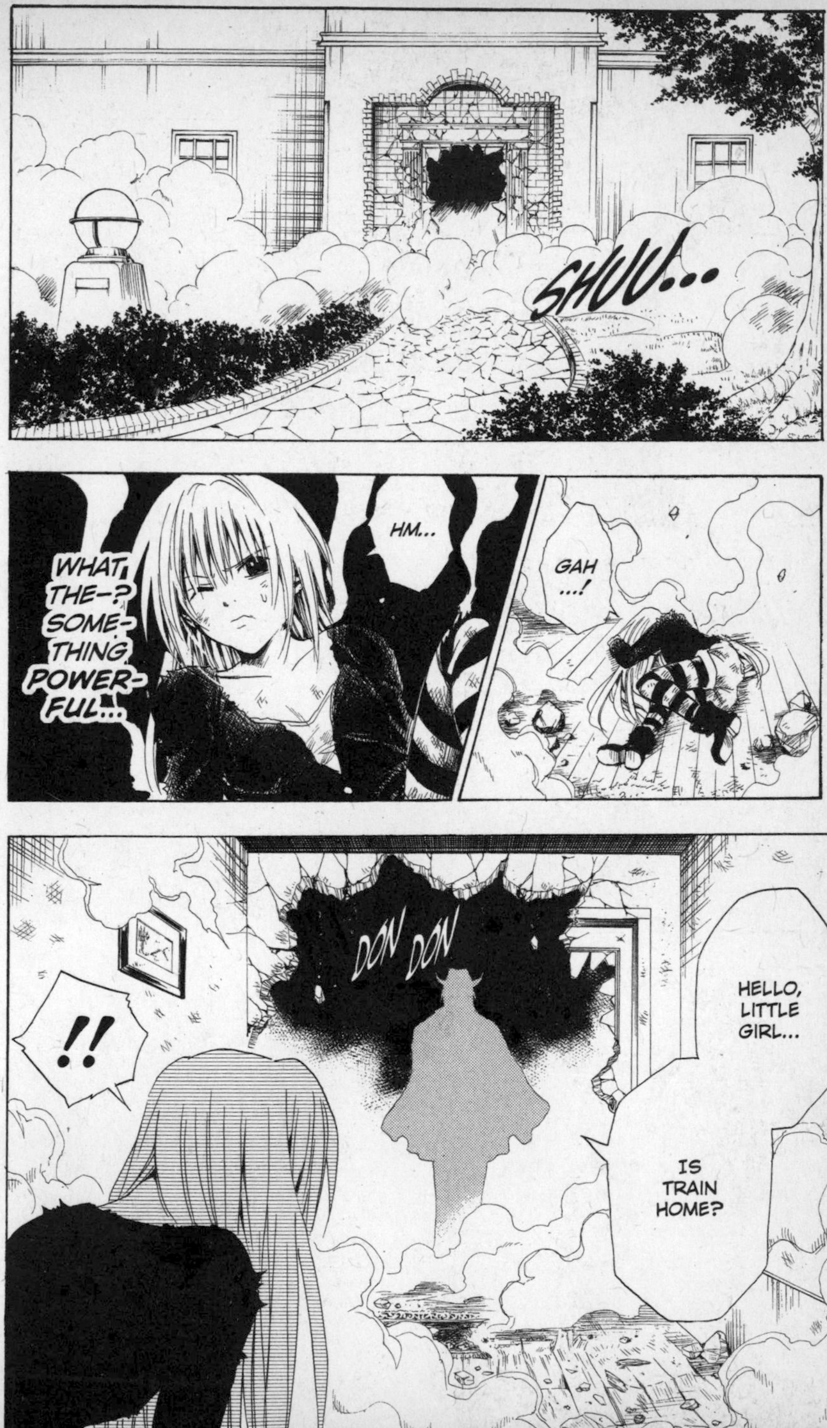
SHUU...
GAH...!
HM...
WHAT THE-? SOMETHING POWERFUL...
HELLO, LITTLE GIRL...
IS TRAIN HOME?
DON DON
!!

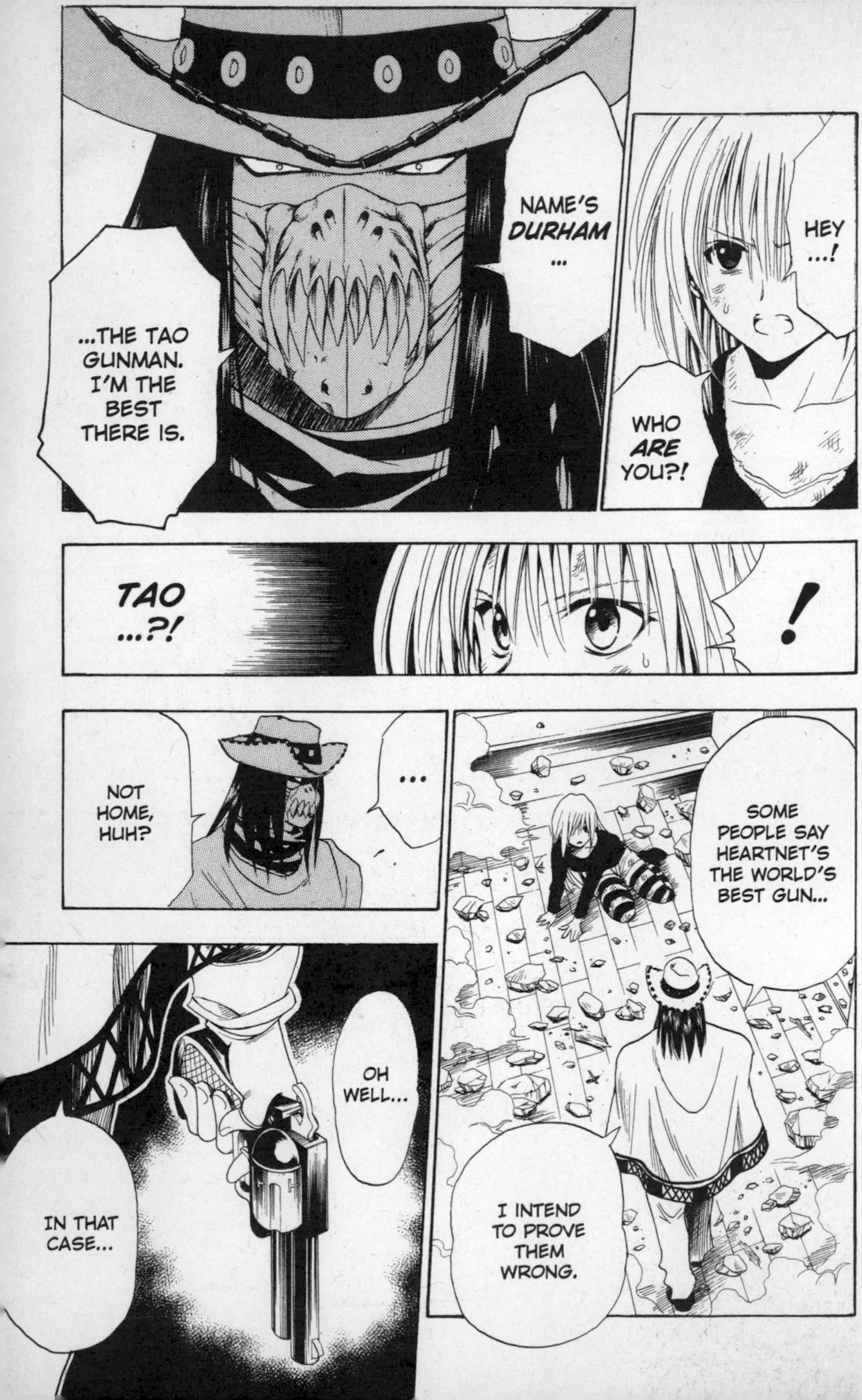
HEY ...!
WHO ARE YOU?!
NAME'S DURHAM ...
...THE TAO GUNMAN. I'M THE BEST THERE IS.
!
TAO ...?!
SOME PEOPLE SAY HEARTNET'S THE WORLD'S BEST GUN...
I INTEND TO PROVE THEM WRONG.
...
NOT HOME, HUH?
OH WELL...
IN THAT CASE...

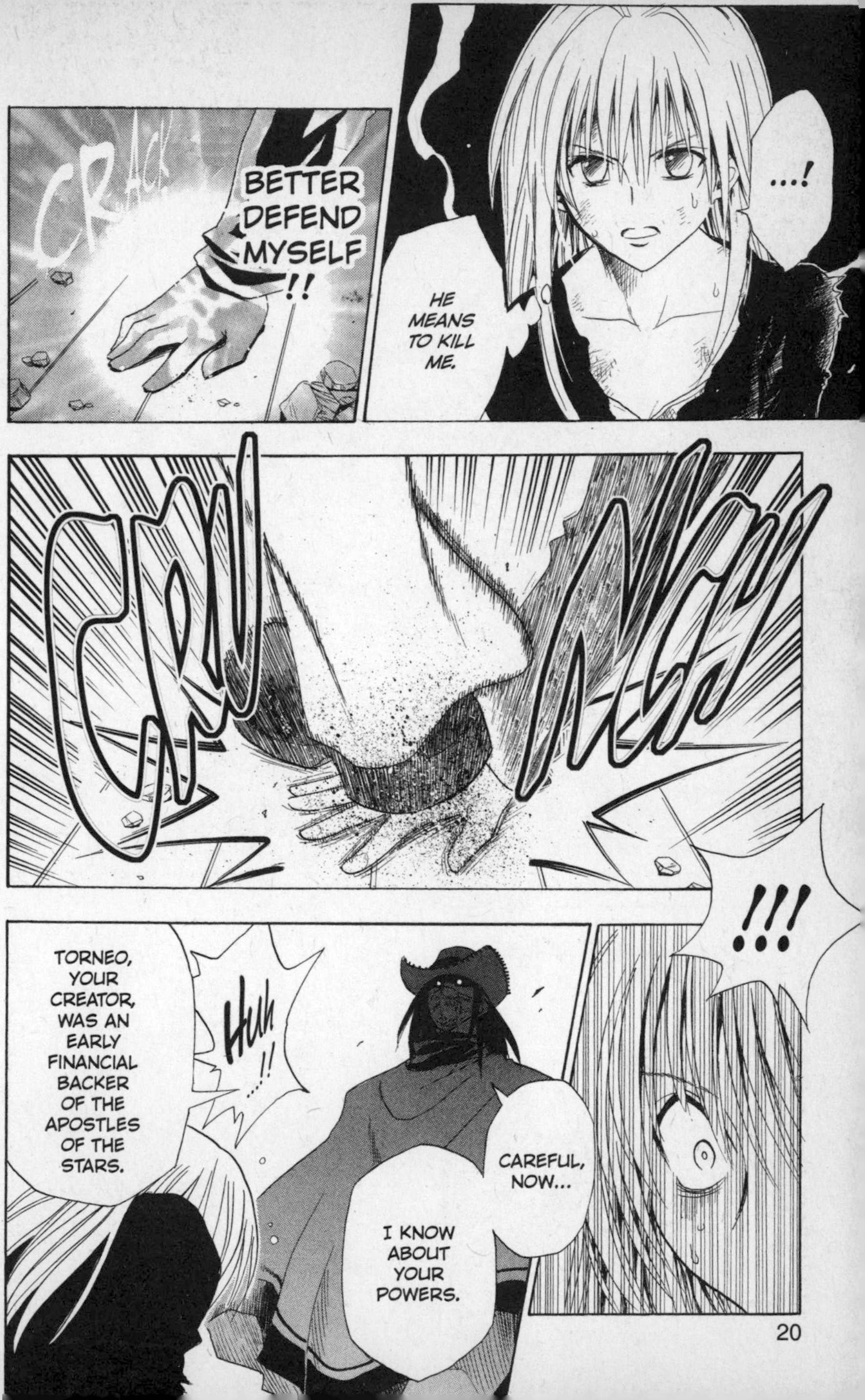

...!
HE MEANS TO KILL ME.
CRACK
BETTER DEFEND MYSELF!!
CRUNCH
!!!
CAREFUL, NOW...
I KNOW ABOUT YOUR POWERS.
Huh...!!
TORNEO, YOUR CREATOR, WAS AN EARLY FINANCIAL BACKER OF THE APOSTLES OF THE STARS.

READ THIS WAY

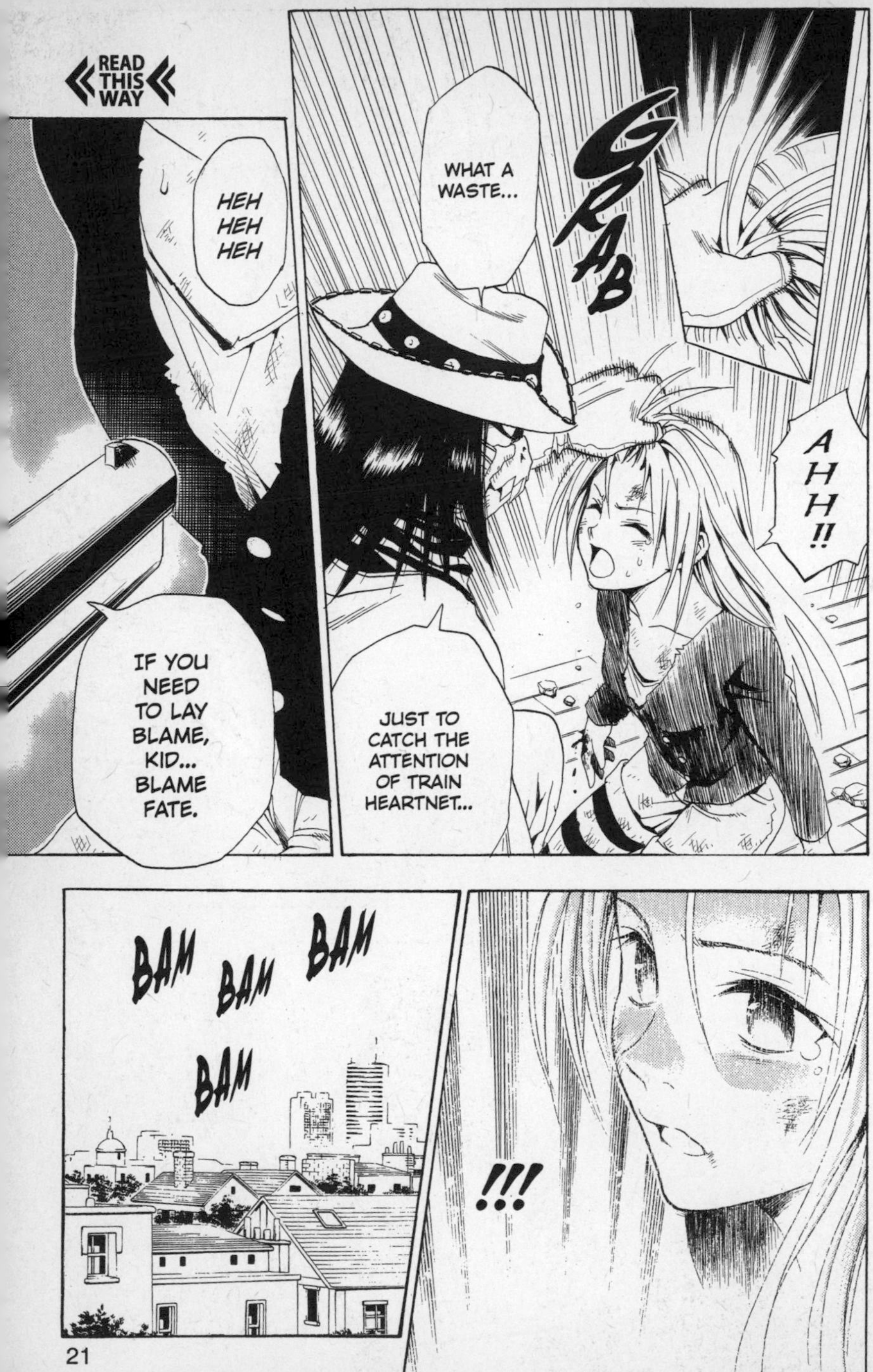
GRAB
AHH!!
WHAT A WASTE...
JUST TO CATCH THE ATTENTION OF TRAIN HEARTNET...
HEH HEH HEH
IF YOU NEED TO LAY BLAME, KID... BLAME FATE.
!!!
BAM
BAM
BAM
BAM

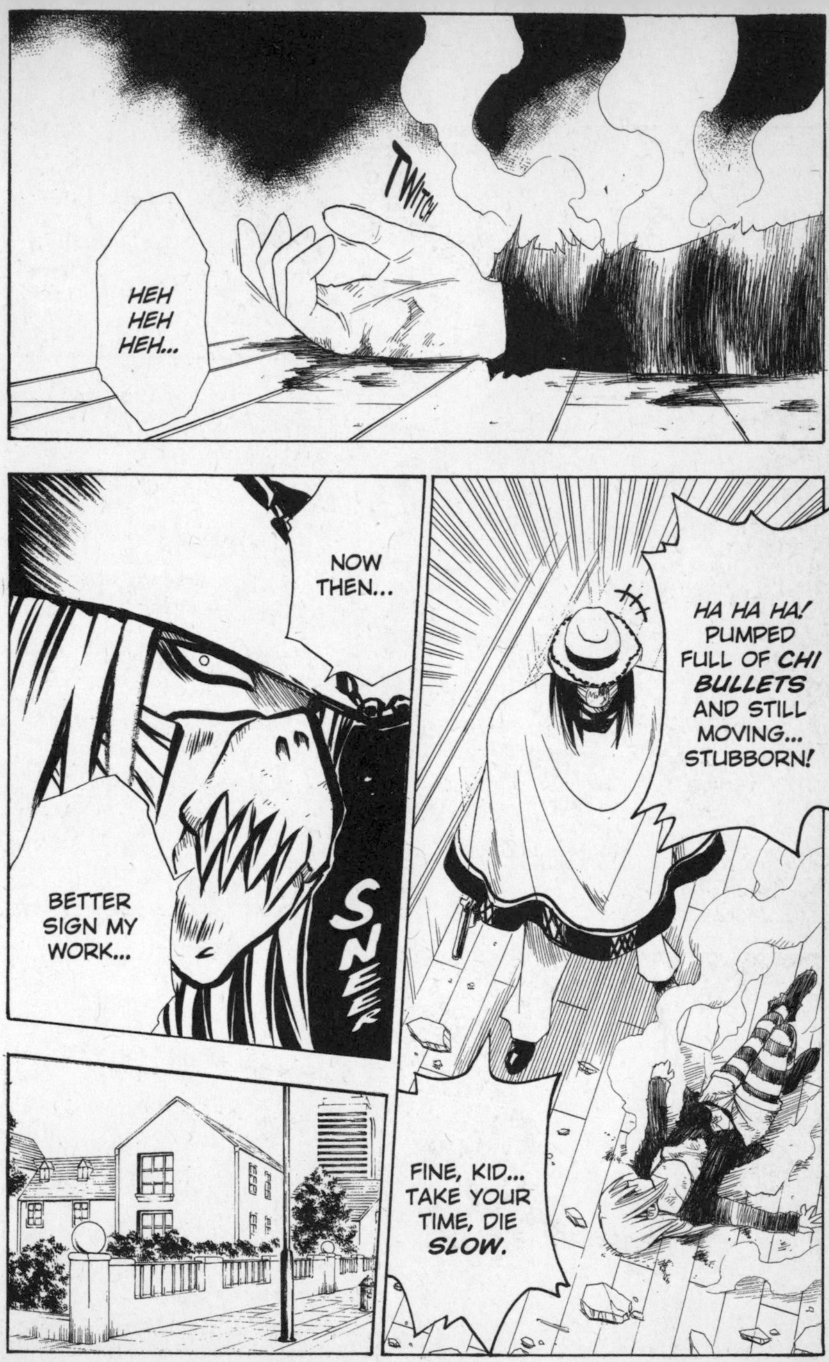
TWITCH
HEH HEH HEH...
HA HA HA! PUMPED FULL OF CHI BULLETS AND STILL MOVING... STUBBORN!
FINE, KID... TAKE YOUR TIME, DIE SLOW.
NOW THEN...
BETTER SIGN MY WORK...
SNEER

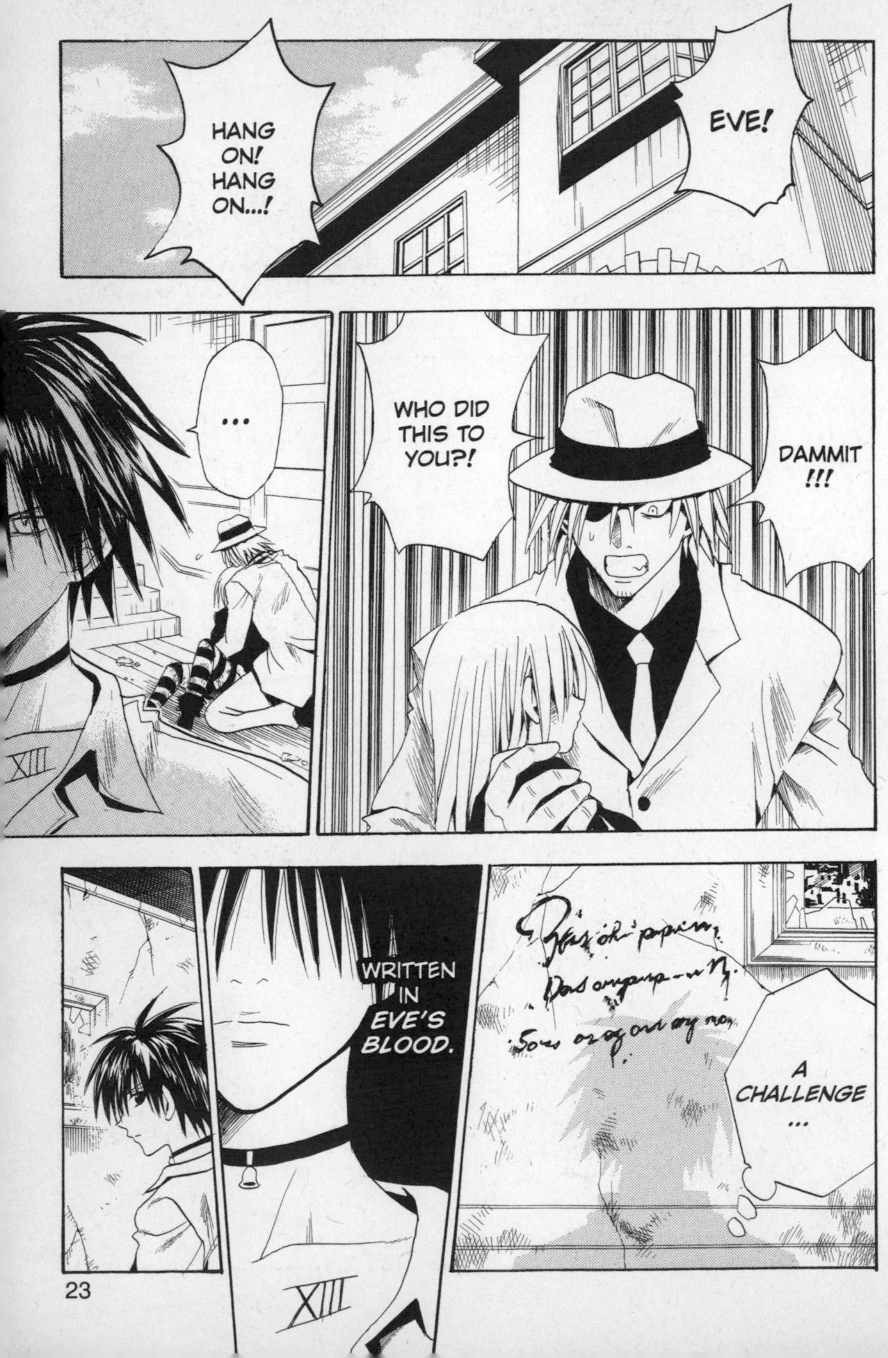
EVE!
HANG ON! HANG ON...!
DAMMIT!!!
WHO DID THIS TO YOU?!
...
A CHALLENGE...
WRITTEN IN EVE'S BLOOD.

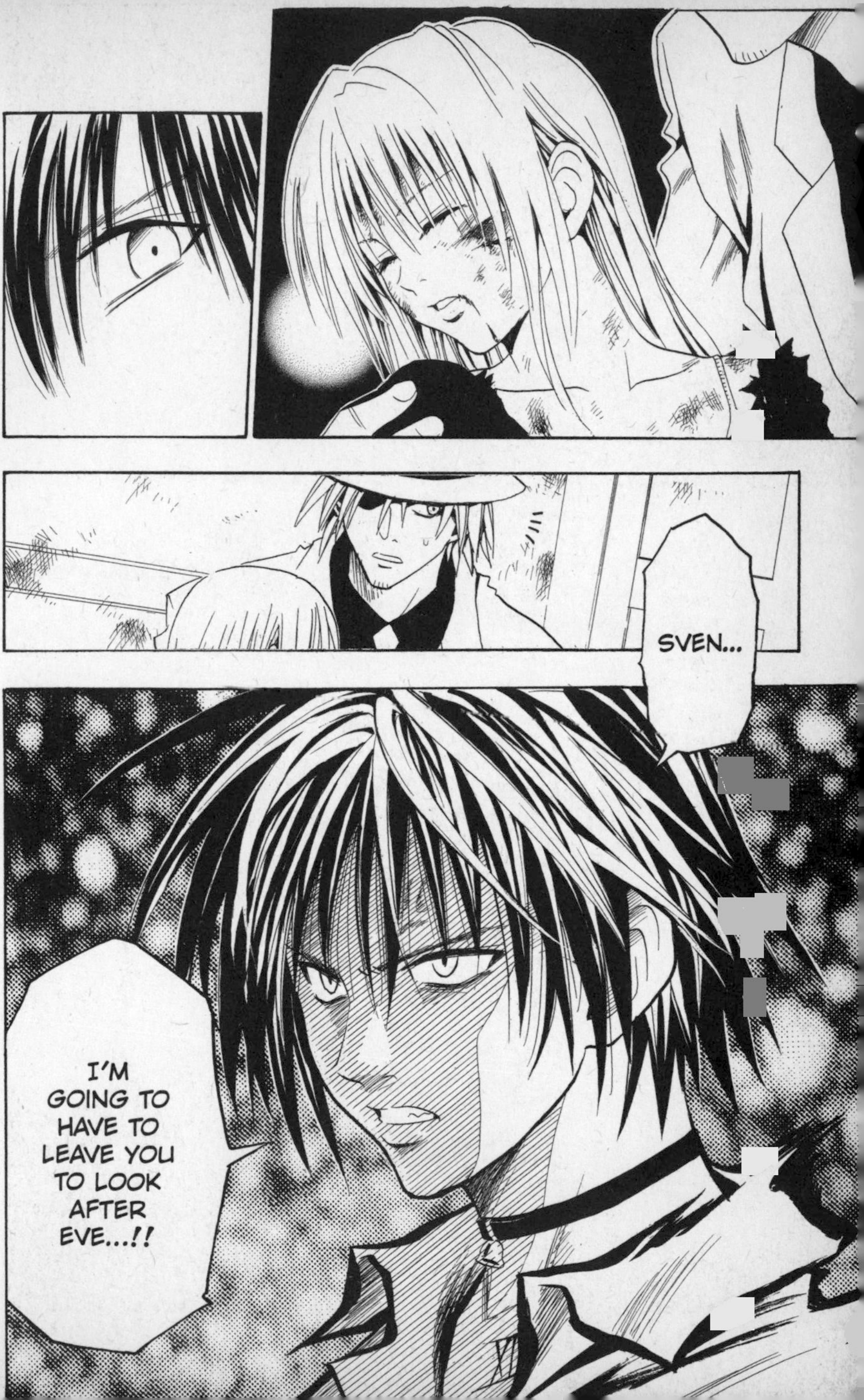
SVEN...
I'M GOING TO HAVE TO LEAVE YOU TO LOOK AFTER EVE...!!

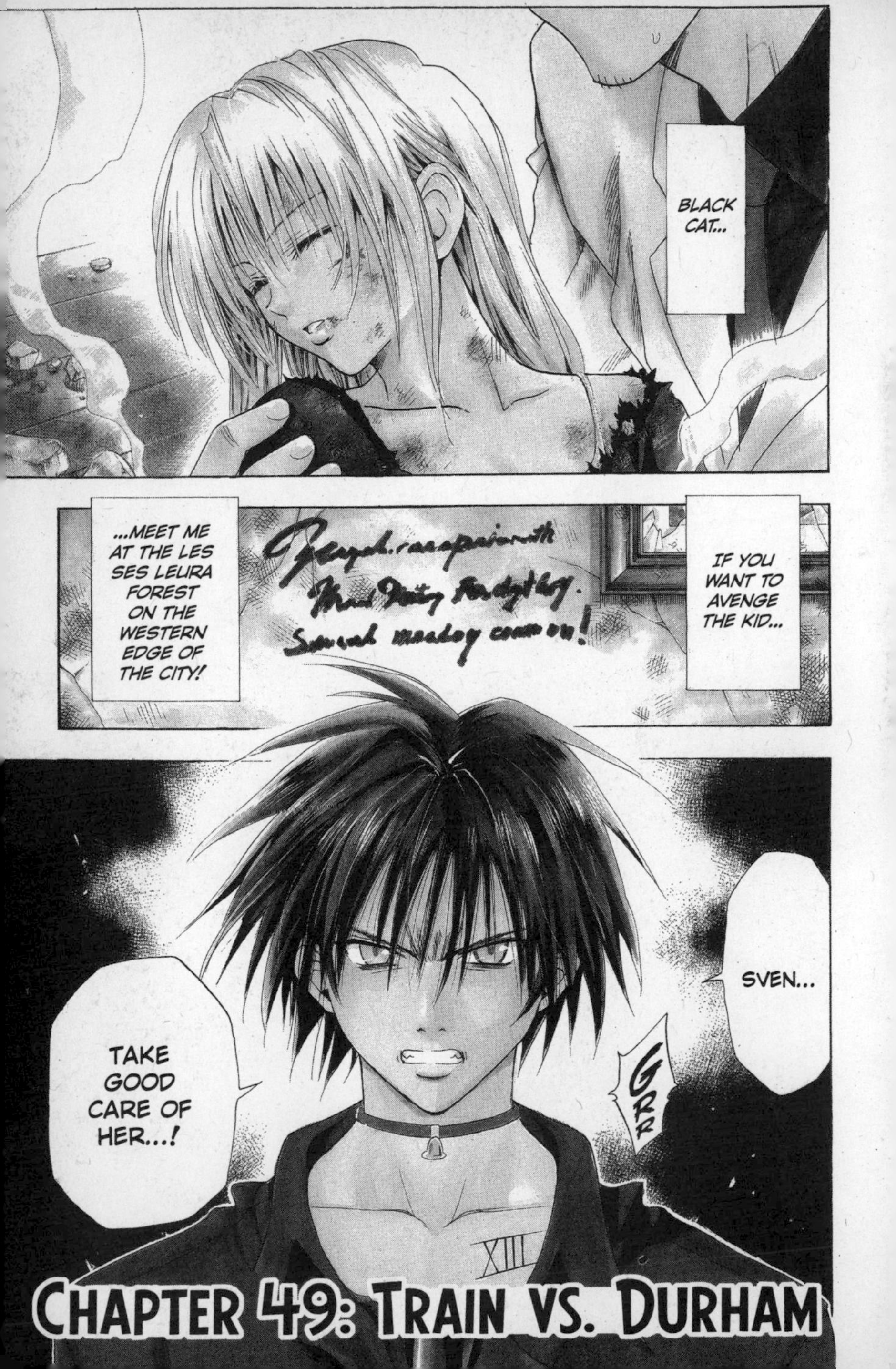
BLACK CAT...
IF YOU WANT TO AVENGE THE KID...
...MEET ME AT THE LES SES LEURA FOREST ON THE WESTERN EDGE OF THE CITY!
SVEN...
GRR
TAKE GOOD CARE OF HER...!

Chapter 49: Train vs. Durham

TRAIN VS. DURHAM

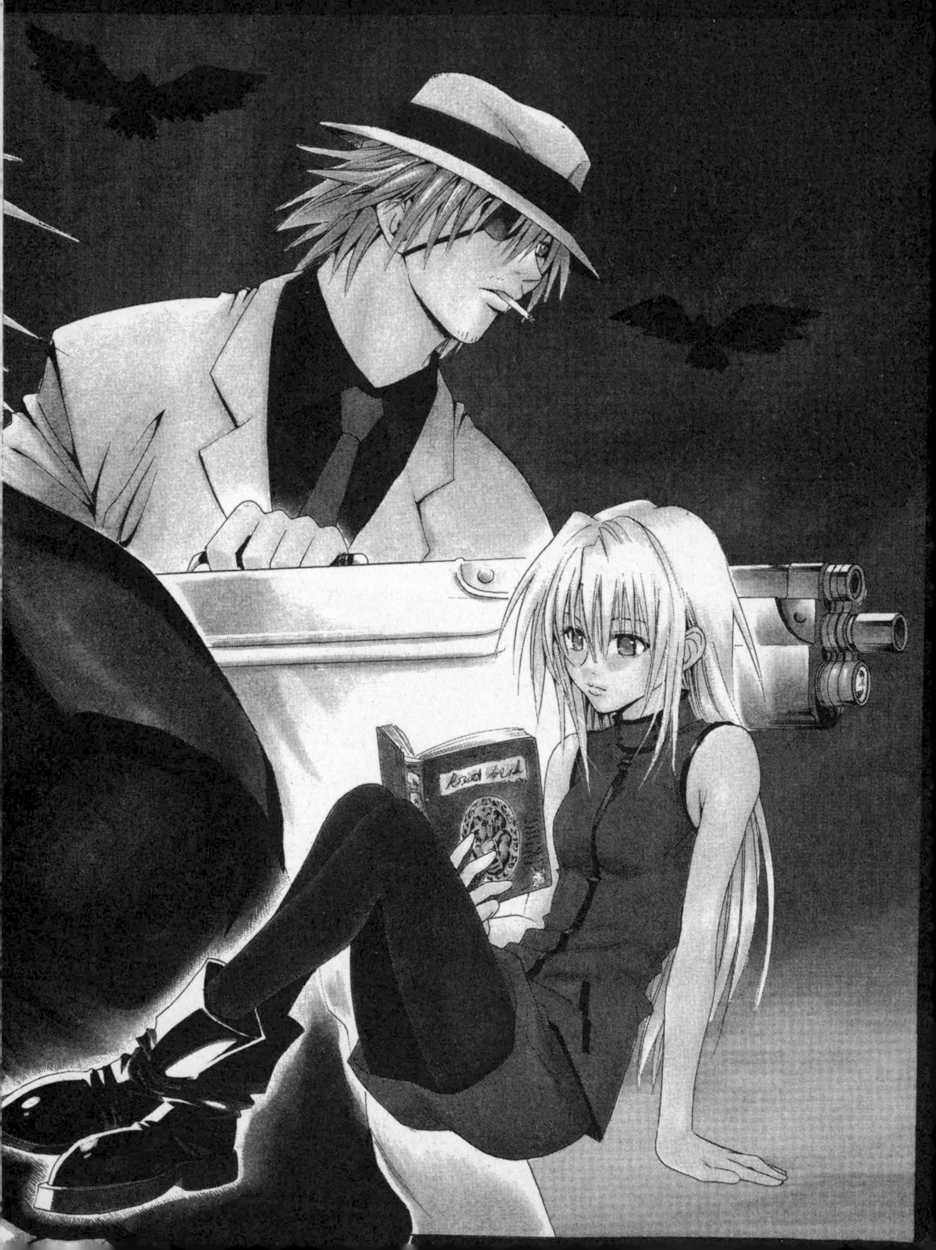

CHAPTER 49:

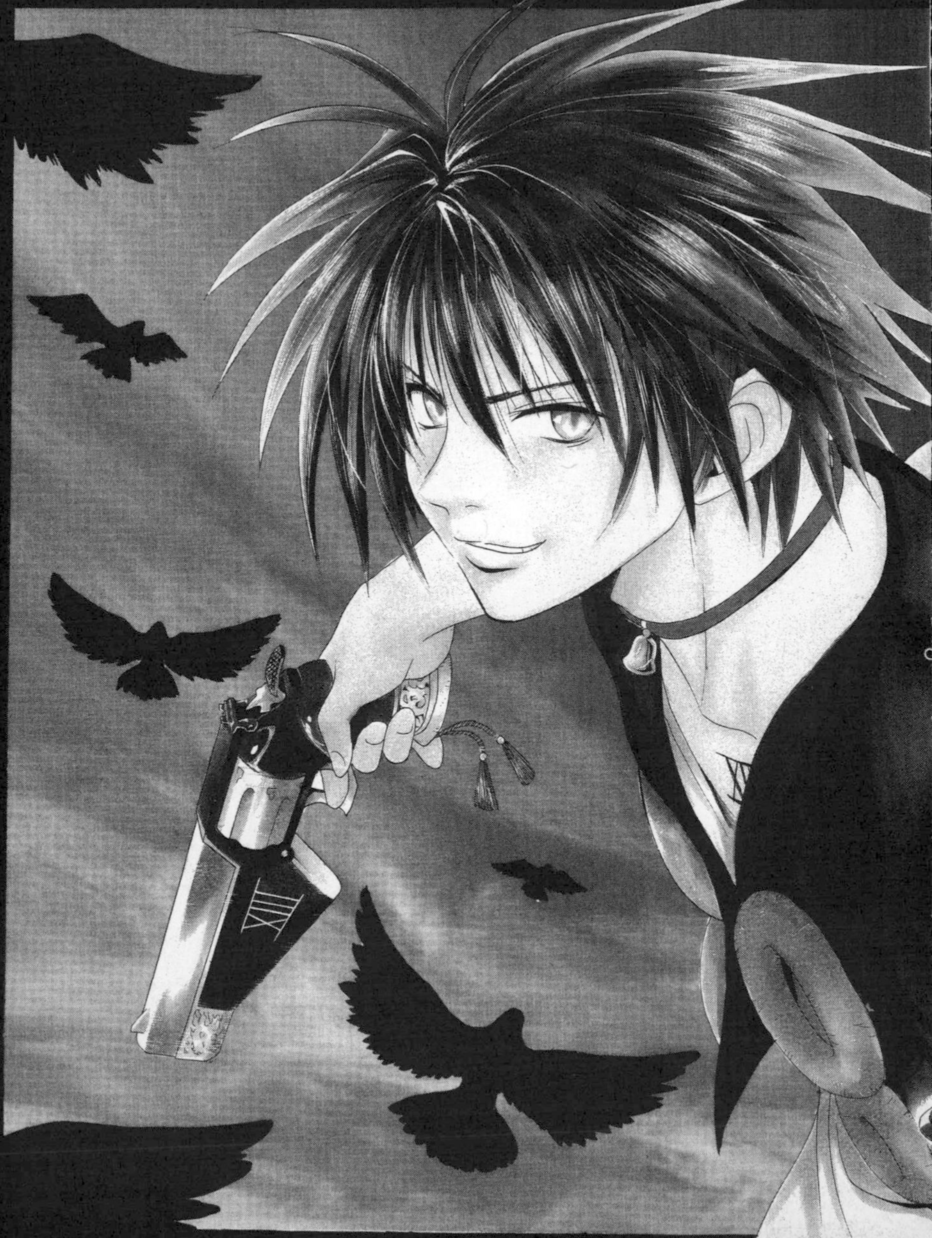

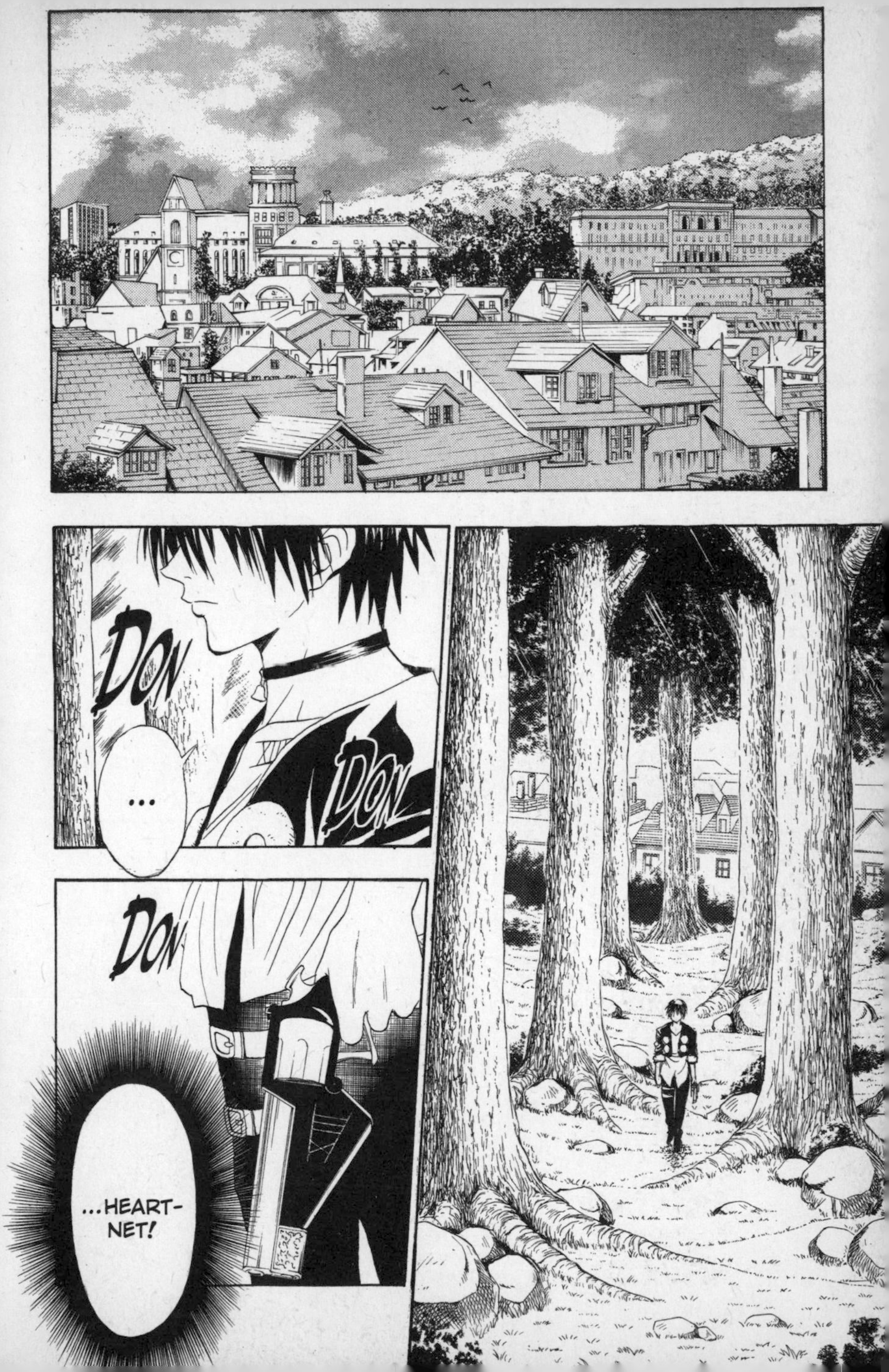
DON
DON
...
DON
...HEART-NET!

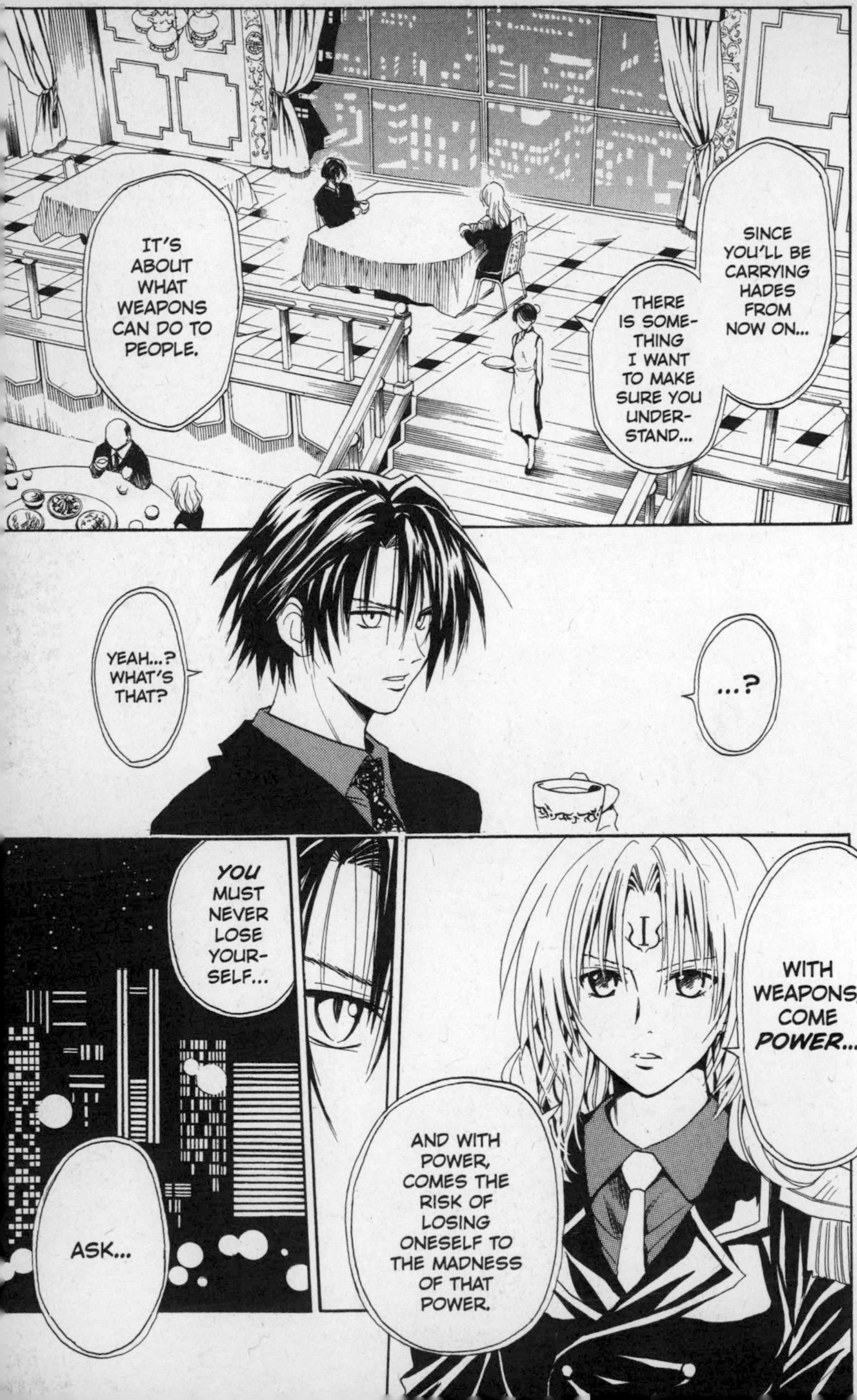

SINCE YOU'LL BE CARRYING HADES FROM NOW ON...
THERE IS SOMETHING I WANT TO MAKE SURE YOU UNDERSTAND...
IT'S ABOUT WHAT WEAPONS CAN DO TO PEOPLE.
...?
YEAH...? WHAT'S THAT?
WITH WEAPONS, COME *POWER*...
AND WITH POWER, COMES THE RISK OF LOSING ONESELF TO THE MADNESS OF THAT POWER.
YOU MUST NEVER LOSE YOURSELF...
ASK...

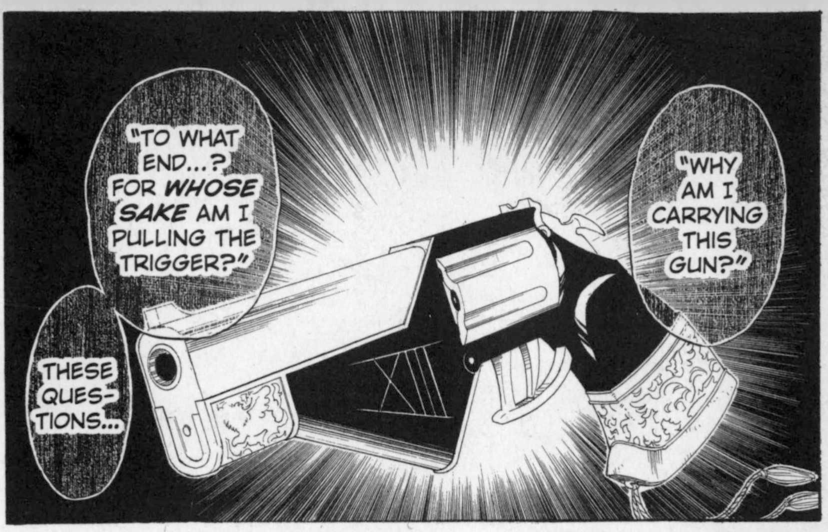
"WHY AM I CARRYING THIS GUN?"
"TO WHAT END...? FOR *WHOSE SAKE* AM I PULLING THE TRIGGER?"
THESE QUES-TIONS...

...MUST ***NEVER*** BE FORGOTTEN.

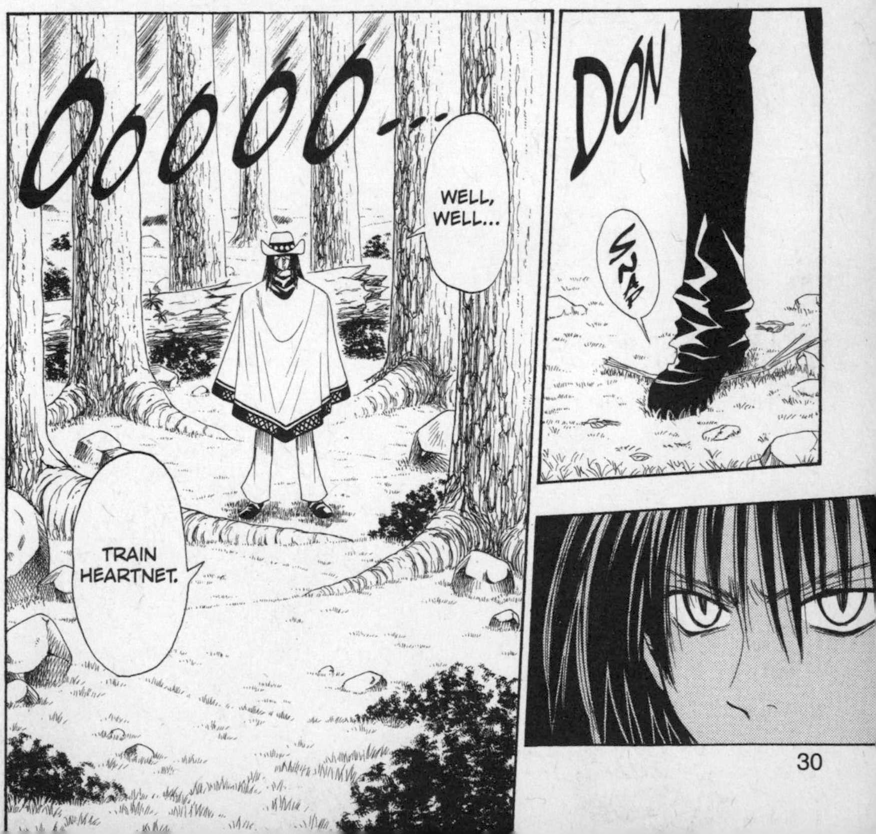
DON
OOOOO...
WELL, WELL...
TRAIN HEARTNET.

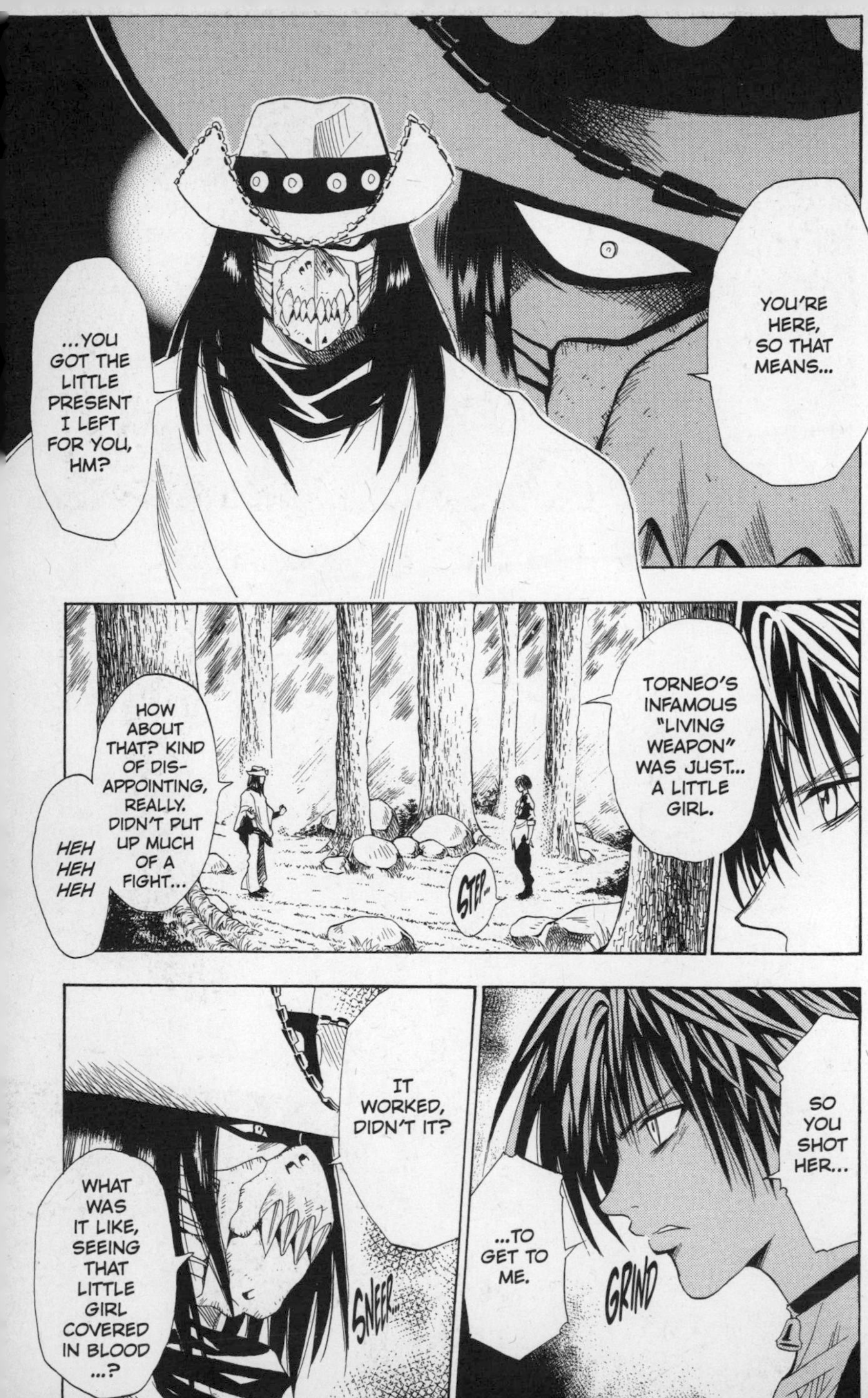
YOU'RE HERE, SO THAT MEANS...
...YOU GOT THE LITTLE PRESENT I LEFT FOR YOU, HM?
TORNEO'S INFAMOUS "LIVING WEAPON" WAS JUST... A LITTLE GIRL.
STEP...
HOW ABOUT THAT? KIND OF DIS-APPOINTING, REALLY. DIDN'T PUT UP MUCH OF A FIGHT...
HEH HEH HEH
SO YOU SHOT HER...
...TO GET TO ME.
GRIND
IT WORKED, DIDN'T IT?
WHAT WAS IT LIKE, SEEING THAT LITTLE GIRL COVERED IN BLOOD ...?
SNEER...

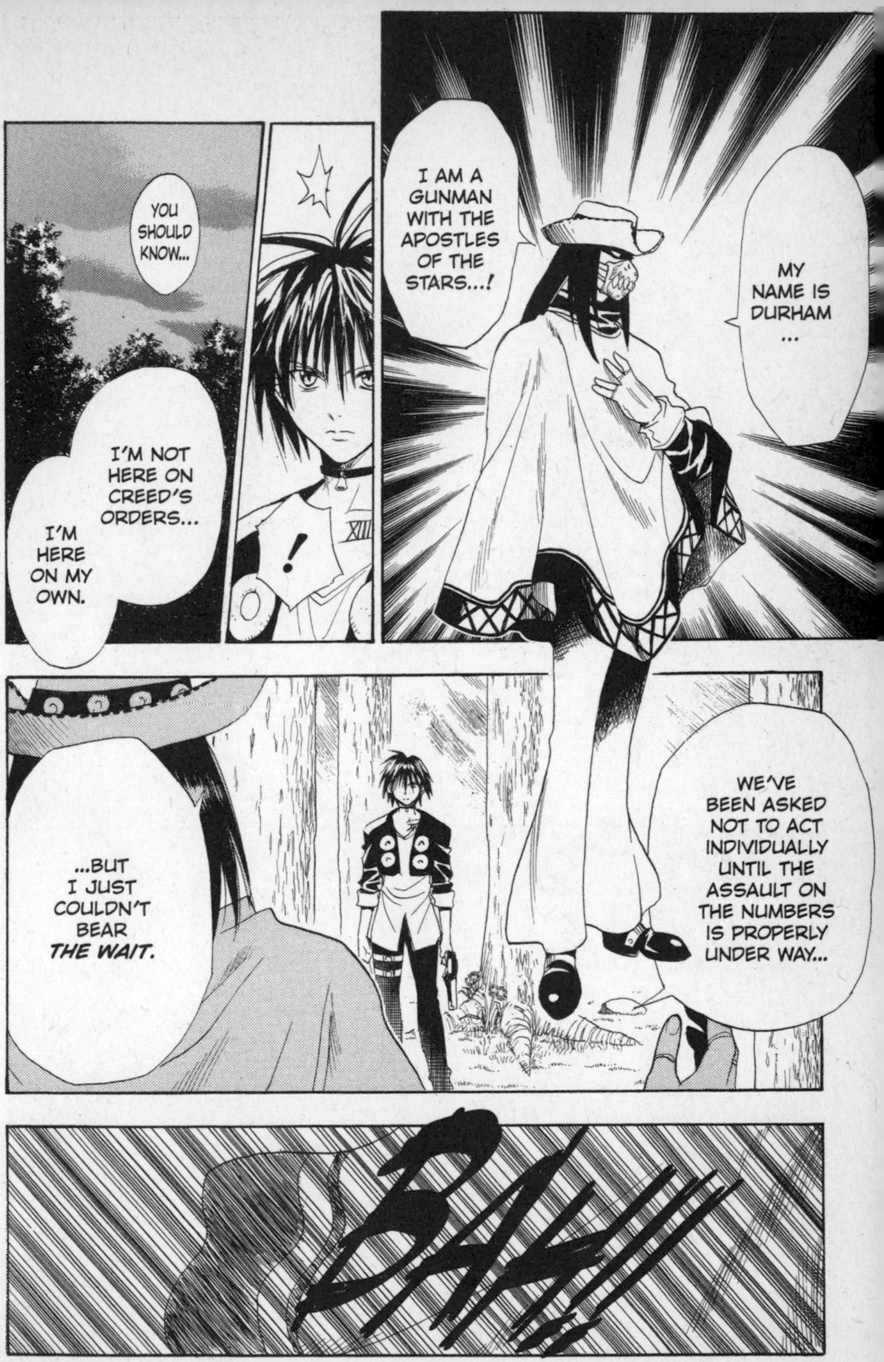
MY NAME IS DURHAM ...
I AM A GUNMAN WITH THE APOSTLES OF THE STARS...!
!
YOU SHOULD KNOW...
I'M NOT HERE ON CREED'S ORDERS...
I'M HERE ON MY OWN.
WE'VE BEEN ASKED NOT TO ACT INDIVIDUALLY UNTIL THE ASSAULT ON THE NUMBERS IS PROPERLY UNDER WAY...
...BUT I JUST COULDN'T BEAR *THE WAIT.*
BAM!

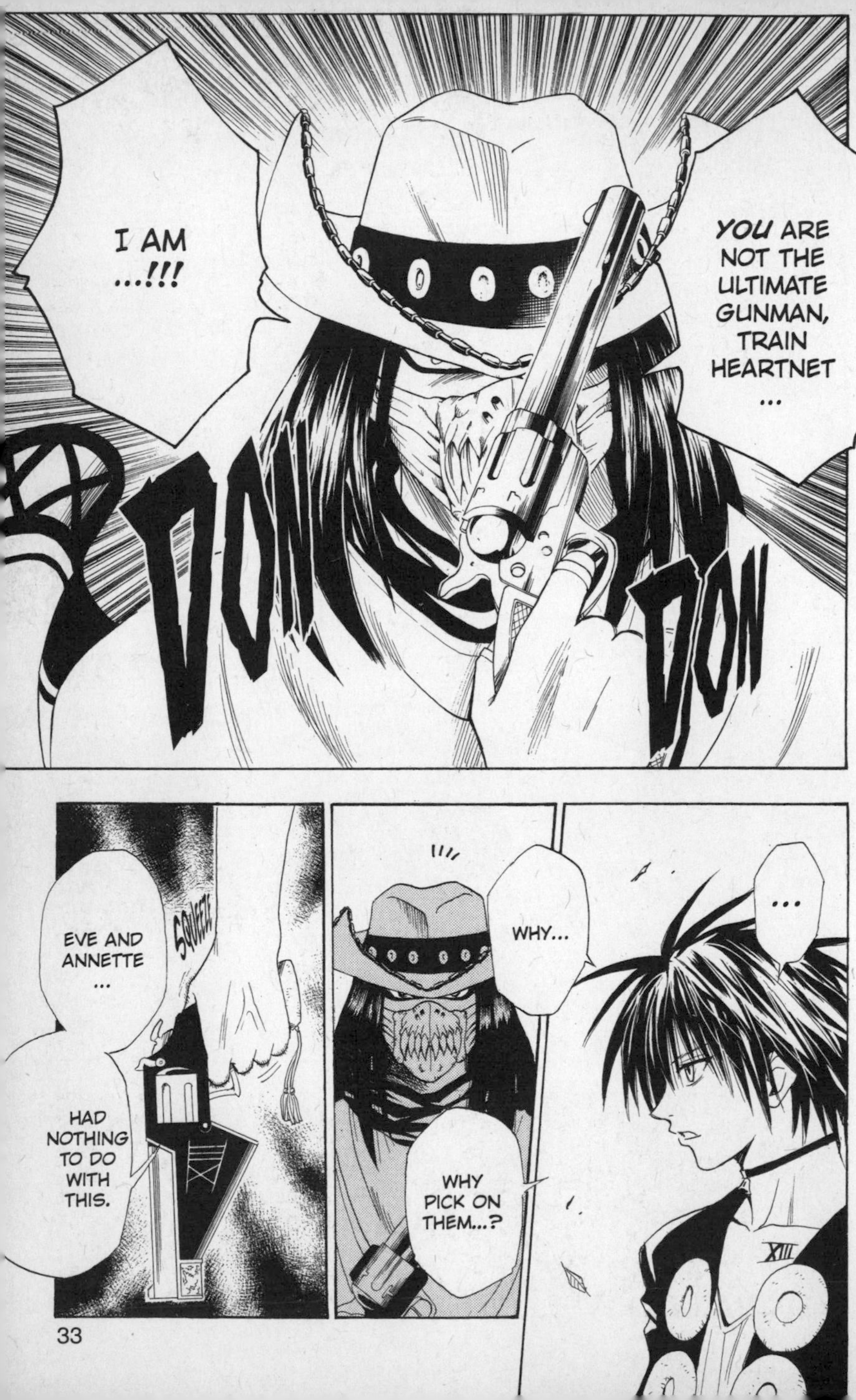
YOU ARE NOT THE ULTIMATE GUNMAN, TRAIN HEARTNET ...
I AM ...!!!
DON
DON
...
WHY...
WHY PICK ON THEM...?
EVE AND ANNETTE ...
SQUEEZE
HAD NOTHING TO DO WITH THIS.

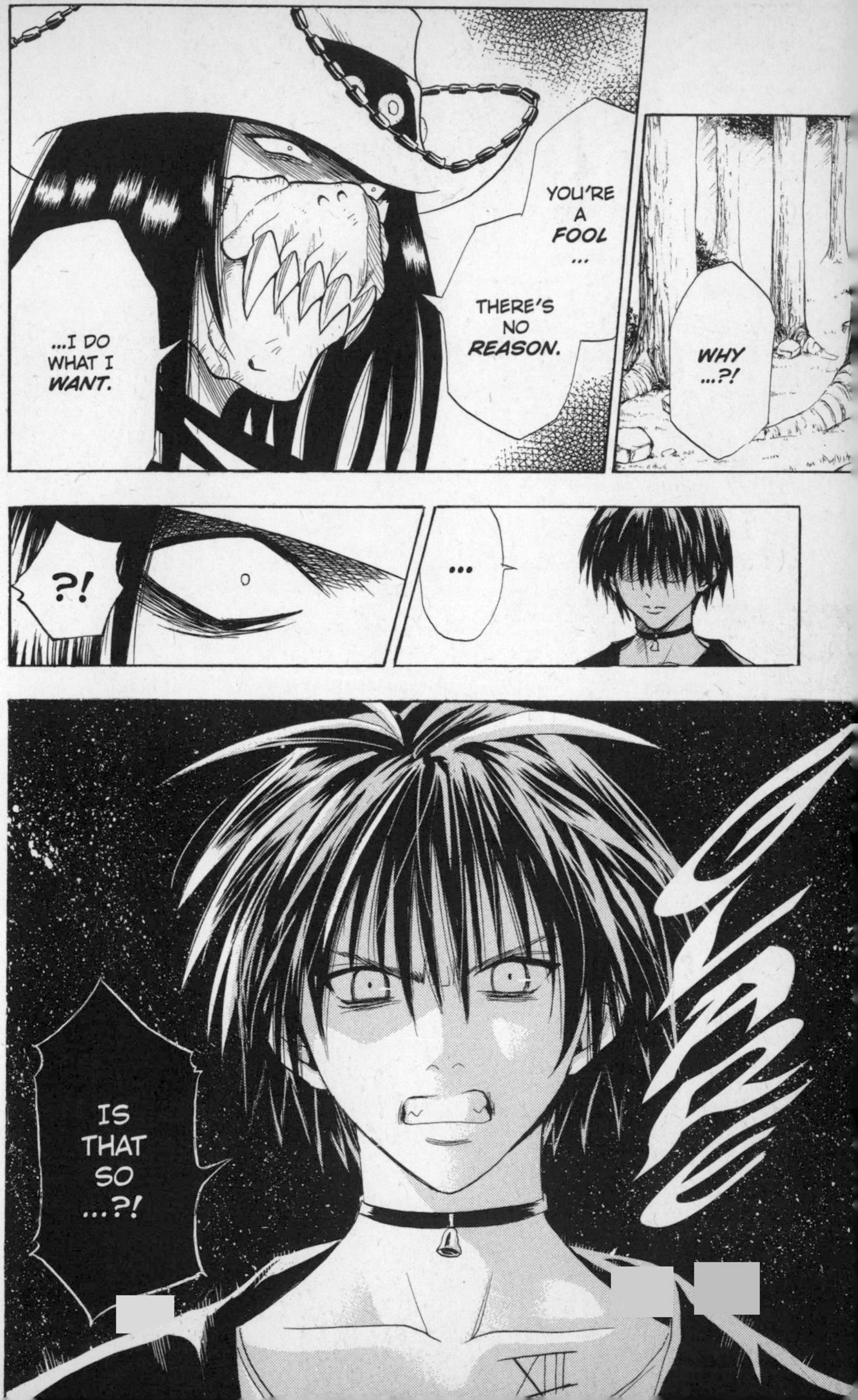
WHY ...?!
YOU'RE A FOOL ...
THERE'S NO REASON.
...I DO WHAT I WANT.
...
?!
IS THAT SO ...?!

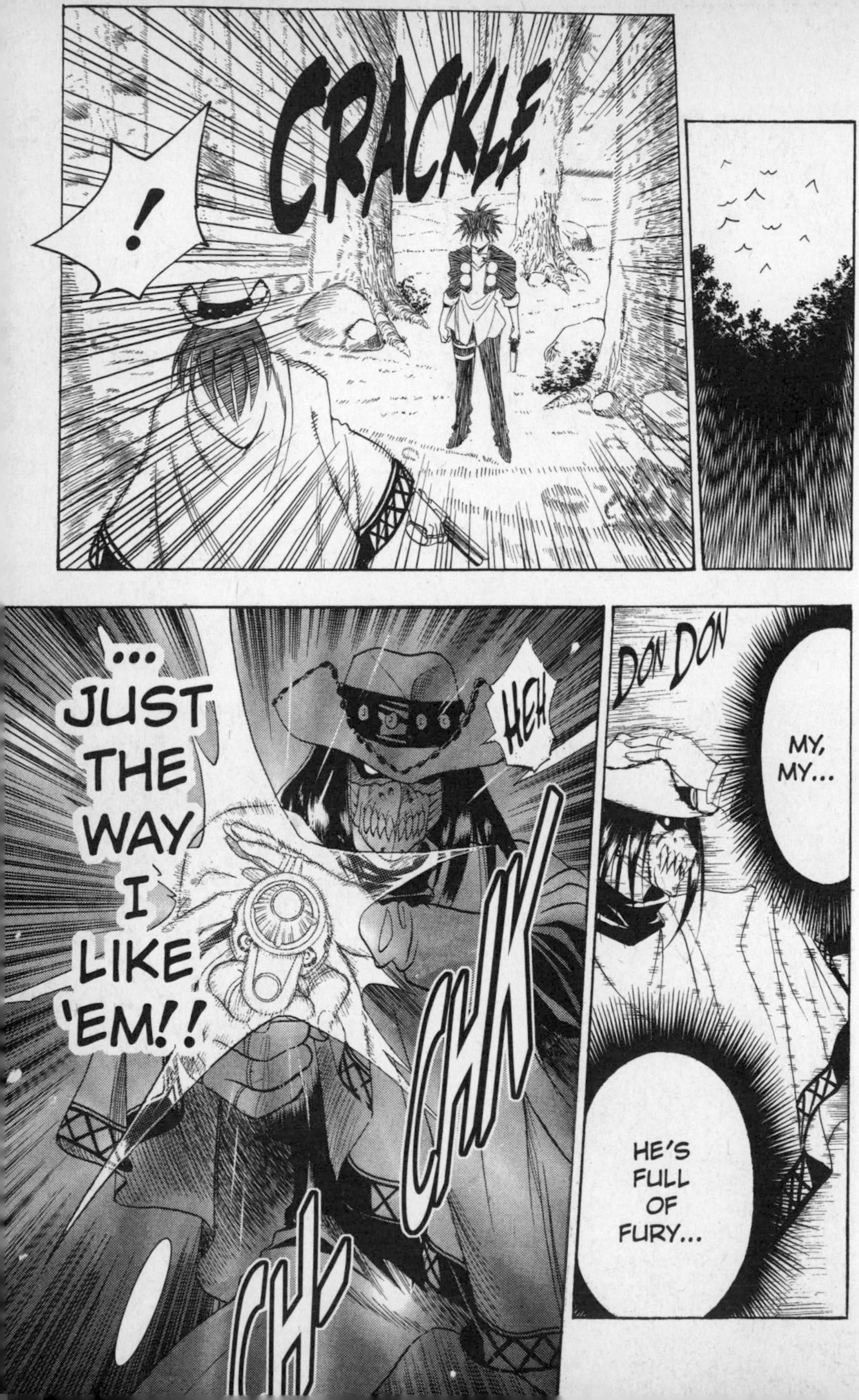

CRACKLE
!
DON DON
MY, MY...
HE'S FULL OF FURY...
HEH
...JUST THE WAY I LIKE 'EM!!
CHK
CHK

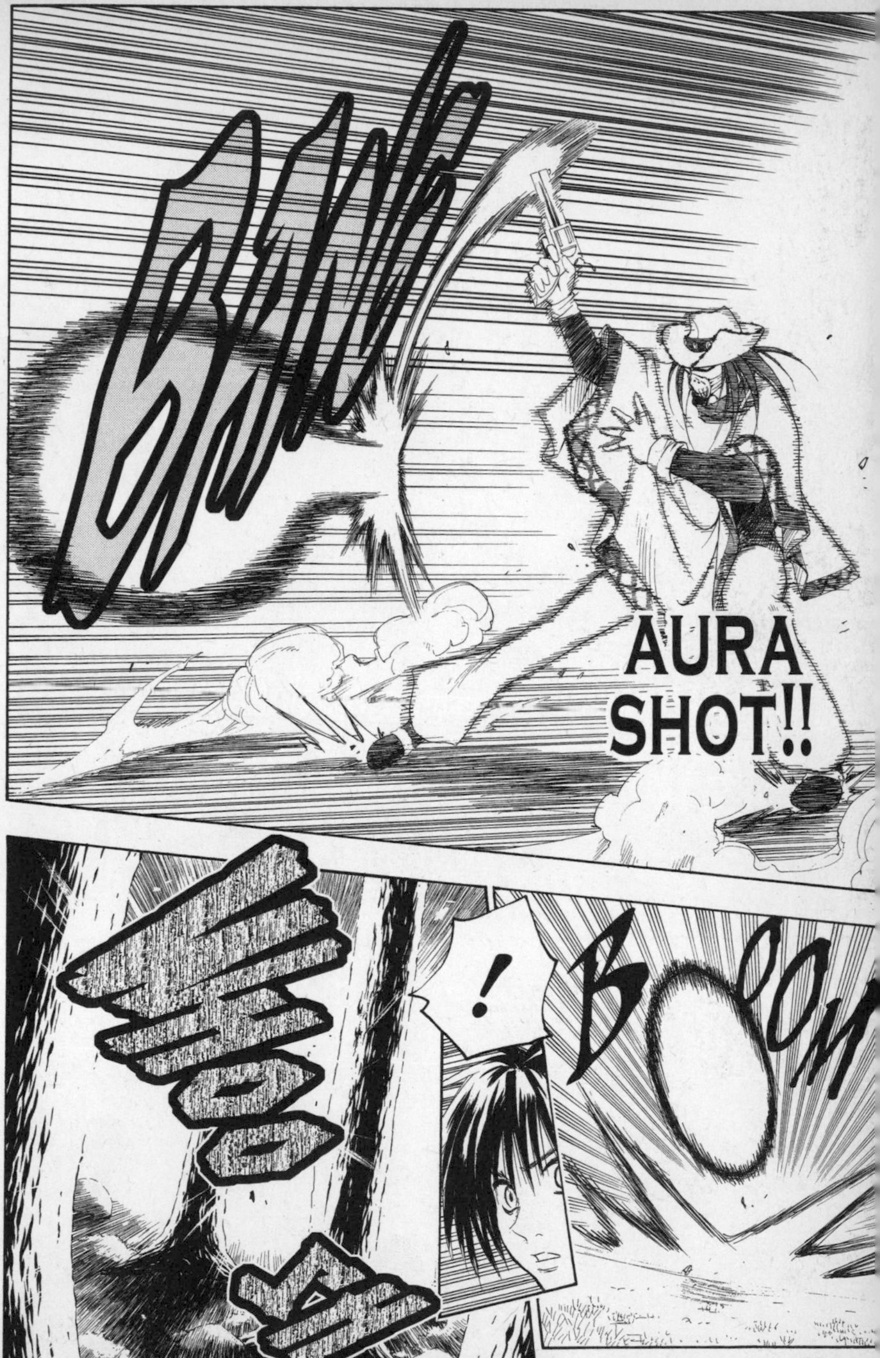
AURA SHOT!!
BOOM
!

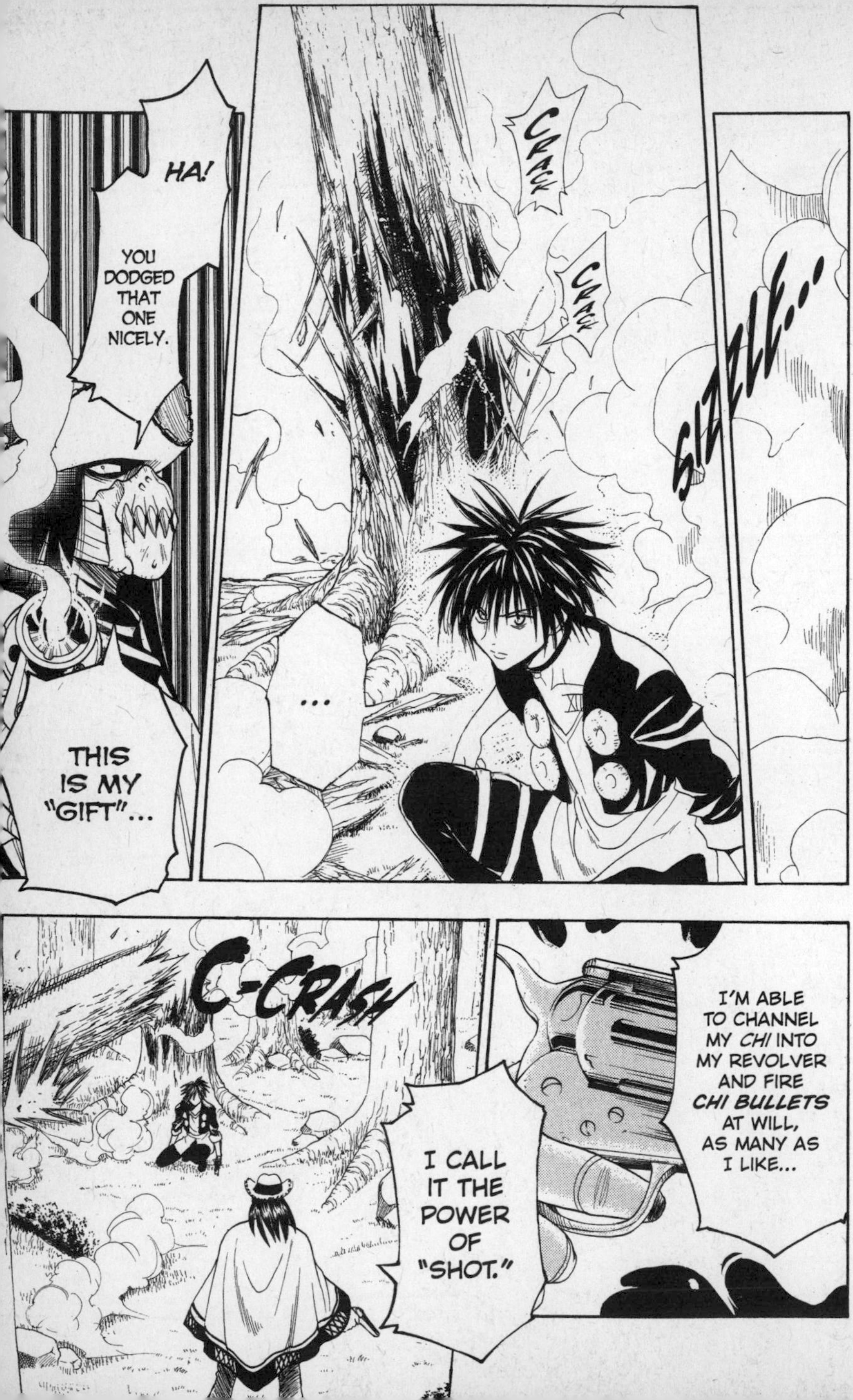
SIZZLE...
CRACK
CRACK
...
HA!
YOU DODGED THAT ONE NICELY.
THIS IS MY "GIFT"...
I'M ABLE TO CHANNEL MY *CHI* INTO MY REVOLVER AND FIRE *CHI BULLETS* AT WILL, AS MANY AS I LIKE...
I CALL IT THE POWER OF "SHOT."
C-CRASH

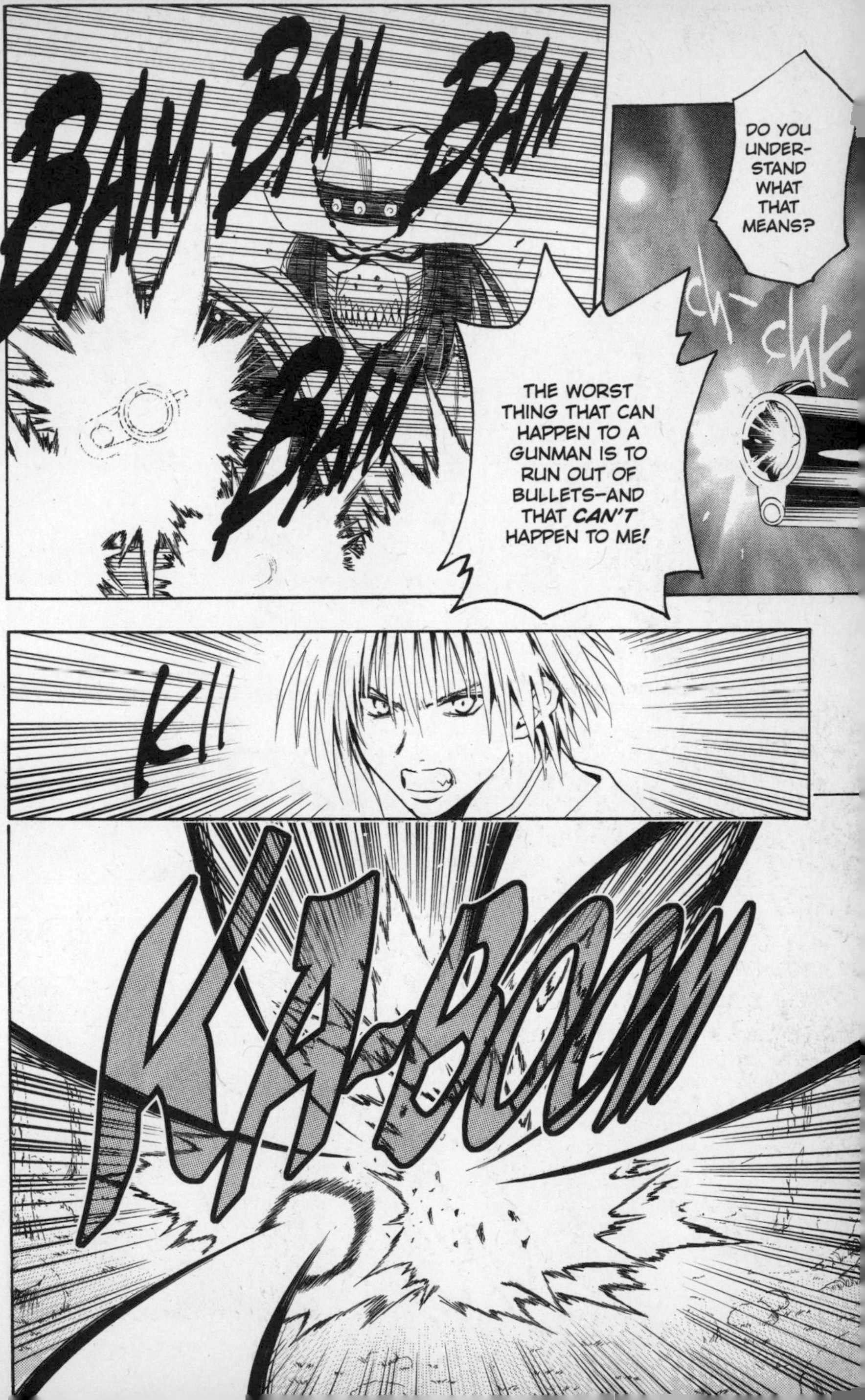
DO YOU UNDER-STAND WHAT THAT MEANS?
ch-chk
BAM BAM BAM
BAM
THE WORST THING THAT CAN HAPPEN TO A GUNMAN IS TO RUN OUT OF BULLETS—AND THAT *CAN'T* HAPPEN TO ME!
KI!
KA-BOOM

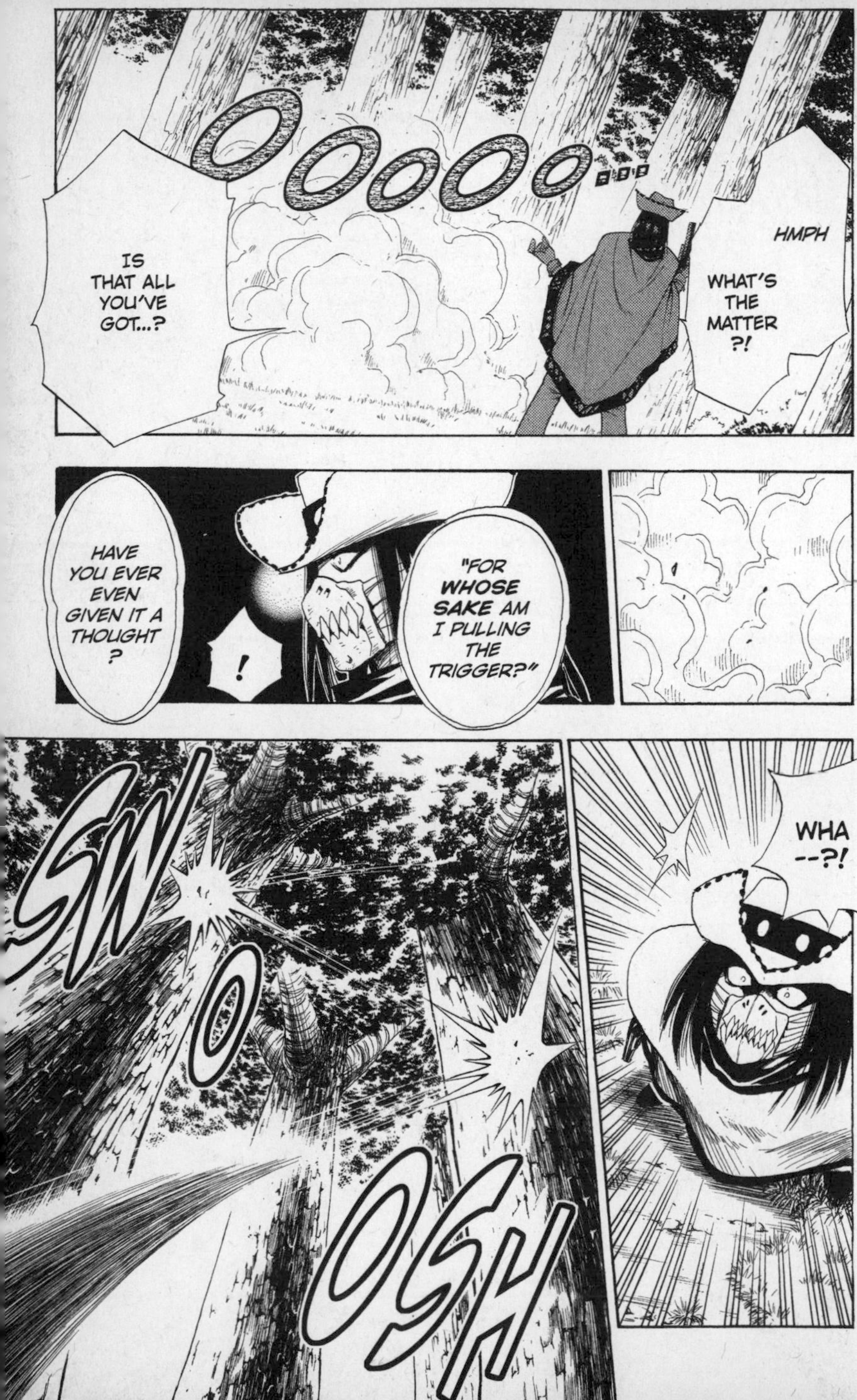
HMPH
WHAT'S THE MATTER ?!
OOOOOO...
IS THAT ALL YOU'VE GOT...?
"FOR WHOSE SAKE AM I PULLING THE TRIGGER?"
!
HAVE YOU EVER EVEN GIVEN IT A THOUGHT ?
WHA --?!
SWOOSH

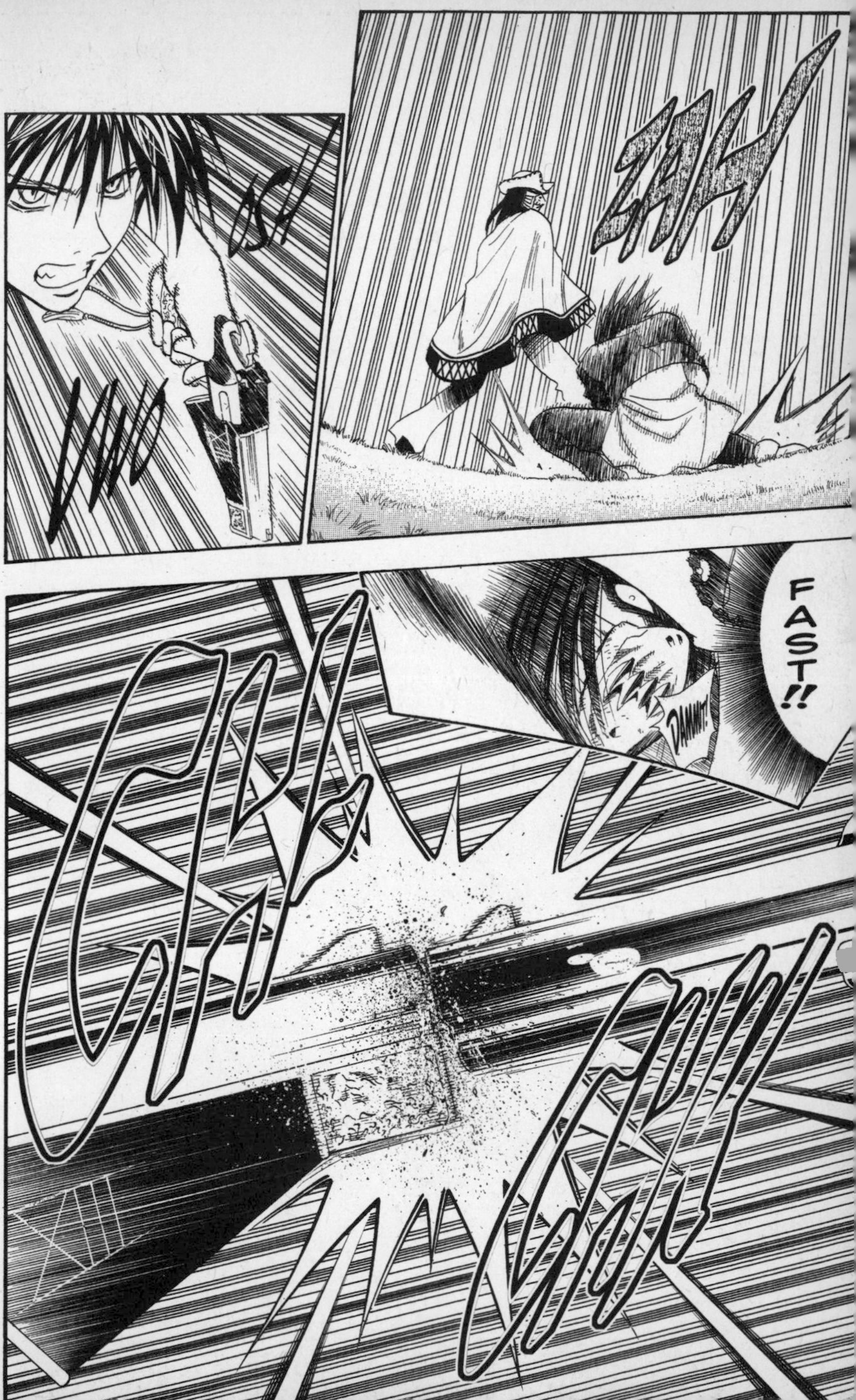
FAST!!
DAMMIT!

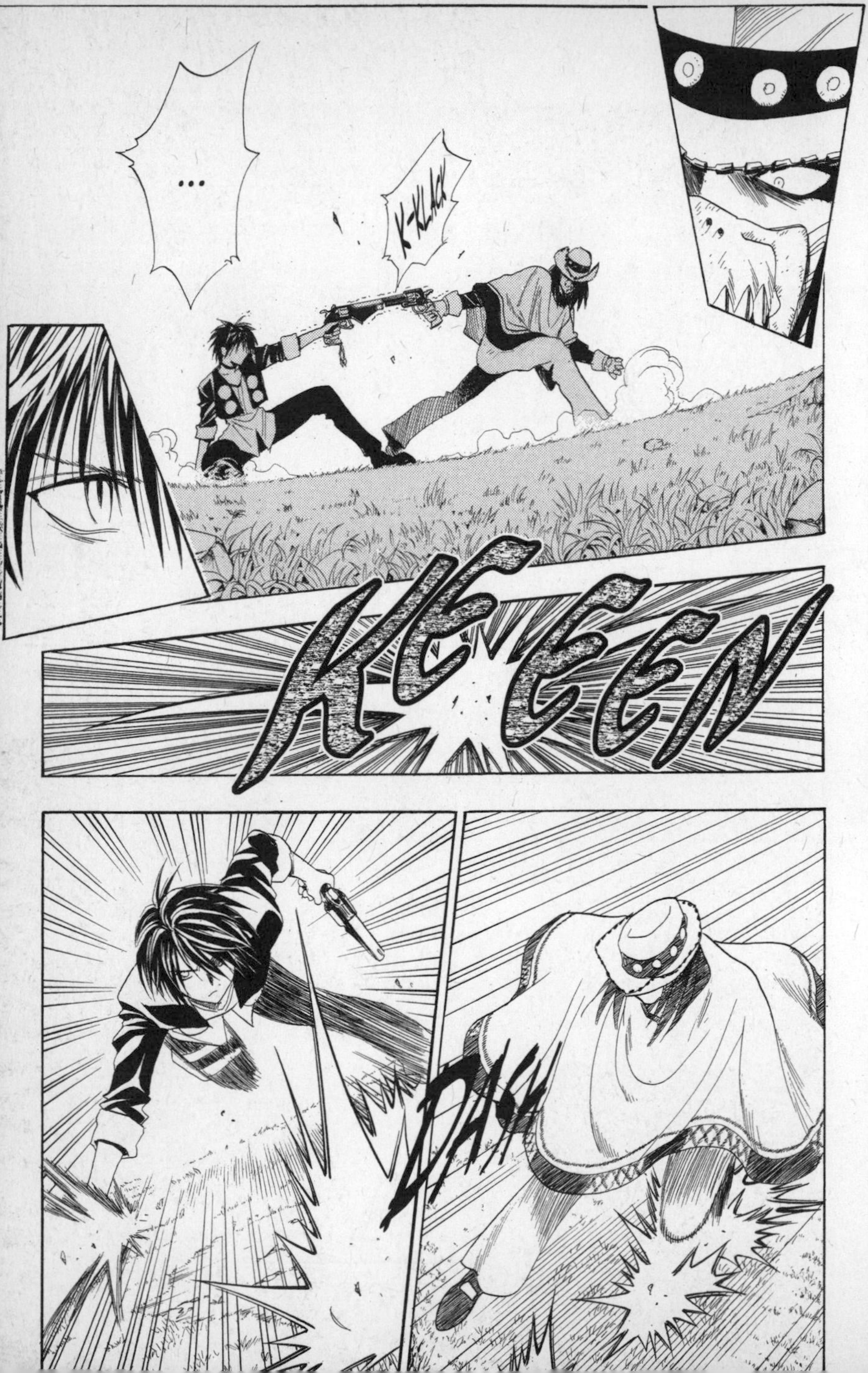

K-KLACK
...
KE EEN
DASH

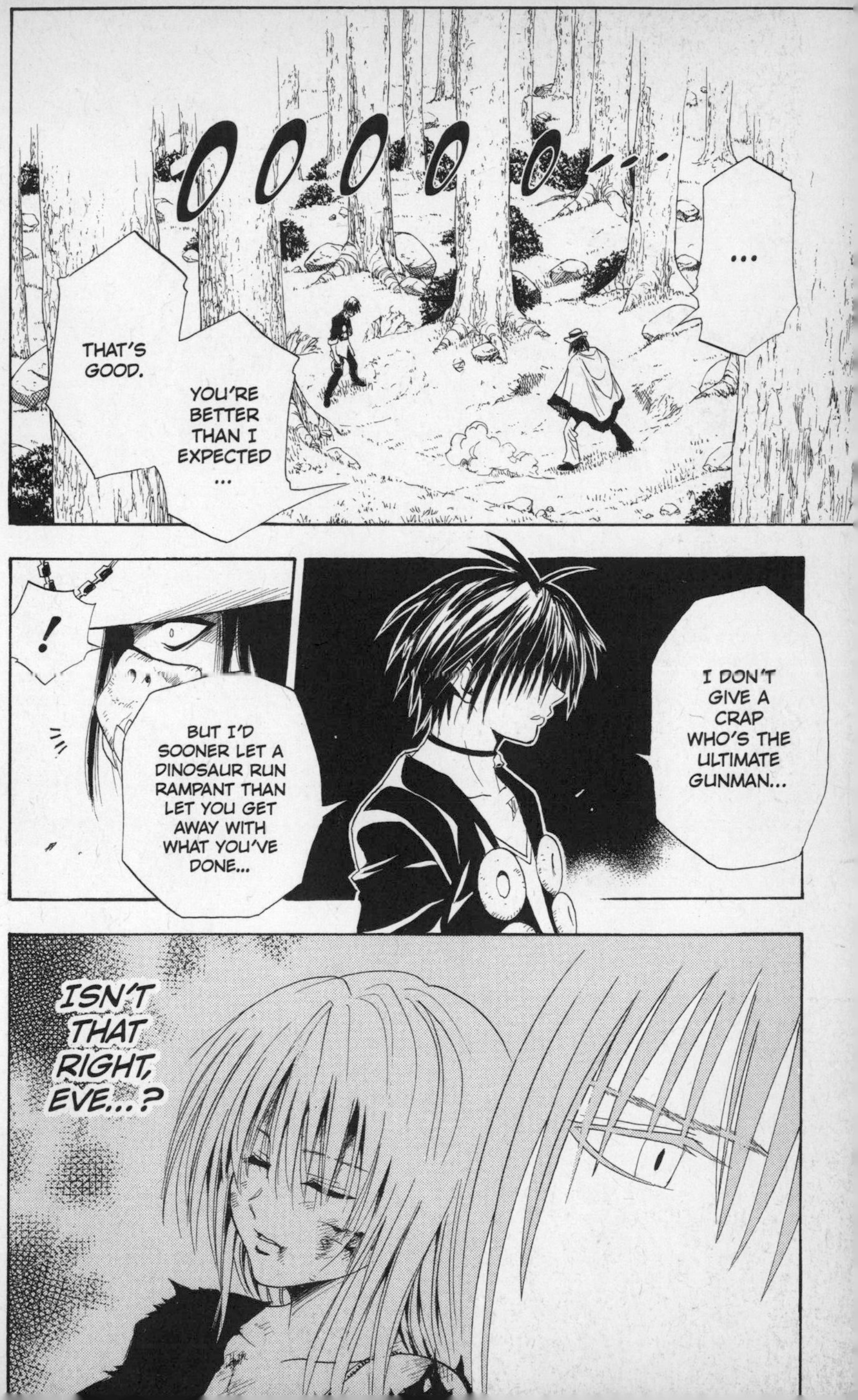
OOOOO...
...
THAT'S GOOD.
YOU'RE BETTER THAN I EXPECTED ...
I DON'T GIVE A CRAP WHO'S THE ULTIMATE GUNMAN...
BUT I'D SOONER LET A DINOSAUR RUN RAMPANT THAN LET YOU GET AWAY WITH WHAT YOU'VE DONE...
!
ISN'T THAT RIGHT, EVE...?

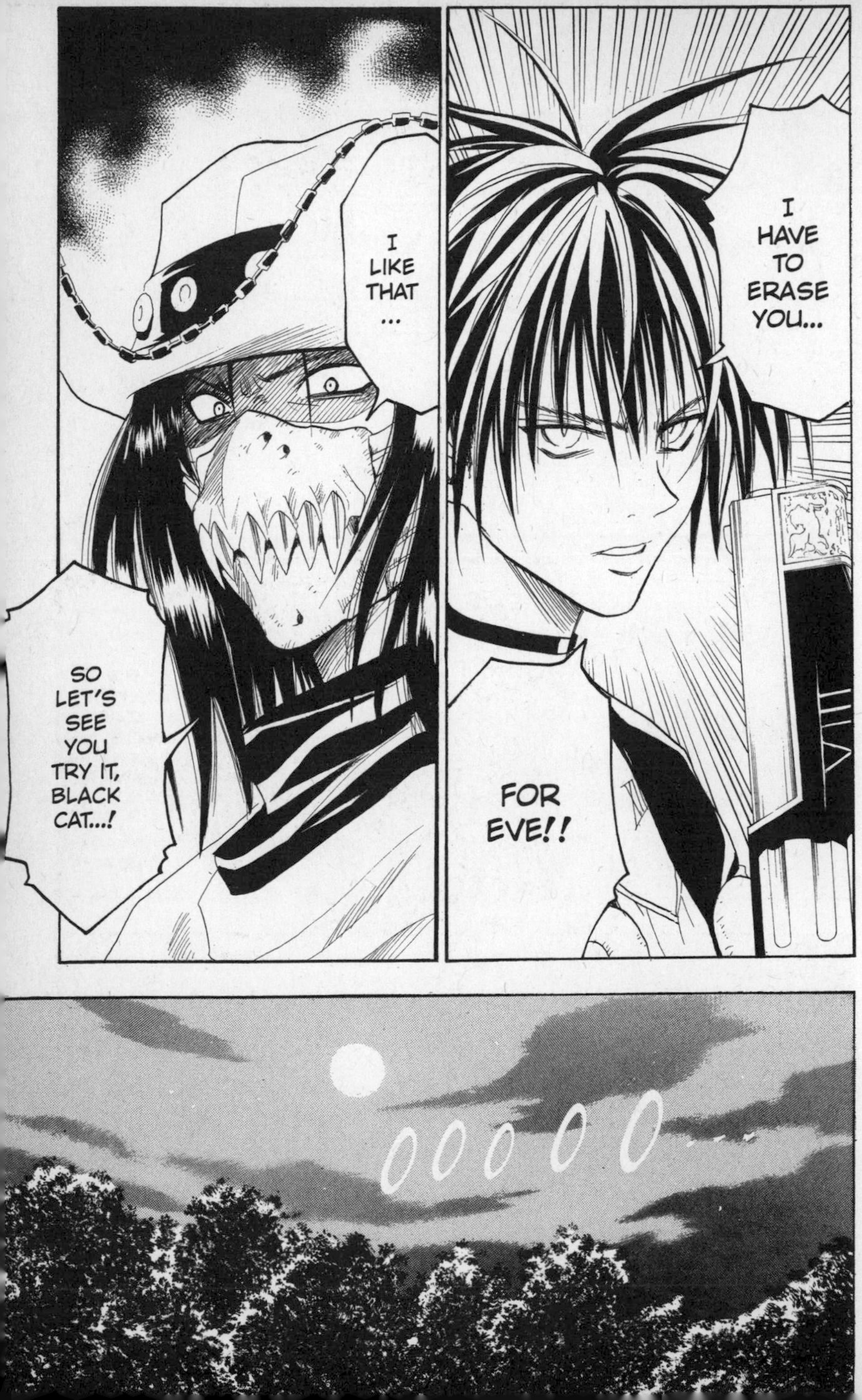
I HAVE TO ERASE YOU...
FOR EVE!!
I LIKE THAT...
SO LET'S SEE YOU TRY IT, BLACK CAT...!

BLACK CAT

profile

SEPHIRIA ARKS

DATA	
BIRTHDATE:	JANUARY 1
AGE:	27
BLOOD TYPE:	A
HEIGHT:	170 CM
WEIGHT:	?
HOBBY:	FLOWER ARRANGEMENT
FAVORITE FOODS:	SUSHI; PREFERS JIPANGU–STYLE CUISINE.
WEAPON:	ICHTHUS
COMMENTS:	SHE IS CHRONO AGENT NUMBER I, AND THEIR LEADER. SHE HAS A COOL DEMEANOR AND IMPECCABLE MANNERS, BUT TO FULFILL A MISSION, SHE'S WILLING TO CALMLY SACRIFICE ANYTHING... OR ANYONE.

Chapter 50: The Duel in the Woods

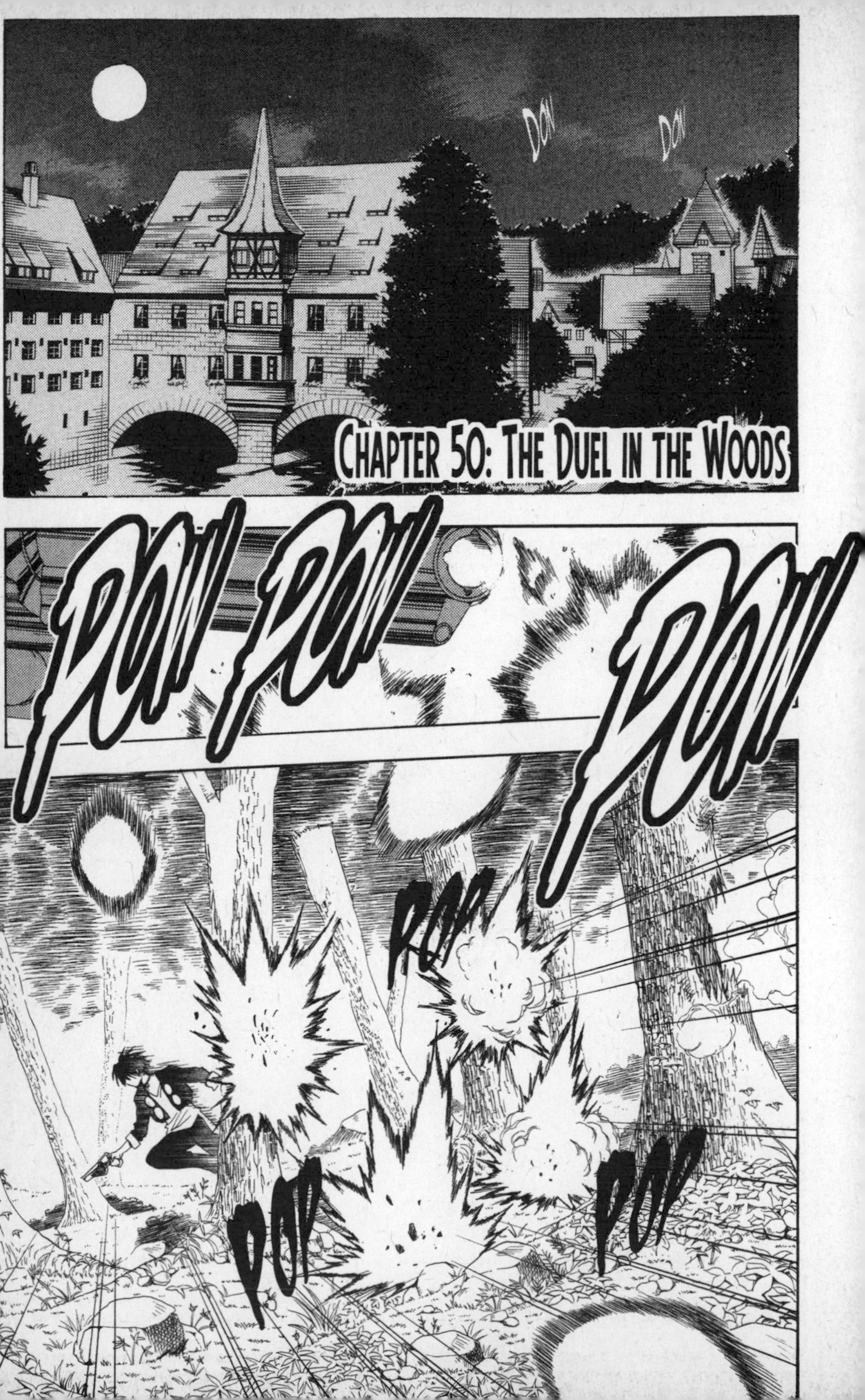
DON
DON
POW
POW
POW
POP
POP
POP
POP

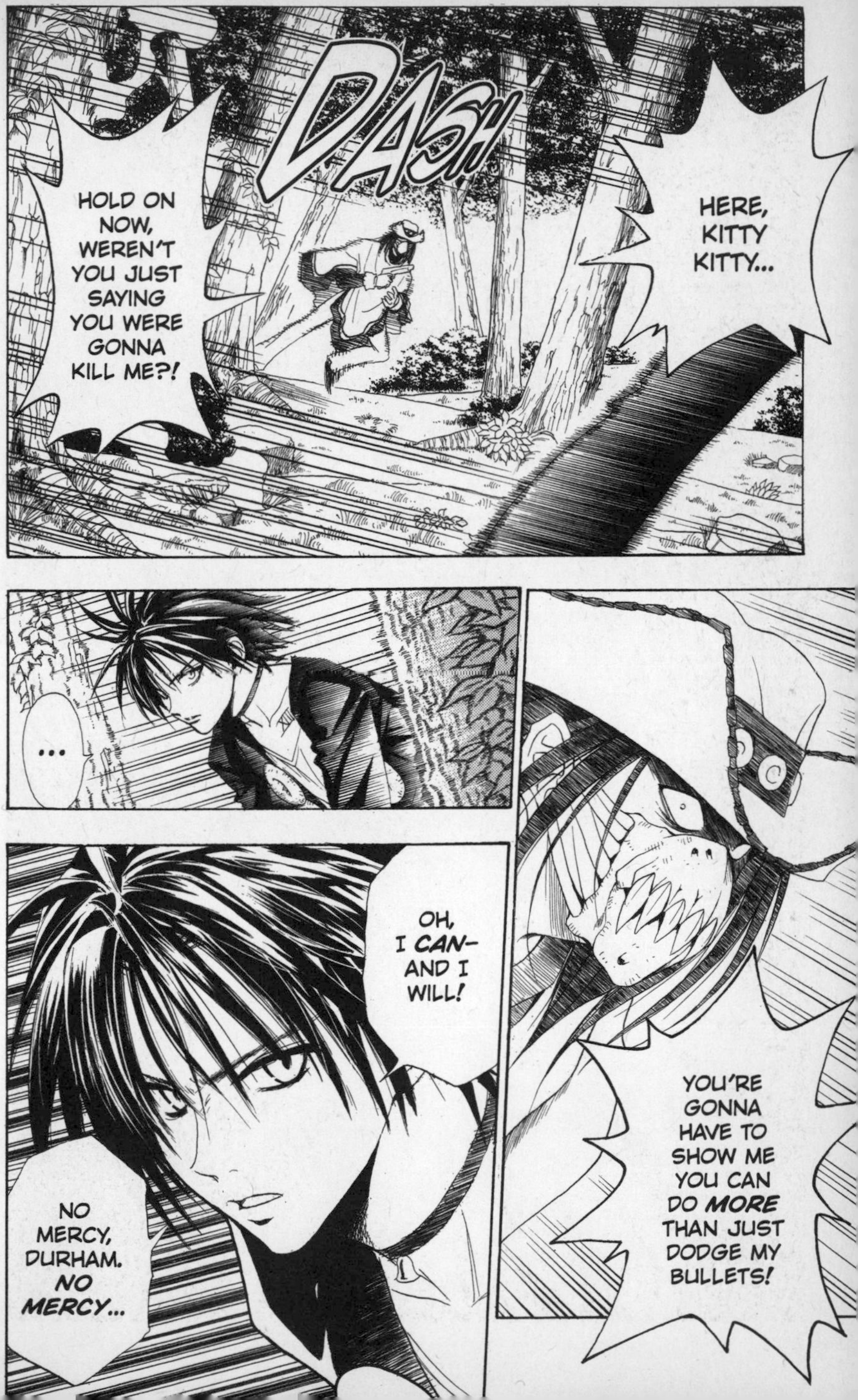
DASH
HERE, KITTY KITTY...
HOLD ON NOW, WEREN'T YOU JUST SAYING YOU WERE GONNA KILL ME?!
YOU'RE GONNA HAVE TO SHOW ME YOU CAN DO ***MORE*** THAN JUST DODGE MY BULLETS!
...
OH, I ***CAN***— AND I WILL!
NO MERCY, DURHAM. ***NO MERCY...***

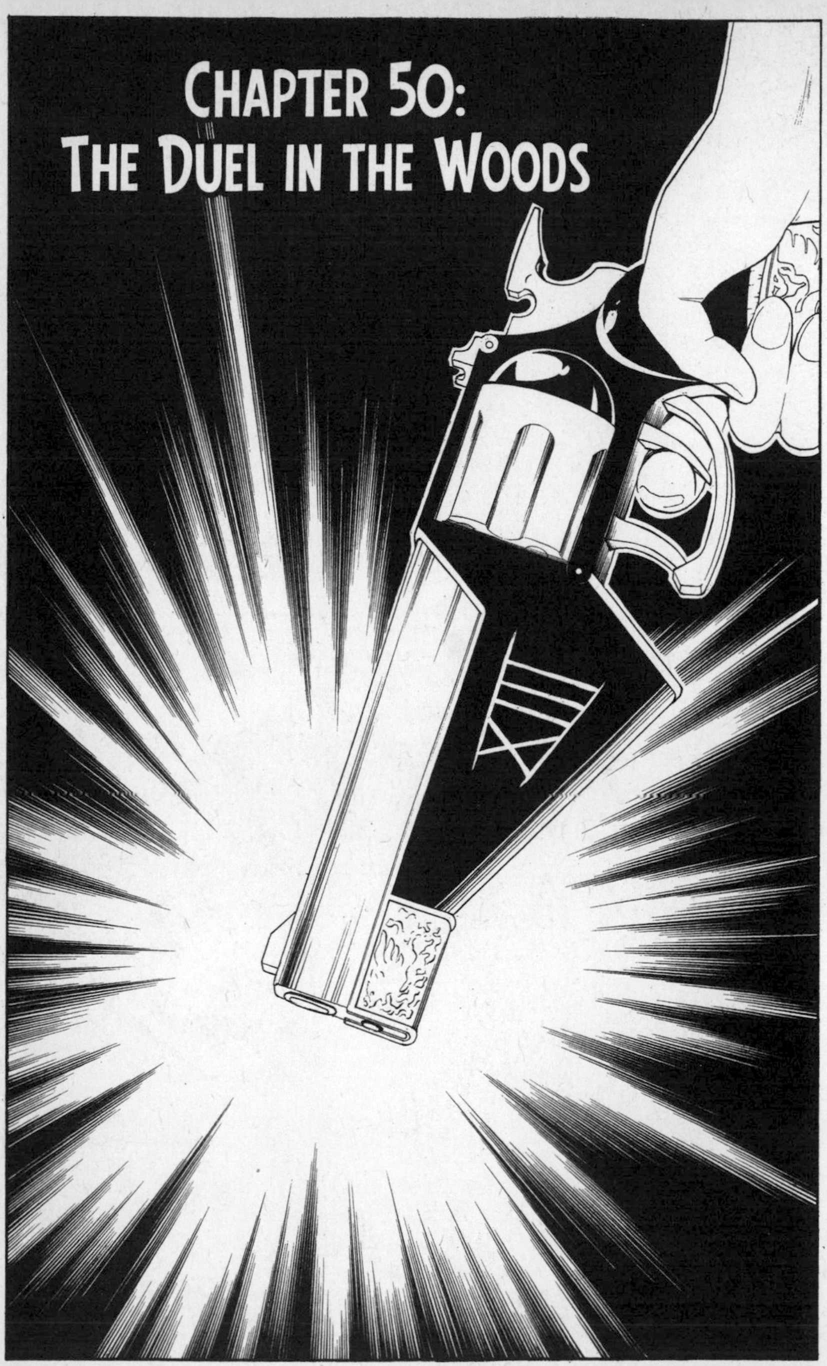
CHAPTER 50:
THE DUEL IN THE WOODS

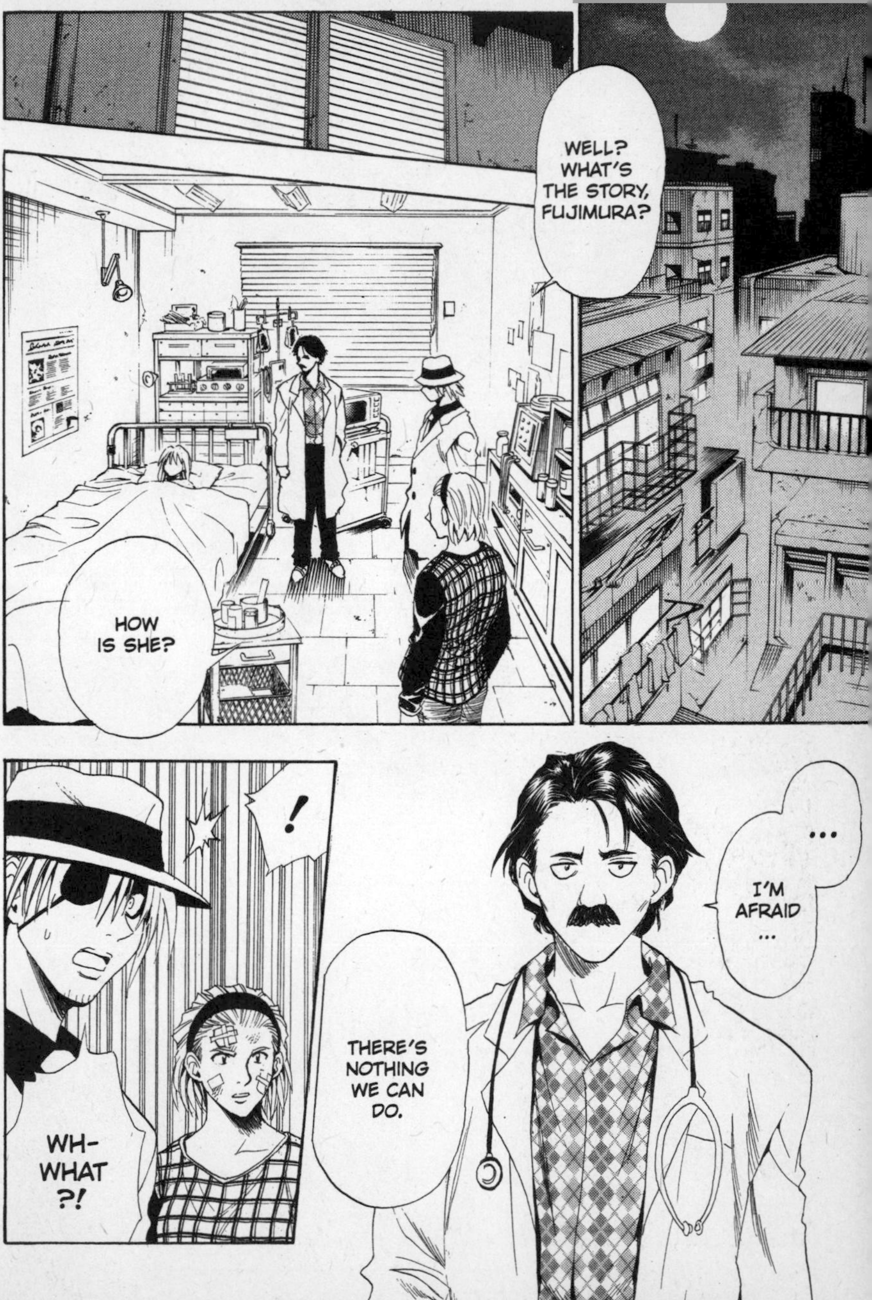
WELL? WHAT'S THE STORY, FUJIMURA?
HOW IS SHE?
... I'M AFRAID ...
THERE'S NOTHING WE CAN DO.
!
WH-WHAT ?!

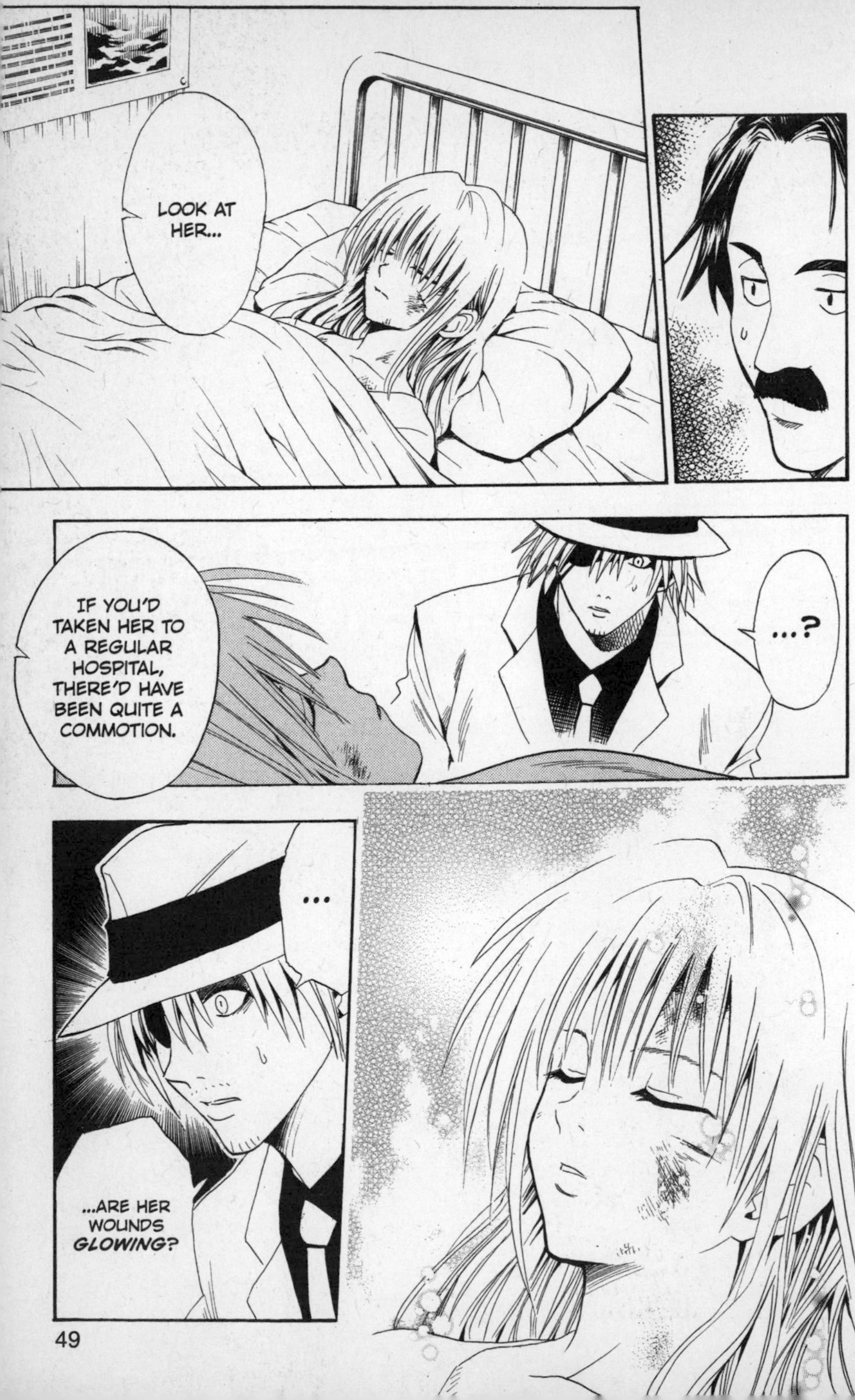
LOOK AT HER...
IF YOU'D TAKEN HER TO A REGULAR HOSPITAL, THERE'D HAVE BEEN QUITE A COMMOTION.
...?
...
...ARE HER WOUNDS *GLOWING*?

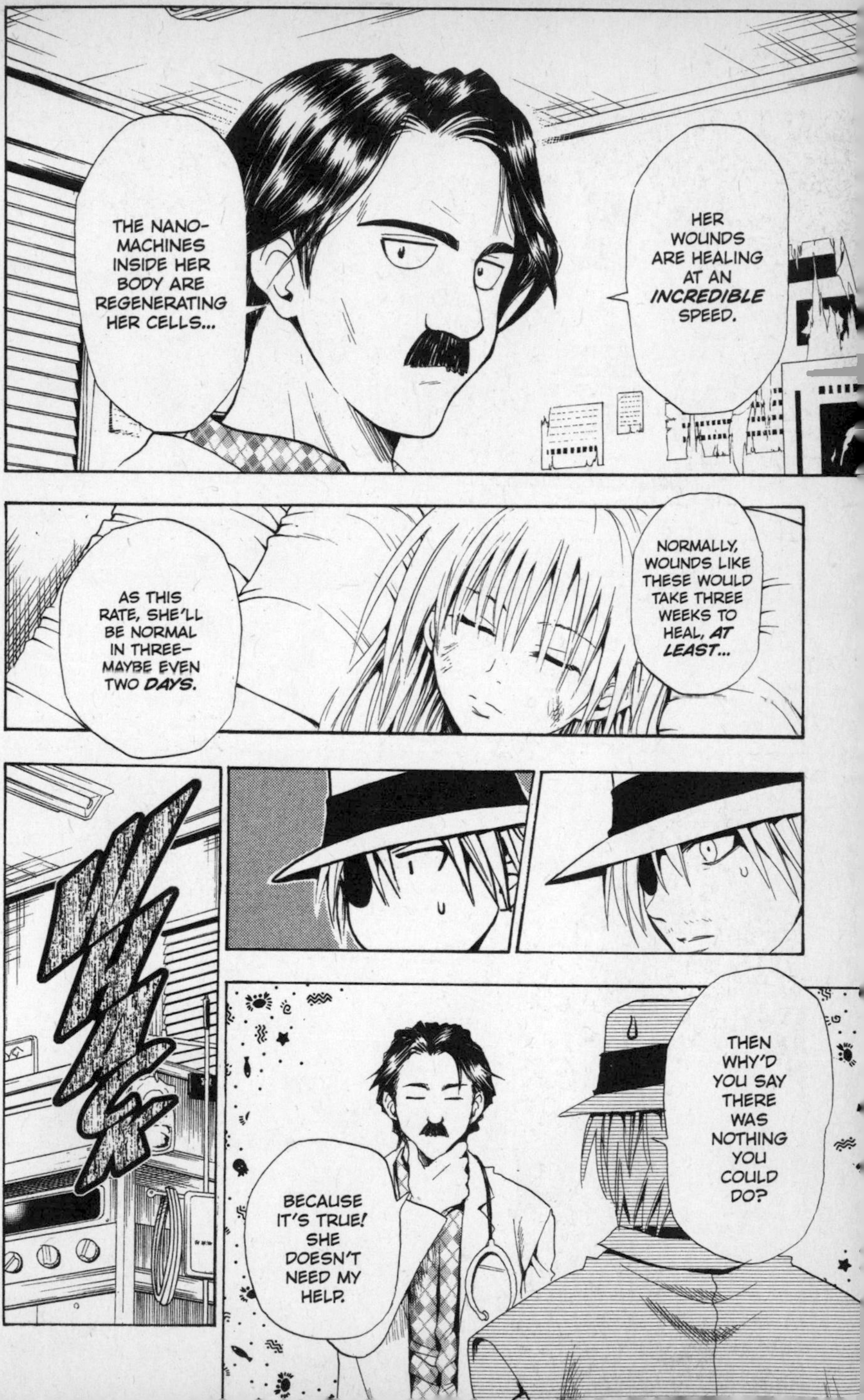
HER WOUNDS ARE HEALING AT AN *INCREDIBLE* SPEED.
THE NANO-MACHINES INSIDE HER BODY ARE REGENERATING HER CELLS...
NORMALLY, WOUNDS LIKE THESE WOULD TAKE THREE WEEKS TO HEAL, *AT LEAST*...
AS THIS RATE, SHE'LL BE NORMAL IN THREE- MAYBE EVEN TWO *DAYS.*
THEN WHY'D YOU SAY THERE WAS NOTHING YOU COULD DO?
BECAUSE IT'S TRUE! SHE DOESN'T NEED MY HELP.

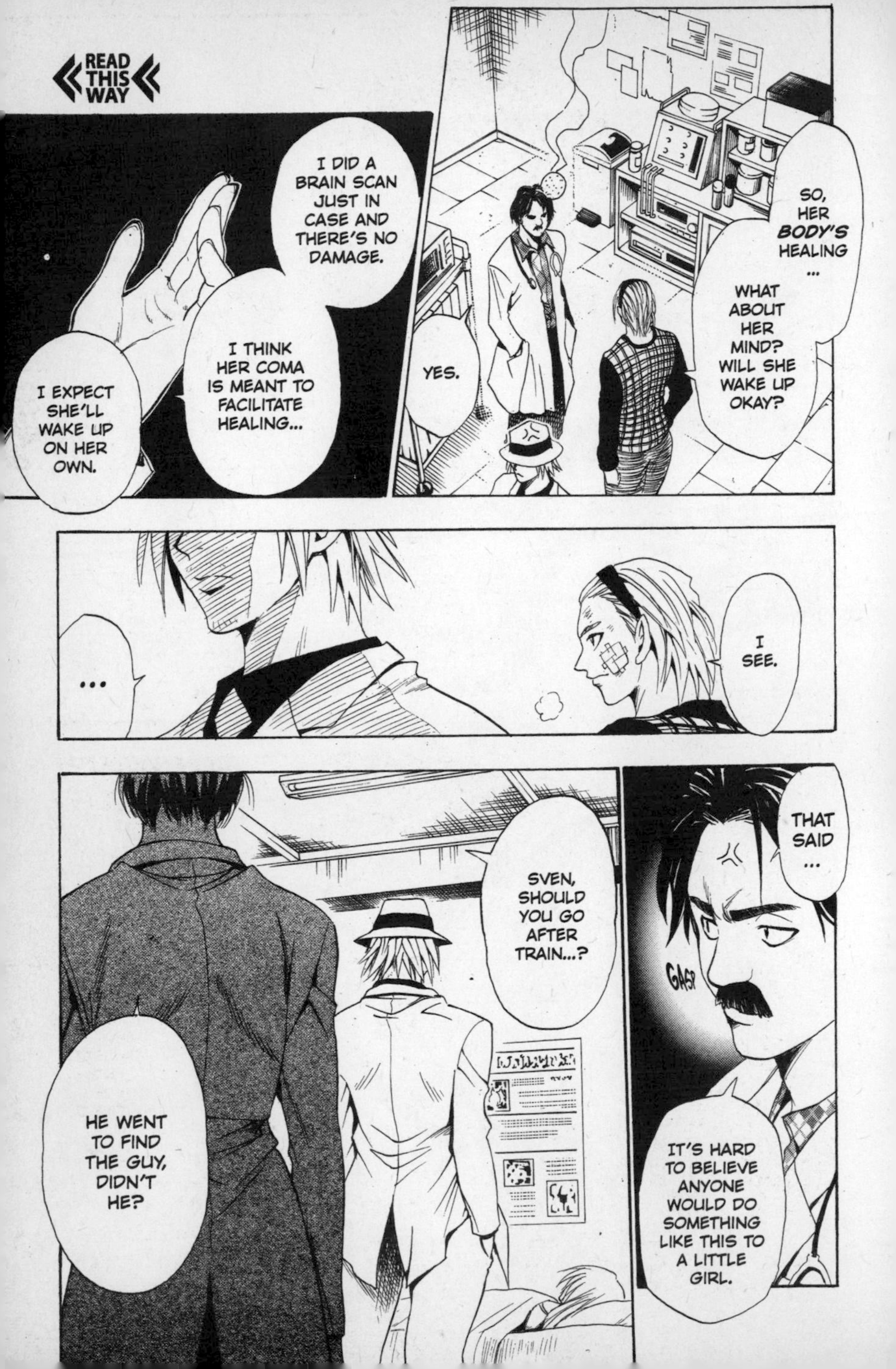
READ THIS WAY
SO, HER BODY'S HEALING ...
WHAT ABOUT HER MIND? WILL SHE WAKE UP OKAY?
YES.
I DID A BRAIN SCAN JUST IN CASE AND THERE'S NO DAMAGE.
I THINK HER COMA IS MEANT TO FACILITATE HEALING...
I EXPECT SHE'LL WAKE UP ON HER OWN.
I SEE.
...
THAT SAID ...
GASP
IT'S HARD TO BELIEVE ANYONE WOULD DO SOMETHING LIKE THIS TO A LITTLE GIRL.
SVEN, SHOULD YOU GO AFTER TRAIN...?
HE WENT TO FIND THE GUY, DIDN'T HE?

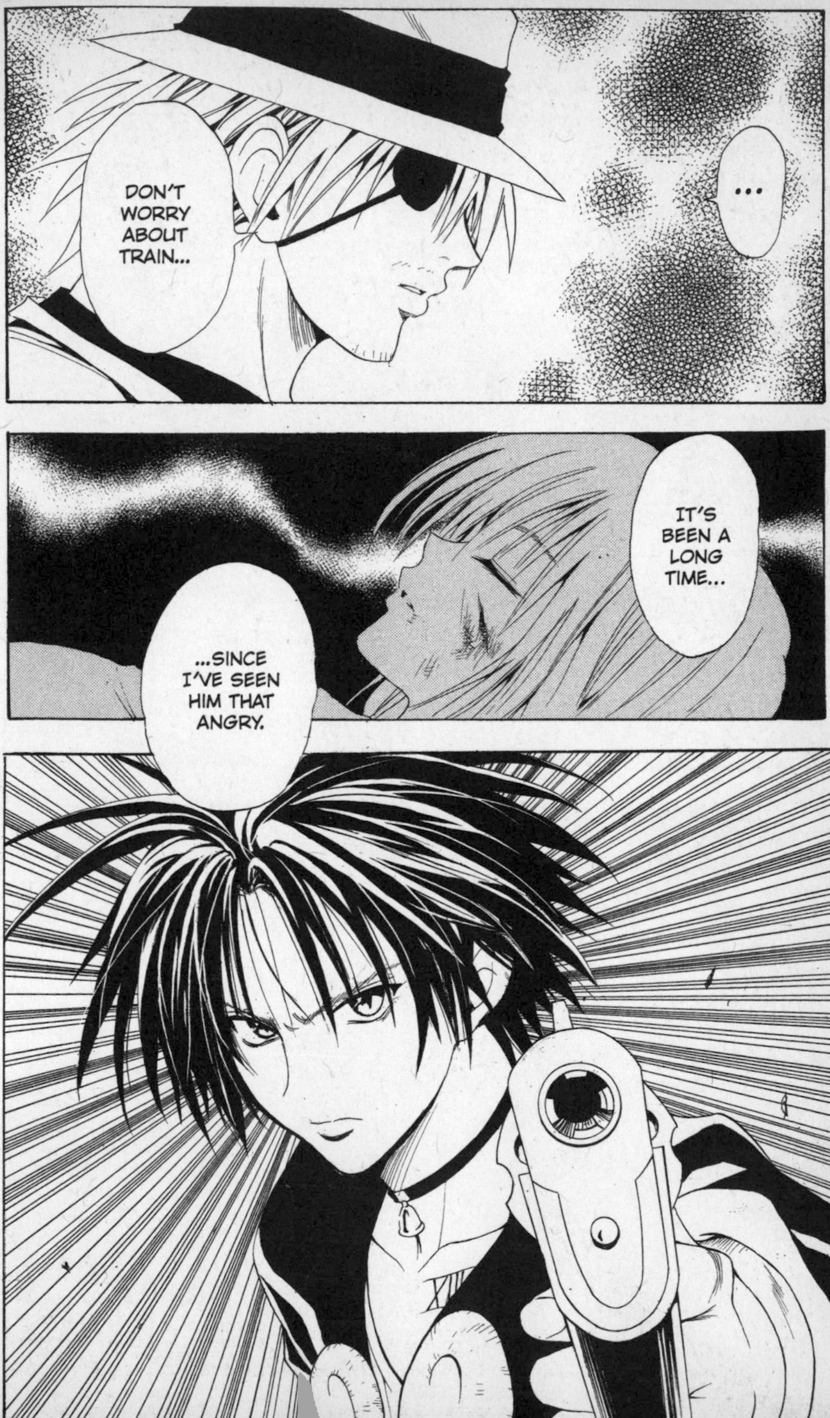
...
DON'T WORRY ABOUT TRAIN...
IT'S BEEN A LONG TIME...
...SINCE I'VE SEEN HIM THAT ANGRY.

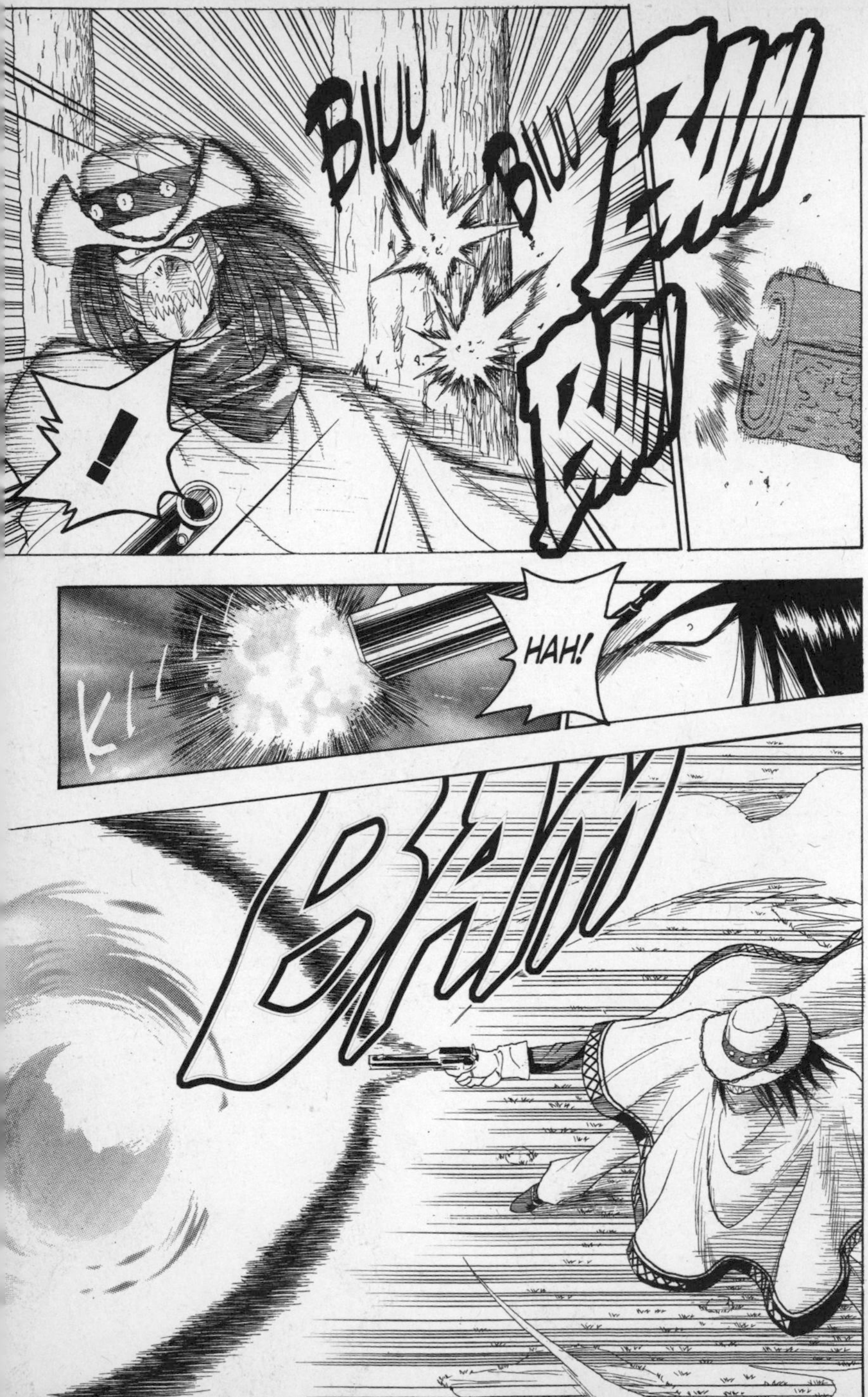
BIUU
BIUU
!
HAH!

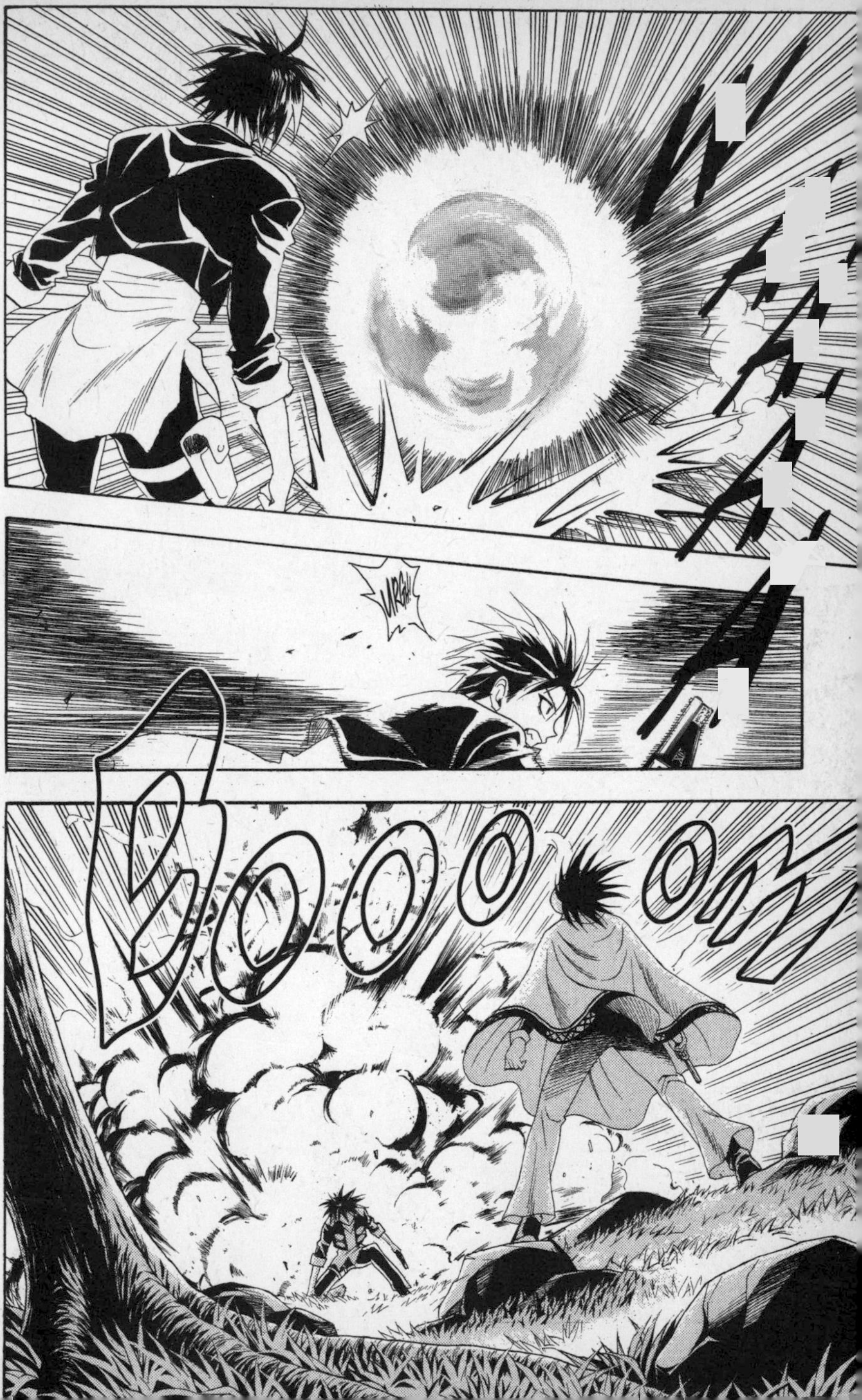
URGH!!
BOOOOOM

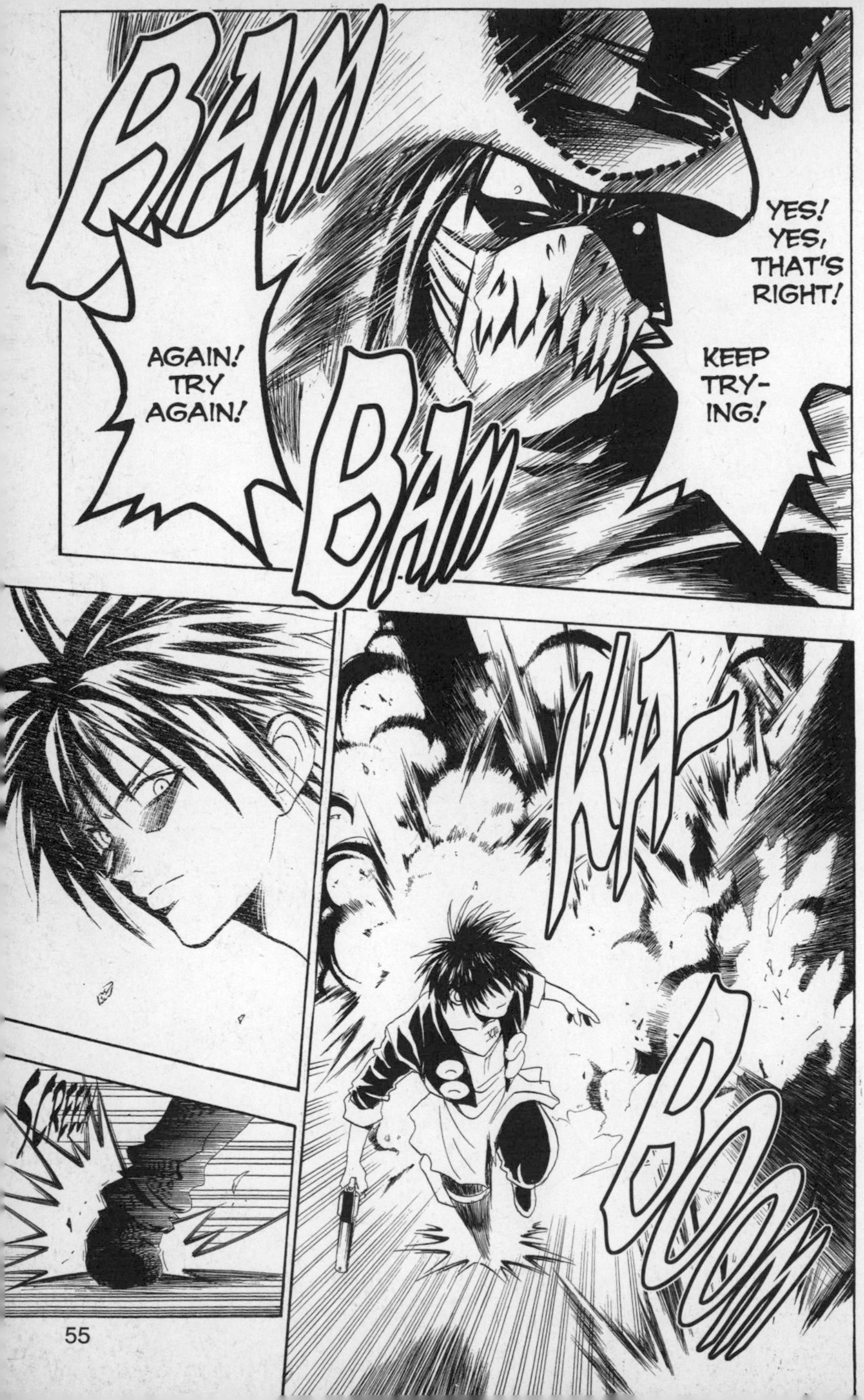
YES! YES, THAT'S RIGHT!
KEEP TRYING!
BAM
AGAIN! TRY AGAIN!
BAM
KA-BOOM
SCREEN

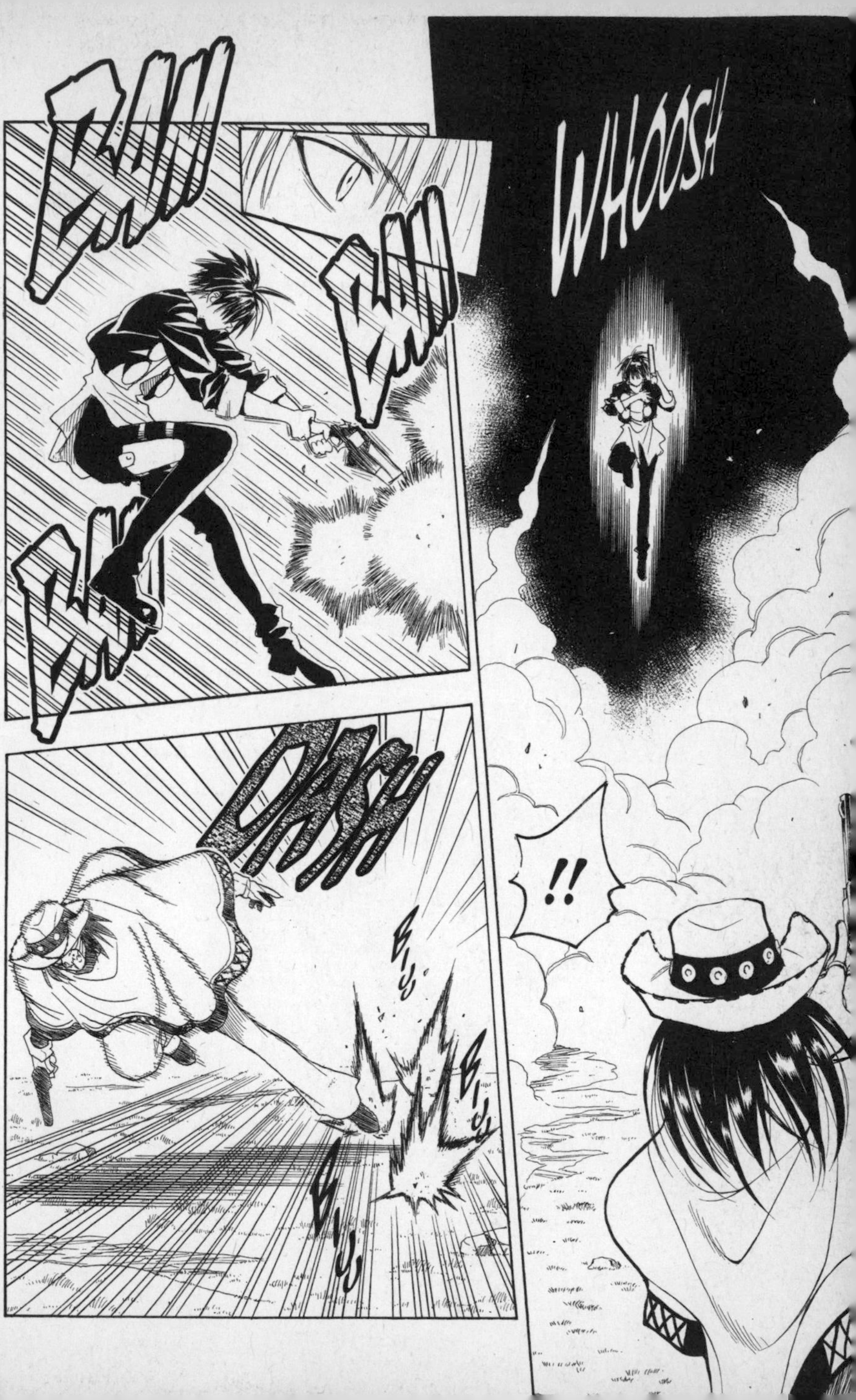
WHOOSH
!!
DASH
BIU
BIU
BIU

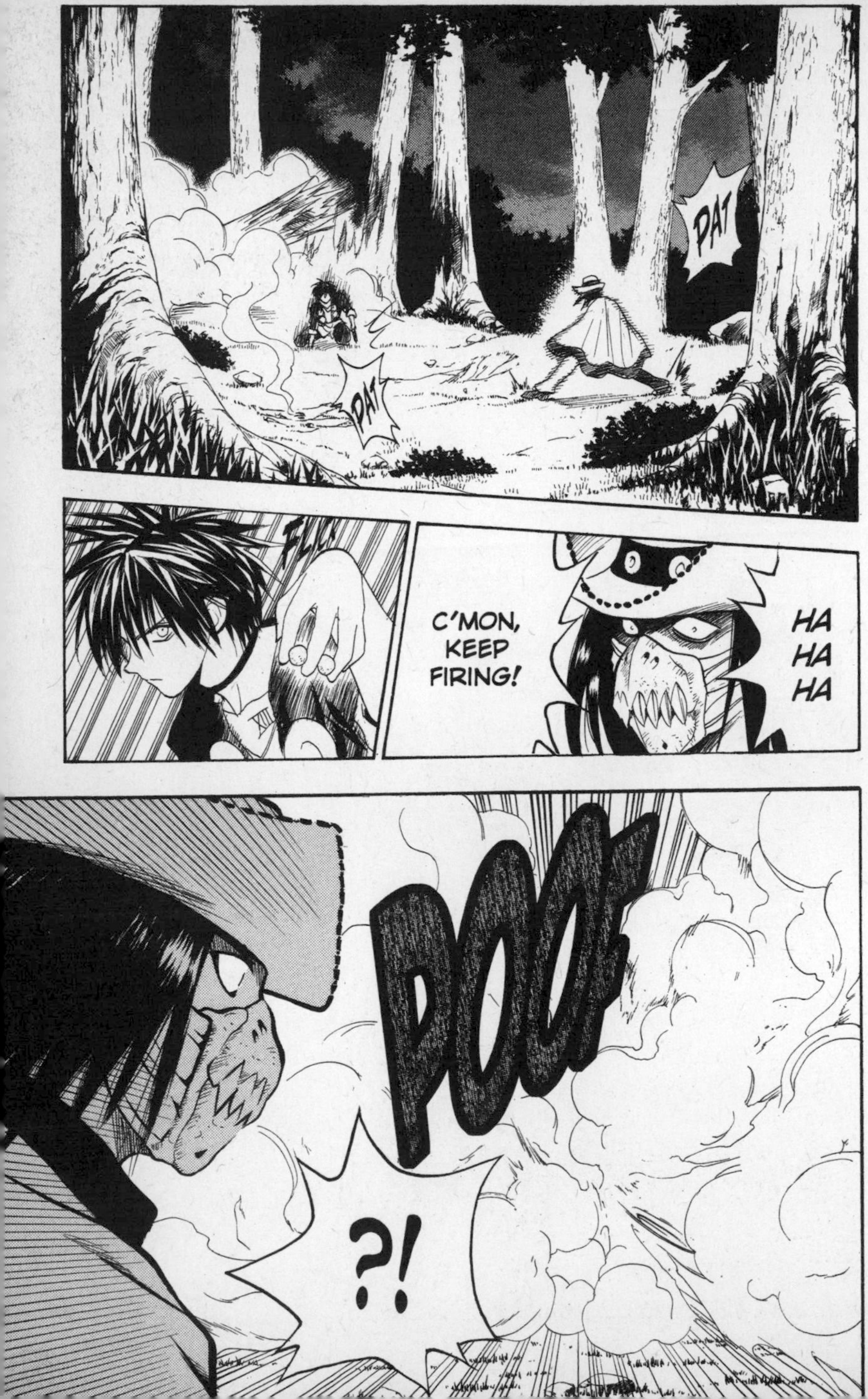
PAT
PAT
HA HA HA
C'MON, KEEP FIRING!
POOF
?!

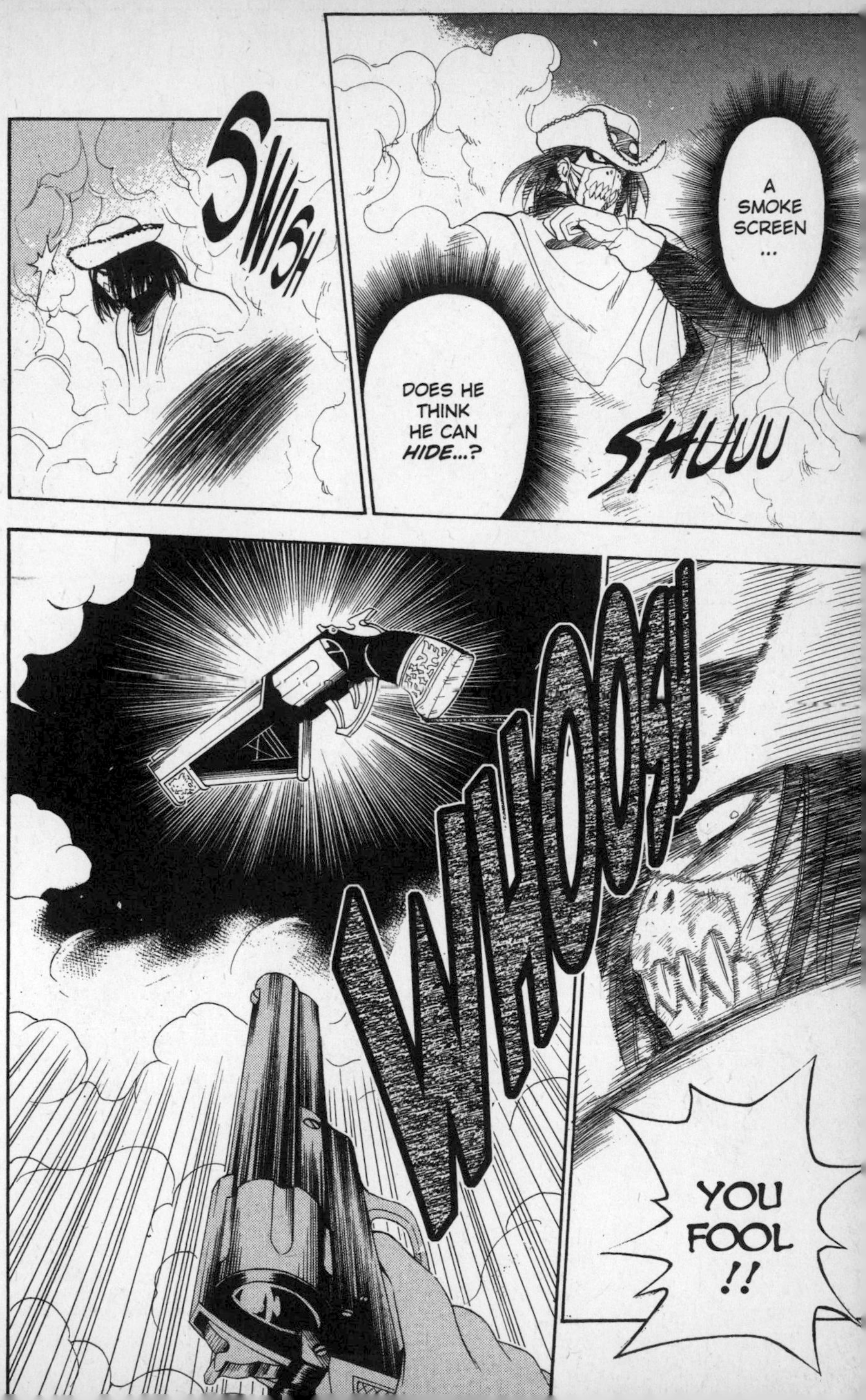
A SMOKE SCREEN ...
DOES HE THINK HE CAN HIDE...?
SHUUU
SWISH
YOU FOOL !!
WHOOSH!!

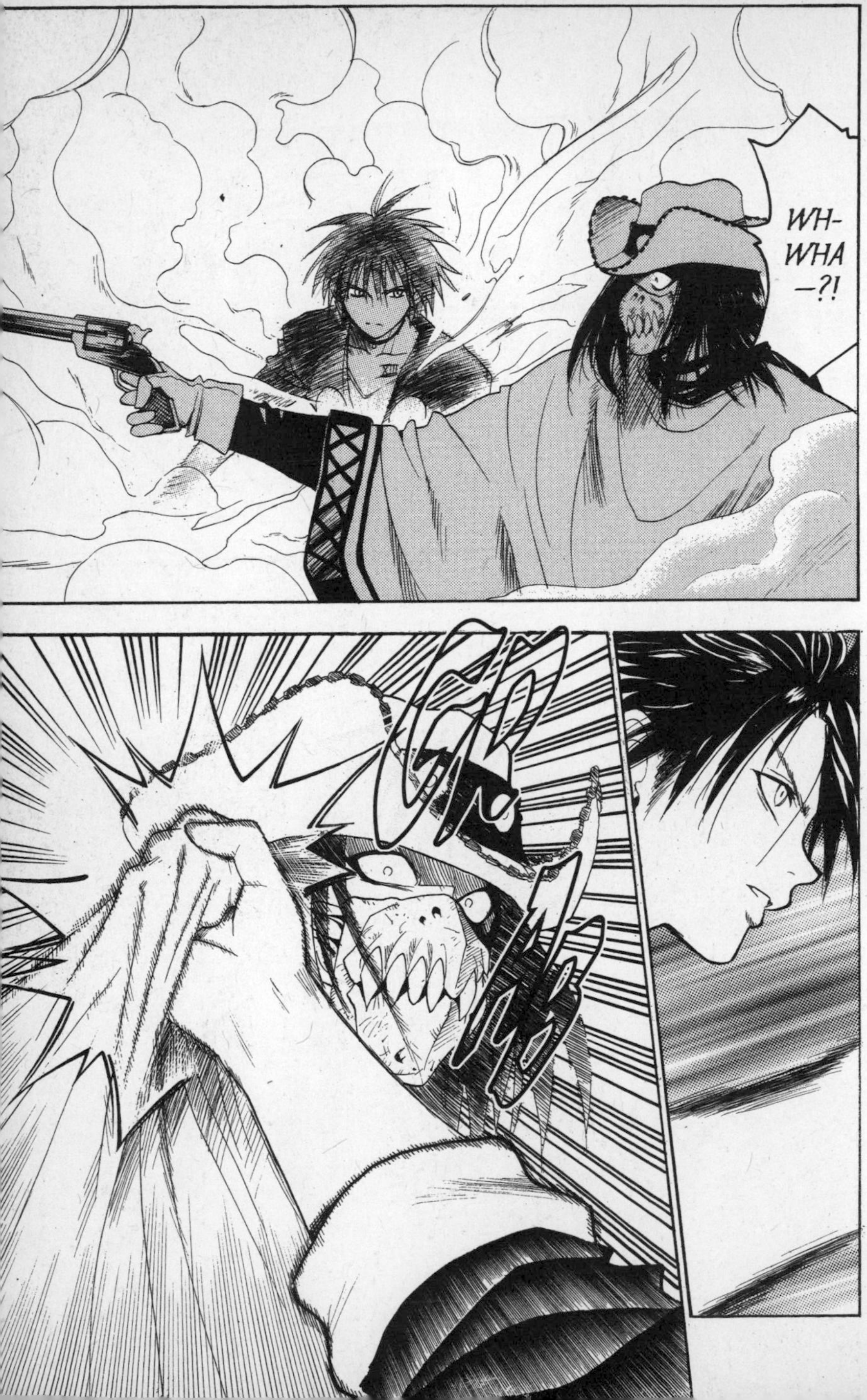
WH-
WHA
—?!

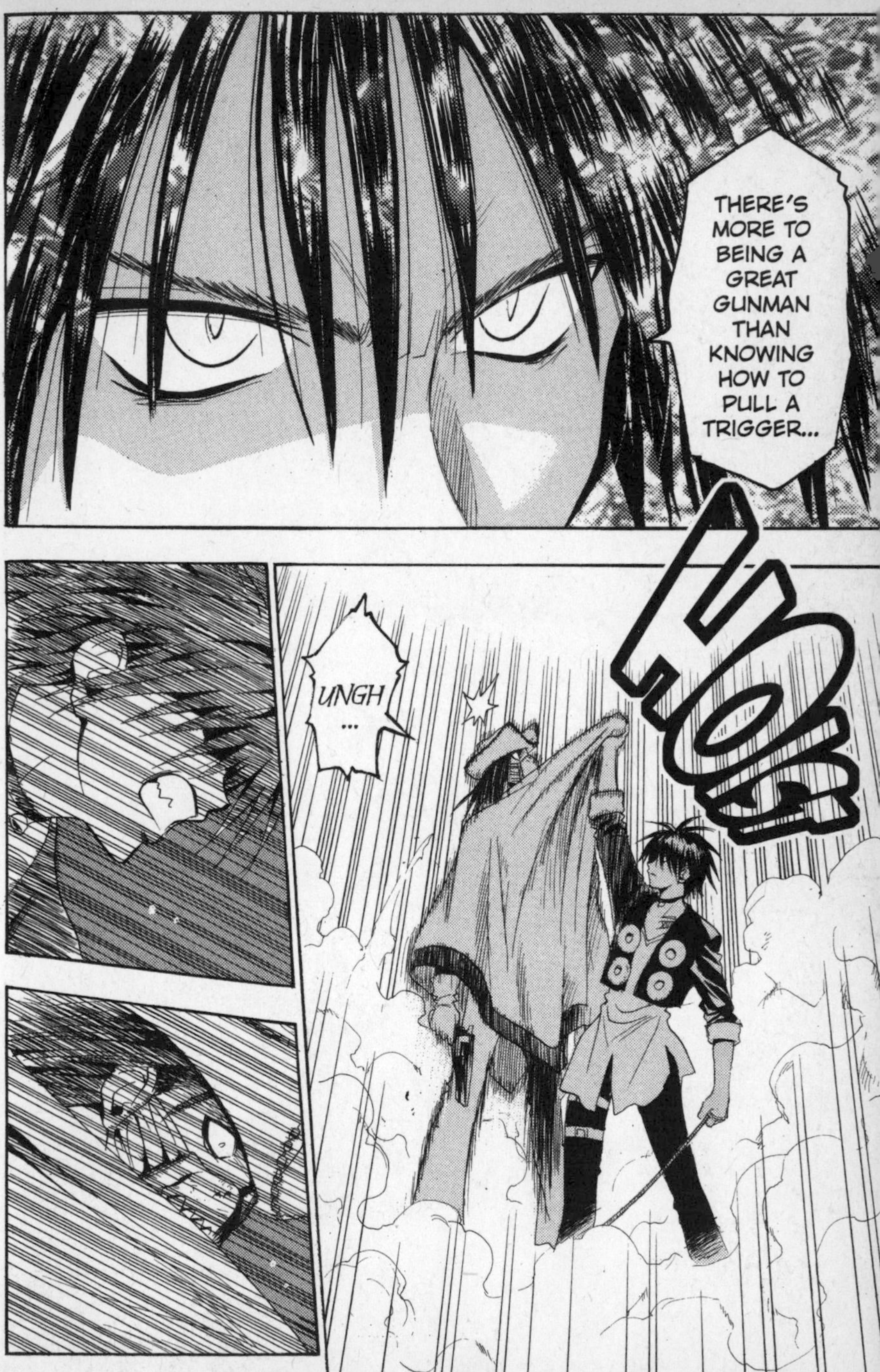
THERE'S MORE TO BEING A GREAT GUNMAN THAN KNOWING HOW TO PULL A TRIGGER...
UNGH ...

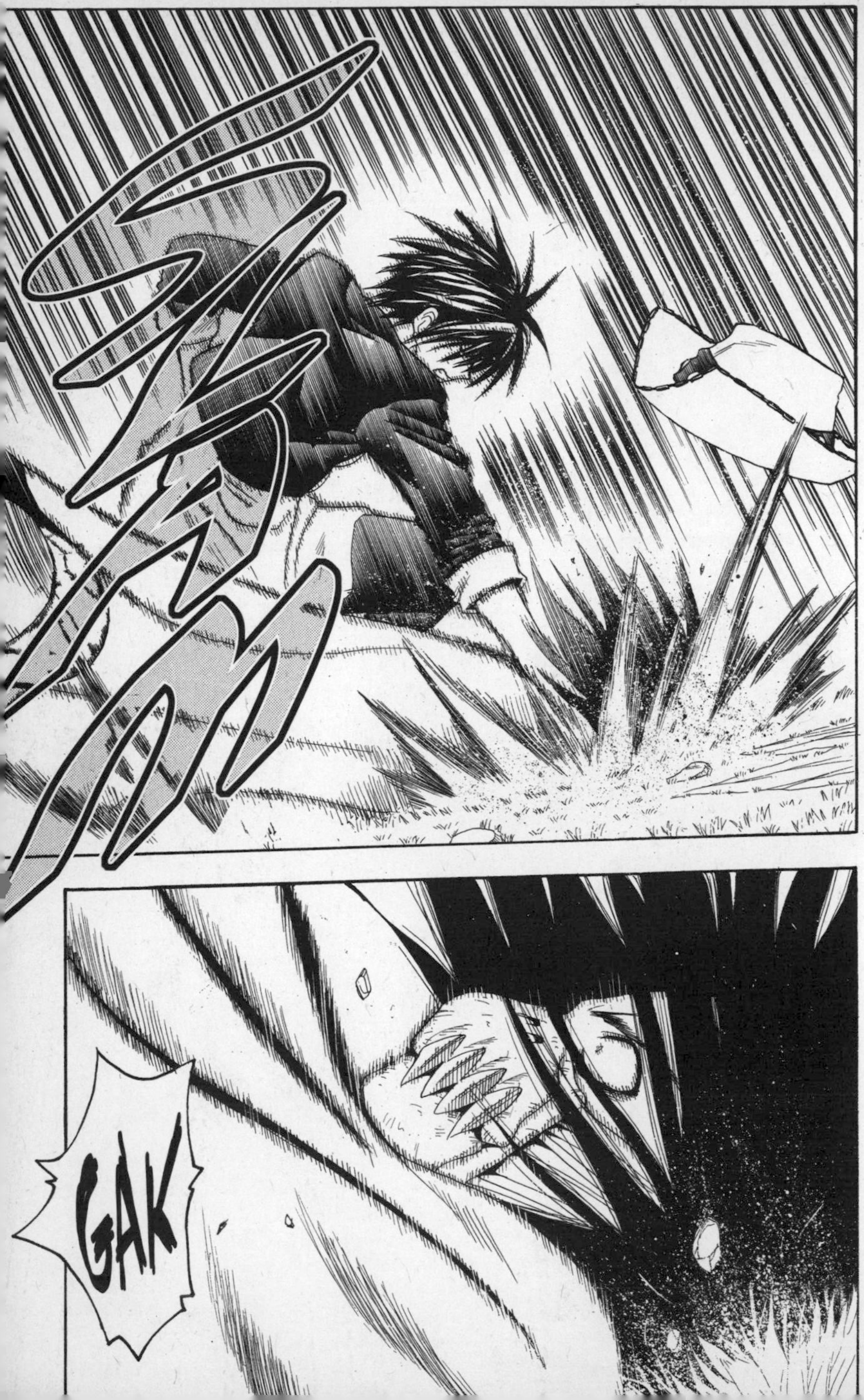
GAK

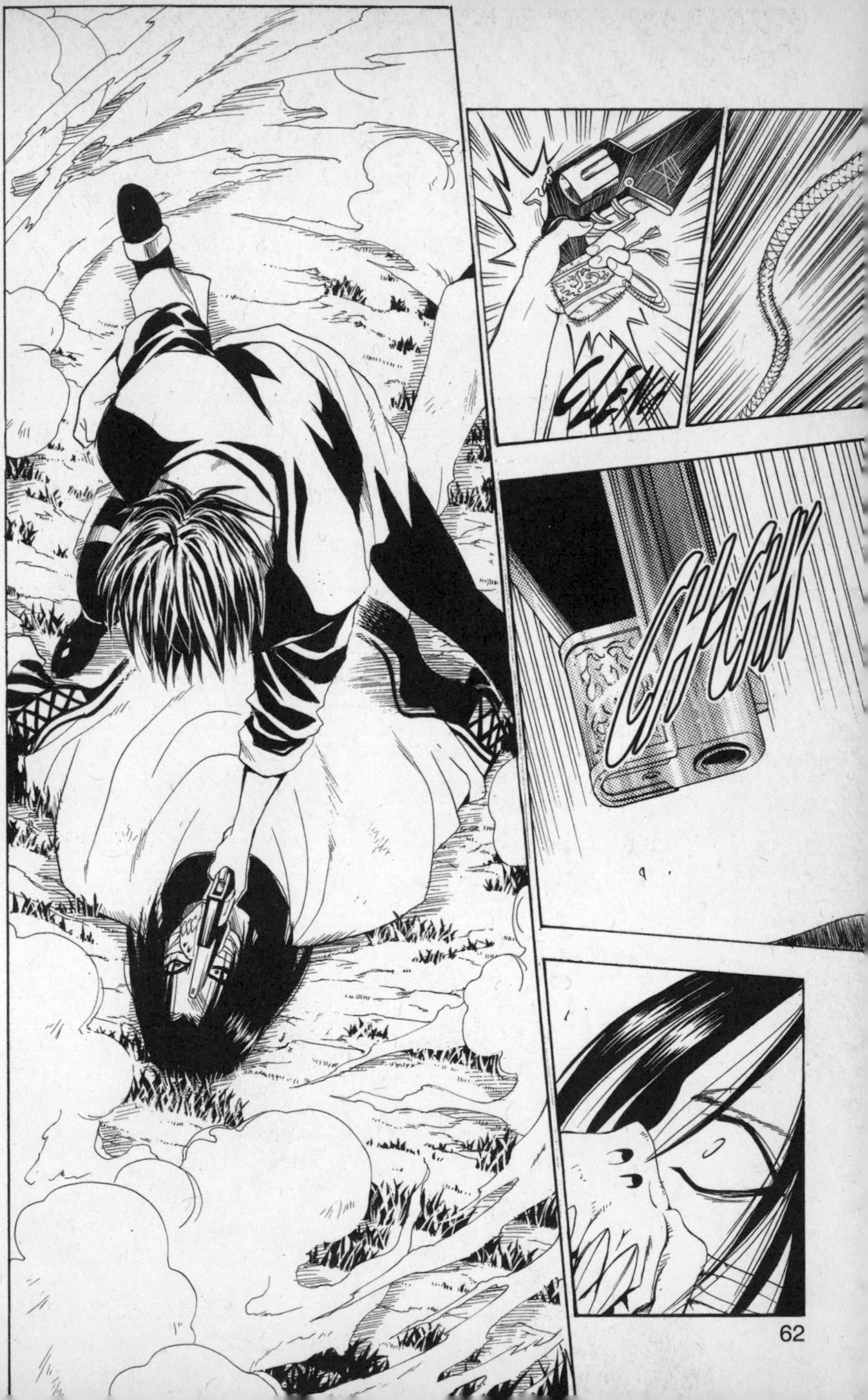
CLENK

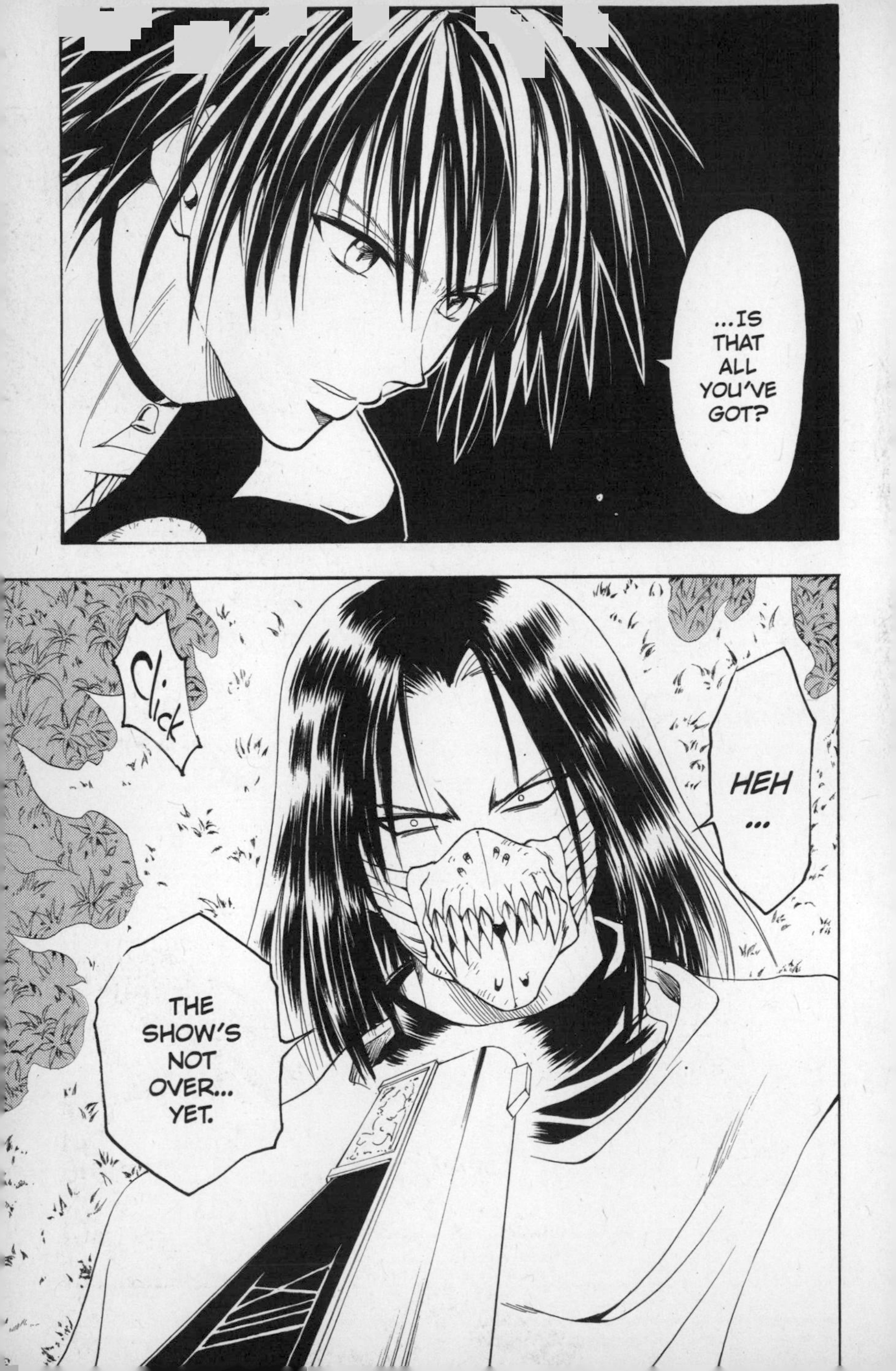
...IS THAT ALL YOU'VE GOT?
Click
HEH ...
THE SHOW'S NOT OVER... YET.

BLACKCAT

profile

DURHAM GLASTER

DATA	
BIRTHDATE:	FEBRUARY 29
AGE:	26
BLOOD TYPE:	A
HEIGHT:	178 CM
WEIGHT:	83 KG
LIKES:	ENJOYS WATCHING VICTIMS WRITHE IN PAIN.
DISLIKES:	SMALL, DARK ROOMS.
POWER:	THE "SHOT"
COMMENTS:	MEMBER, APOSTLES OF THE STARS. FORMERLY A CRIMINAL. HAS THE *TAO* ABILITY TO CHANNEL HIS *CHI* THOUGH HIS GUN AND FIRE IT AS A BULLET.

Chapter 51:
Train vs. Durham: The Showdown

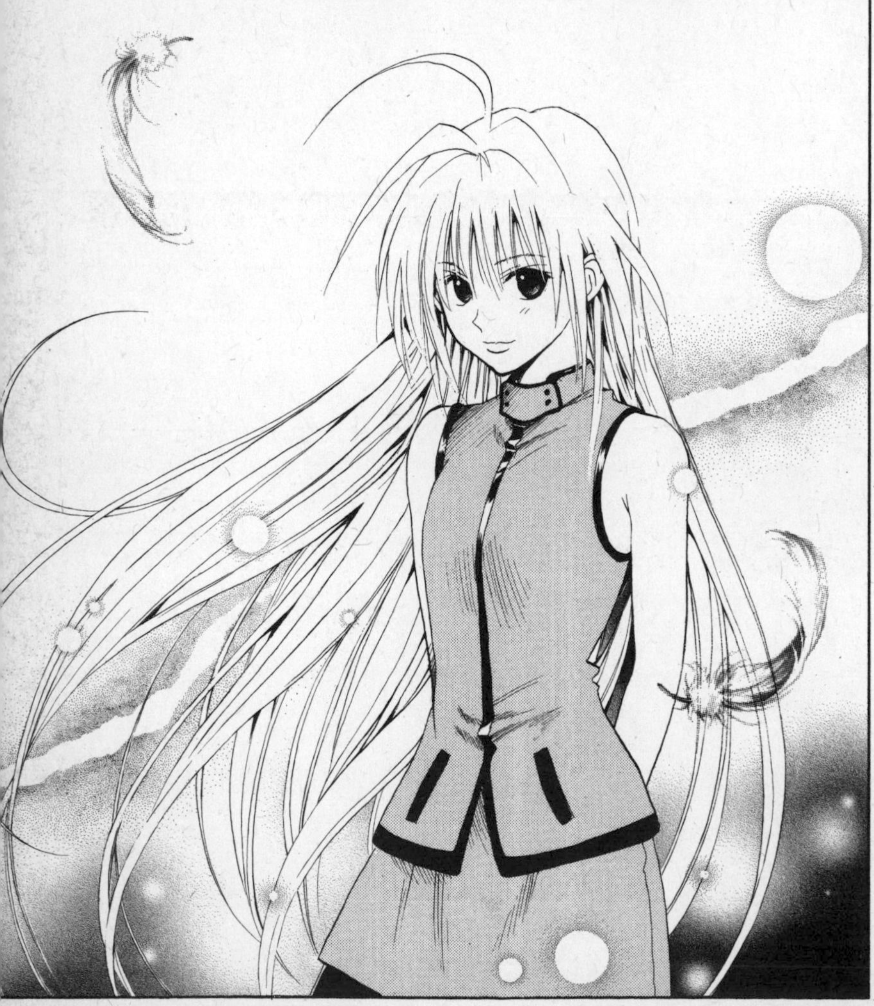

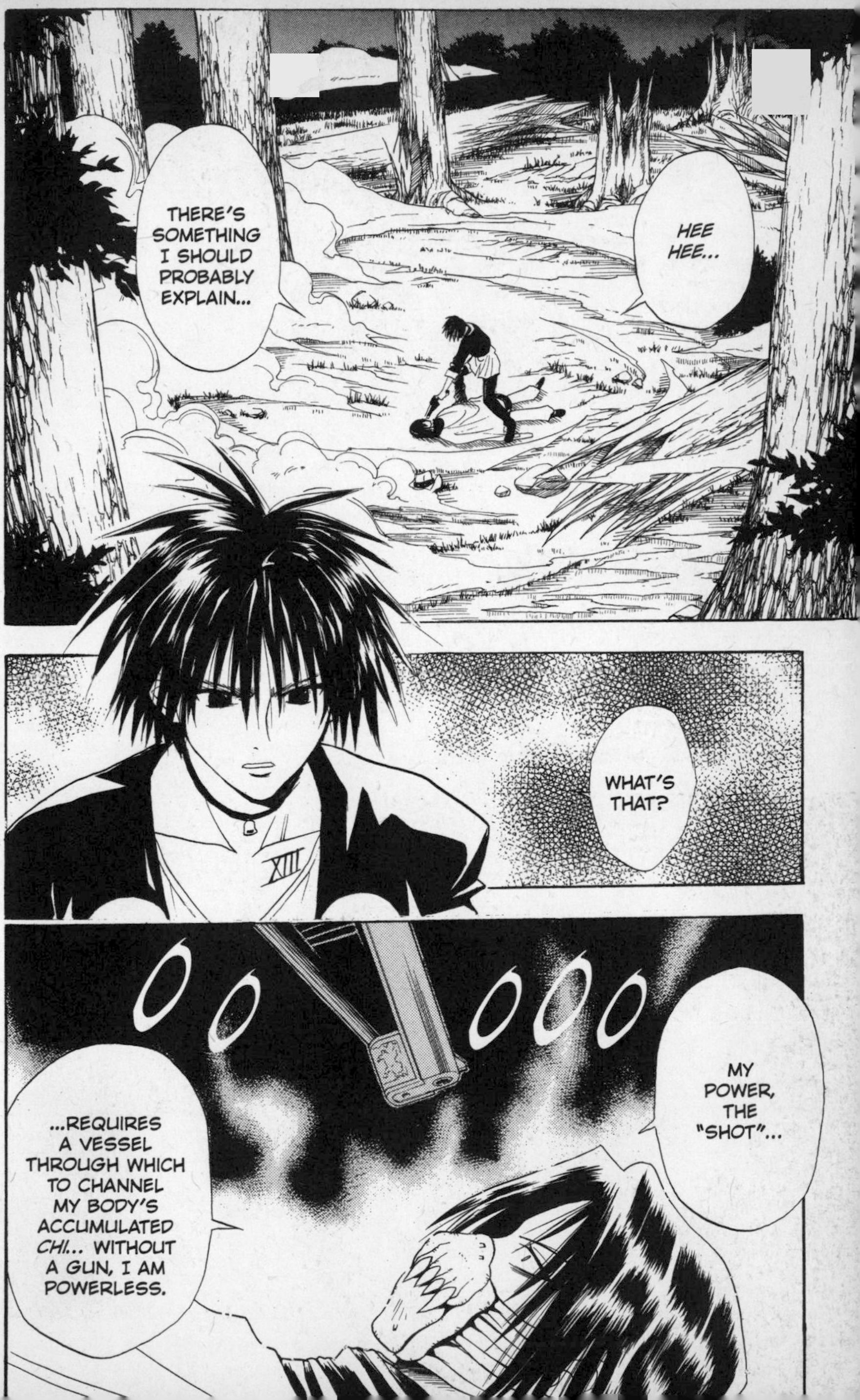
HEE HEE...
THERE'S SOMETHING I SHOULD PROBABLY EXPLAIN...
WHAT'S THAT?
MY POWER, THE "SHOT"...
...REQUIRES A VESSEL THROUGH WHICH TO CHANNEL MY BODY'S ACCUMULATED *CHI*... WITHOUT A GUN, I AM POWERLESS.

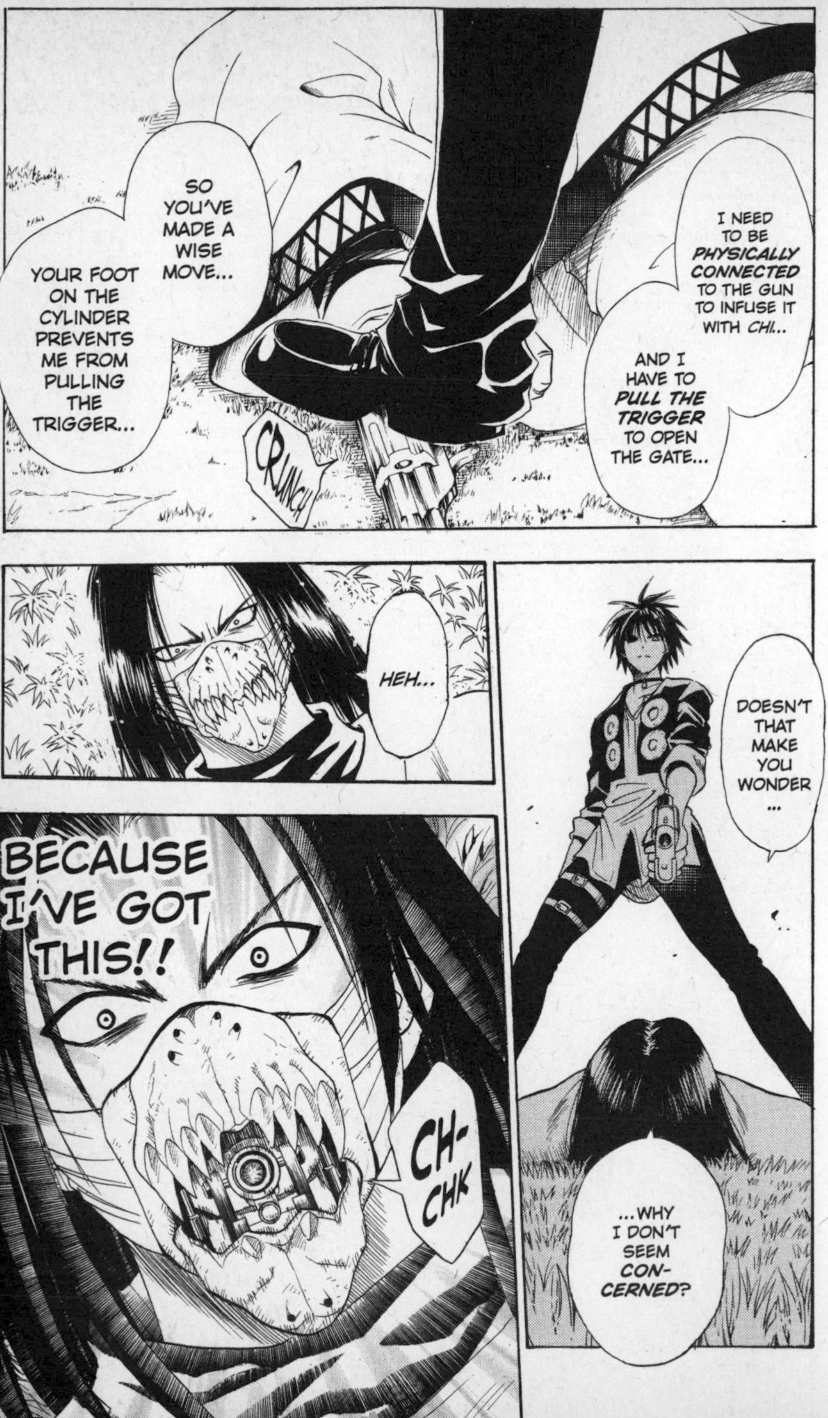
I NEED TO BE *PHYSICALLY CONNECTED* TO THE GUN TO INFUSE IT WITH *CHI*...
AND I HAVE TO *PULL THE TRIGGER* TO OPEN THE GATE...
CRUNCH
SO YOU'VE MADE A WISE MOVE...
YOUR FOOT ON THE CYLINDER PREVENTS ME FROM PULLING THE TRIGGER...
DOESN'T THAT MAKE YOU WONDER...
...WHY I DON'T SEEM *CON-CERNED*?
HEH...
BECAUSE I'VE GOT THIS!!
CH-CHK

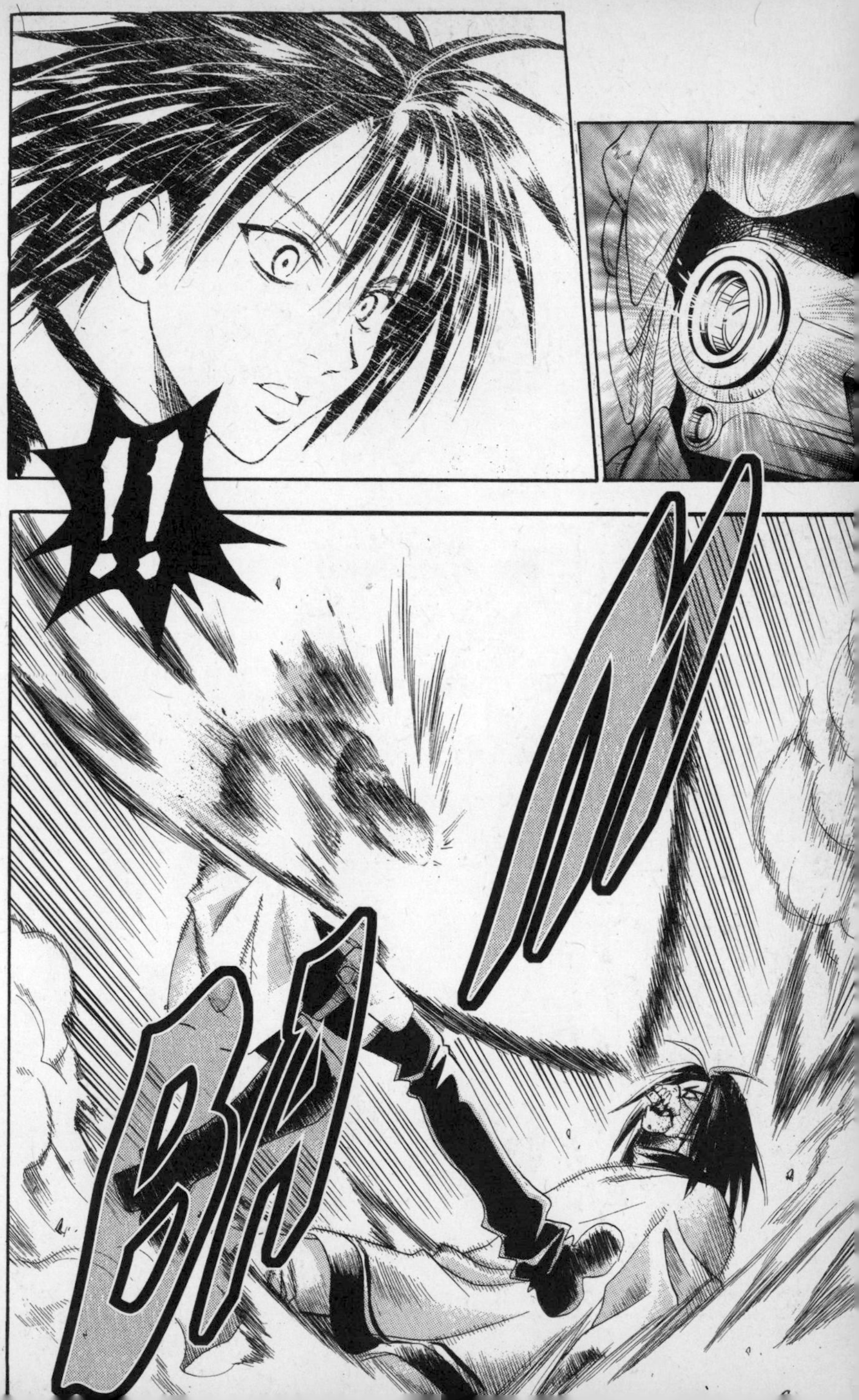
!!

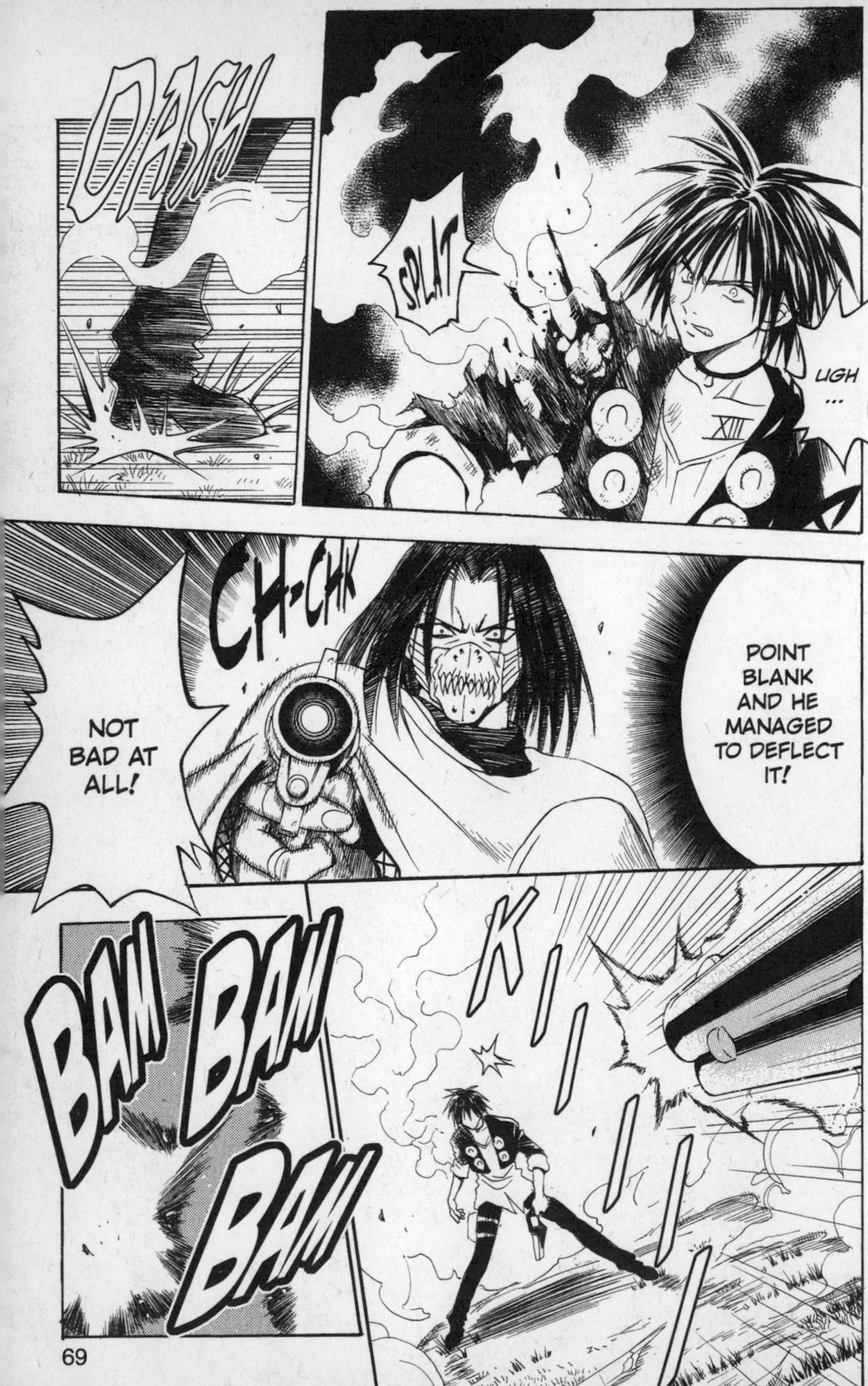
SPLAT
UGH ...
DASH
POINT BLANK AND HE MANAGED TO DEFLECT IT!
CH-CHK
NOT BAD AT ALL!
KIIIIII
BAM BAM BAM

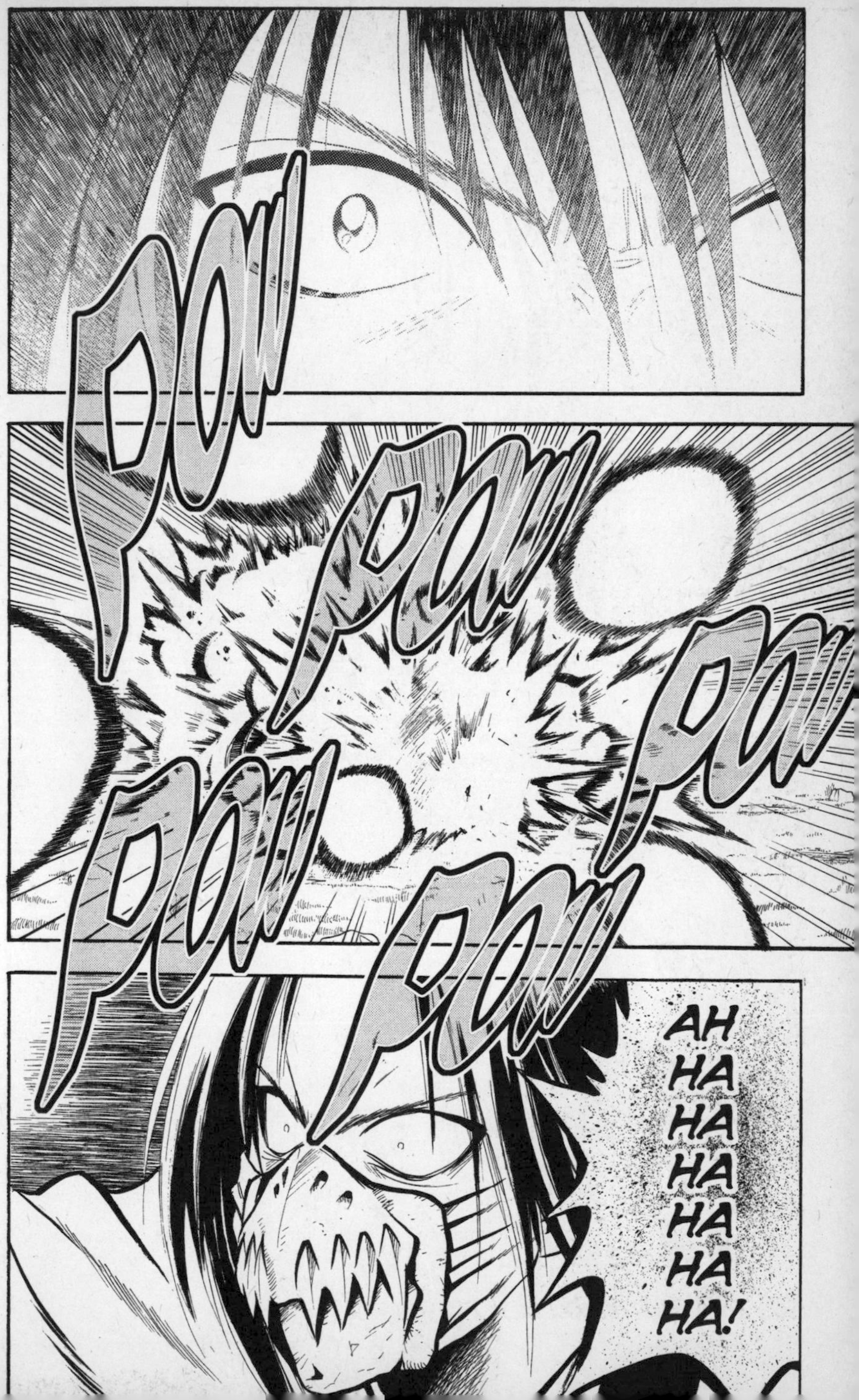
PAU
PAU
PAU
PAU
PAU
AH HA HA HA HA HA HA HA!

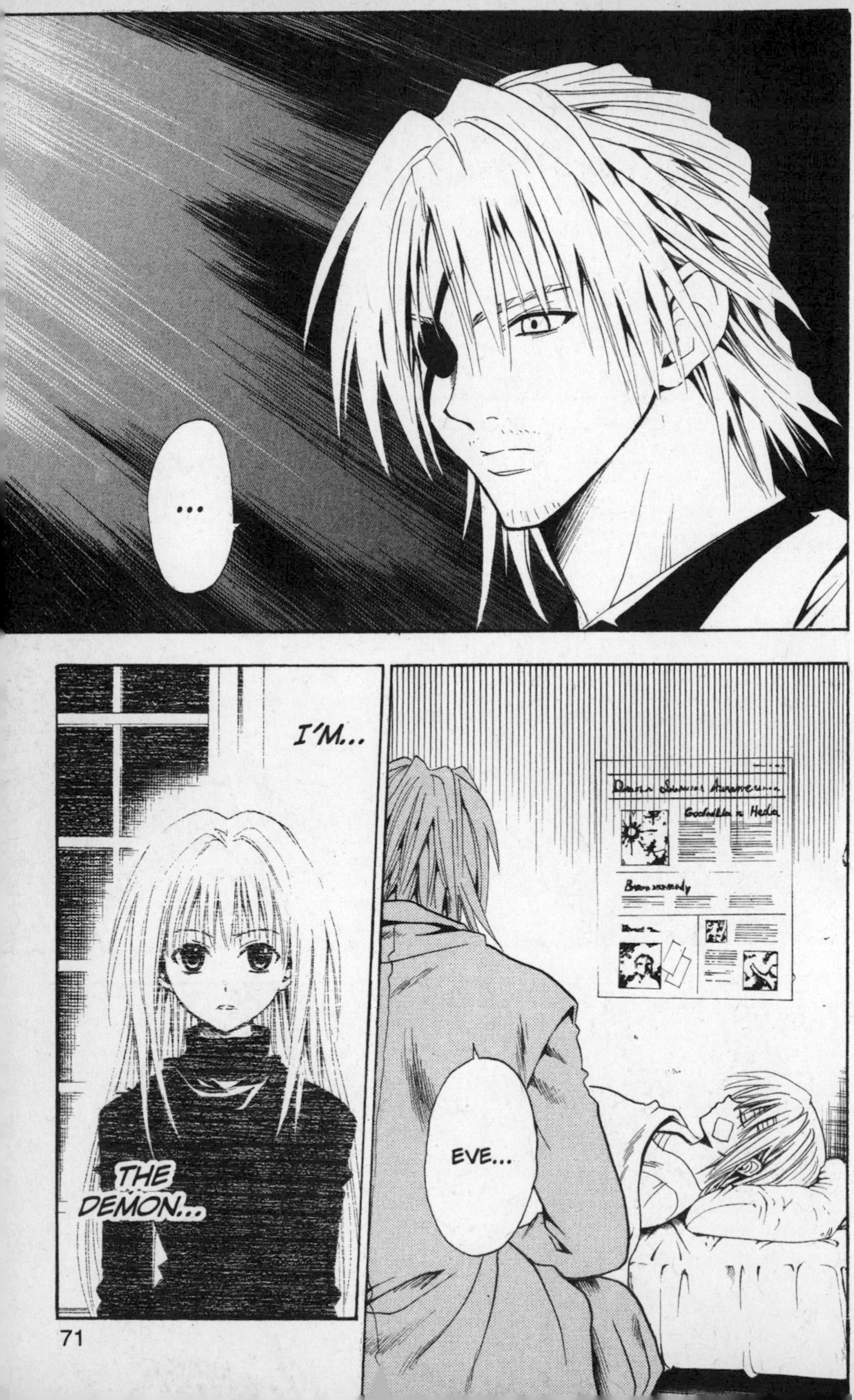
...
EVE...
I'M...
THE DEMON...

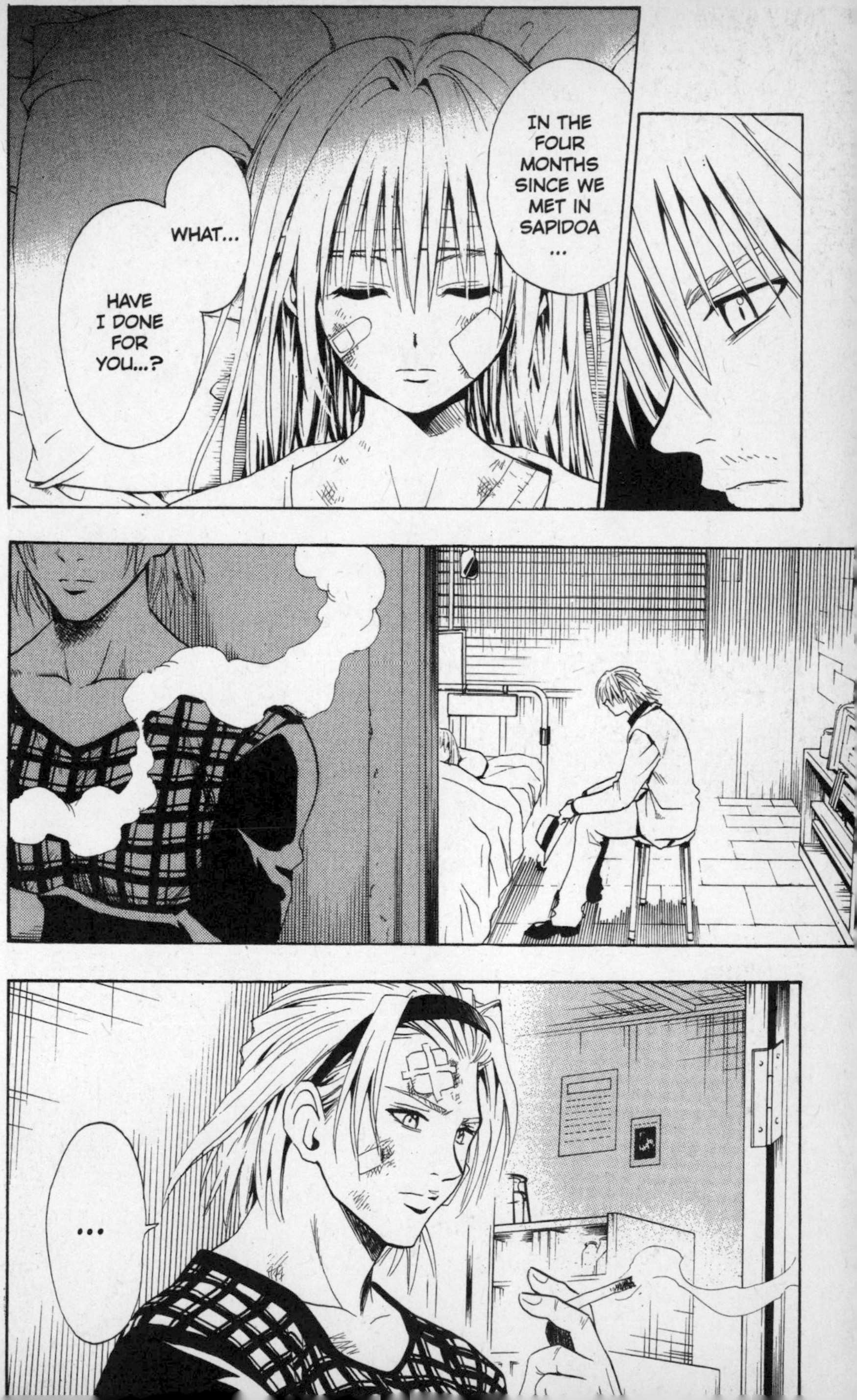
IN THE FOUR MONTHS SINCE WE MET IN SAPIDOA...
WHAT...
HAVE I DONE FOR YOU...?
...

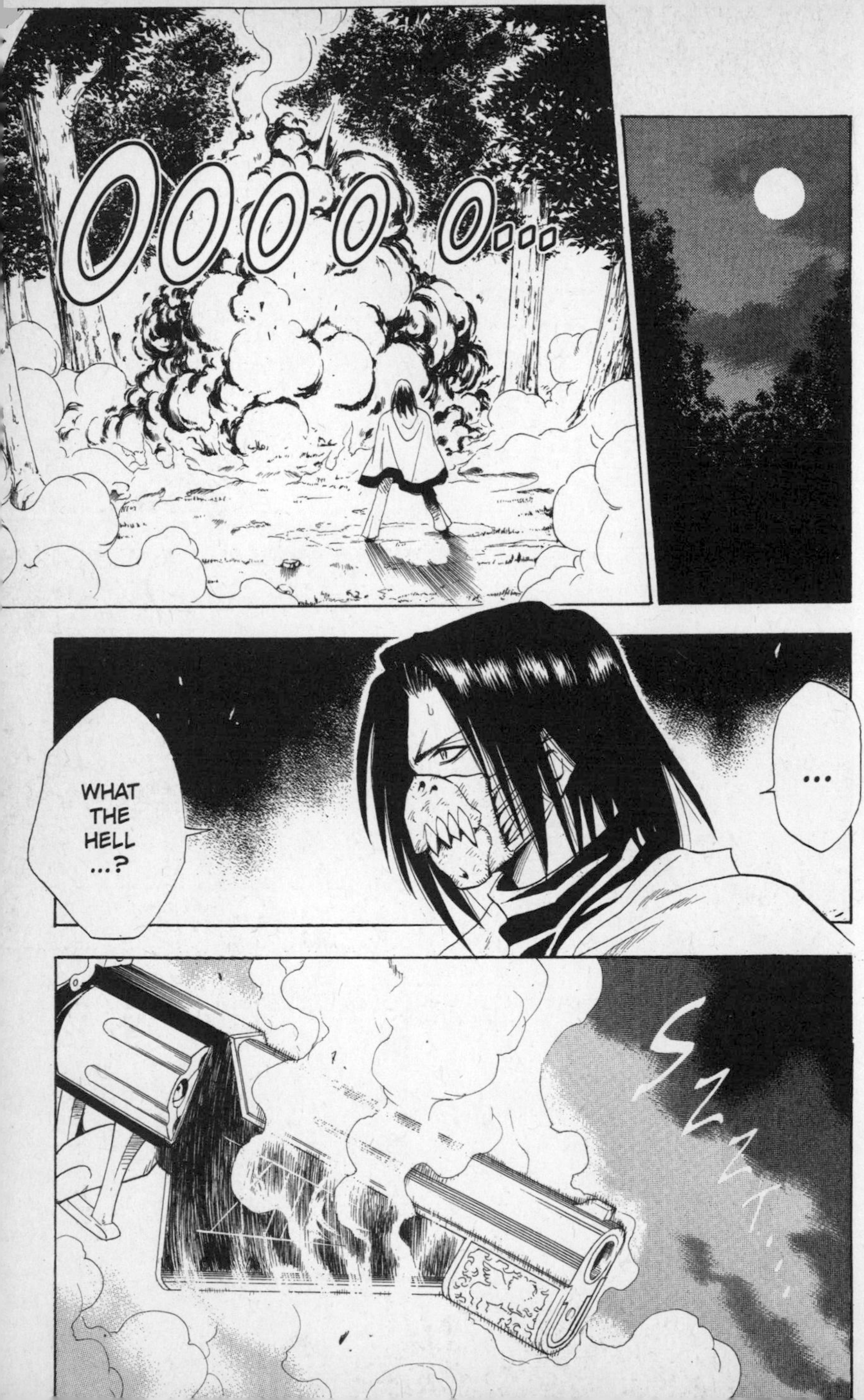
OOOO O...
...
WHAT THE HELL ...?
SZZZK...

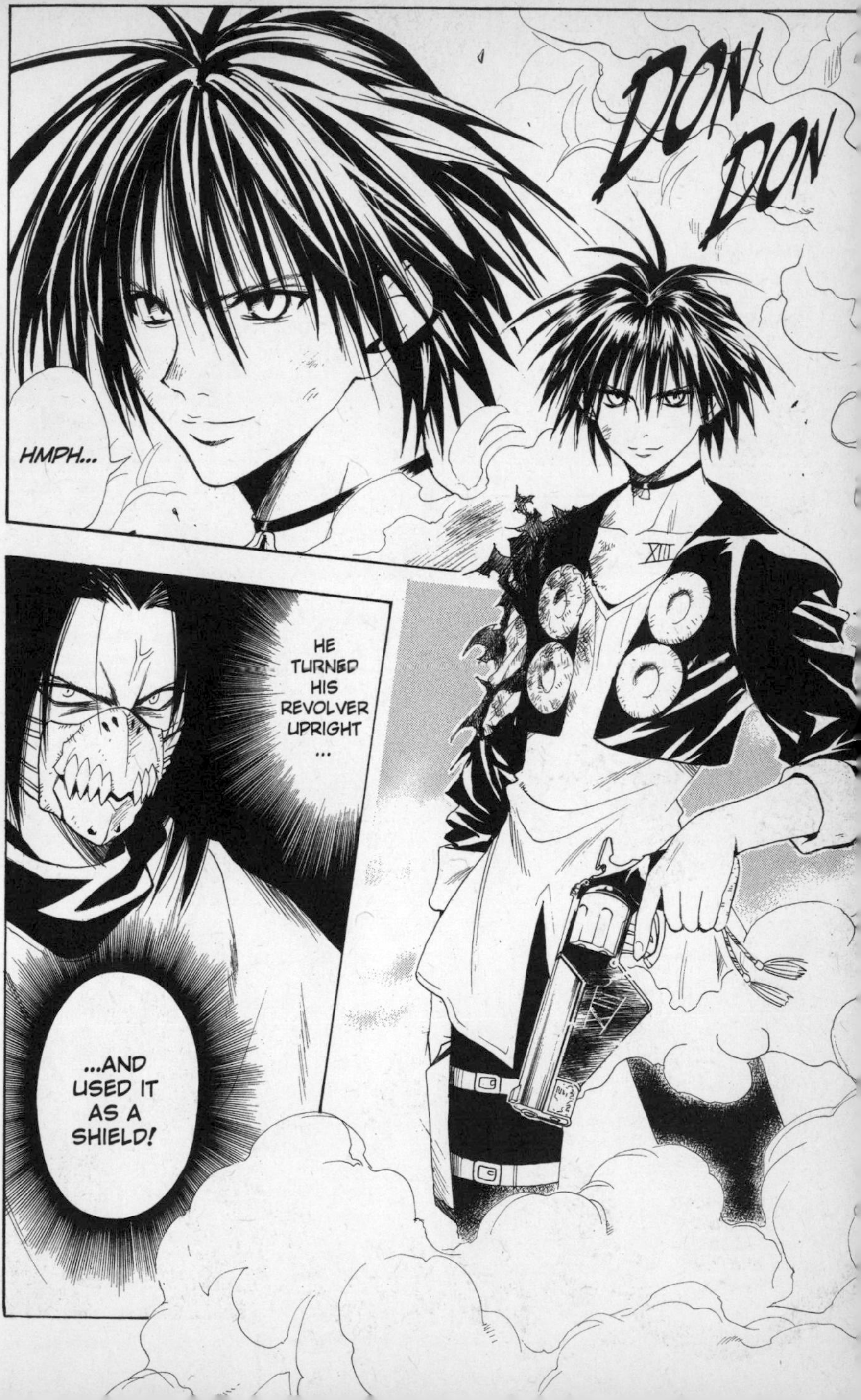
DON DON
HMPH...
HE TURNED HIS REVOLVER UPRIGHT...
...AND USED IT AS A SHIELD!

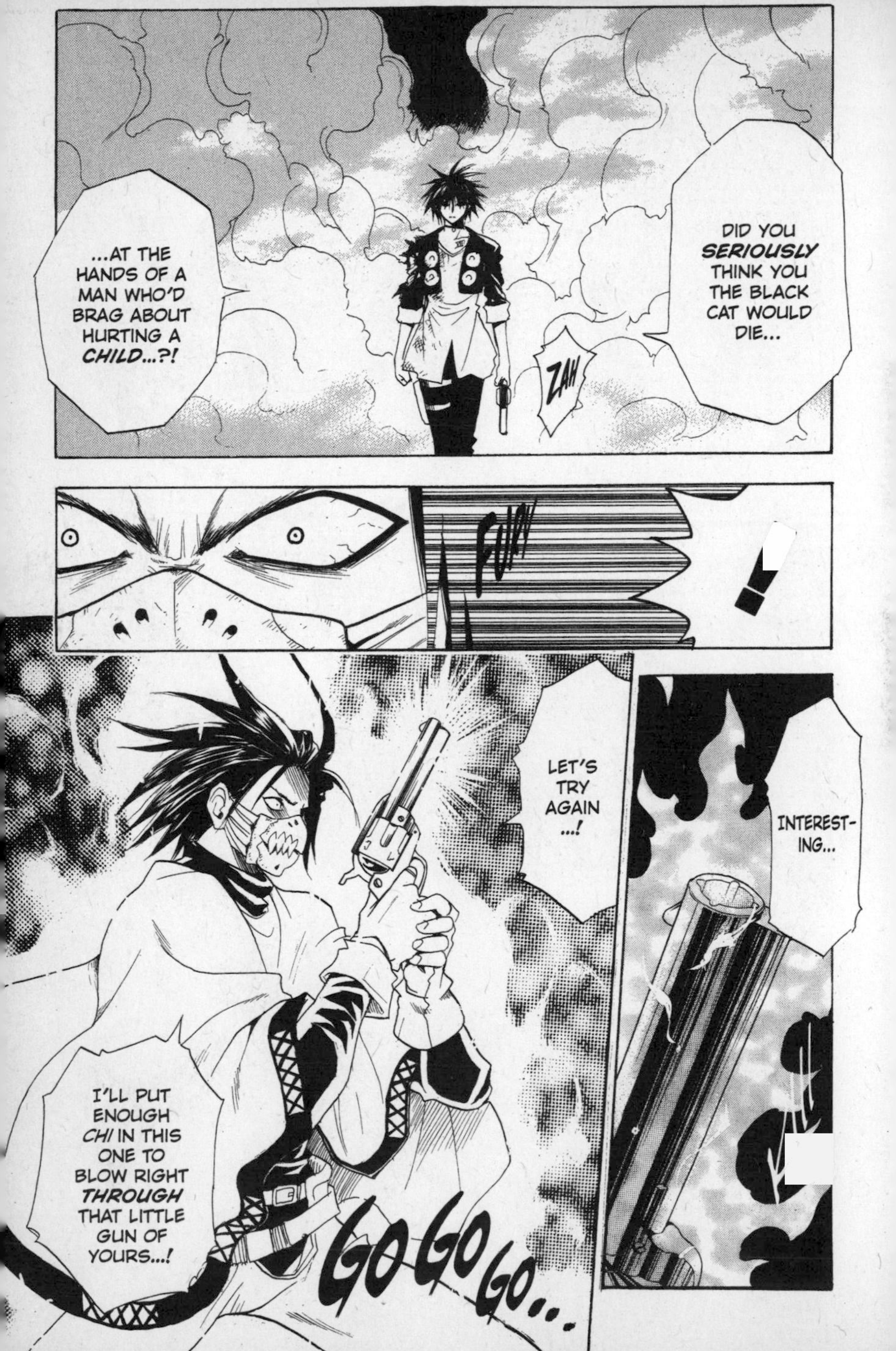
DID YOU SERIOUSLY THINK YOU THE BLACK CAT WOULD DIE...
ZAH
...AT THE HANDS OF A MAN WHO'D BRAG ABOUT HURTING A CHILD...?!
!
INTEREST-ING...
LET'S TRY AGAIN...!
I'LL PUT ENOUGH CHI IN THIS ONE TO BLOW RIGHT THROUGH THAT LITTLE GUN OF YOURS...!
GO GO GO...

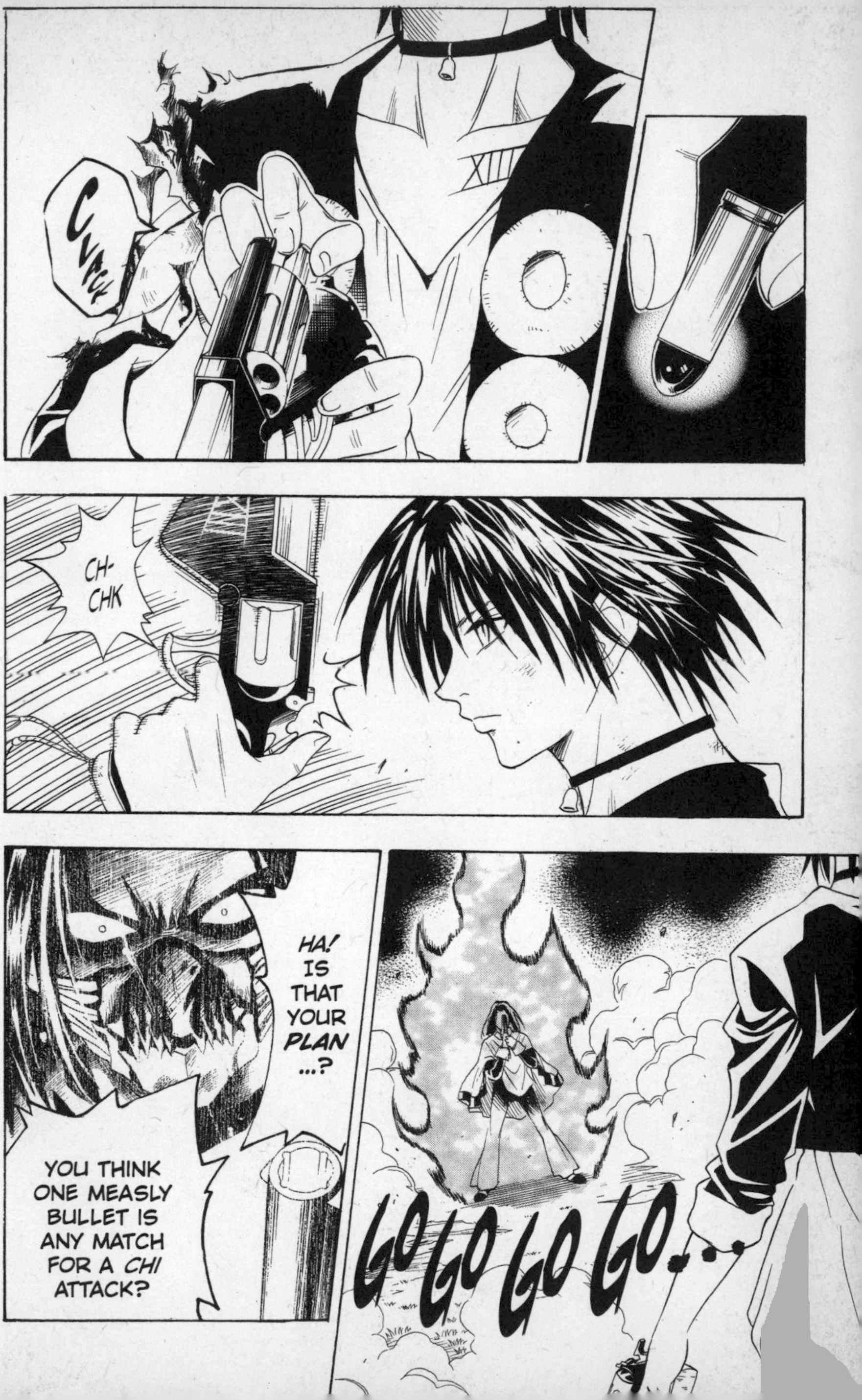
CLACK
CH-CHK
HA! IS THAT YOUR PLAN ...?
YOU THINK ONE MEASLY BULLET IS ANY MATCH FOR A CHI ATTACK?
GO GO GO GO GO...

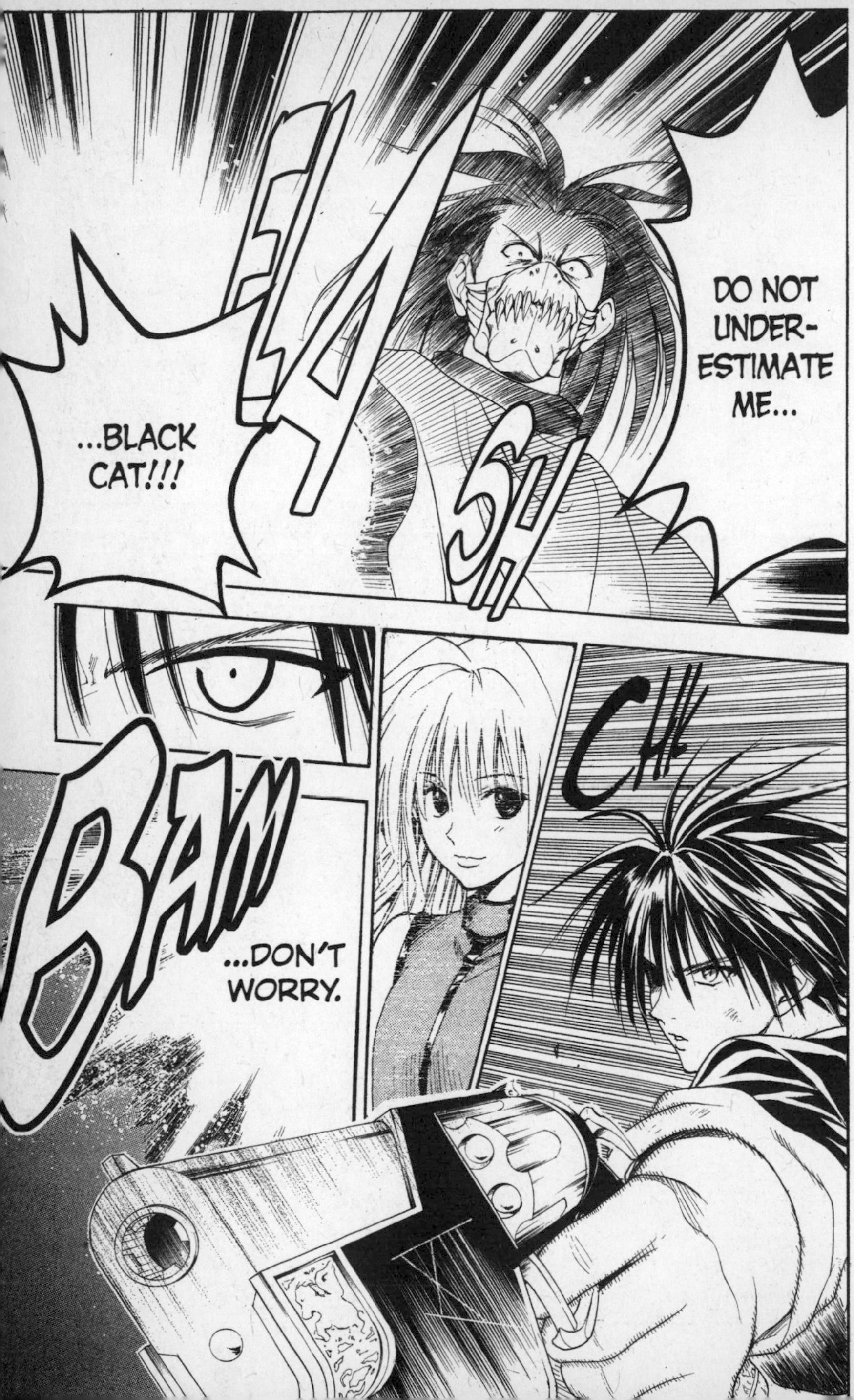
DO NOT UNDER-ESTIMATE ME...
...BLACK CAT!!!
...DON'T WORRY.

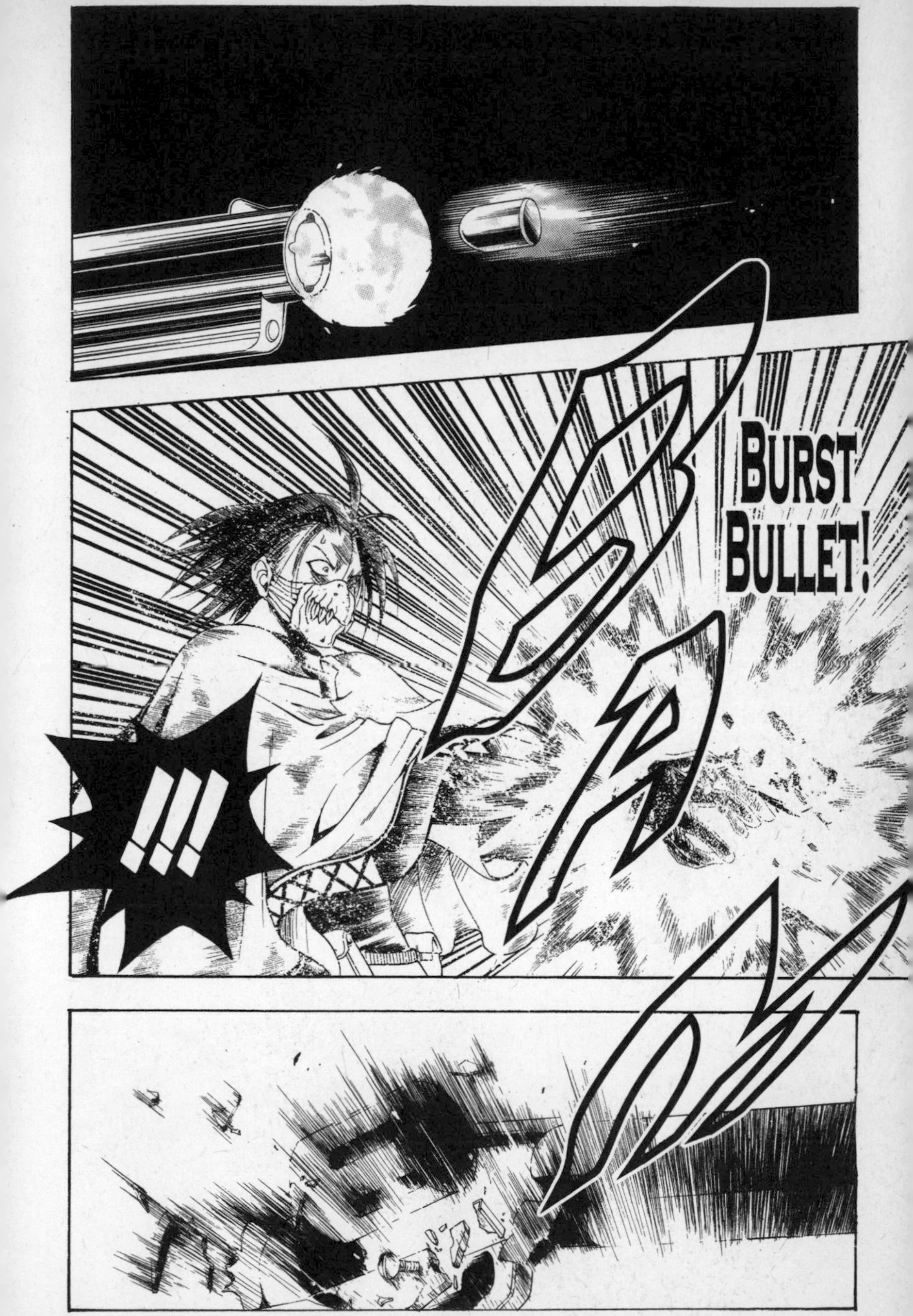
BURST BULLET!
!!!

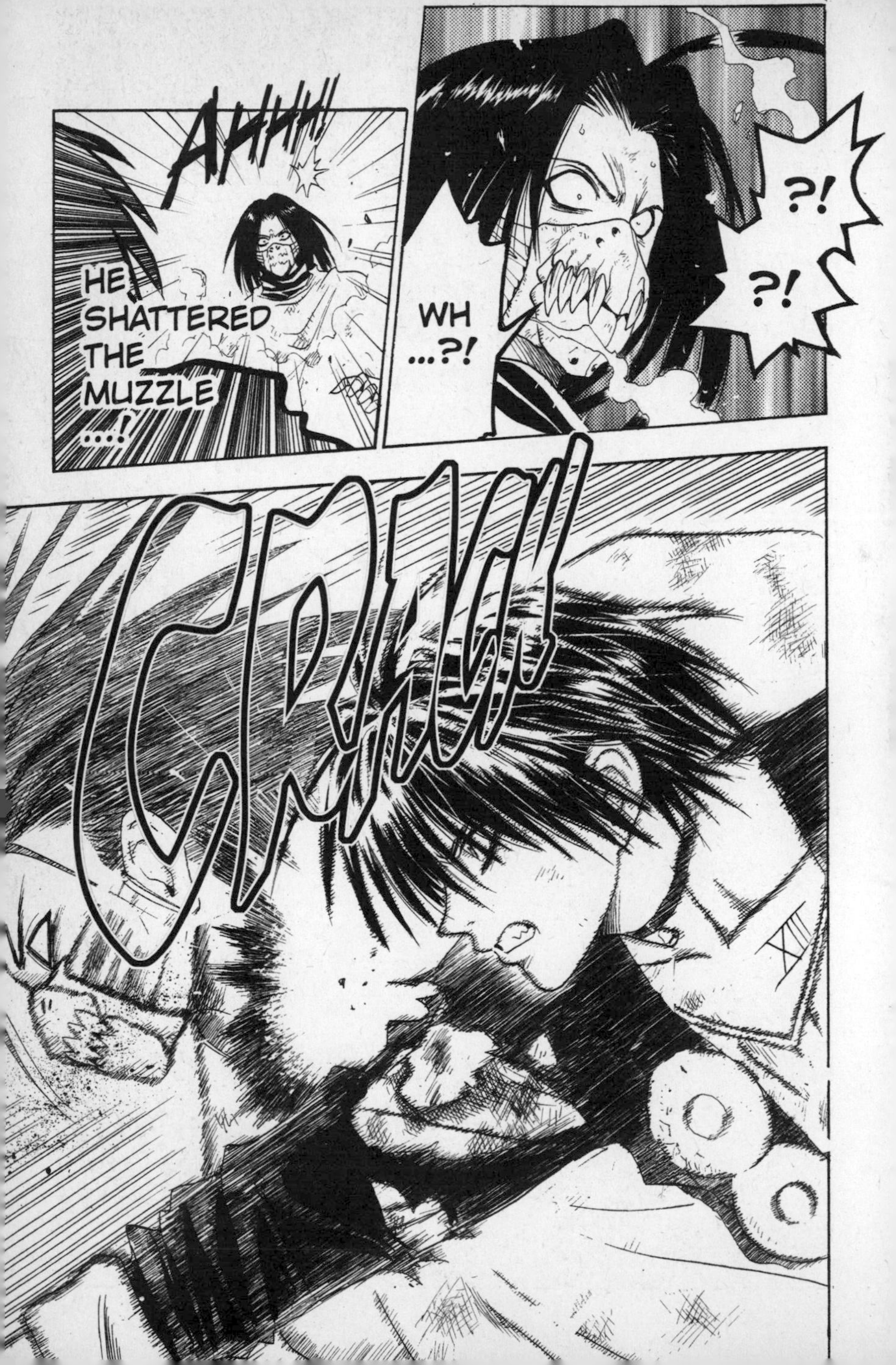
?!
?!
WH ...?!
AHHH!!
HE SHATTERED THE MUZZLE ...!

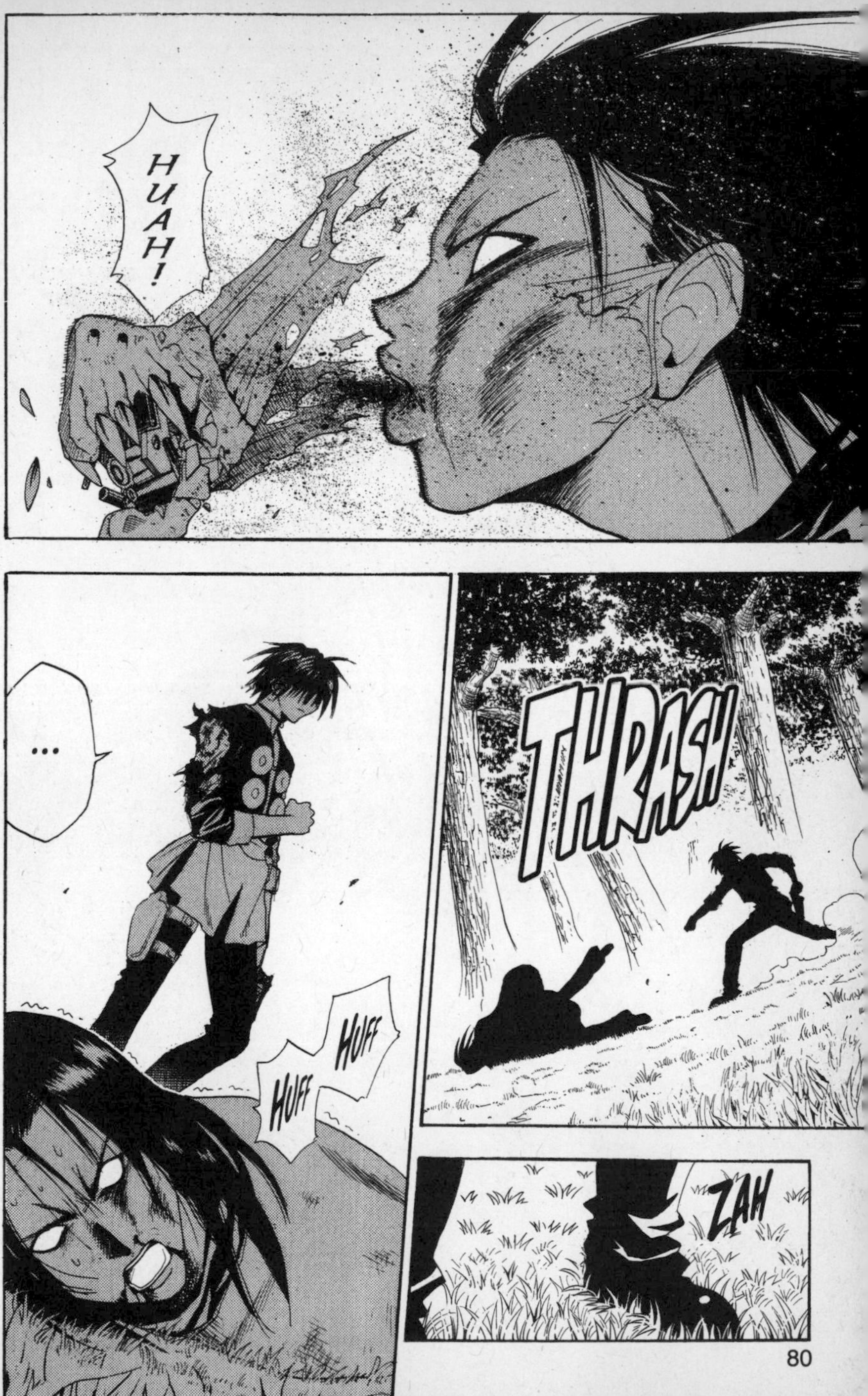
HUAH!
THRASH
ZAH
...
HUFF
HUFF

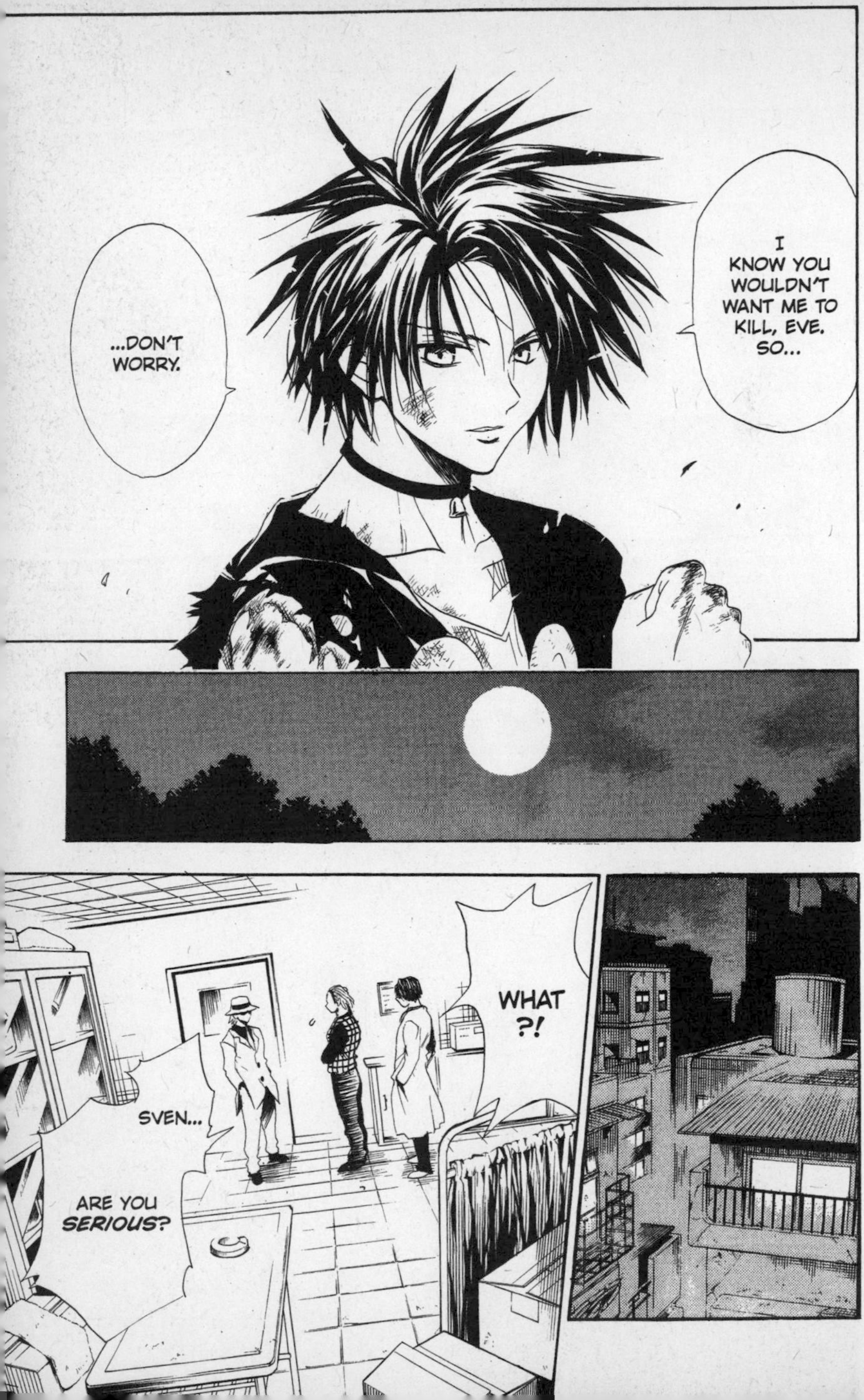
I KNOW YOU WOULDN'T WANT ME TO KILL, EVE. SO...
...DON'T WORRY.
WHAT ?!
SVEN...
ARE YOU *SERIOUS?*

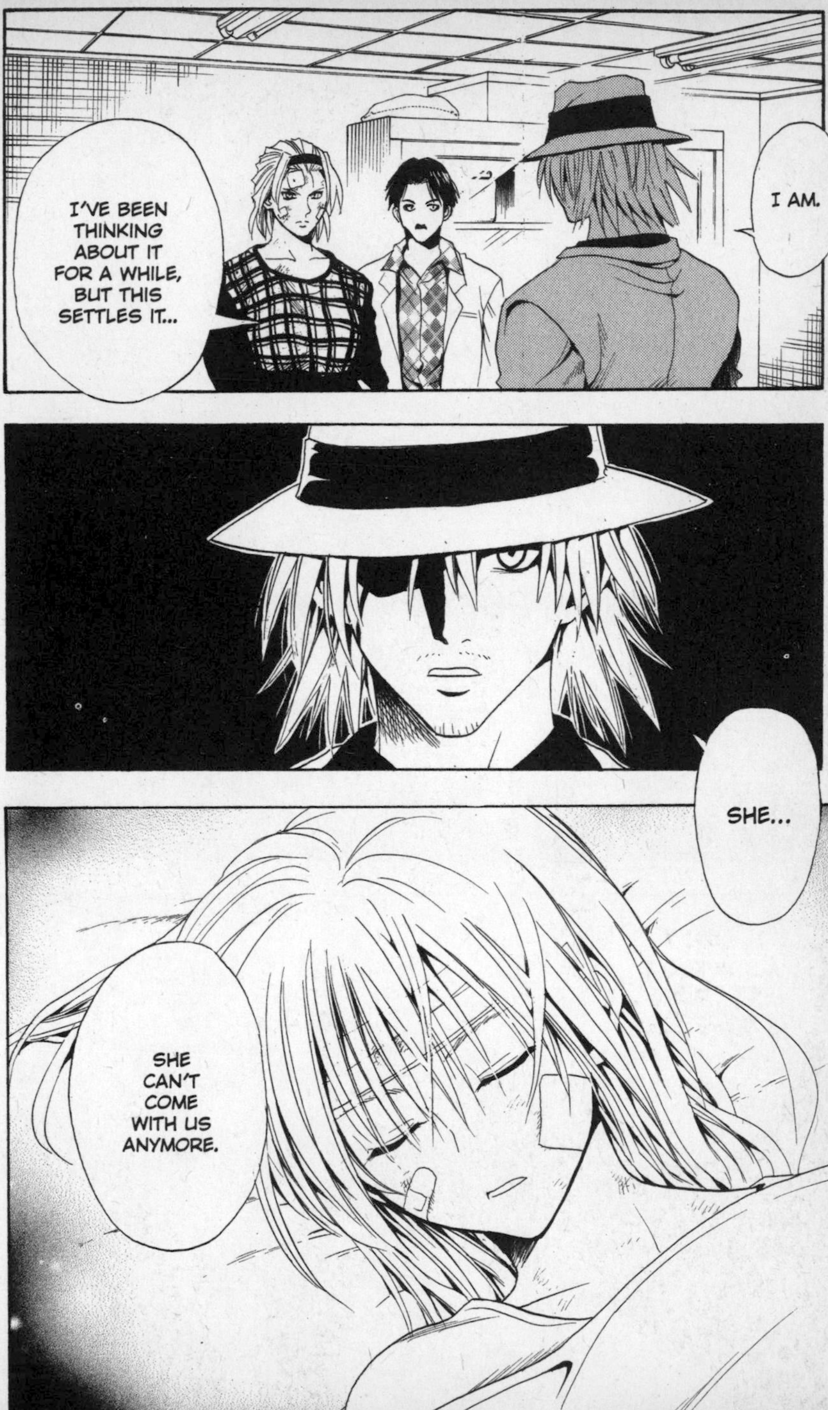
I AM.
I'VE BEEN THINKING ABOUT IT FOR A WHILE, BUT THIS SETTLES IT...
SHE...
SHE CAN'T COME WITH US ANYMORE.

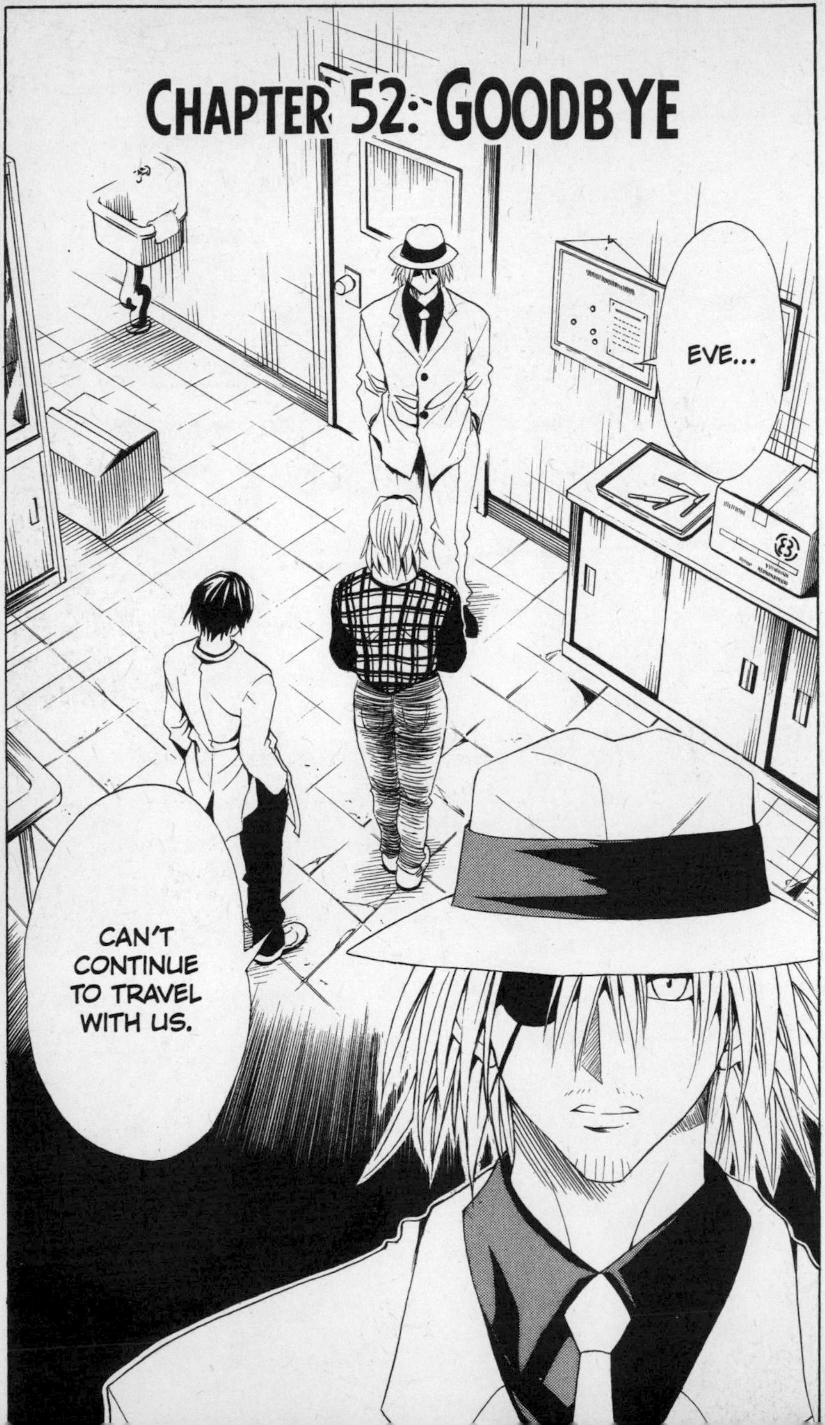
CHAPTER 52: GOODBYE
EVE...
CAN'T CONTINUE TO TRAVEL WITH US.

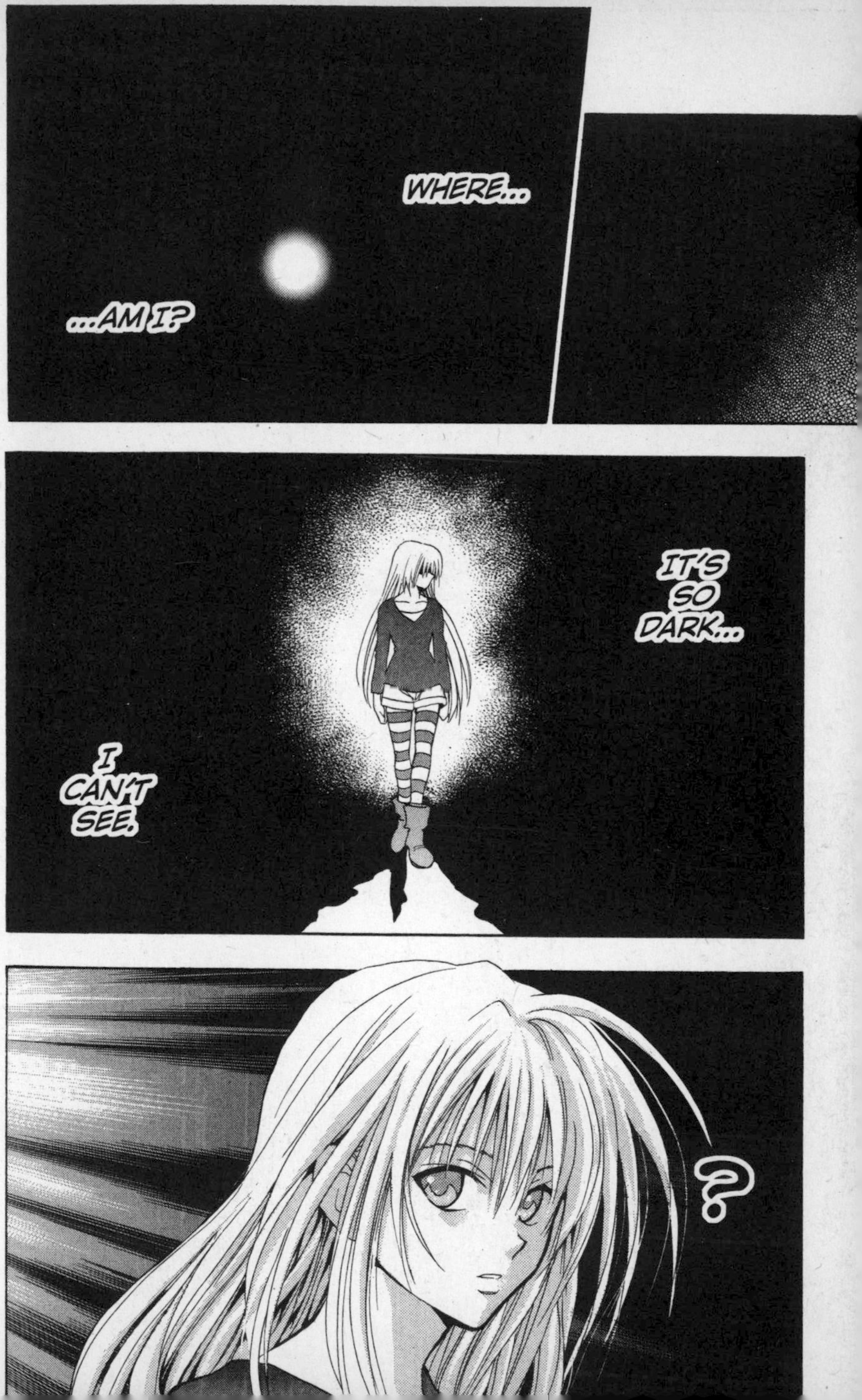
WHERE...
...AM I?
IT'S SO DARK...
I CAN'T SEE.
?

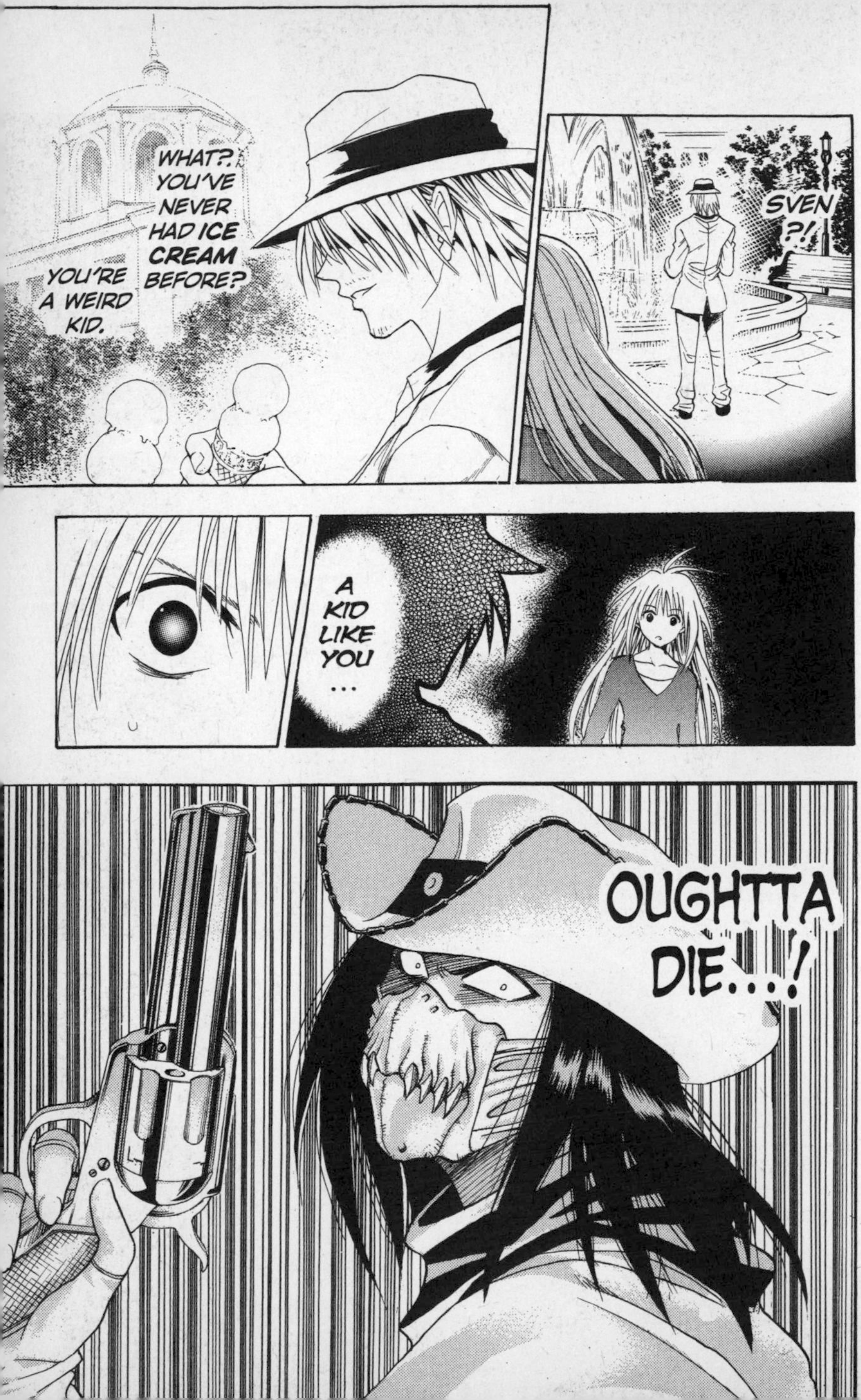
SVEN ?!
WHAT?. YOU'VE NEVER HAD ICE CREAM BEFORE?
YOU'RE A WEIRD KID.
A KID LIKE YOU ...
OUGHTTA DIE...!

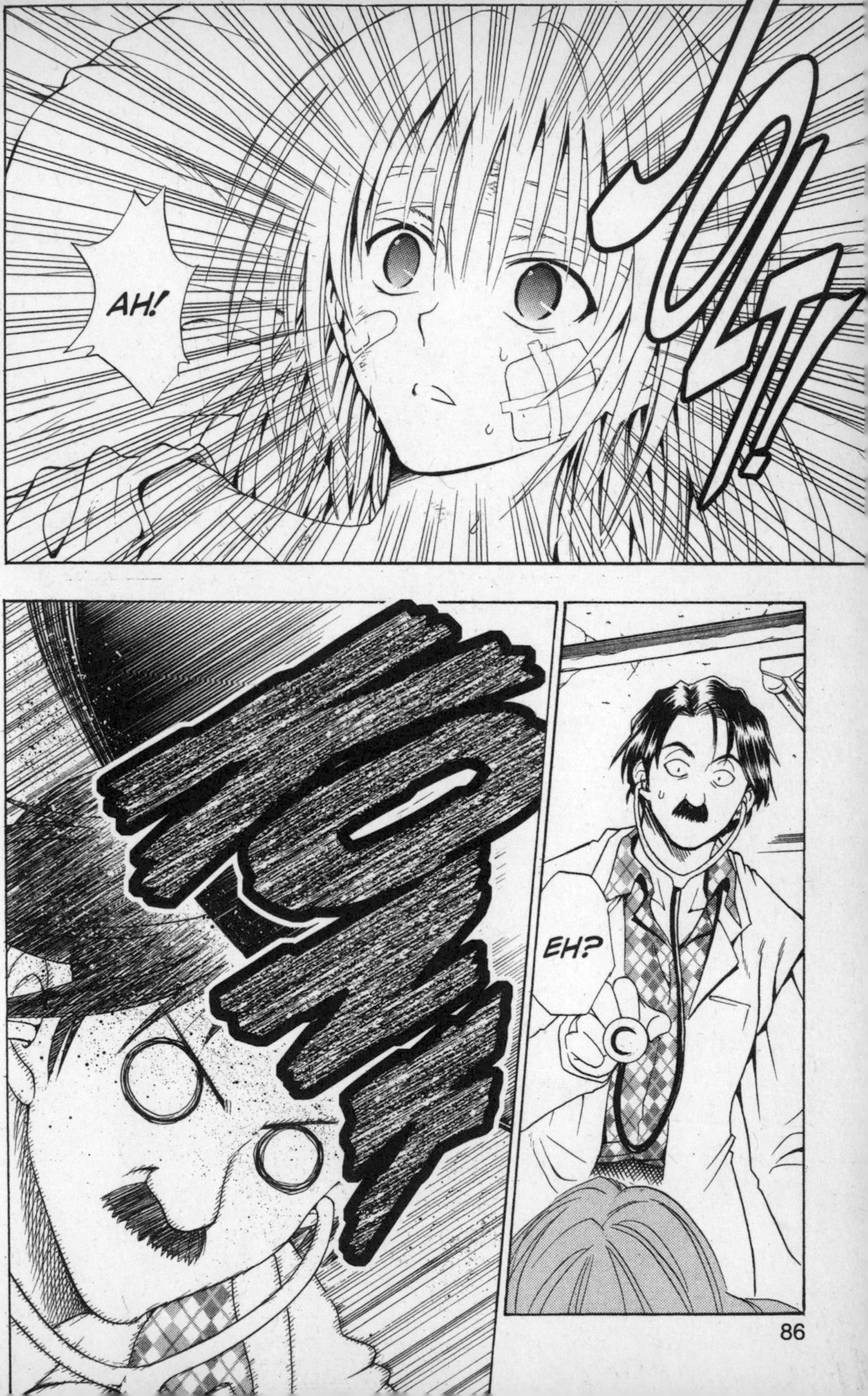
JOLT!!
AH!
EH?

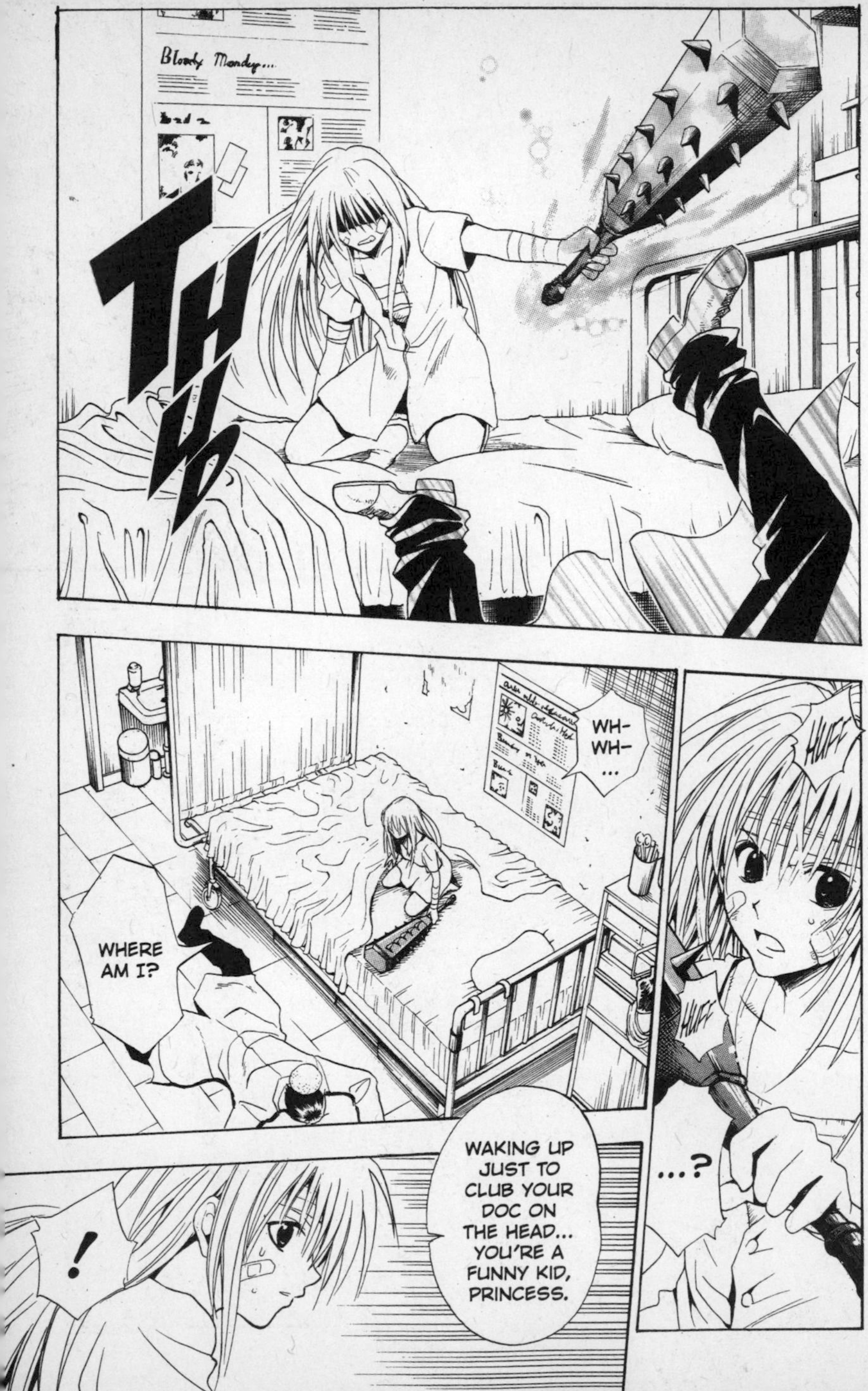
Bloody Monday...
THUD
HUFF
HUFF
...?
WH-WH-...
WHERE AM I?
WAKING UP JUST TO CLUB YOUR DOC ON THE HEAD... YOU'RE A FUNNY KID, PRINCESS.
!

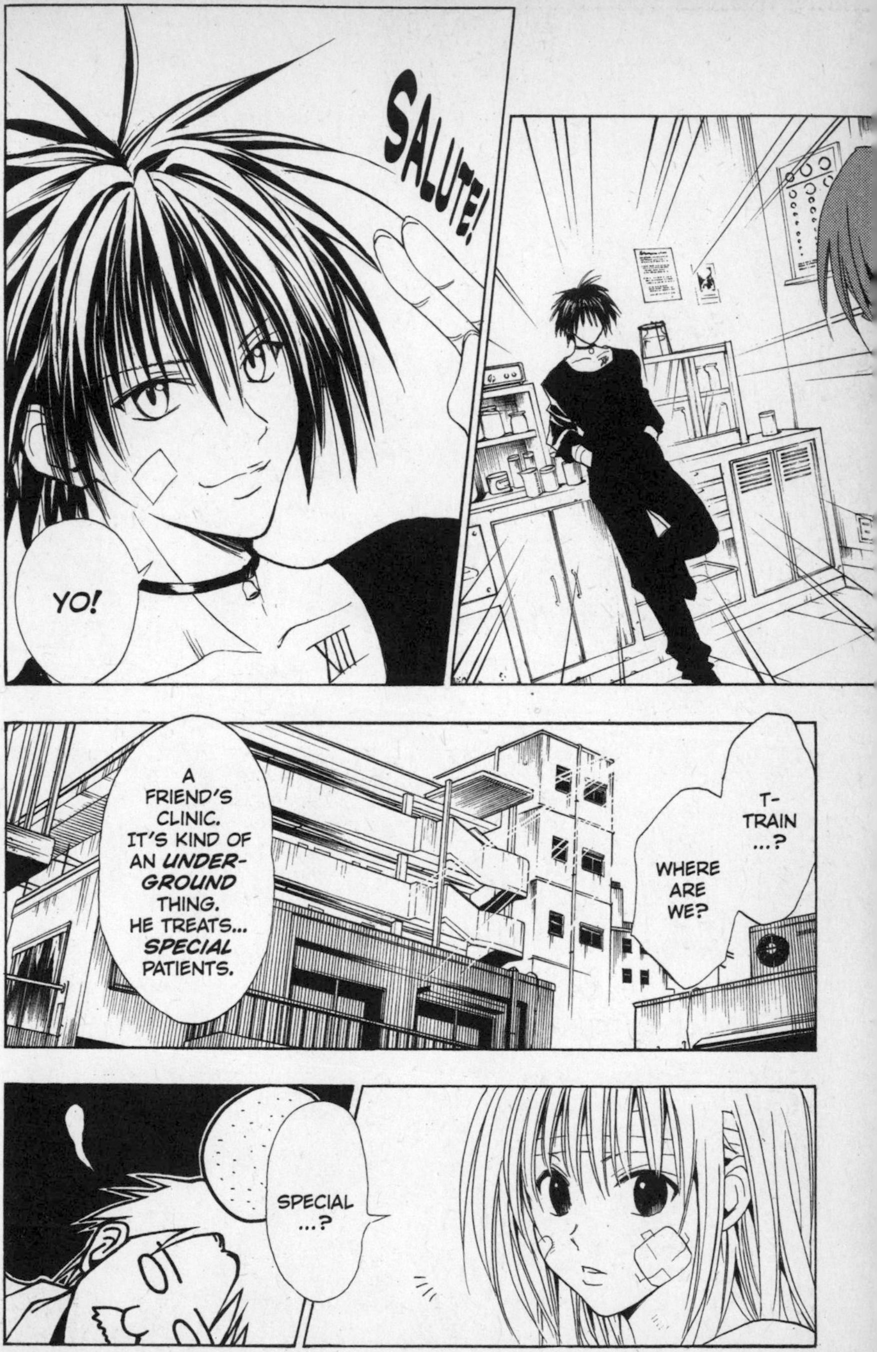
SALUTE!
YO!
T-TRAIN ...?
WHERE ARE WE?
A FRIEND'S CLINIC. IT'S KIND OF AN UNDERGROUND THING. HE TREATS... SPECIAL PATIENTS.
SPECIAL ...?

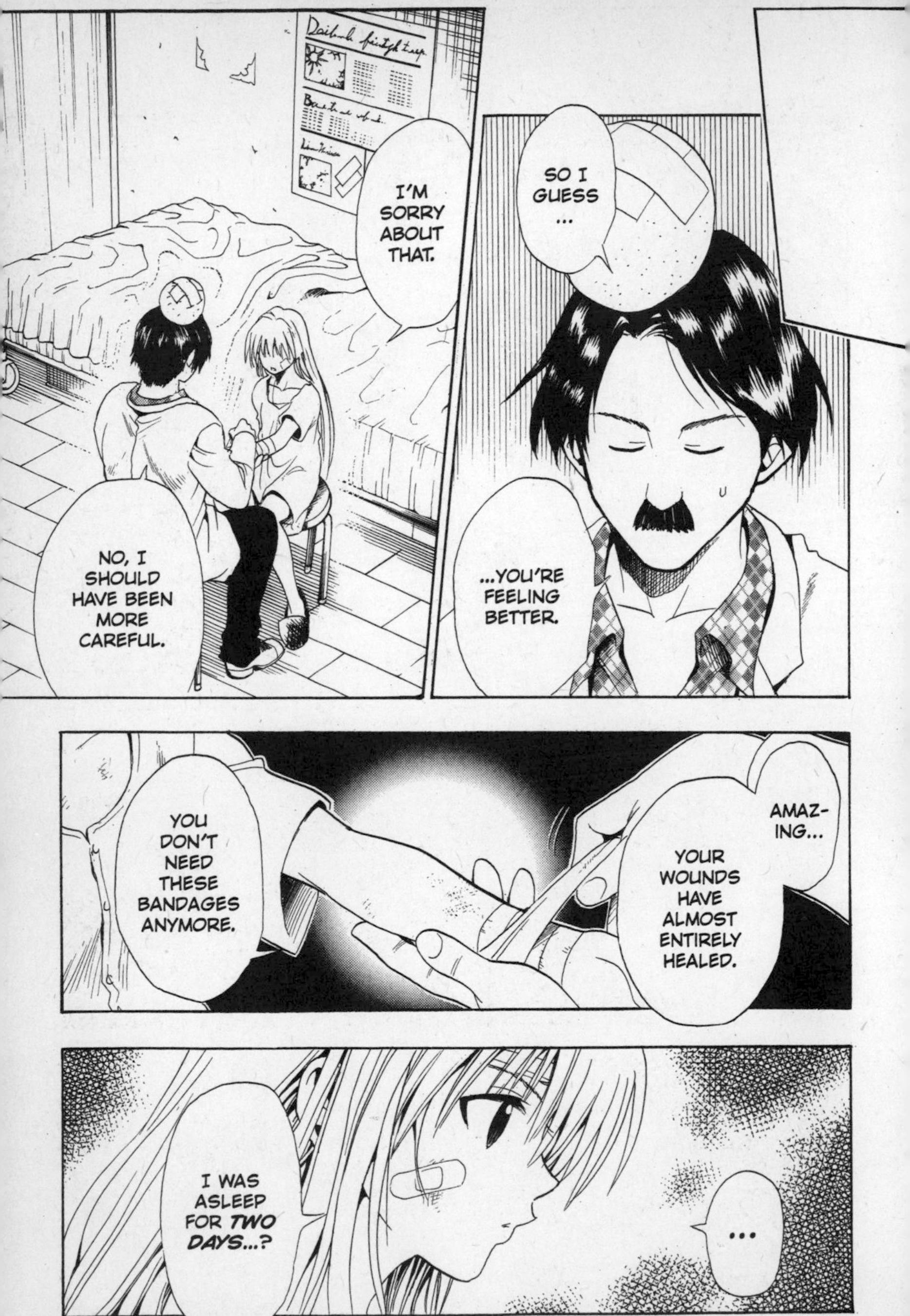
SO I GUESS ...
...YOU'RE FEELING BETTER.
I'M SORRY ABOUT THAT.
NO, I SHOULD HAVE BEEN MORE CAREFUL.
AMAZ-ING...
YOUR WOUNDS HAVE ALMOST ENTIRELY HEALED.
YOU DON'T NEED THESE BANDAGES ANYMORE.
...
I WAS ASLEEP FOR *TWO DAYS*...?

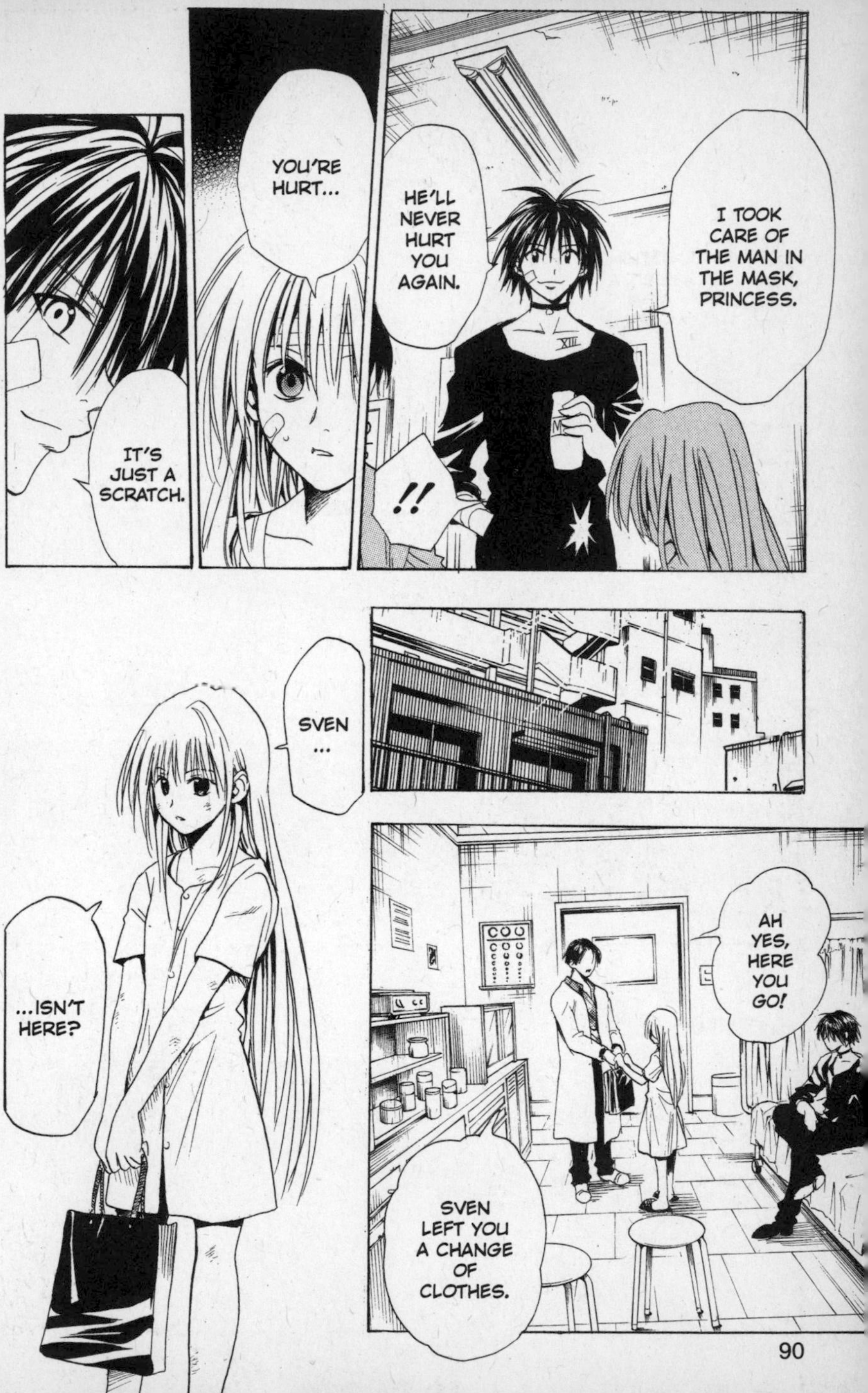
I TOOK CARE OF THE MAN IN THE MASK, PRINCESS.
HE'LL NEVER HURT YOU AGAIN.
!!
YOU'RE HURT...
IT'S JUST A SCRATCH.
AH YES, HERE YOU GO!
SVEN LEFT YOU A CHANGE OF CLOTHES.
SVEN ...
...ISN'T HERE?

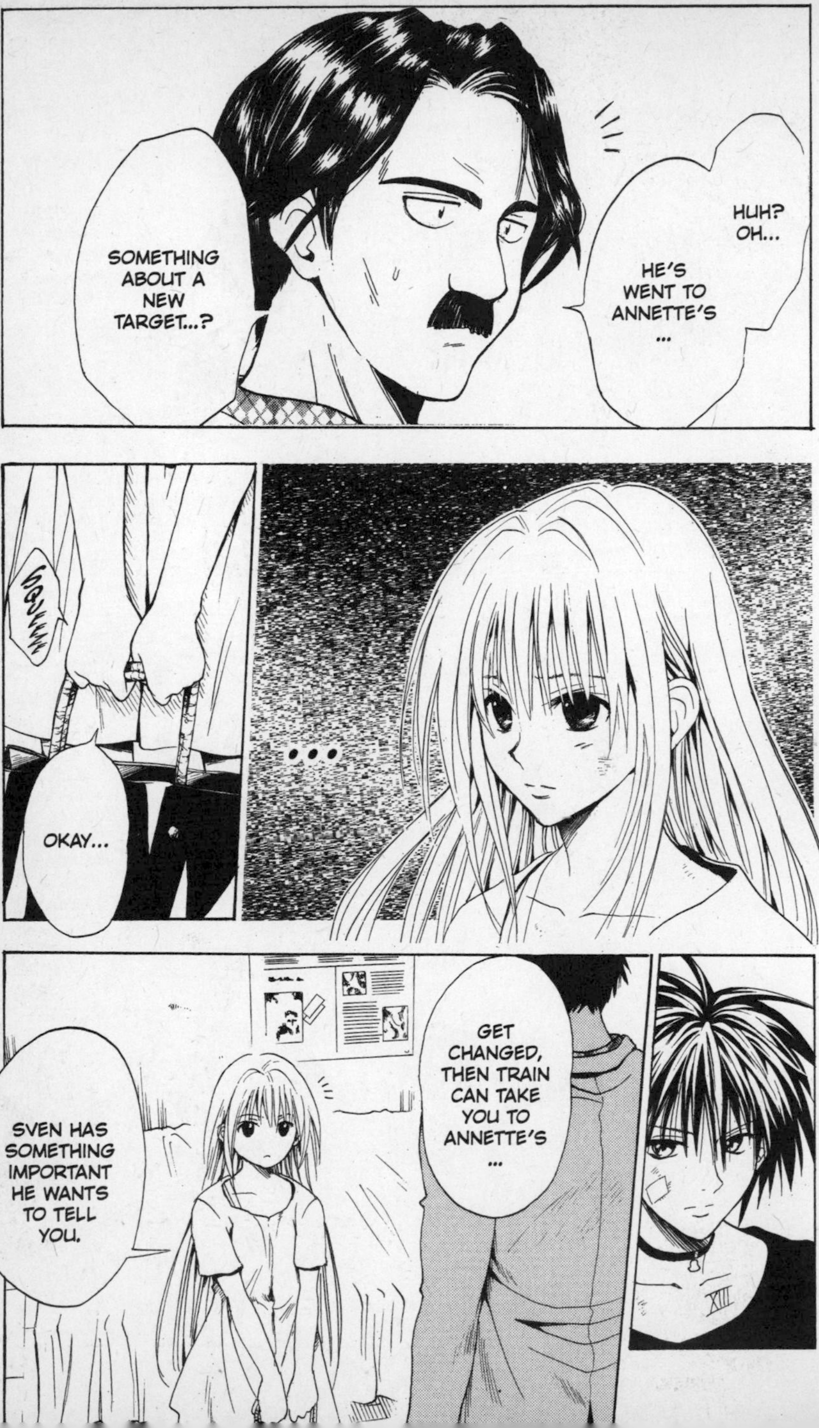
HUH? OH...
HE'S WENT TO ANNETTE'S ...
SOMETHING ABOUT A NEW TARGET...?
...
OKAY...
GET CHANGED, THEN TRAIN CAN TAKE YOU TO ANNETTE'S ...
SVEN HAS SOMETHING IMPORTANT HE WANTS TO TELL YOU.

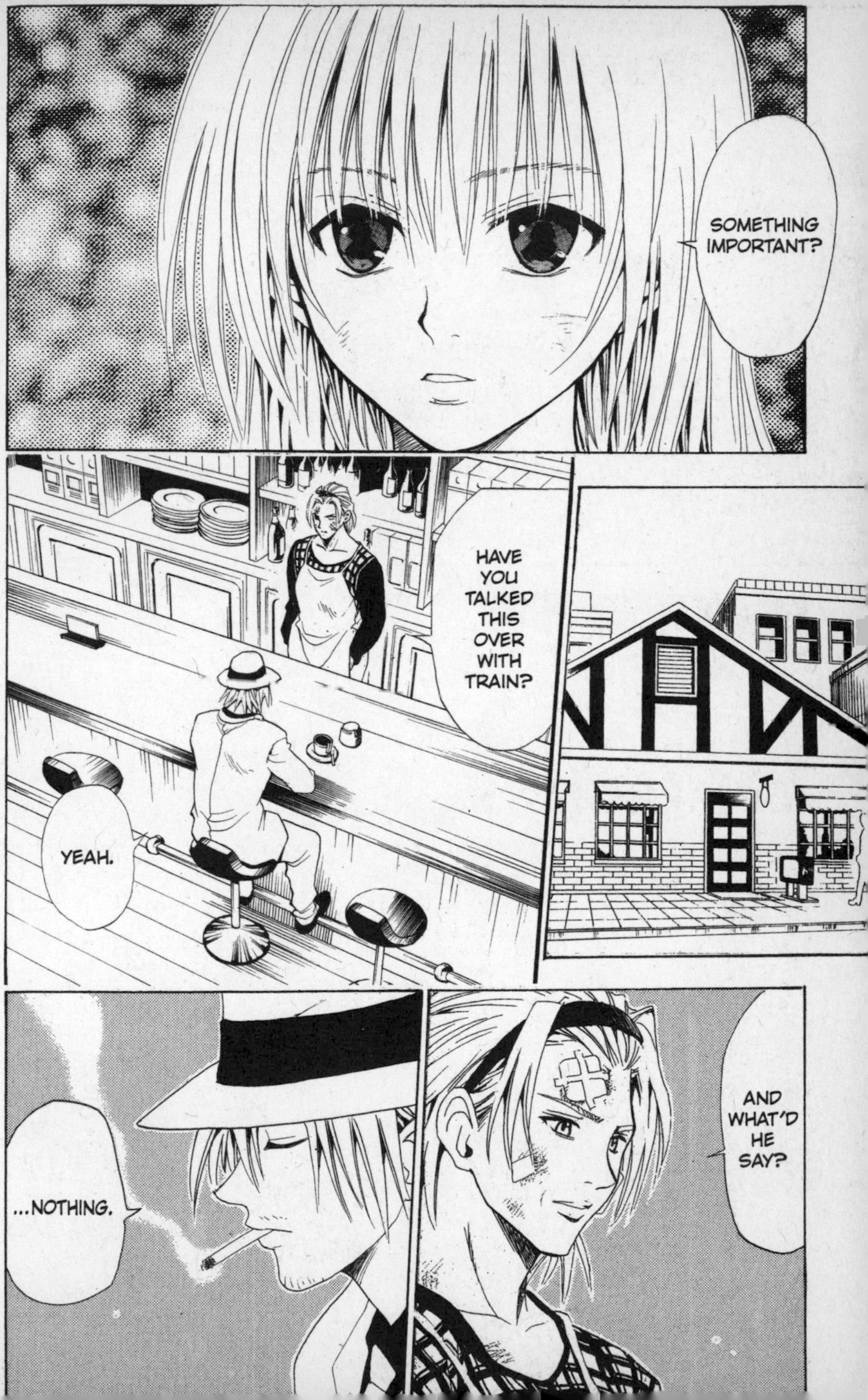
SOMETHING IMPORTANT?
HAVE YOU TALKED THIS OVER WITH TRAIN?
YEAH.
AND WHAT'D HE SAY?
...NOTHING.

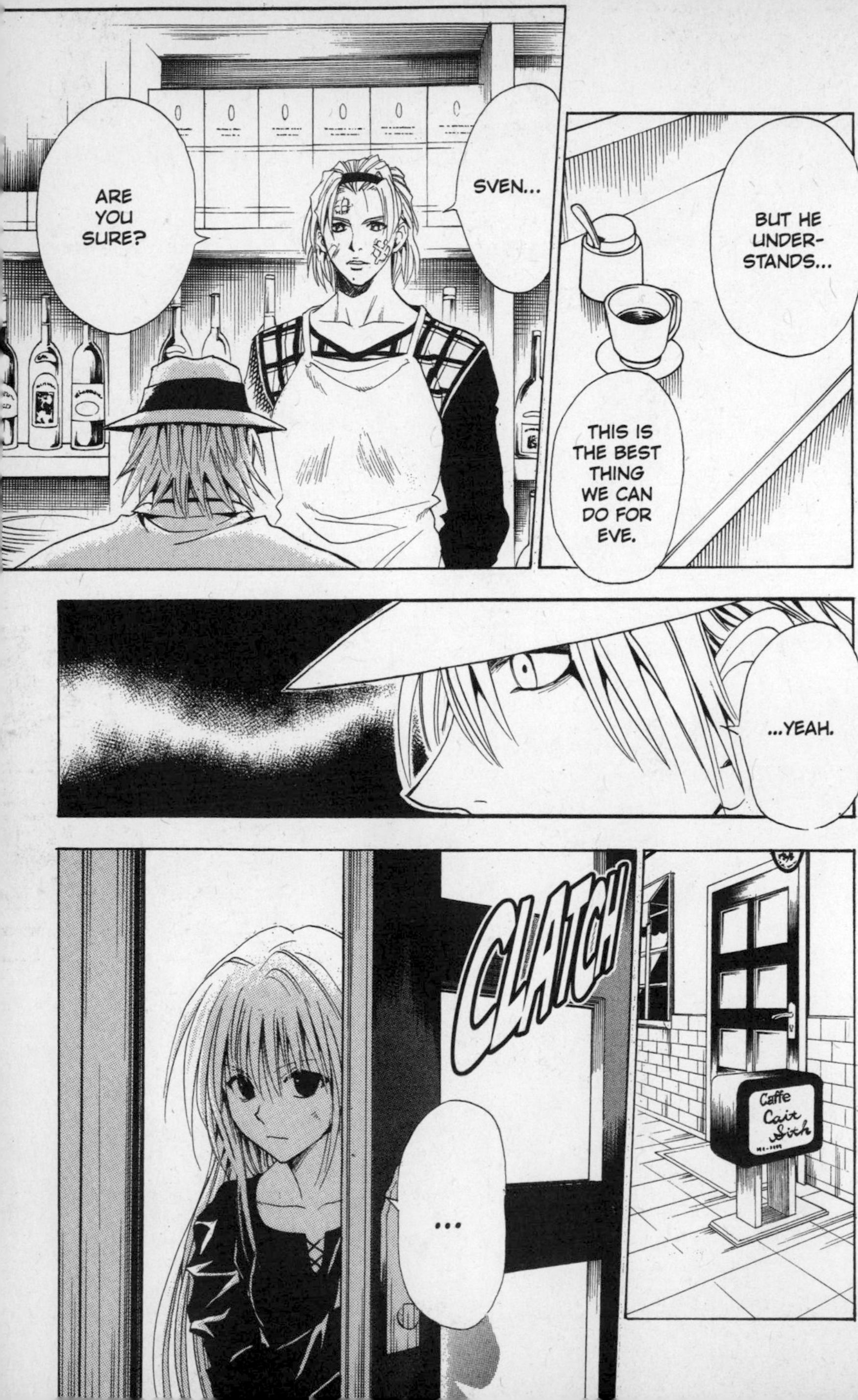
BUT HE UNDER-STANDS...
THIS IS THE BEST THING WE CAN DO FOR EVE.
SVEN...
ARE YOU SURE?
...YEAH.
CLATCH
Caffe Cait Sith
...

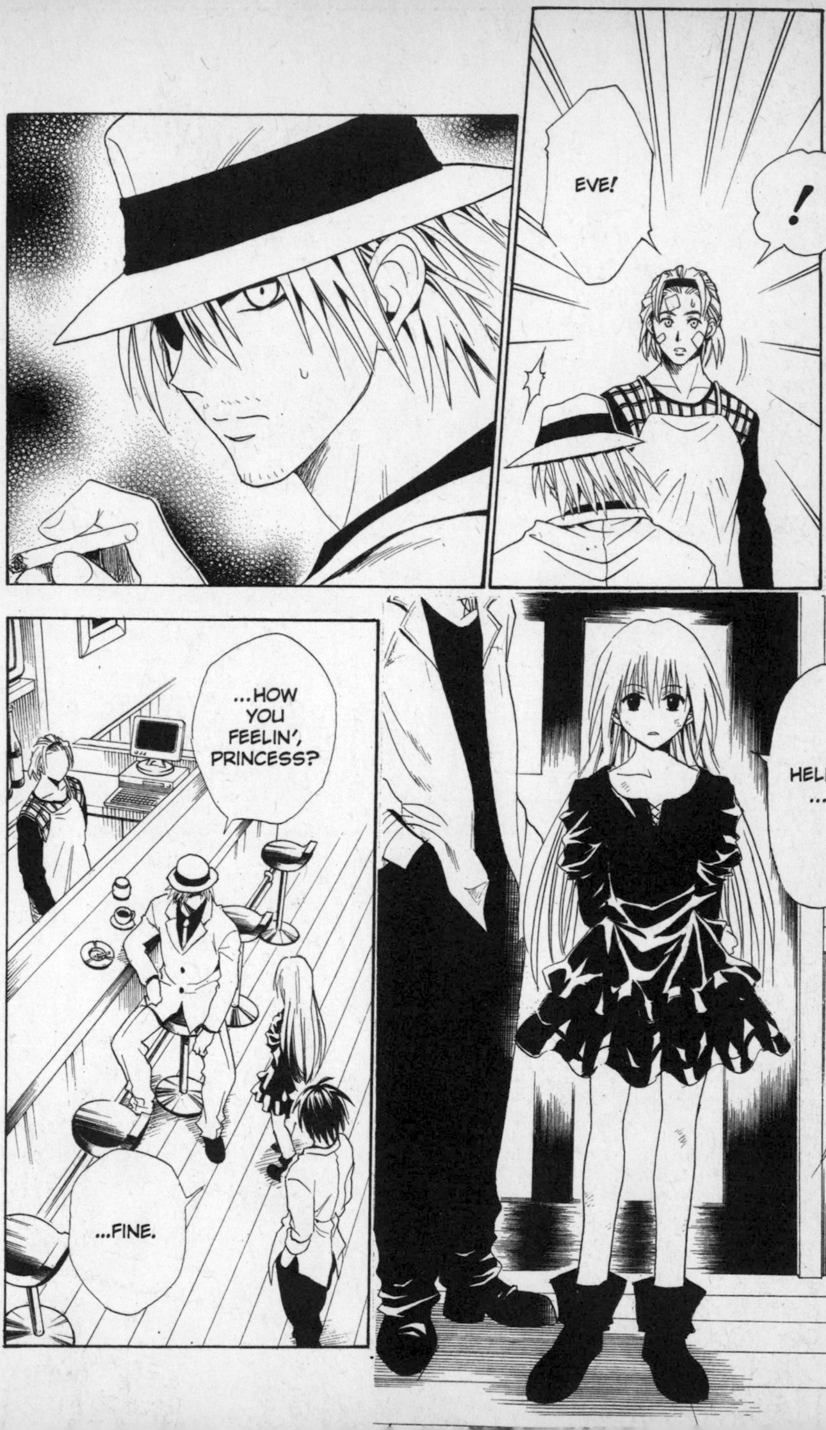
EVE!
!
HELLO ...
...HOW YOU FEELIN', PRINCESS?
...FINE.

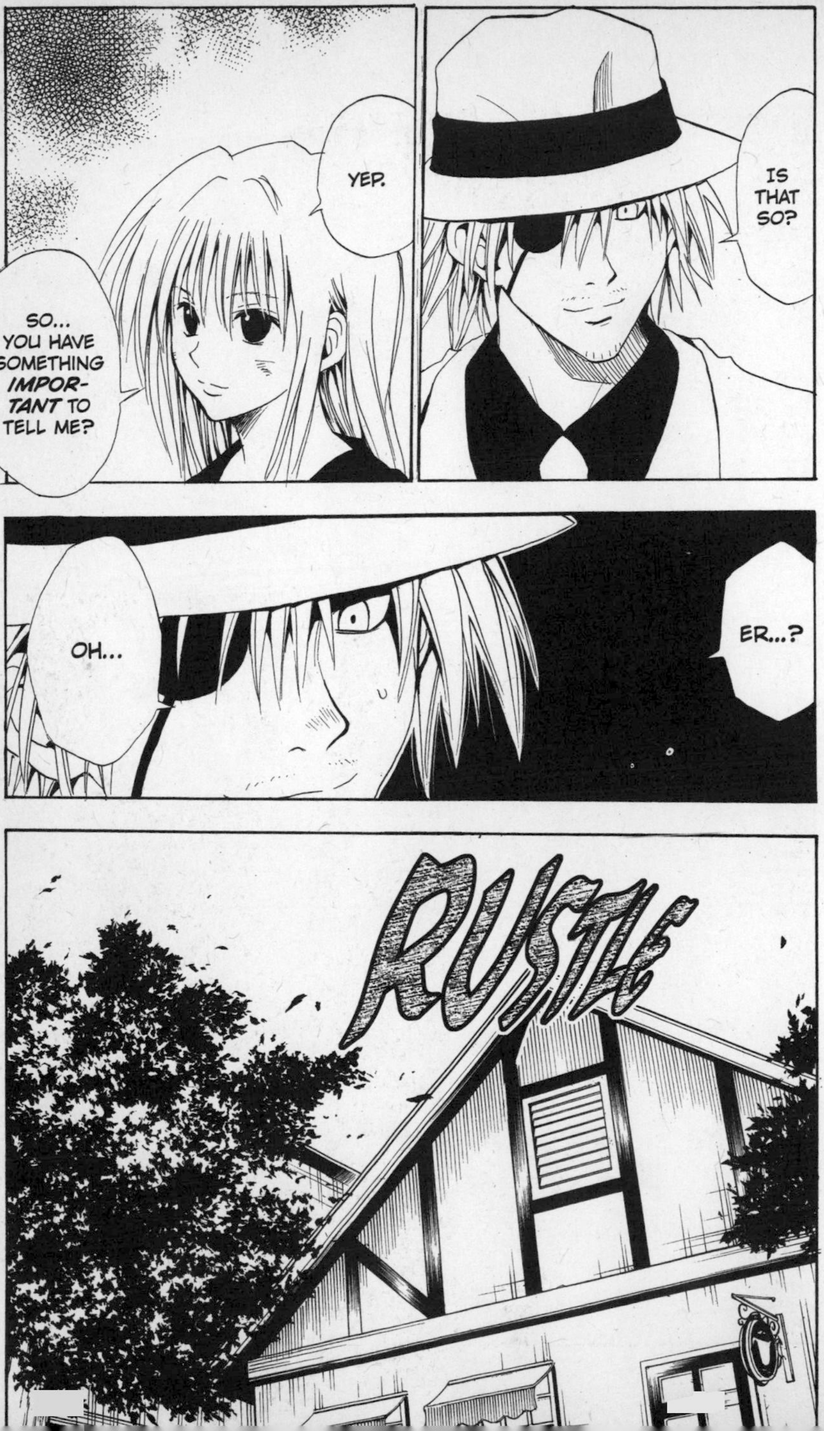
IS THAT SO?
YEP.
SO... YOU HAVE SOMETHING *IMPORTANT* TO TELL ME?
ER...?
OH...
RUSTLE

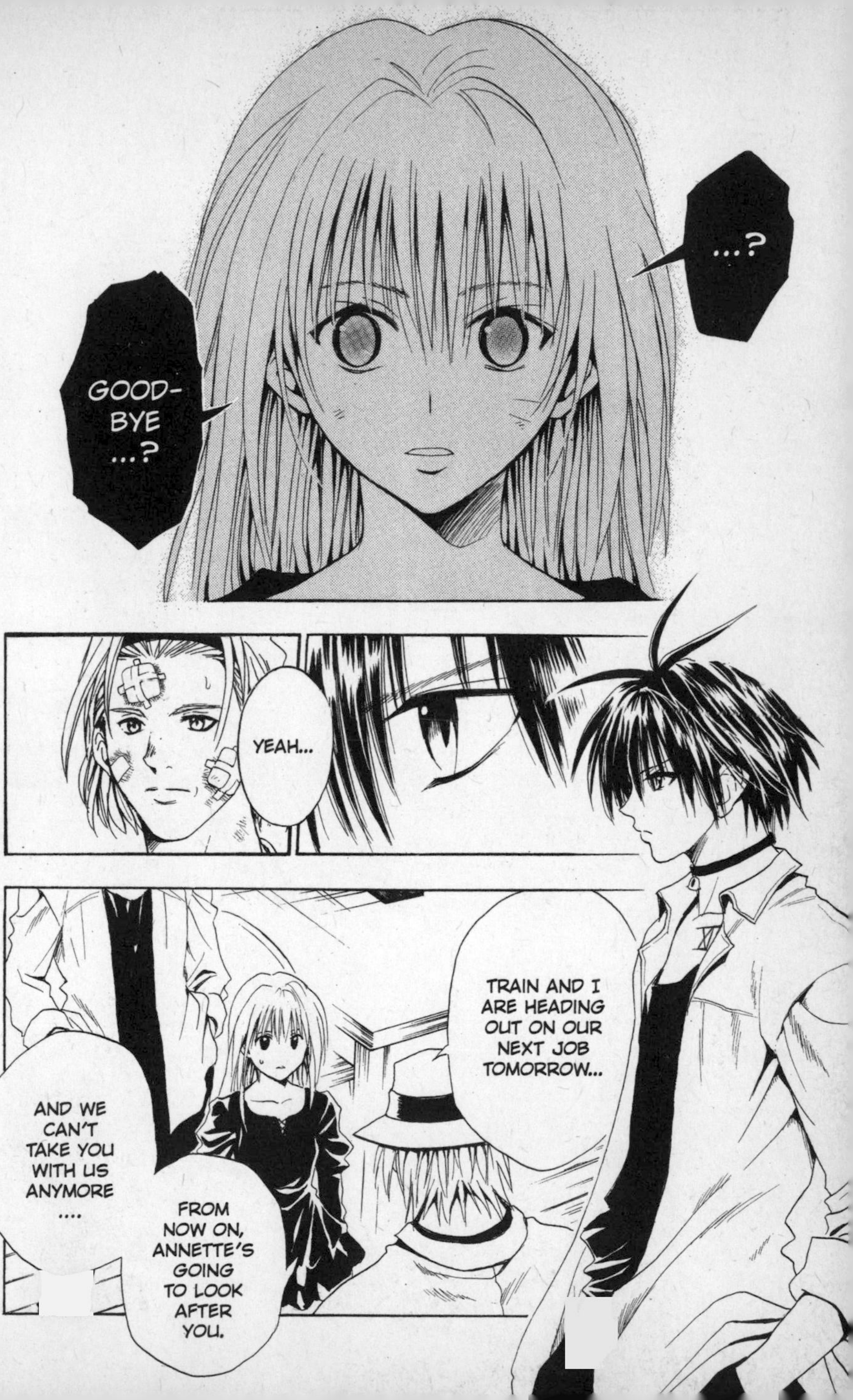
...?
GOOD-BYE ...?
YEAH...
TRAIN AND I ARE HEADING OUT ON OUR NEXT JOB TOMORROW...
AND WE CAN'T TAKE YOU WITH US ANYMORE ....
FROM NOW ON, ANNETTE'S GOING TO LOOK AFTER YOU.

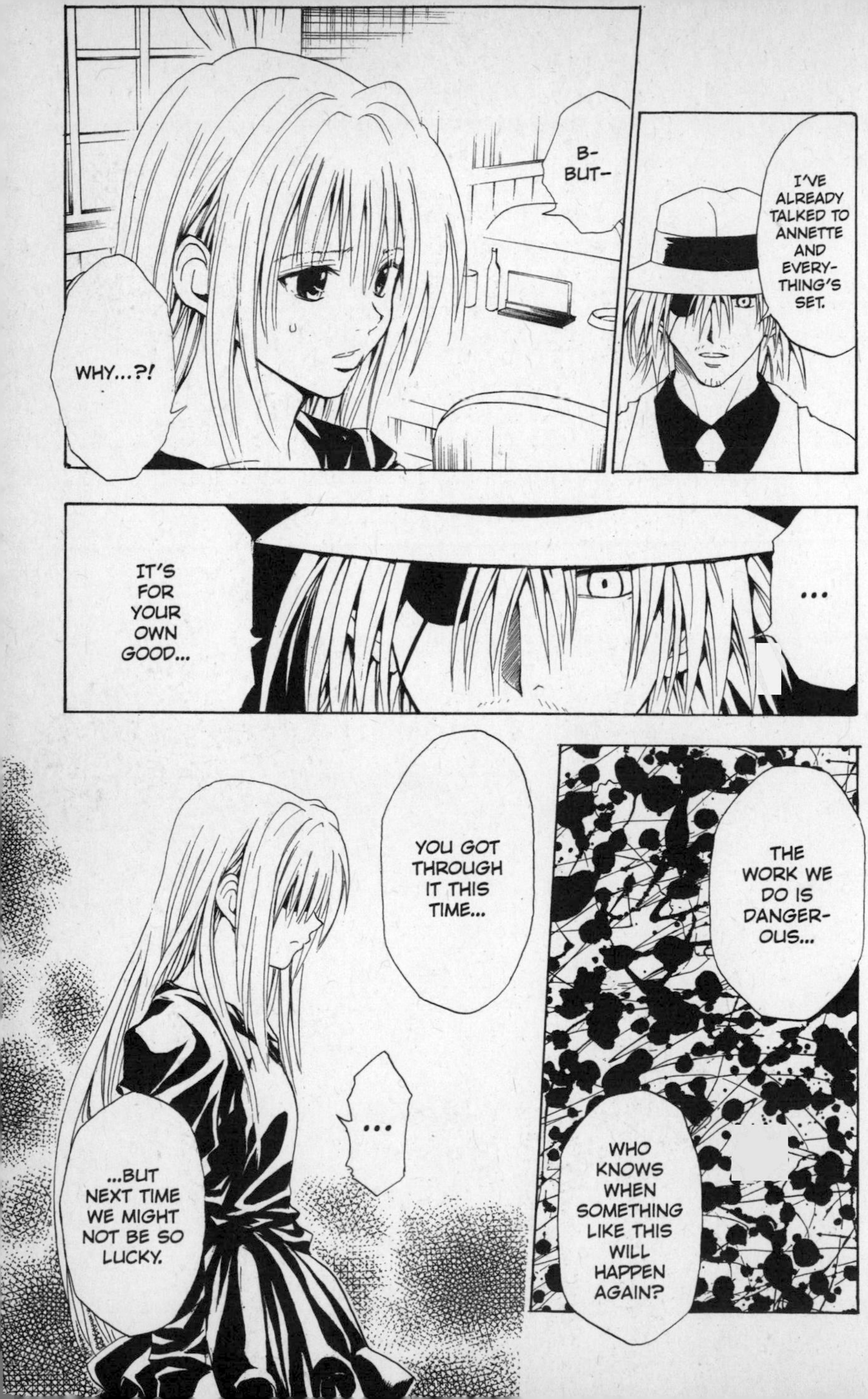
I'VE ALREADY TALKED TO ANNETTE AND EVERYTHING'S SET.
B-BUT-
WHY...?!
...
IT'S FOR YOUR OWN GOOD...
THE WORK WE DO IS DANGEROUS...
WHO KNOWS WHEN SOMETHING LIKE THIS WILL HAPPEN AGAIN?
YOU GOT THROUGH IT THIS TIME...
...
...BUT NEXT TIME WE MIGHT NOT BE SO LUCKY.

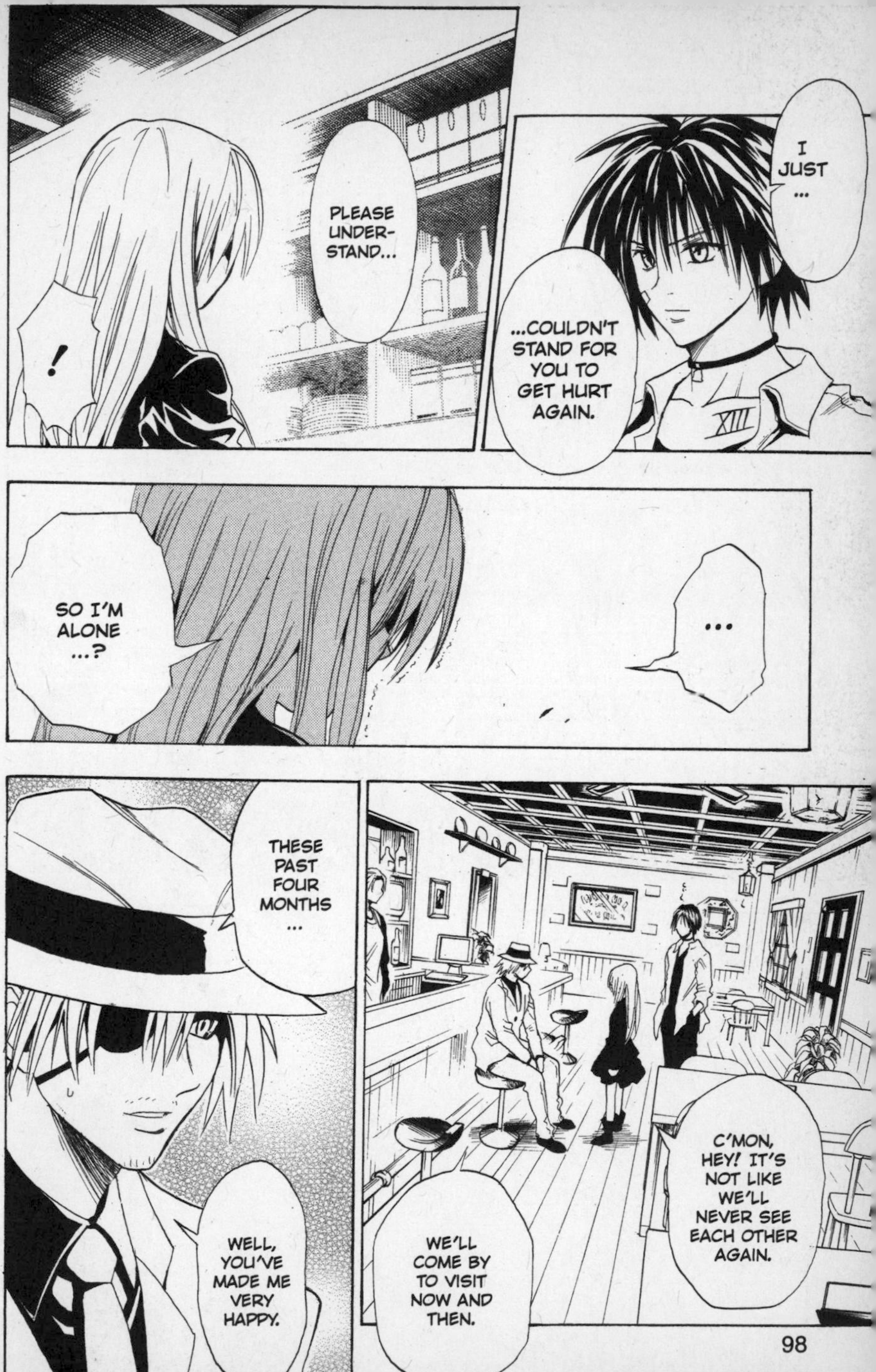
I JUST ...
...COULDN'T STAND FOR YOU TO GET HURT AGAIN.
PLEASE UNDER-STAND...
!
...
SO I'M ALONE ...?
C'MON, HEY! IT'S NOT LIKE WE'LL NEVER SEE EACH OTHER AGAIN.
WE'LL COME BY TO VISIT NOW AND THEN.
THESE PAST FOUR MONTHS ...
WELL, YOU'VE MADE ME VERY HAPPY.

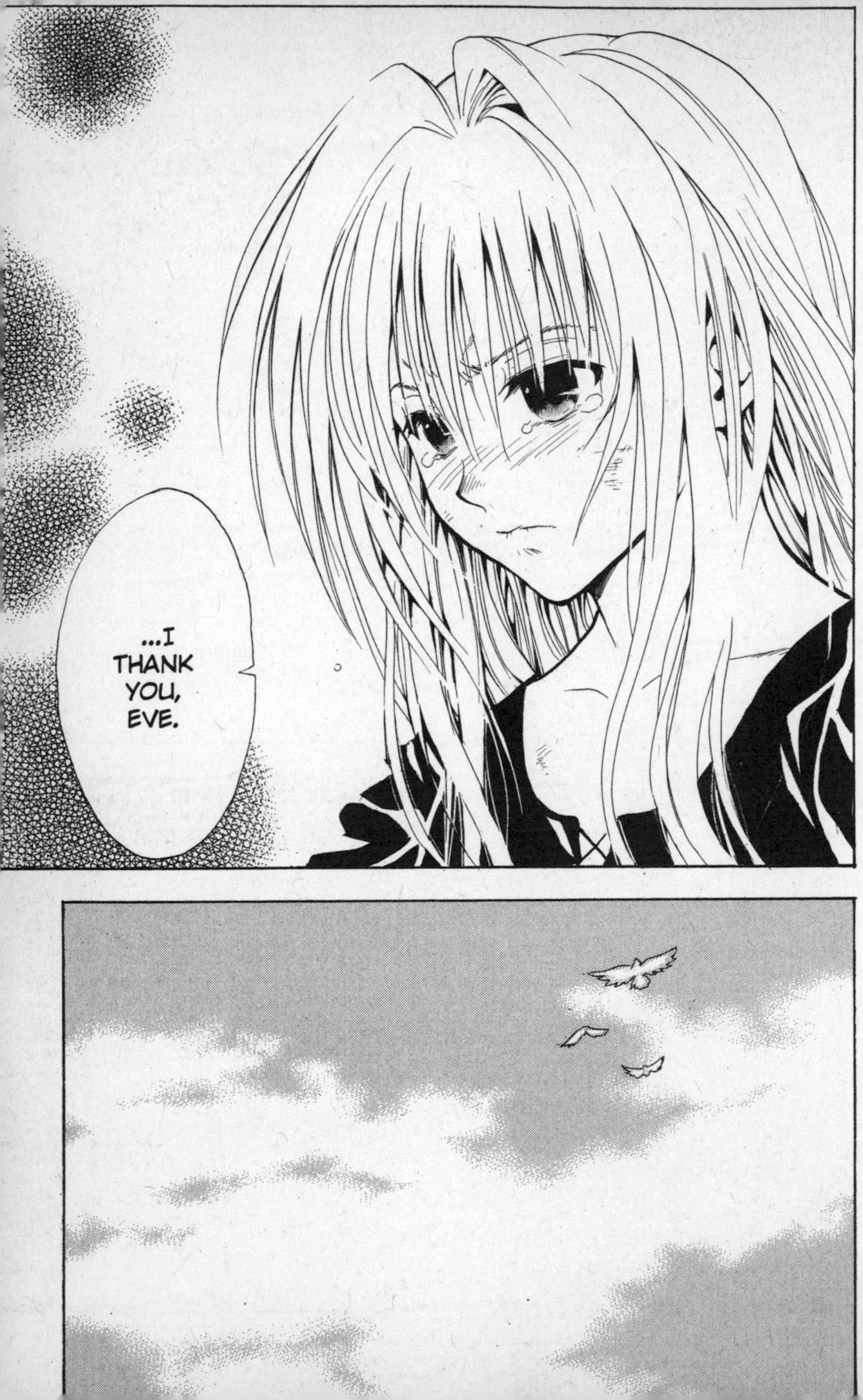
...I THANK YOU, EVE.

profile

ANNETTE PIAS

DATA	
BIRTHDATE:	MAY 17
AGE:	44
BLOOD TYPE:	B
HEIGHT:	172 CM
WEIGHT:	62 KG
HOBBY:	BILLIARDS
COMMENTS:	RETIRED SWEEPER AND OWNER OF CAFFE CAIT SITH. NOW, MAKES USE OF HER CONNECTIONS AND DATA-MINING SKILLS TO WORK AS AN INFORMANT. OLD FRIEND OF SVEN'S.

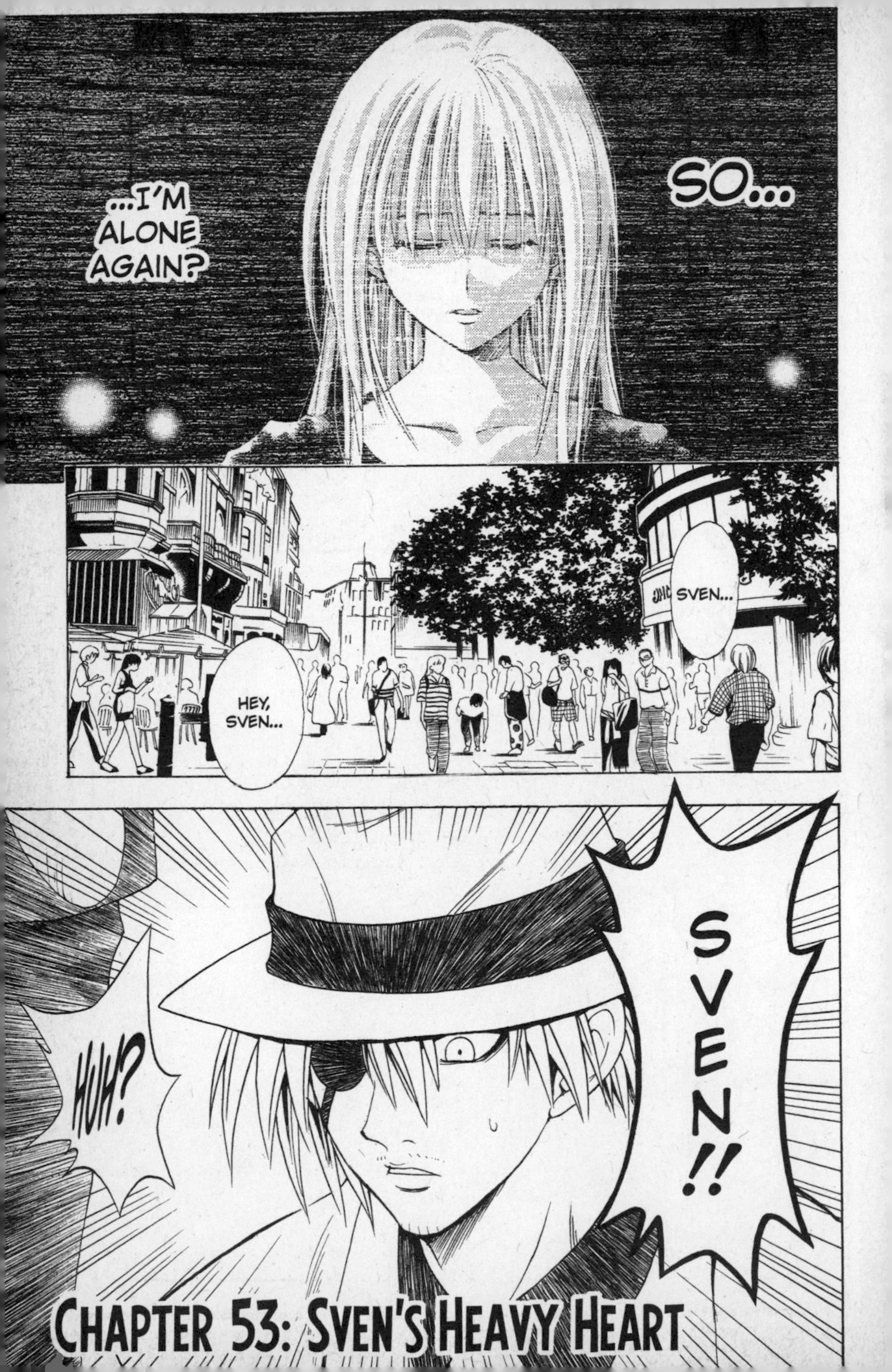
SO...
...I'M ALONE AGAIN?
SVEN...
HEY, SVEN...
SVEN!!
HUH?
Chapter 53: Sven's Heavy Heart

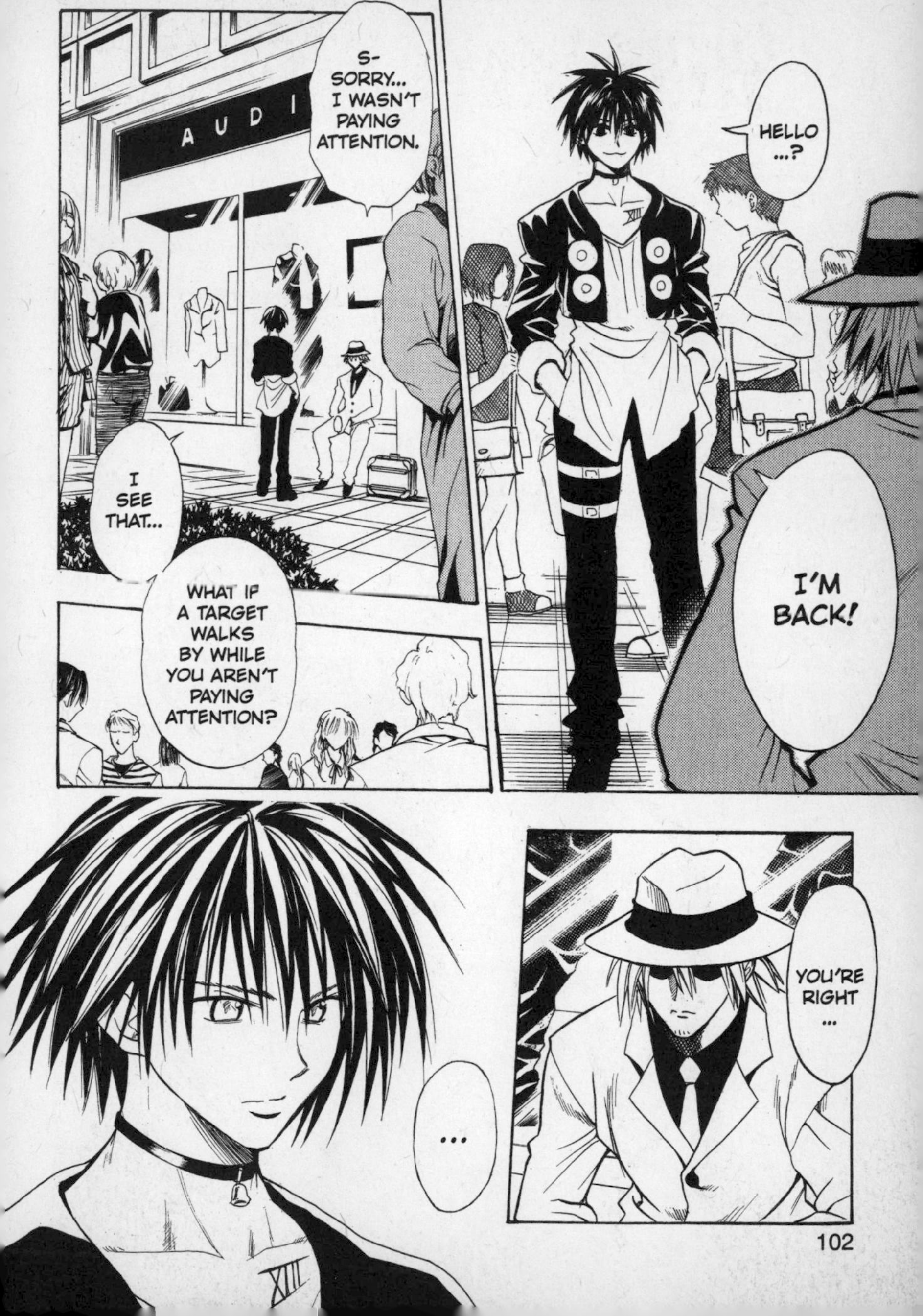
HELLO ...?
I'M BACK!
S-SORRY... I WASN'T PAYING ATTENTION.
I SEE THAT...
WHAT IF A TARGET WALKS BY WHILE YOU AREN'T PAYING ATTENTION?
YOU'RE RIGHT ...
...

Chapter 53: Sven's Heavy Heart

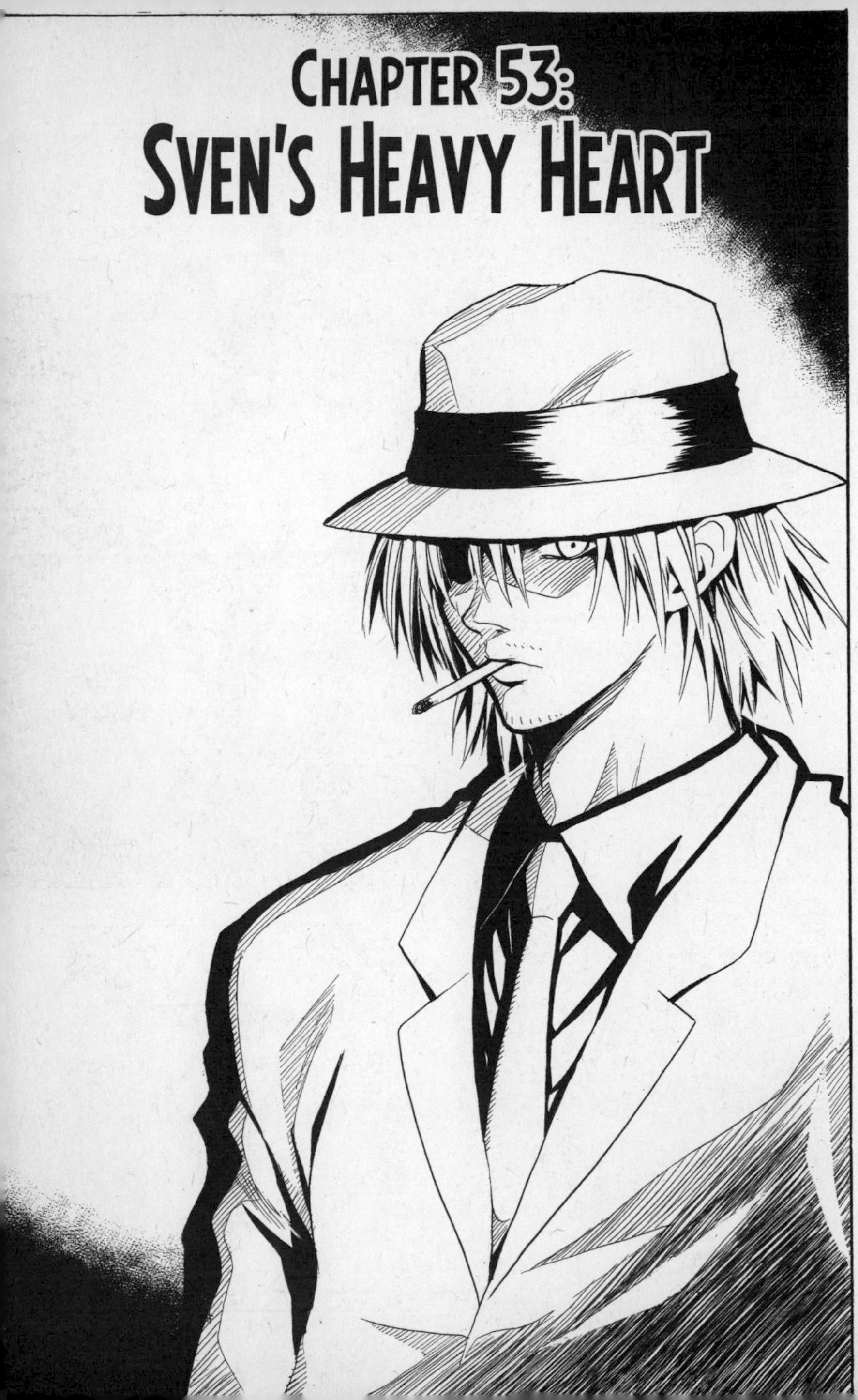

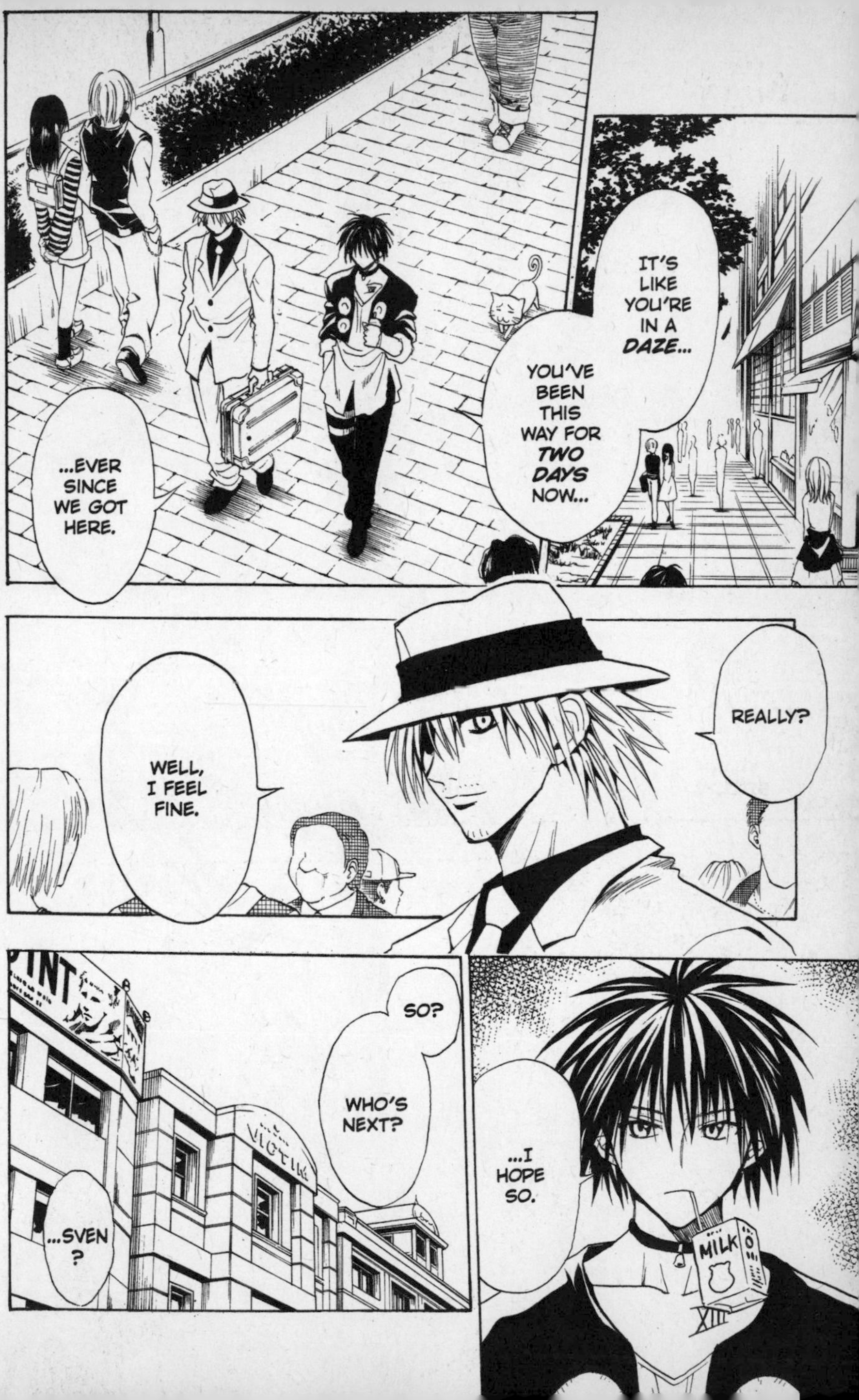
IT'S LIKE YOU'RE IN A *DAZE*...
YOU'VE BEEN THIS WAY FOR **TWO DAYS** NOW...
...EVER SINCE WE GOT HERE.
REALLY?
WELL, I FEEL FINE.
...I HOPE SO.
SO?
WHO'S NEXT?
...SVEN?
MILK

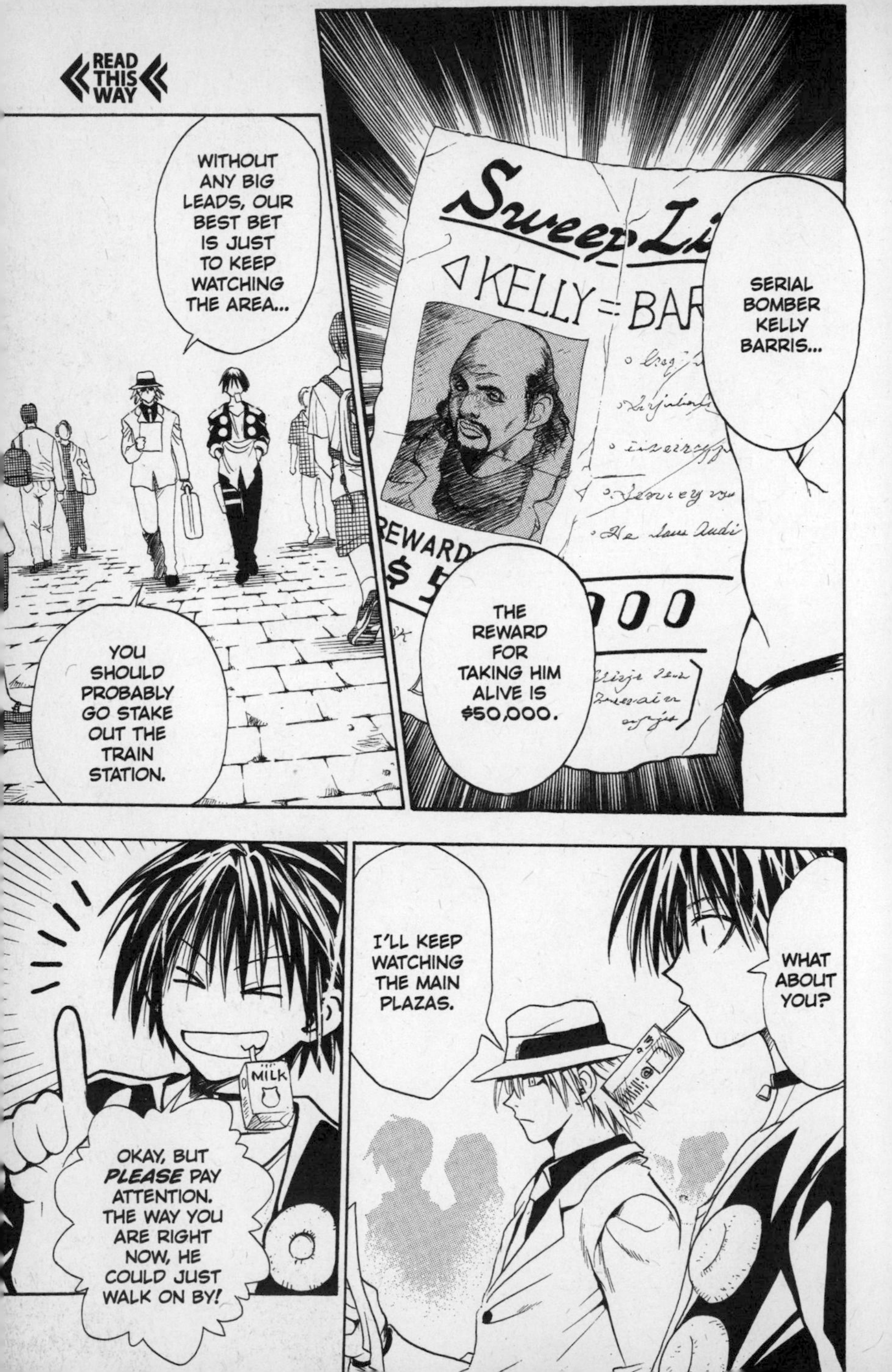
READ THIS WAY
Sweep
KELLY
SERIAL BOMBER KELLY BARRIS...
THE REWARD FOR TAKING HIM ALIVE IS $50,000.
WITHOUT ANY BIG LEADS, OUR BEST BET IS JUST TO KEEP WATCHING THE AREA...
YOU SHOULD PROBABLY GO STAKE OUT THE TRAIN STATION.
WHAT ABOUT YOU?
I'LL KEEP WATCHING THE MAIN PLAZAS.
MILK
OKAY, BUT *PLEASE* PAY ATTENTION. THE WAY YOU ARE RIGHT NOW, HE COULD JUST WALK ON BY!

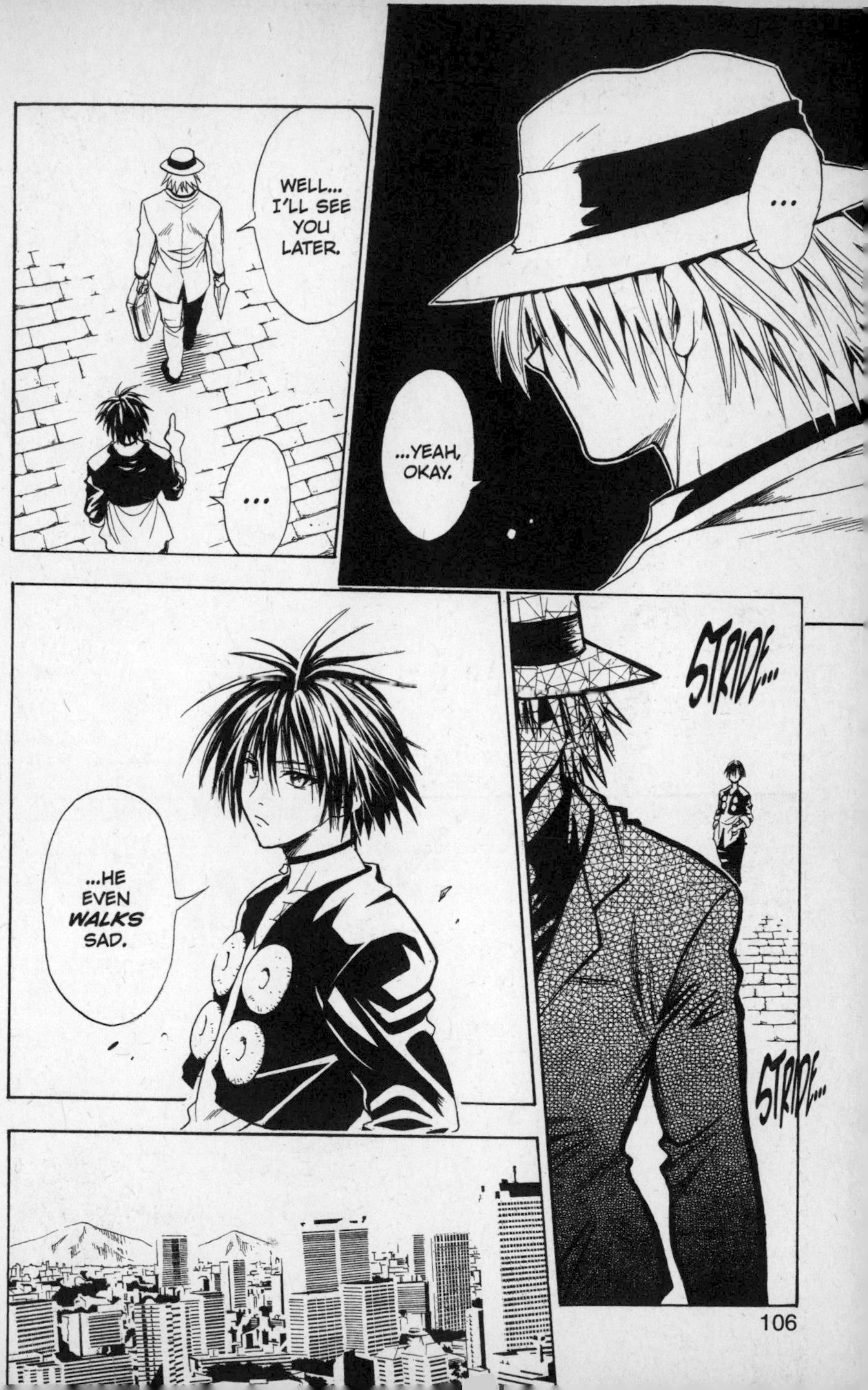
...
...YEAH, OKAY.
WELL... I'LL SEE YOU LATER.
...
STRIDE...
STRIDE...
...HE EVEN *WALKS* SAD.

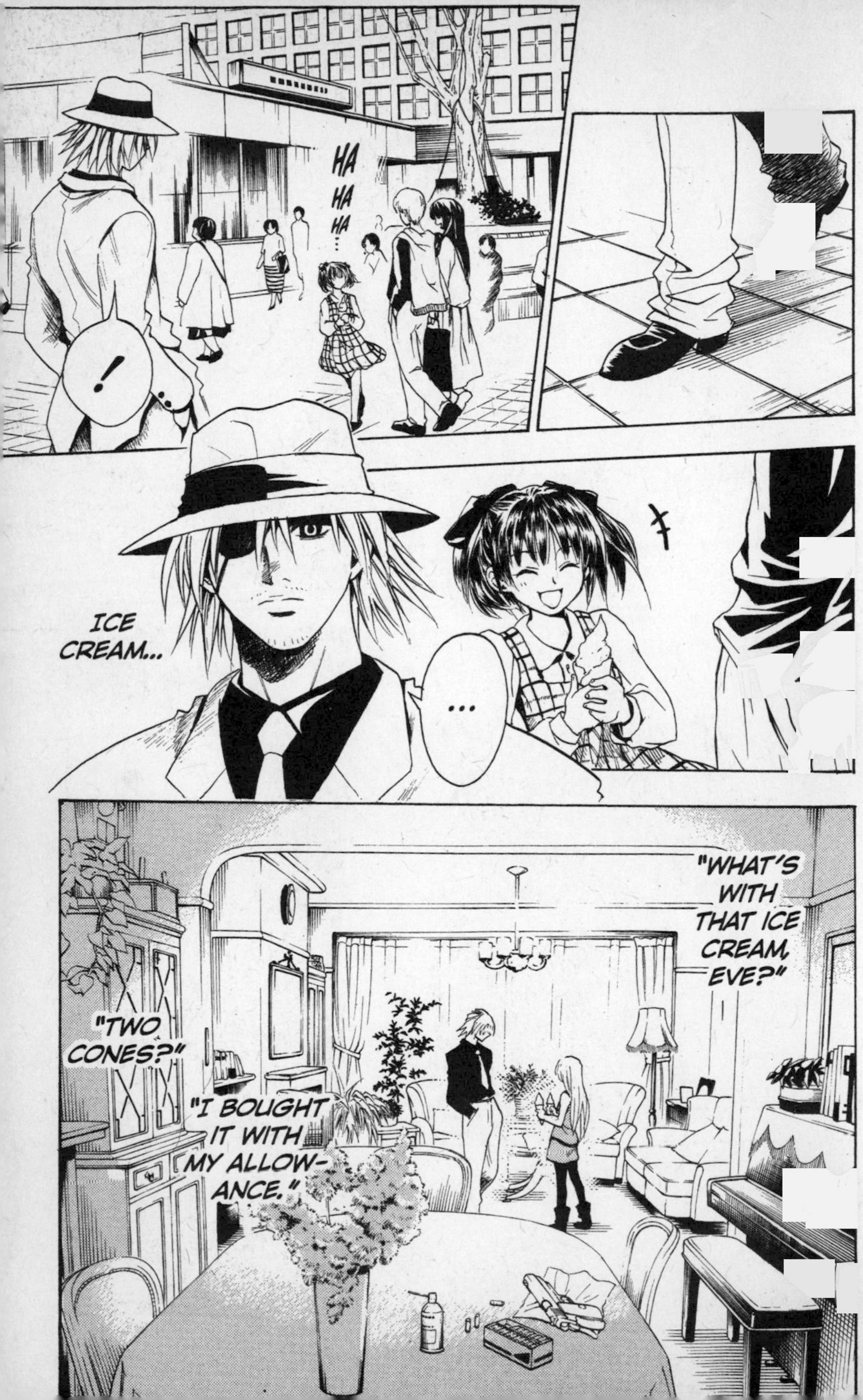
HA HA HA...
!
...
ICE CREAM...
"WHAT'S WITH THAT ICE CREAM, EVE?"
"TWO CONES?"
"I BOUGHT IT WITH MY ALLOW- ANCE."

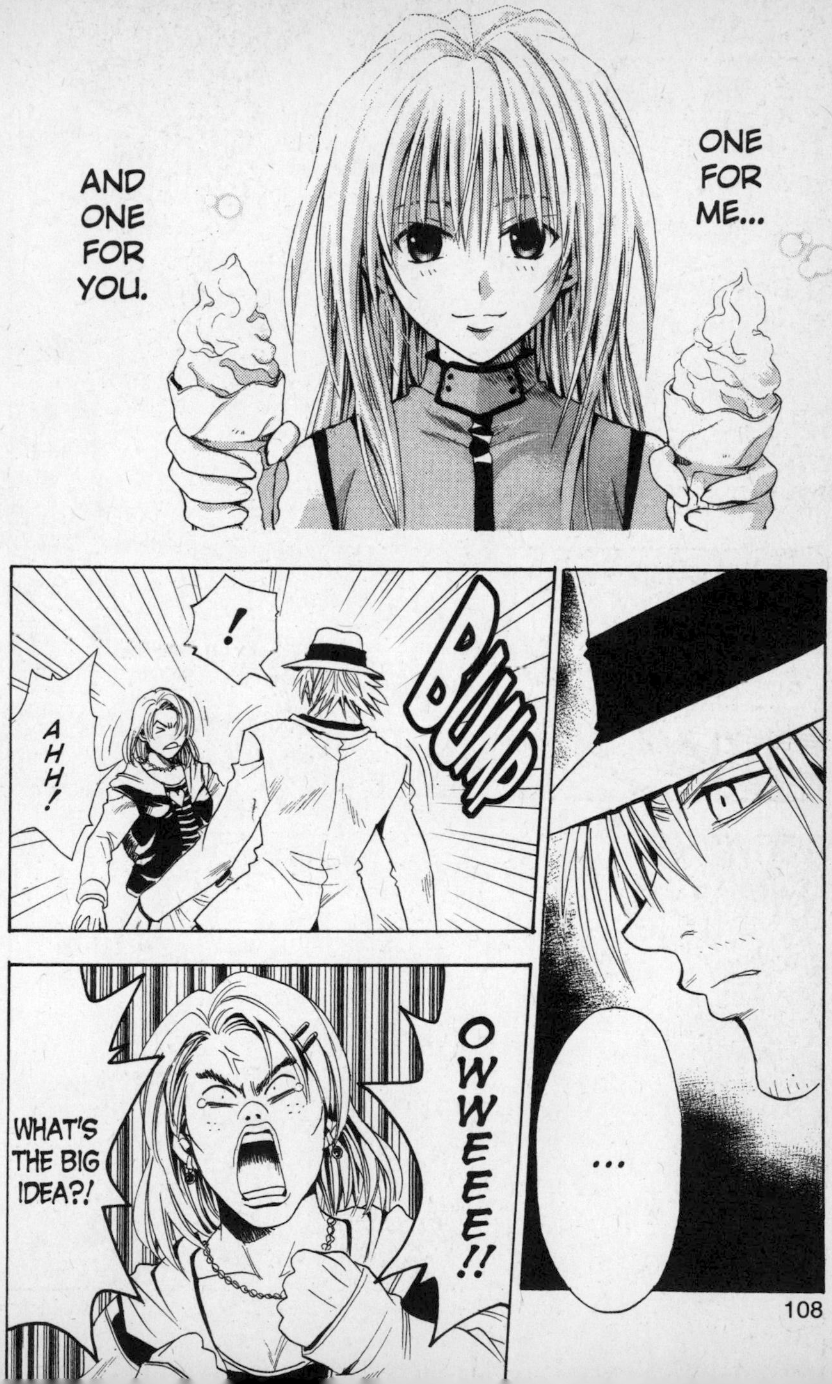
ONE FOR ME...
AND ONE FOR YOU.
...
!
BUMP
AHH!
OWWEEE!!
WHAT'S THE BIG IDEA?!

READ THIS WAY

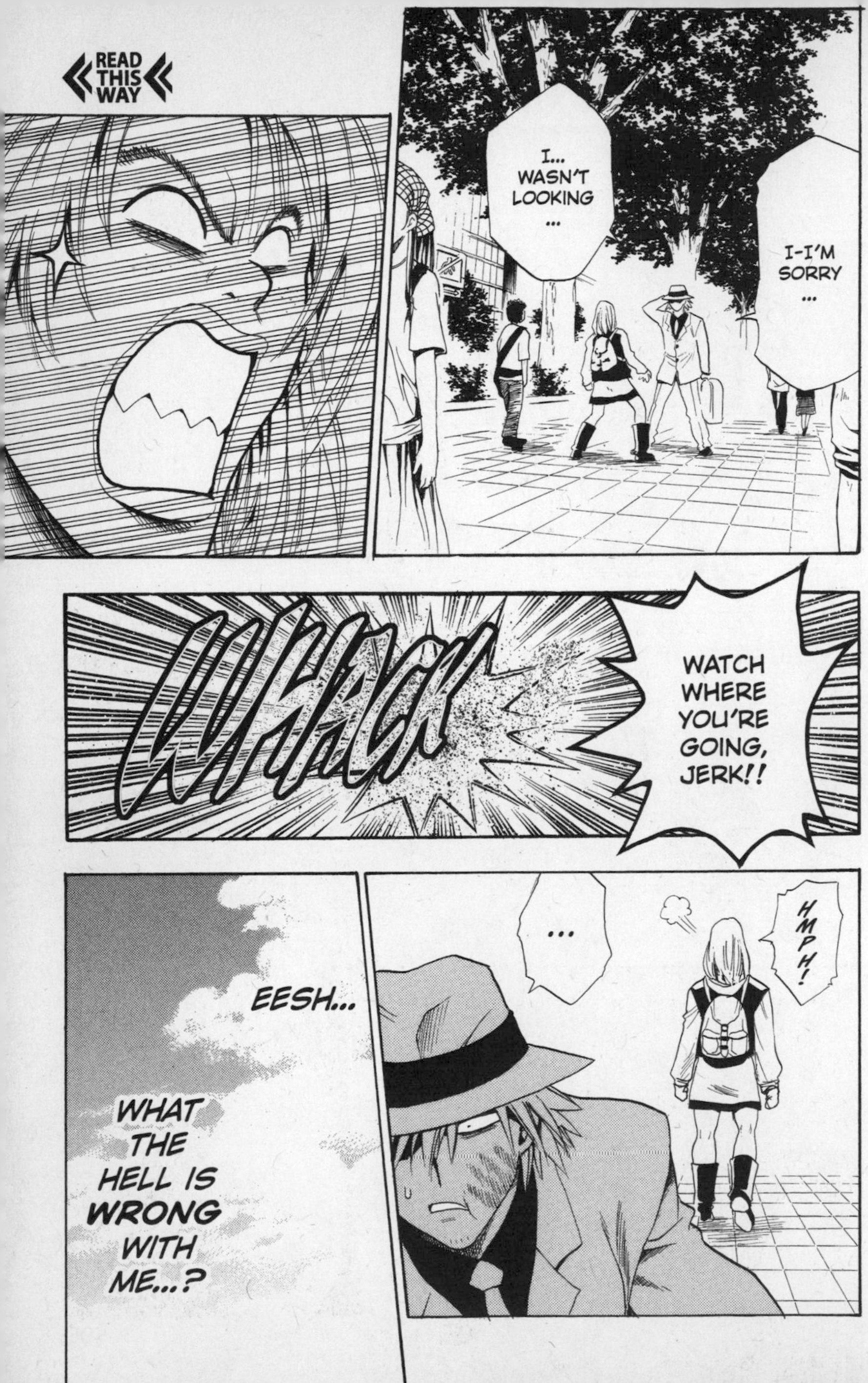
I-I'M SORRY...
I... WASN'T LOOKING...
WHACK
WATCH WHERE YOU'RE GOING, JERK!!
HMPH!
...
EESH...
WHAT THE HELL IS WRONG WITH ME...?

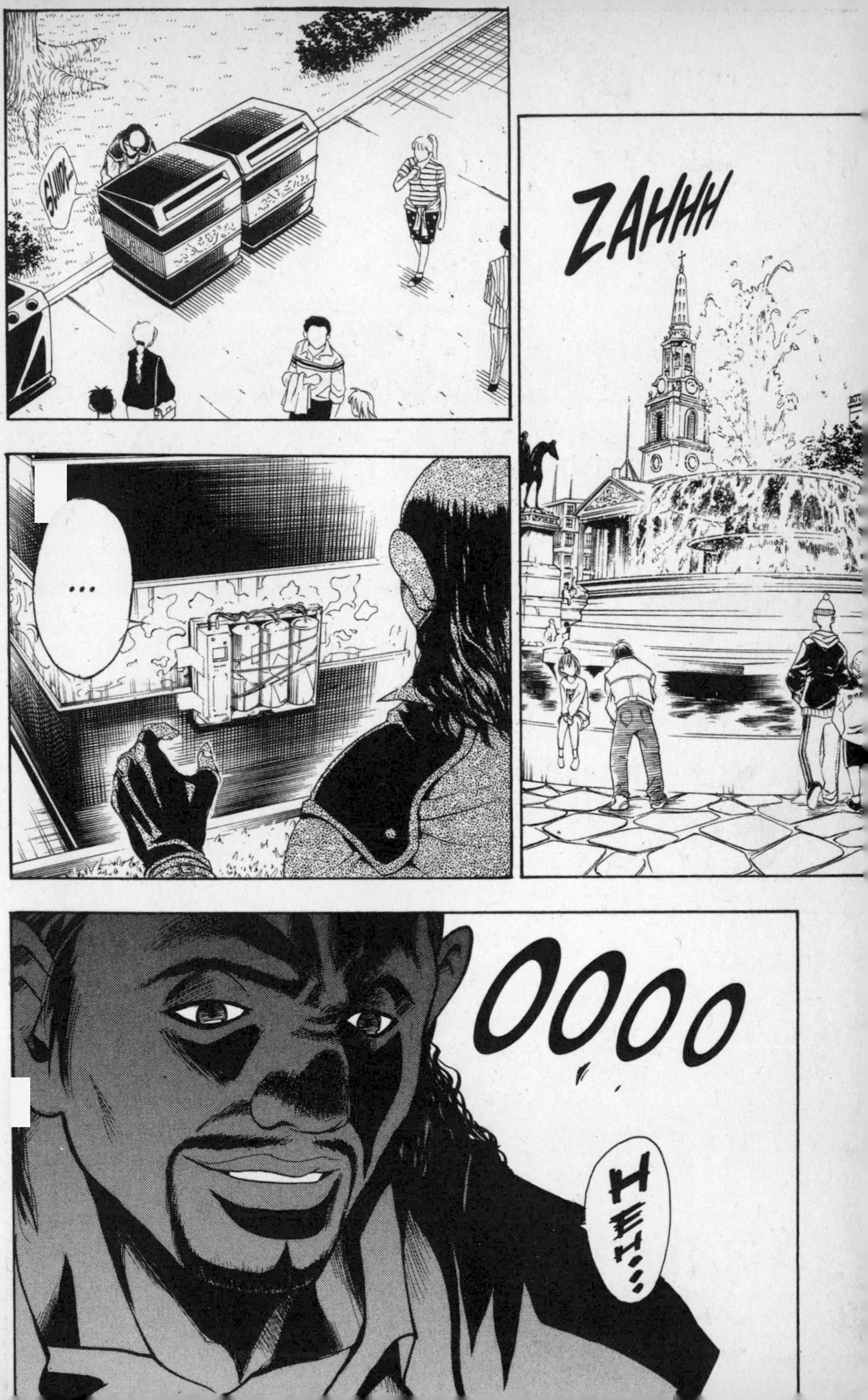
ZAHHH
SLIIDE...
...
OOOO
HEH!!

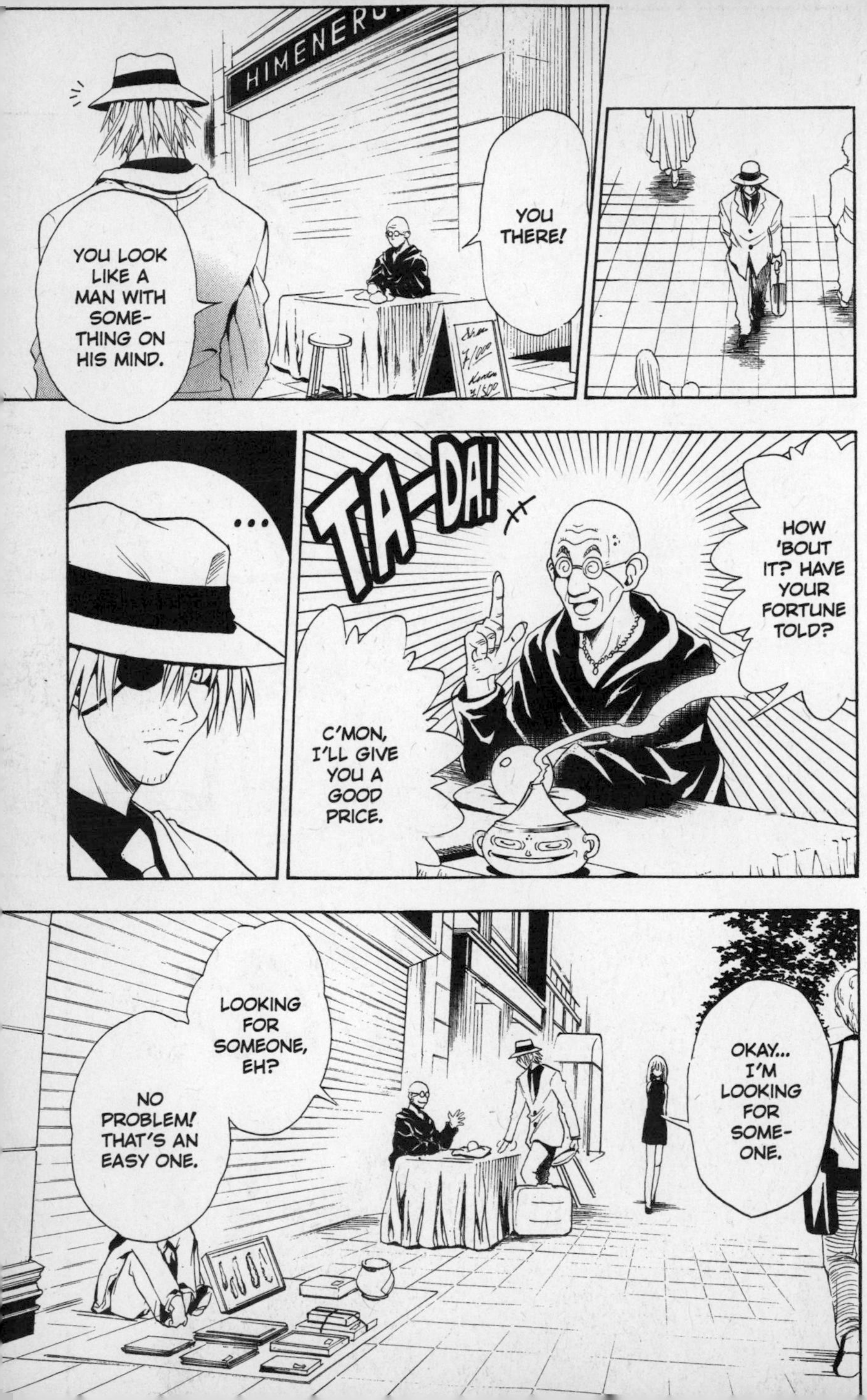
HIMENERU
YOU THERE!
YOU LOOK LIKE A MAN WITH SOME-THING ON HIS MIND.
HOW 'BOUT IT? HAVE YOUR FORTUNE TOLD?
TA-DA!
C'MON, I'LL GIVE YOU A GOOD PRICE.
...
OKAY... I'M LOOKING FOR SOME-ONE.
LOOKING FOR SOMEONE, EH?
NO PROBLEM! THAT'S AN EASY ONE.

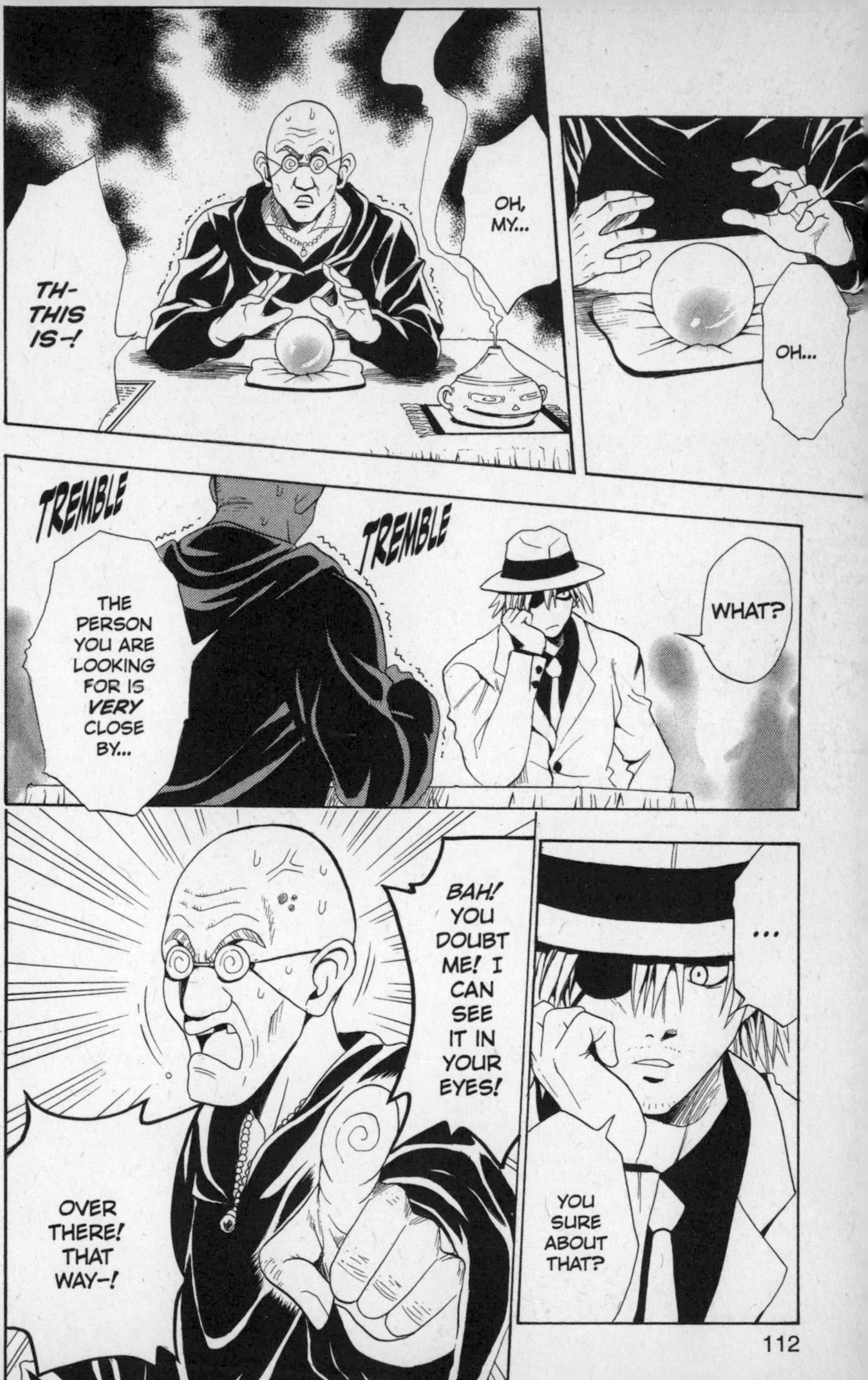
OH...
OH, MY...
TH-THIS IS-!
TREMBLE
TREMBLE
WHAT?
THE PERSON YOU ARE LOOKING FOR IS *VERY* CLOSE BY...
...
YOU SURE ABOUT THAT?
BAH! YOU DOUBT ME! I CAN SEE IT IN YOUR EYES!
OVER THERE! THAT WAY-!

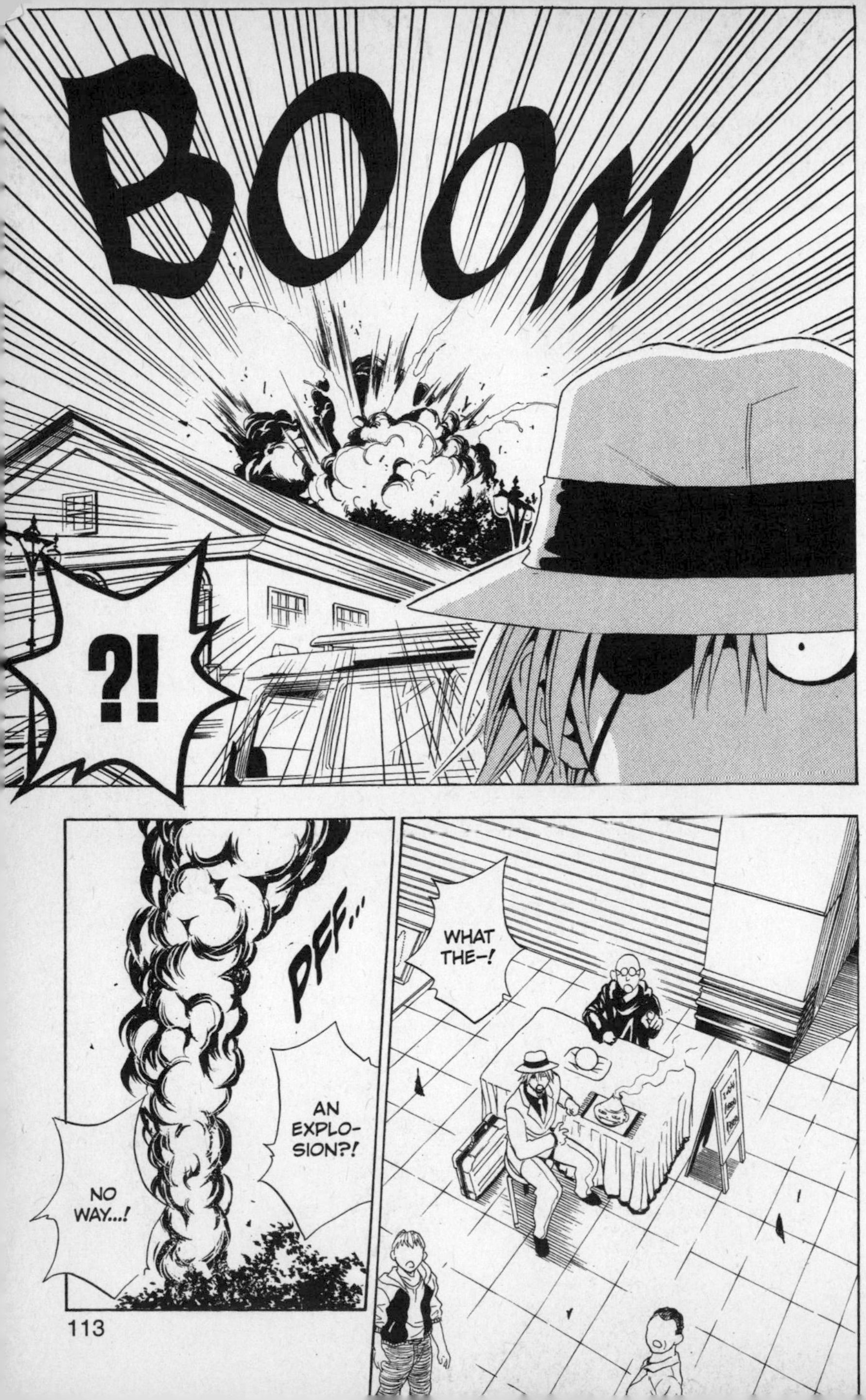
BOOM
?!
WHAT THE–!
PFF...
AN EXPLO-SION?!
NO WAY...!

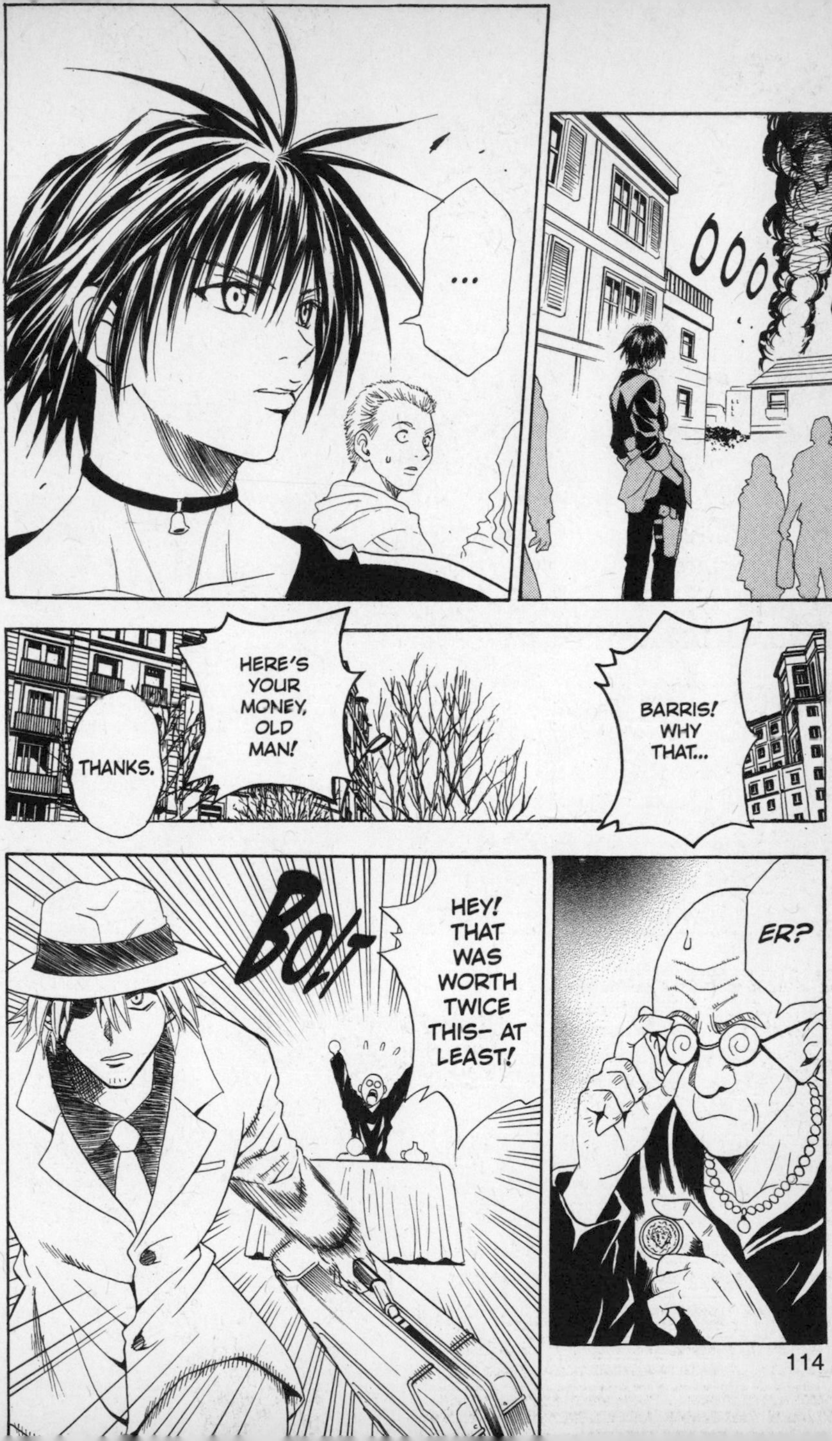
OOOO...
...
BARRIS! WHY THAT...
HERE'S YOUR MONEY, OLD MAN!
THANKS.
ER?
BOLT
HEY! THAT WAS WORTH TWICE THIS- AT LEAST!

READ THIS WAY

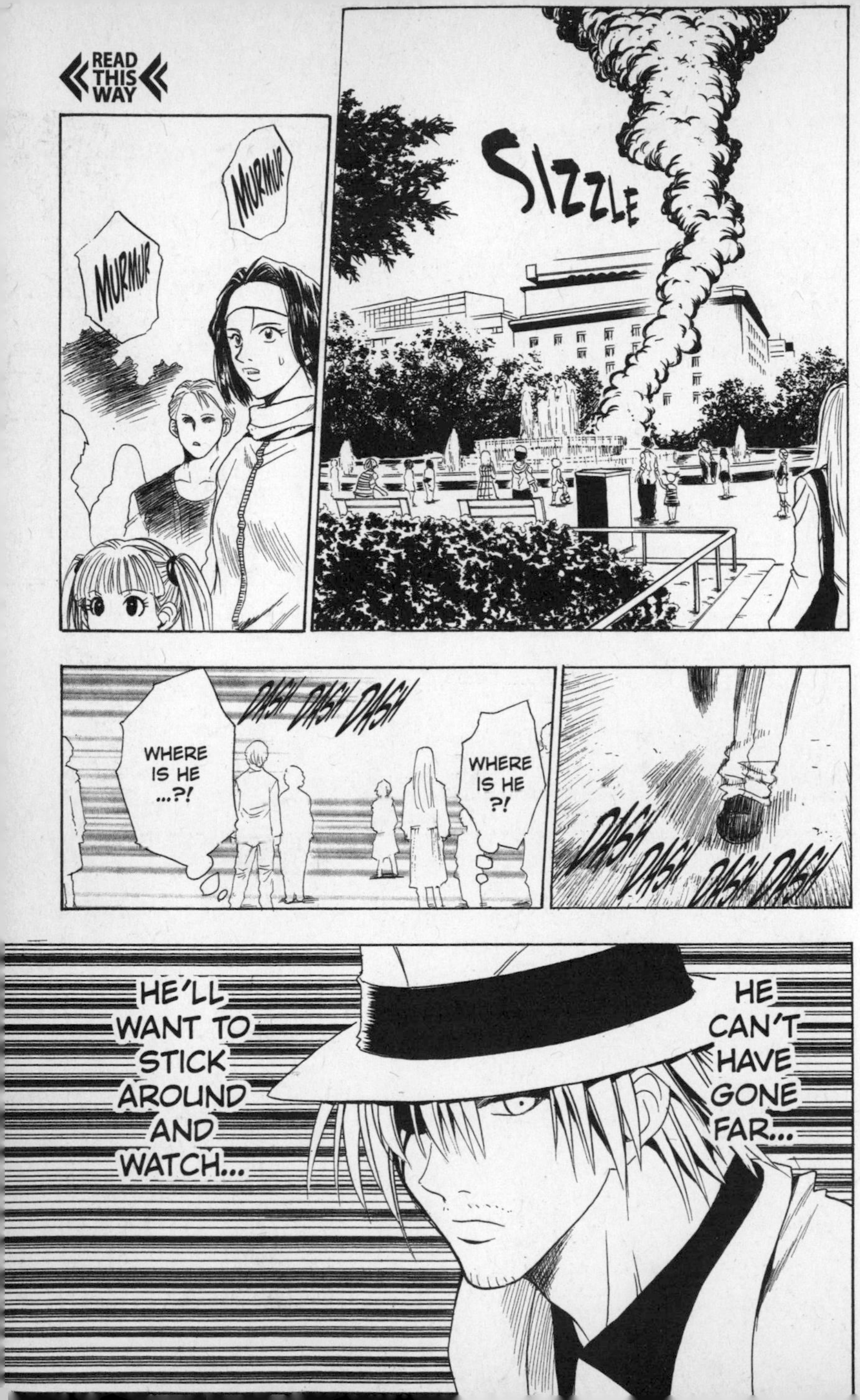
SIZZLE
MURMUR
MURMUR
DASH DASH DASH DASH
DASH DASH DASH
WHERE IS HE ?!
WHERE IS HE ...?!
HE CAN'T HAVE GONE FAR...
HE'LL WANT TO STICK AROUND AND WATCH...

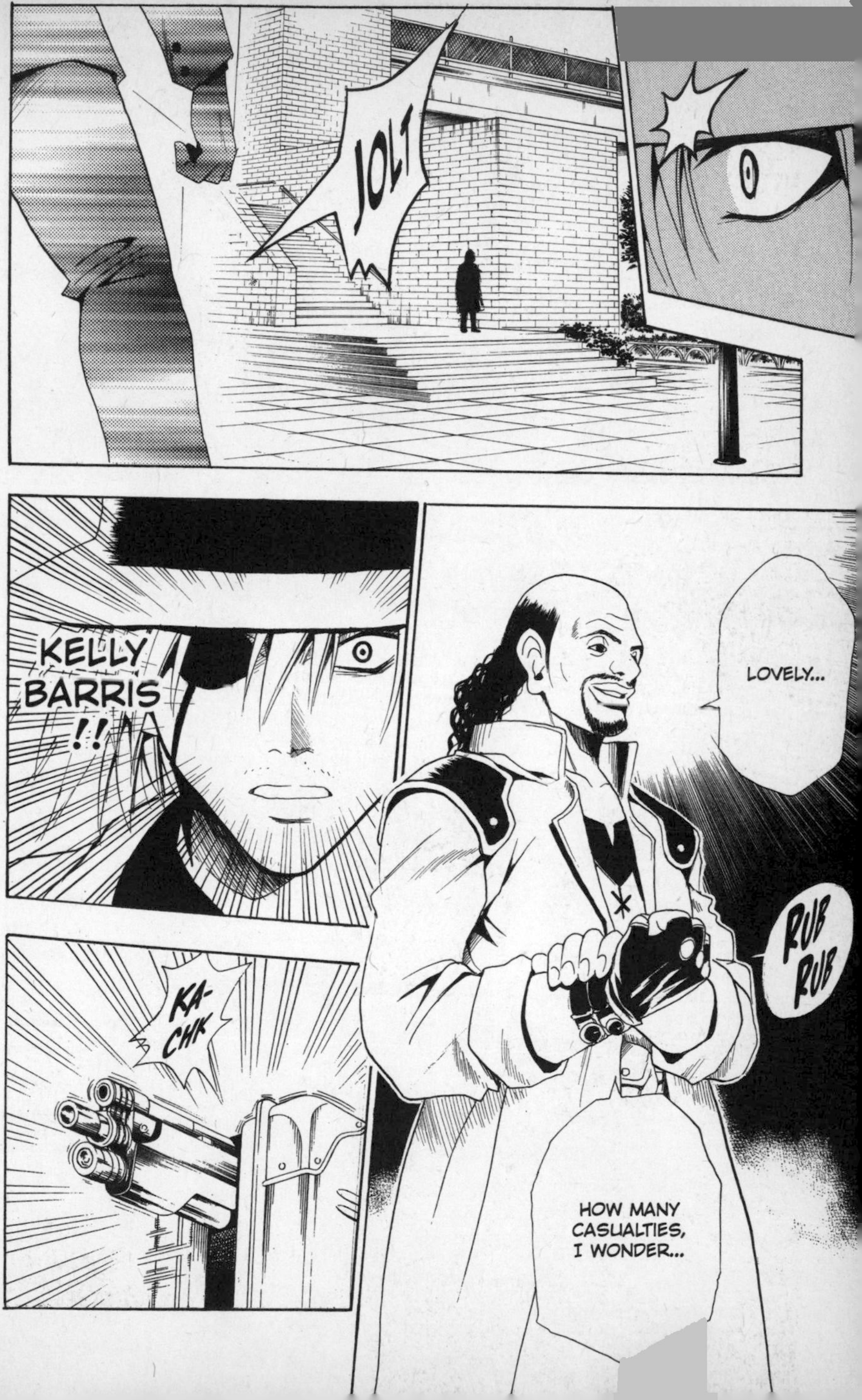
JOLT
LOVELY...
RUB RUB
HOW MANY CASUALTIES, I WONDER...
KELLY BARRIS!!
KA-CHK

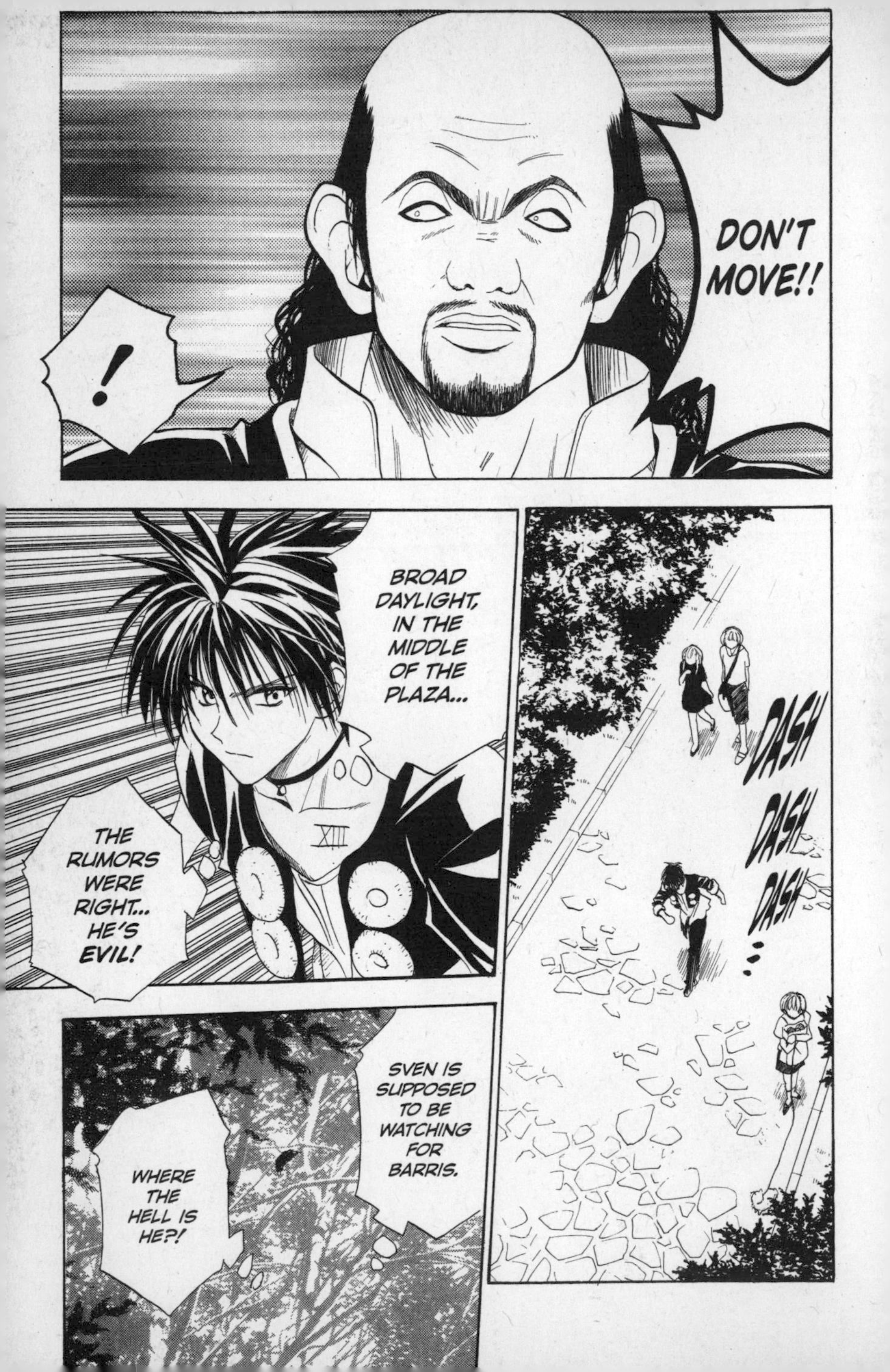
DON'T MOVE!!
!
DASH
DASH
DASH
...
BROAD DAYLIGHT, IN THE MIDDLE OF THE PLAZA...
THE RUMORS WERE RIGHT... HE'S EVIL!
SVEN IS SUPPOSED TO BE WATCHING FOR BARRIS.
WHERE THE HELL IS HE?!

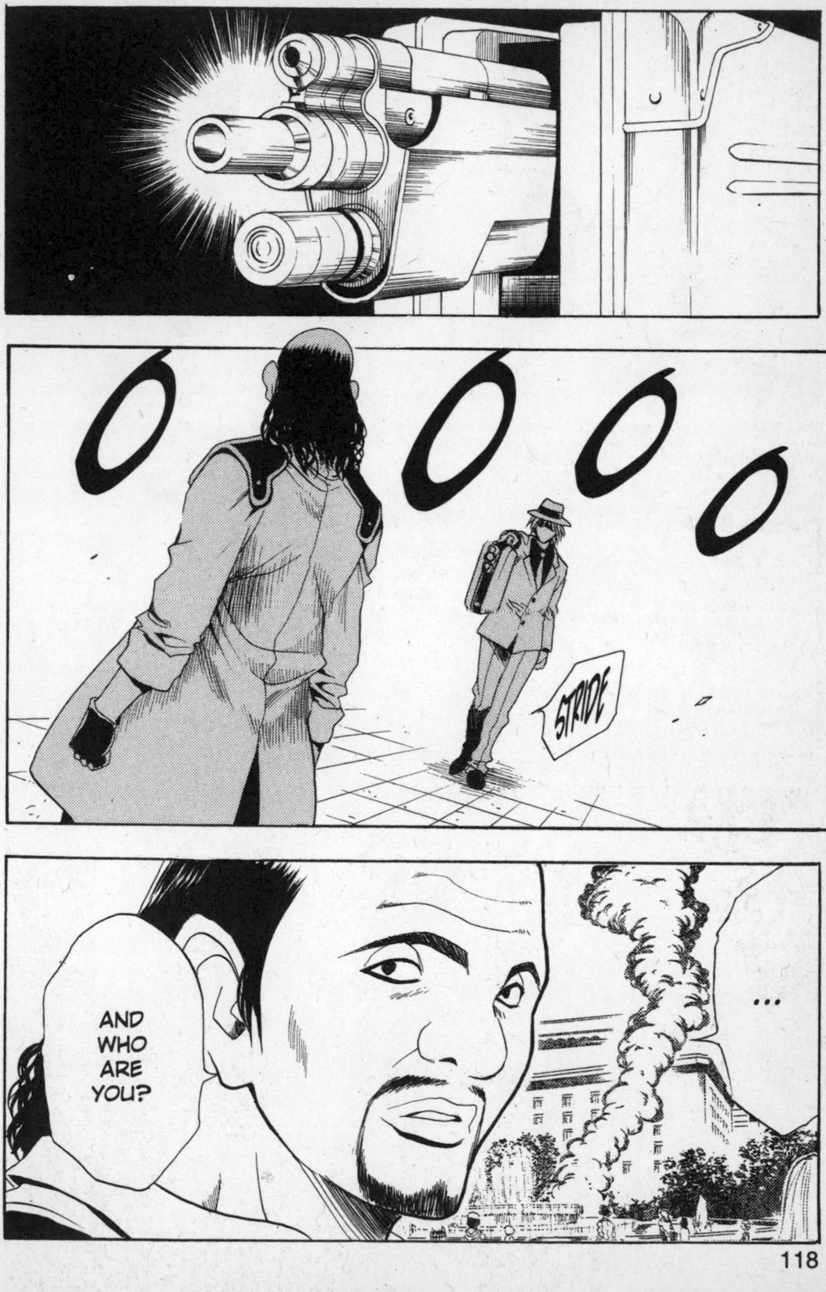
OOOO
STRIDE
...
AND WHO ARE YOU?

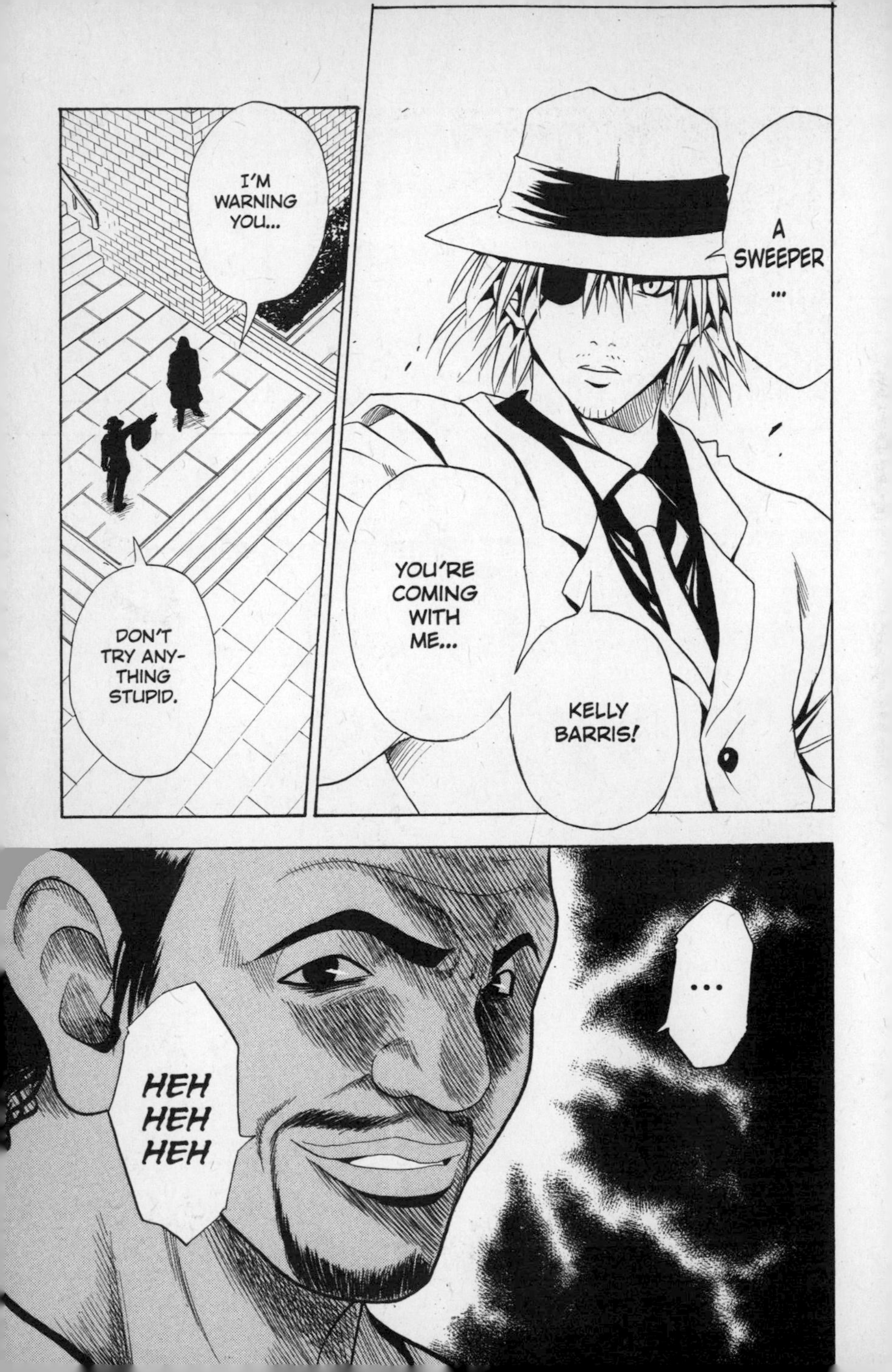
A SWEEPER ...
YOU'RE COMING WITH ME...
KELLY BARRIS!
I'M WARNING YOU...
DON'T TRY ANY-THING STUPID.
...
HEH HEH HEH

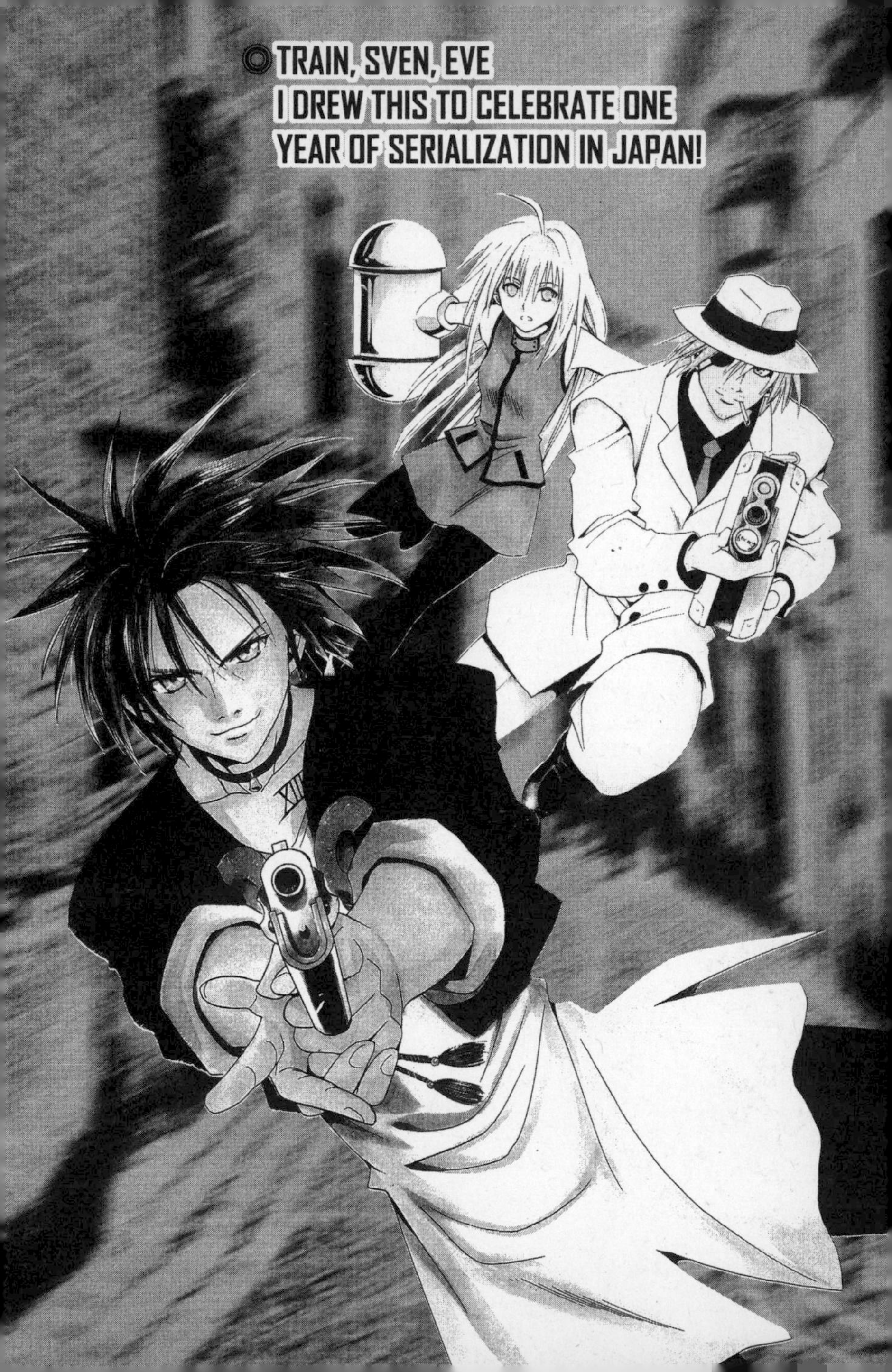

TRAIN, SVEN, EVE
I DREW THIS TO CELEBRATE ONE YEAR OF SERIALIZATION IN JAPAN!

Chapter 54: Hostage

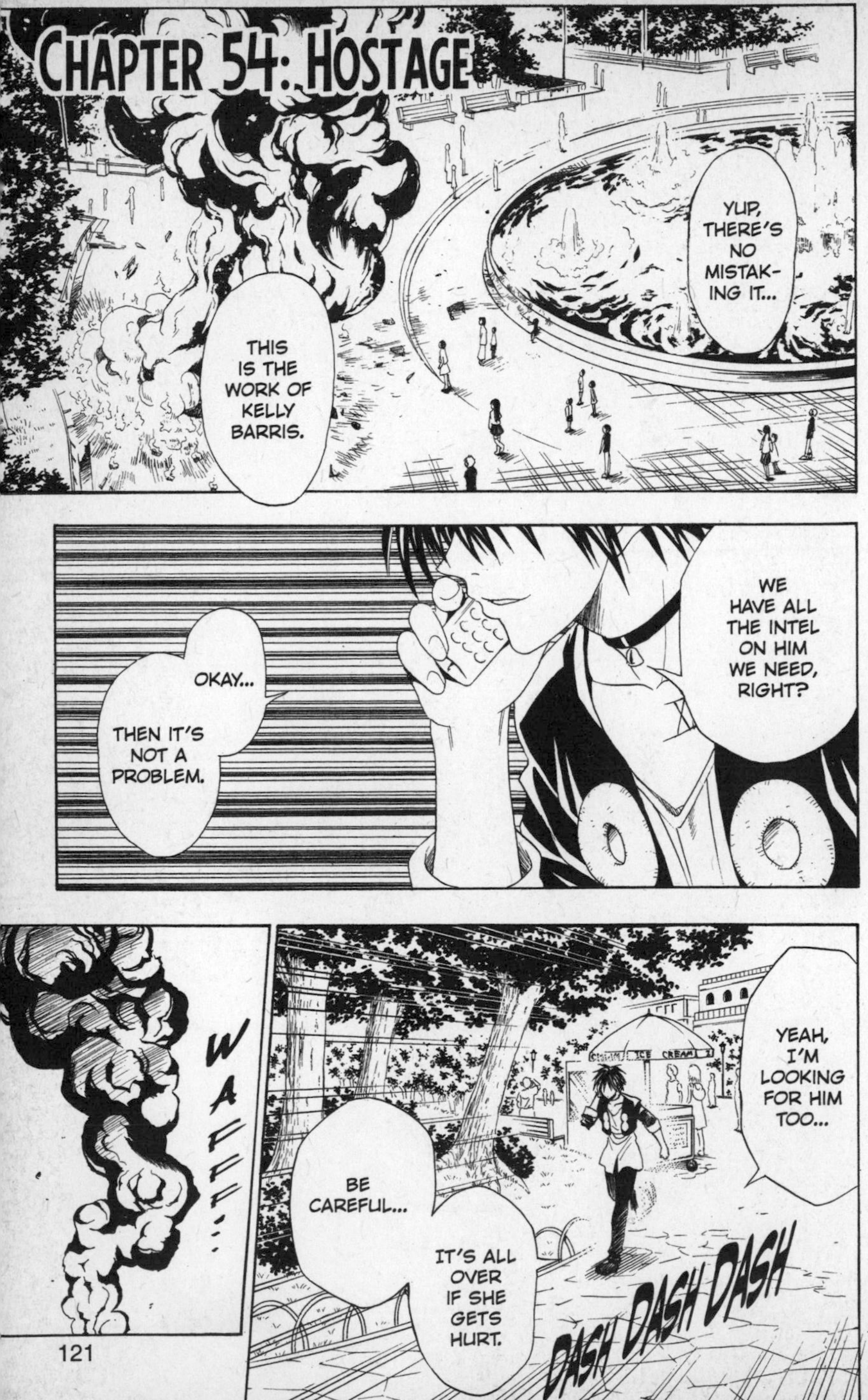

YUP, THERE'S NO MISTAKING IT...
THIS IS THE WORK OF KELLY BARRIS.
WE HAVE ALL THE INTEL ON HIM WE NEED, RIGHT?
OKAY...
THEN IT'S NOT A PROBLEM.
YEAH, I'M LOOKING FOR HIM TOO...
BE CAREFUL...
IT'S ALL OVER IF SHE GETS HURT.
DASH DASH DASH
WAFFF...

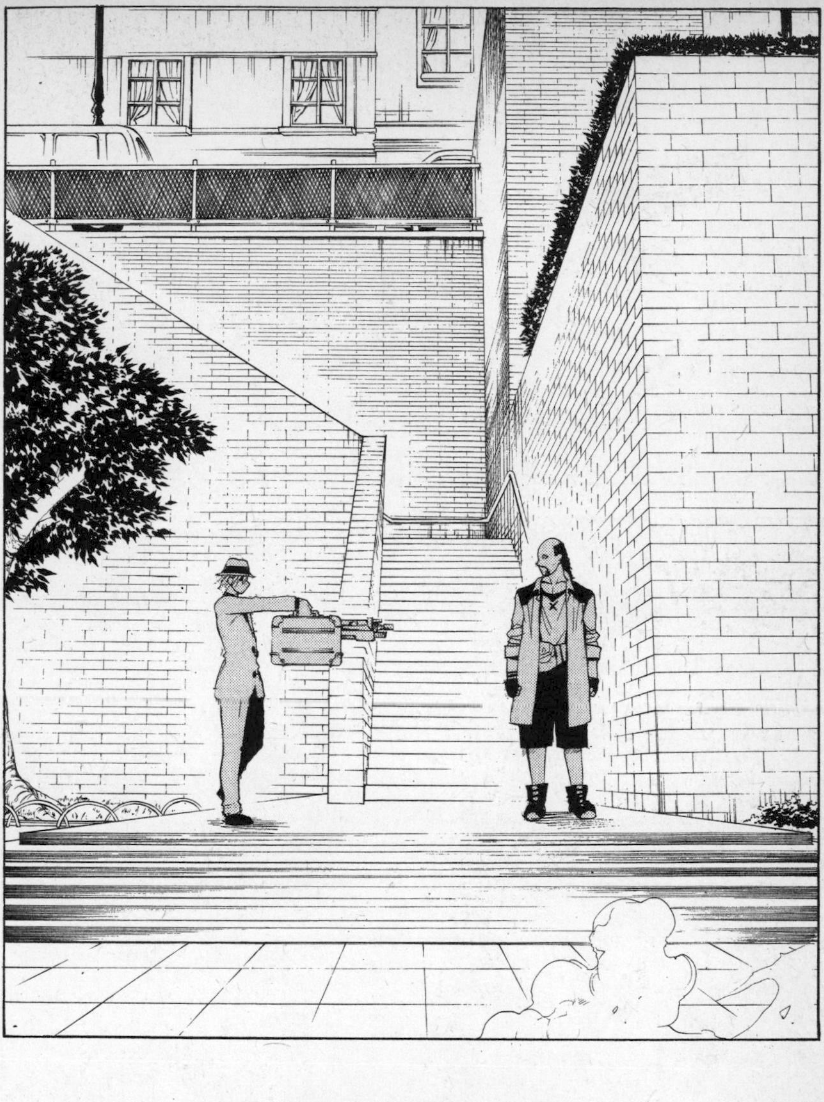

Chapter 54:
Hostage

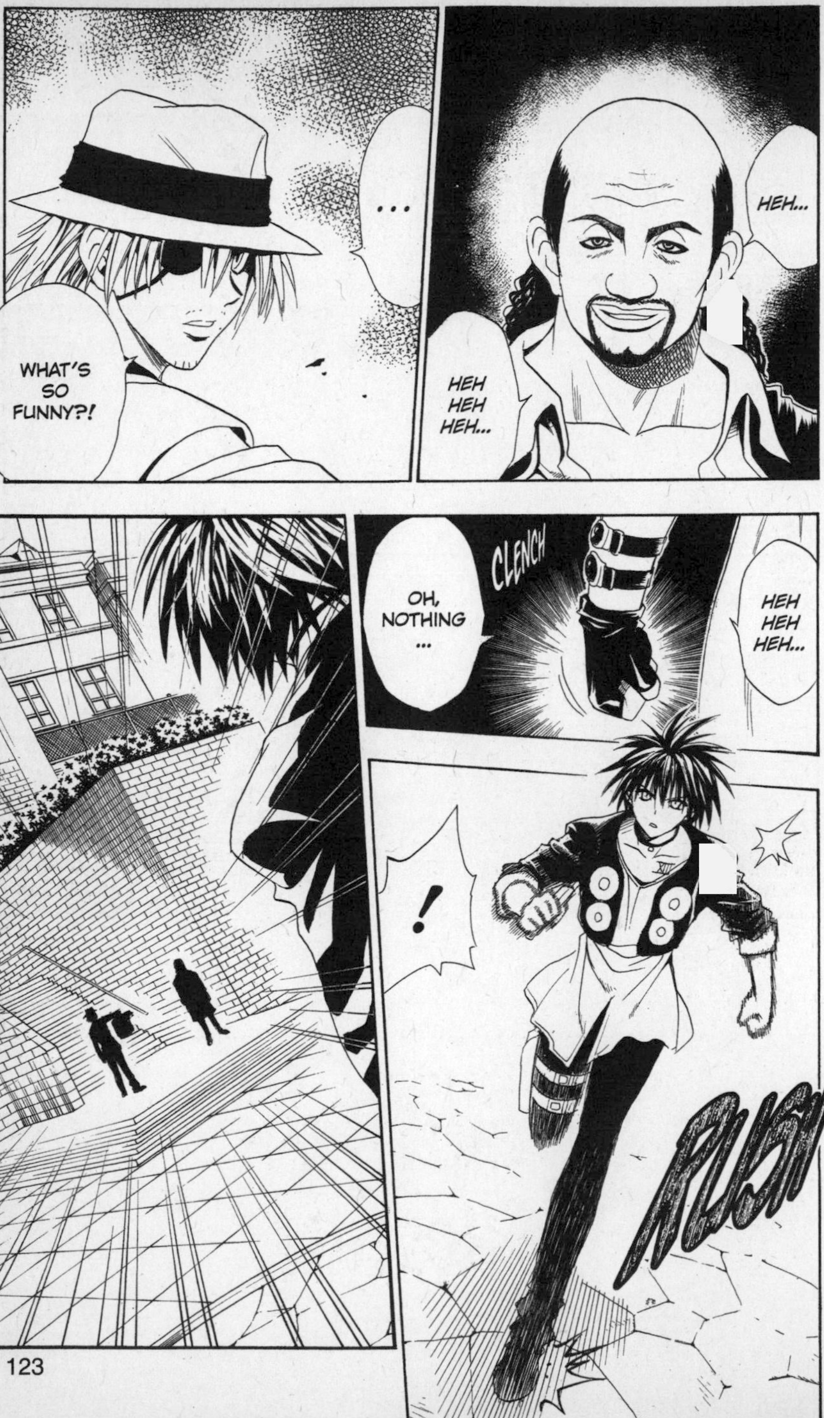
HEH...
HEH HEH HEH...
...
WHAT'S SO FUNNY?!
HEH HEH HEH...
CLENCH
OH, NOTHING ...
!
RUSH

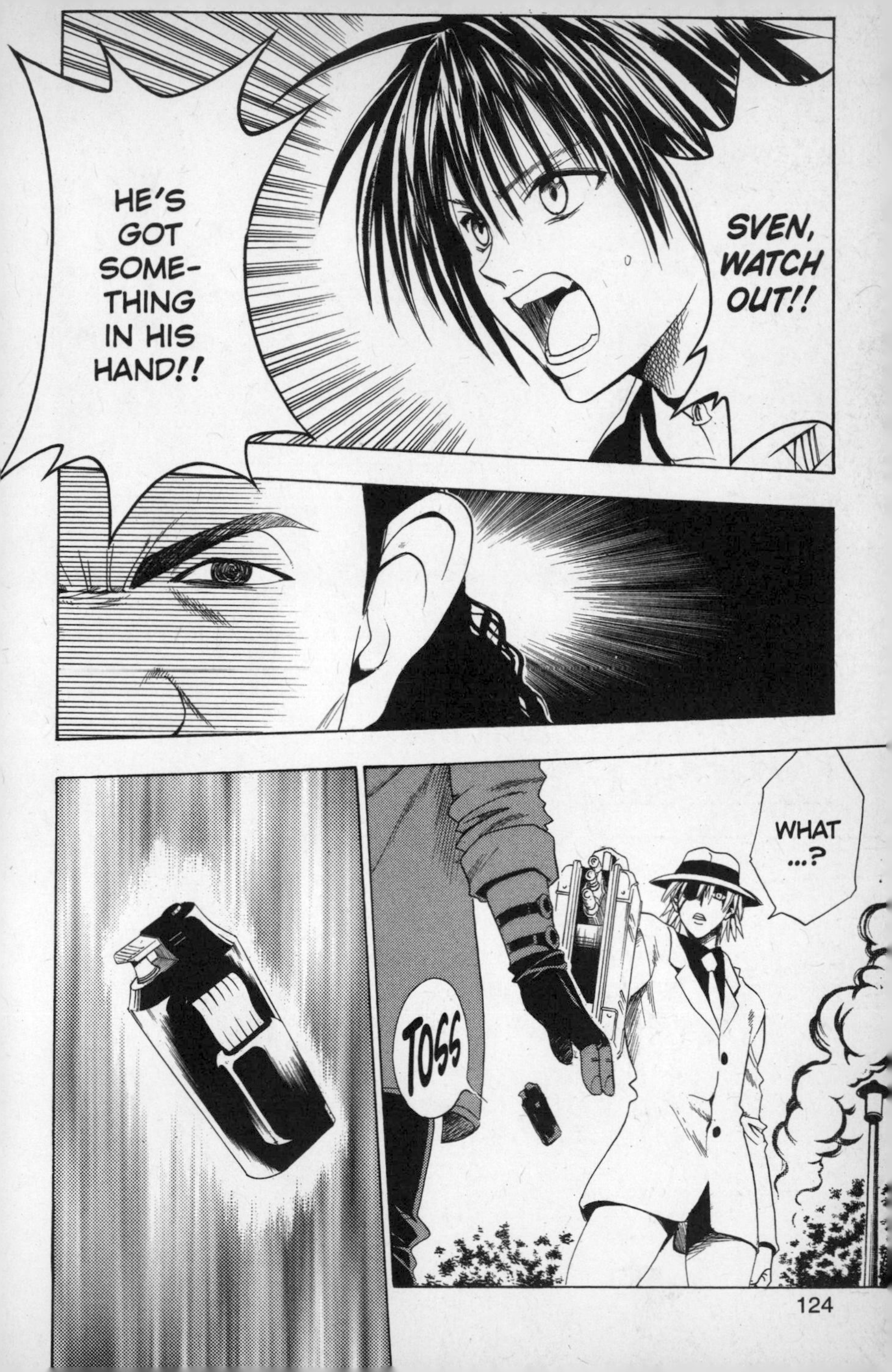
SVEN, WATCH OUT!!
HE'S GOT SOME-THING IN HIS HAND!!
WHAT ...?
TOSS

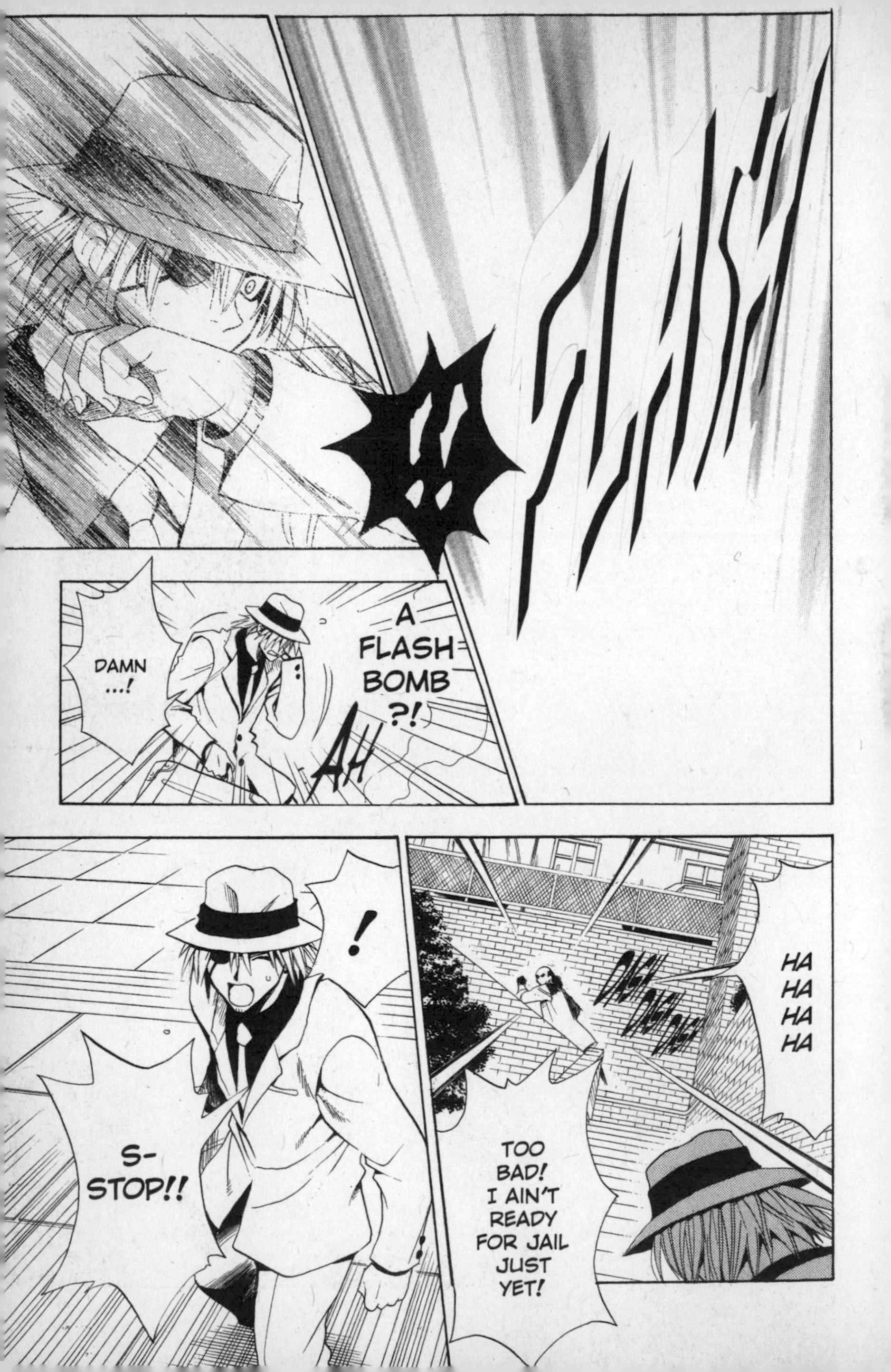
A FLASH BOMB ?!
AH
DAMN ...!
HA HA HA HA
DASH DASH DASH
TOO BAD! I AIN'T READY FOR JAIL JUST YET!
!
S- STOP!!

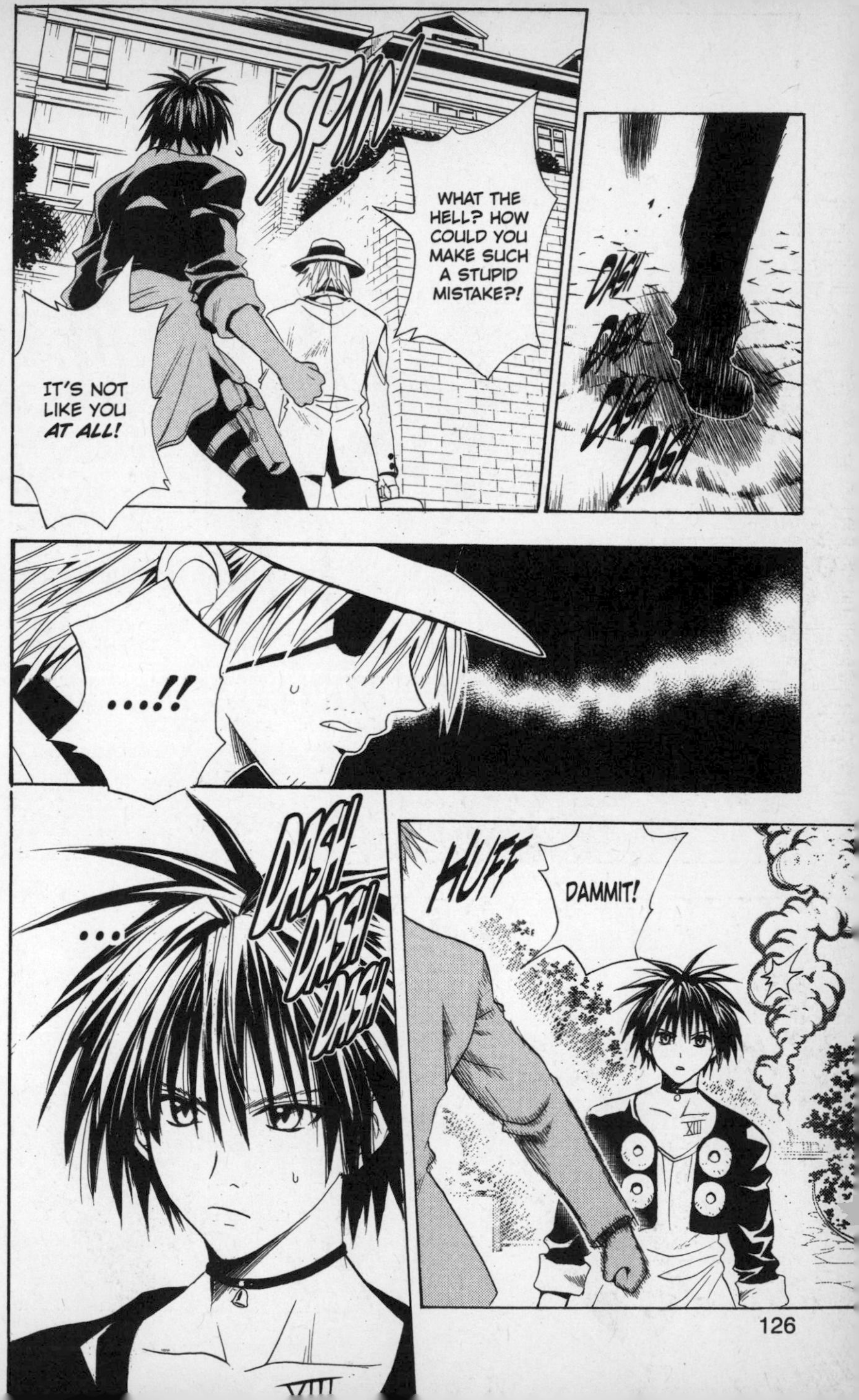

DASH DASH DASH DASH
SPIN
WHAT THE HELL? HOW COULD YOU MAKE SUCH A STUPID MISTAKE?!
IT'S NOT LIKE YOU *AT ALL!*
...!!
HUFF
DAMMIT!
DASH DASH DASH
...

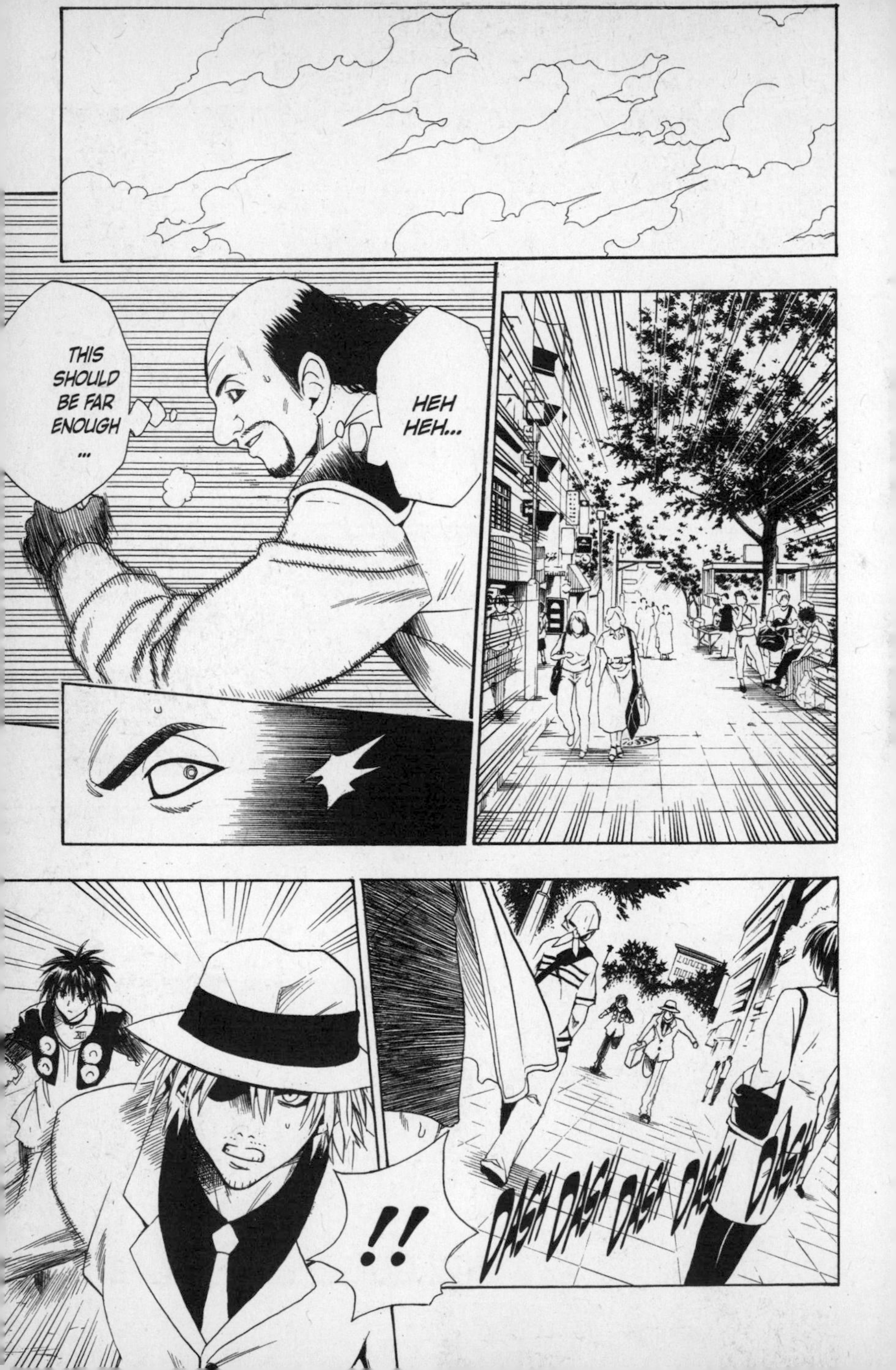
HEH HEH...
THIS SHOULD BE FAR ENOUGH...
DASH DASH DASH DASH DASH
!!

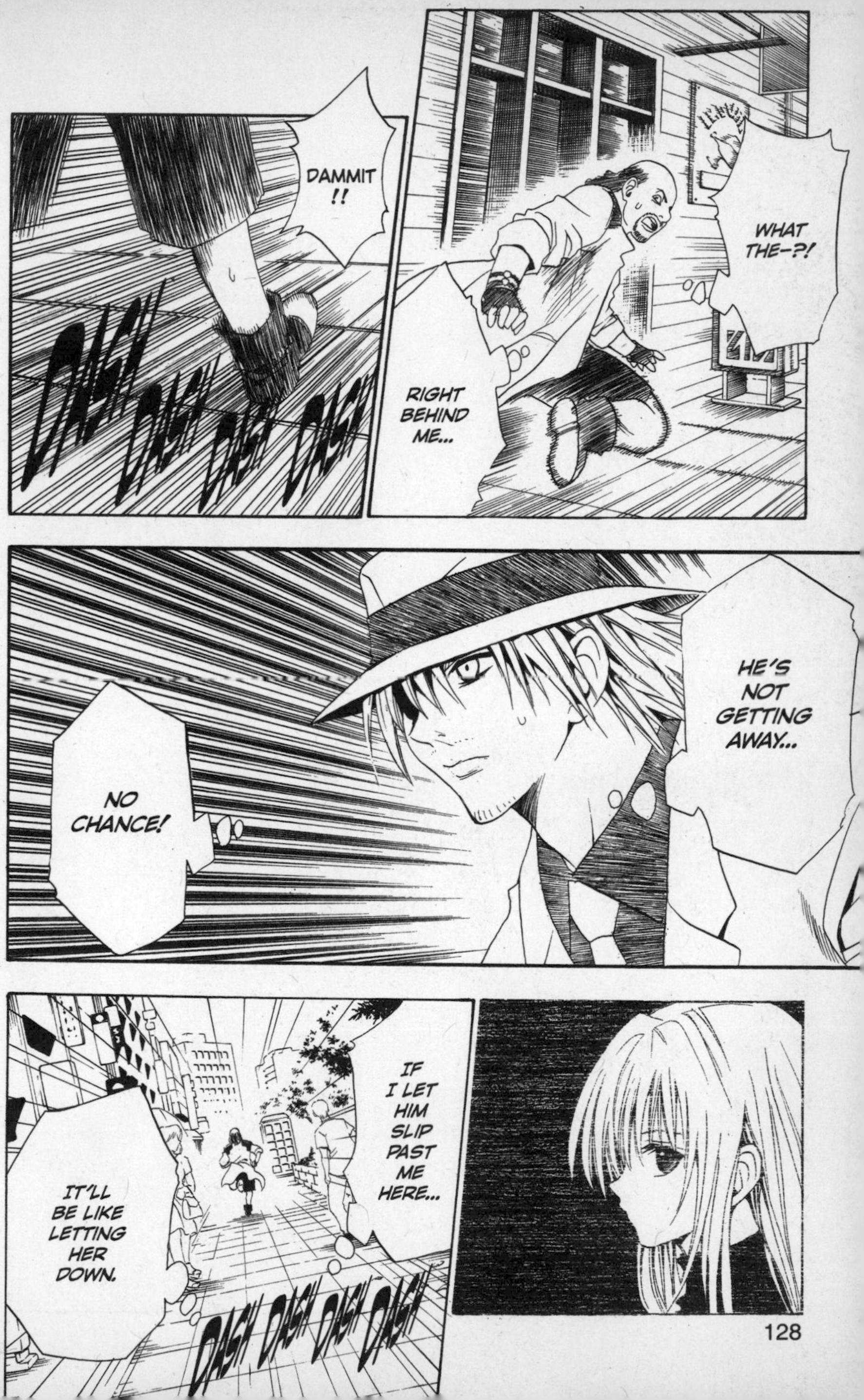
WHAT THE-?!
RIGHT BEHIND ME...
DAMMIT !!
DASH DASH DASH DASH
HE'S NOT GETTING AWAY...
NO CHANCE!
IF I LET HIM SLIP PAST ME HERE...
IT'LL BE LIKE LETTING HER DOWN.
DASH DASH DASH DASH

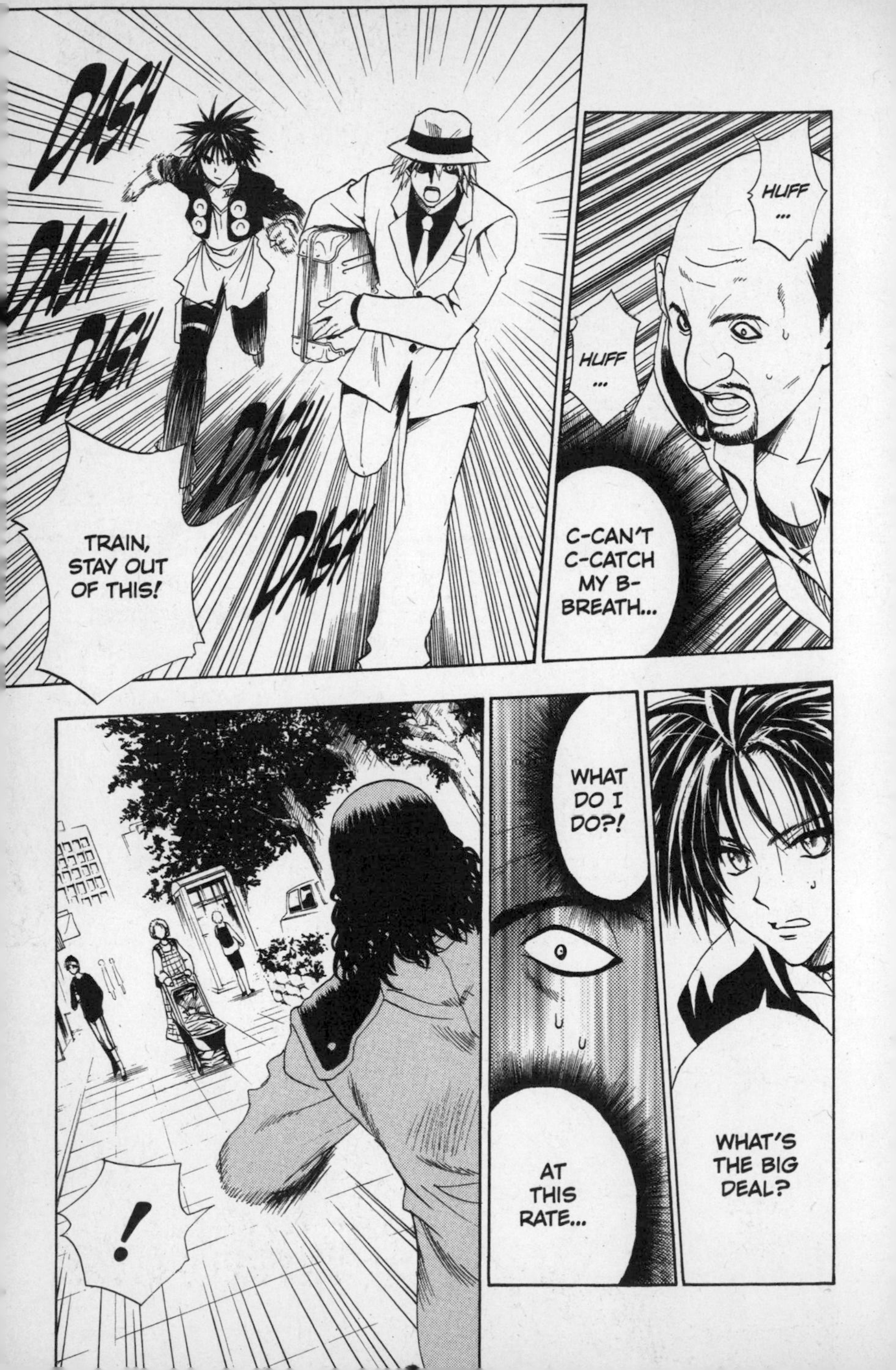
HUFF ...
HUFF ...
C-CAN'T C-CATCH MY B-BREATH...
DASH DASH DASH
DASH DASH
TRAIN, STAY OUT OF THIS!
WHAT'S THE BIG DEAL?
WHAT DO I DO?!
AT THIS RATE...
!

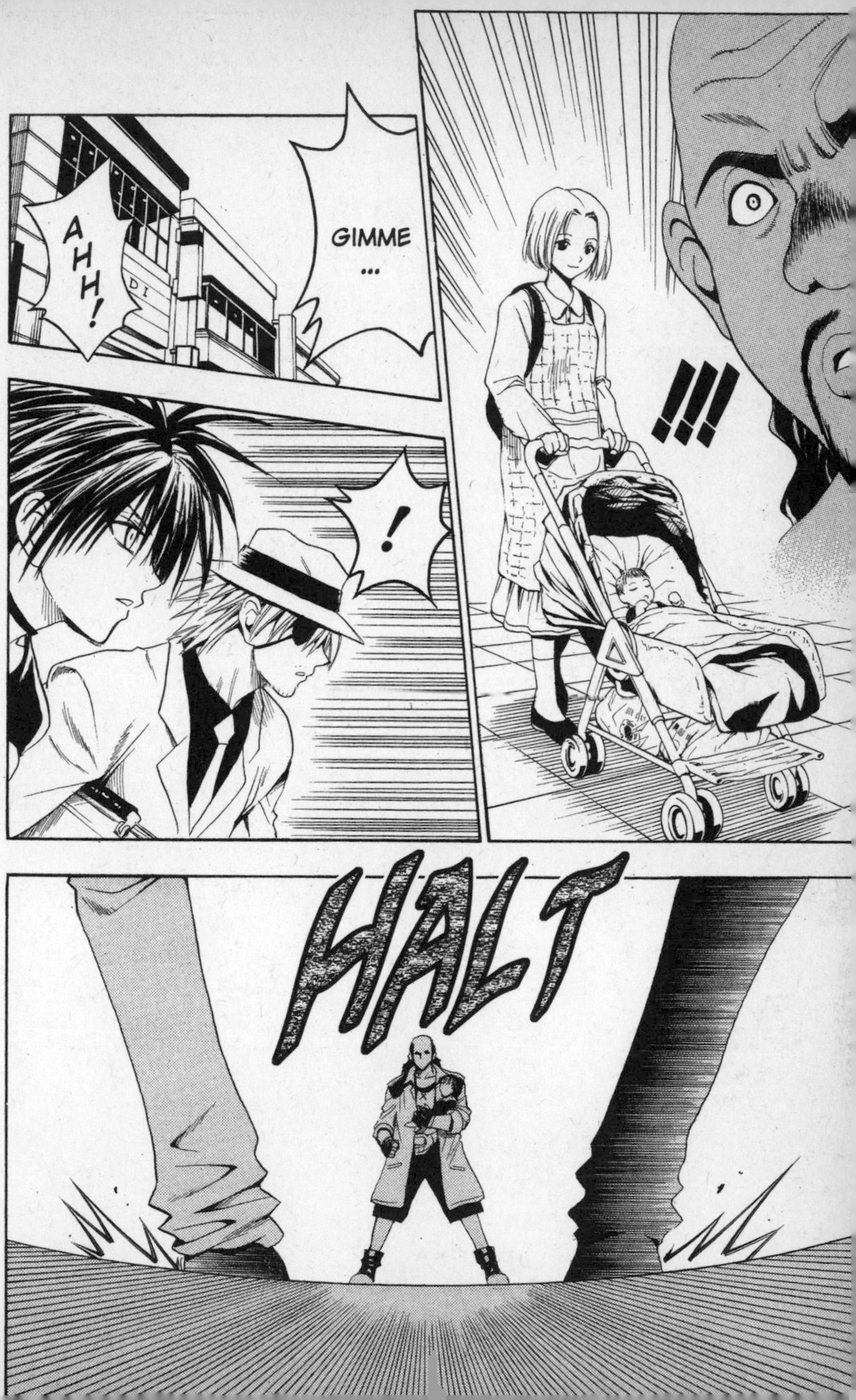
!!!
GIMME ...
AHH!
DI
!
HALT

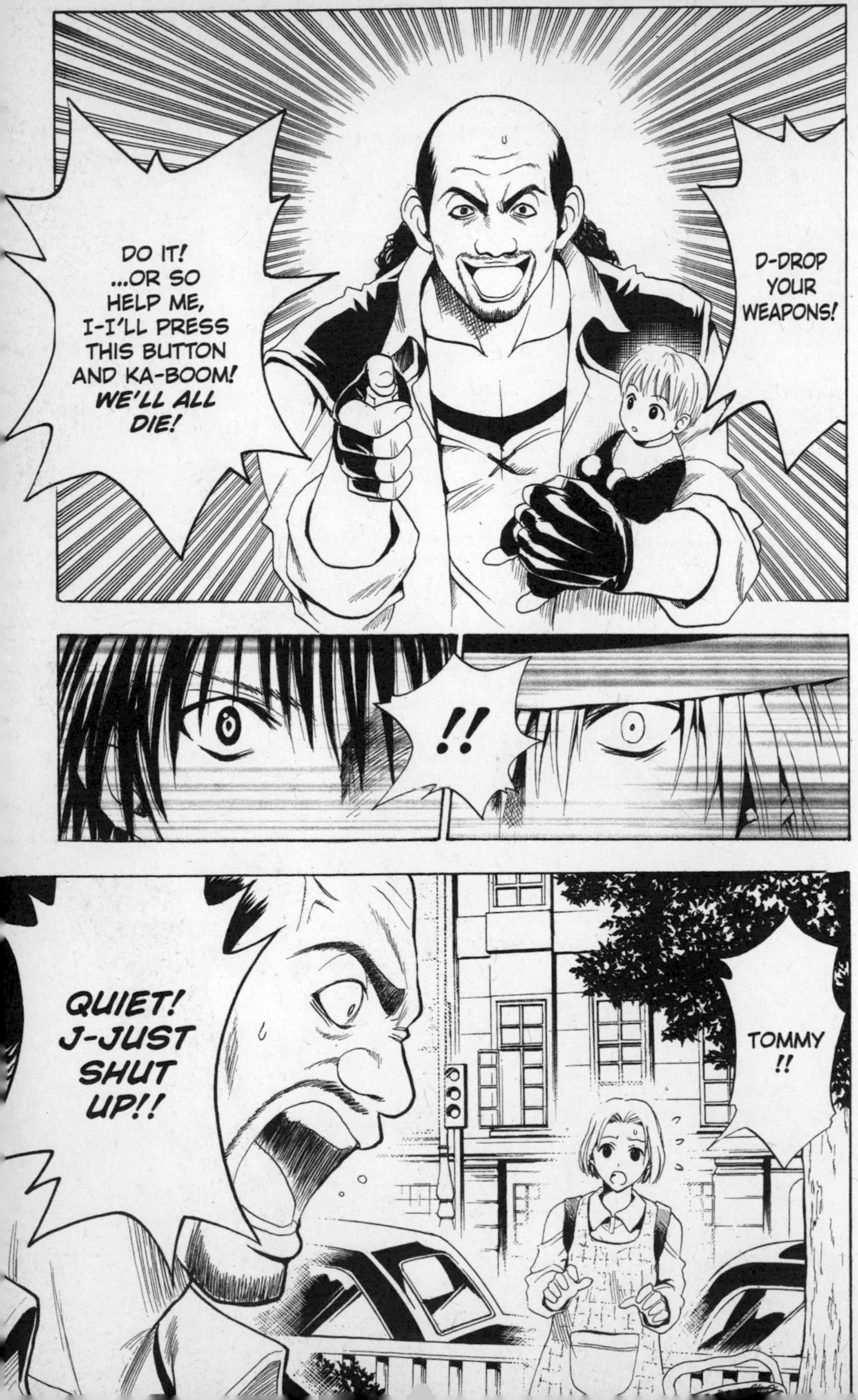
D-DROP YOUR WEAPONS!
DO IT! ...OR SO HELP ME, I-I'LL PRESS THIS BUTTON AND KA-BOOM! *WE'LL ALL DIE!*
!!
TOMMY !!
QUIET! J-JUST SHUT UP!!

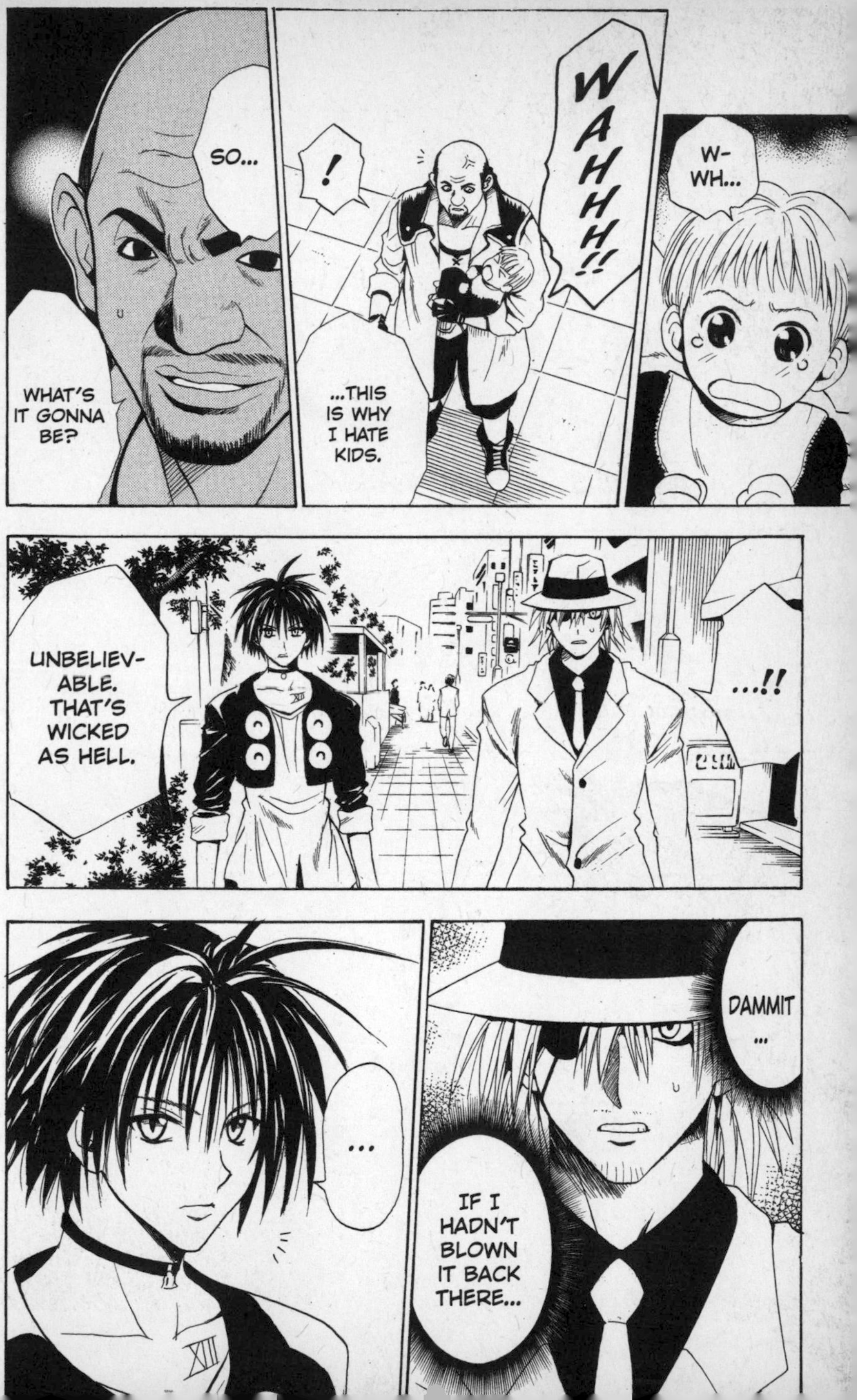
W- WH...
WAHHHH!!
!
...THIS IS WHY I HATE KIDS.
SO...
WHAT'S IT GONNA BE?
...!!
UNBELIEVABLE. THAT'S WICKED AS HELL.
DAMMIT ...
IF I HADN'T BLOWN IT BACK THERE...
...

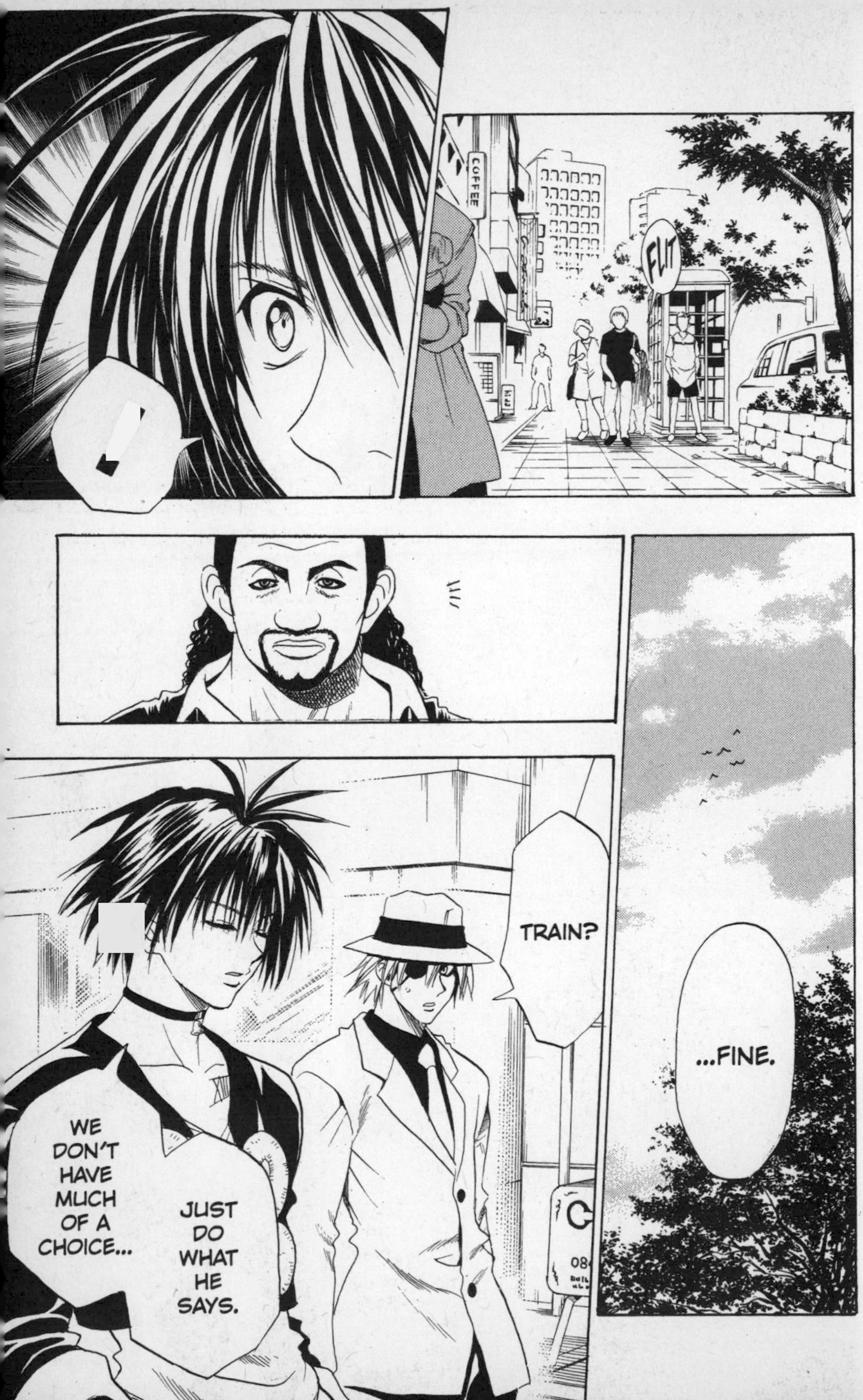
COFFEE
FLIT
!
TRAIN?
WE DON'T HAVE MUCH OF A CHOICE...
JUST DO WHAT HE SAYS.
...FINE.

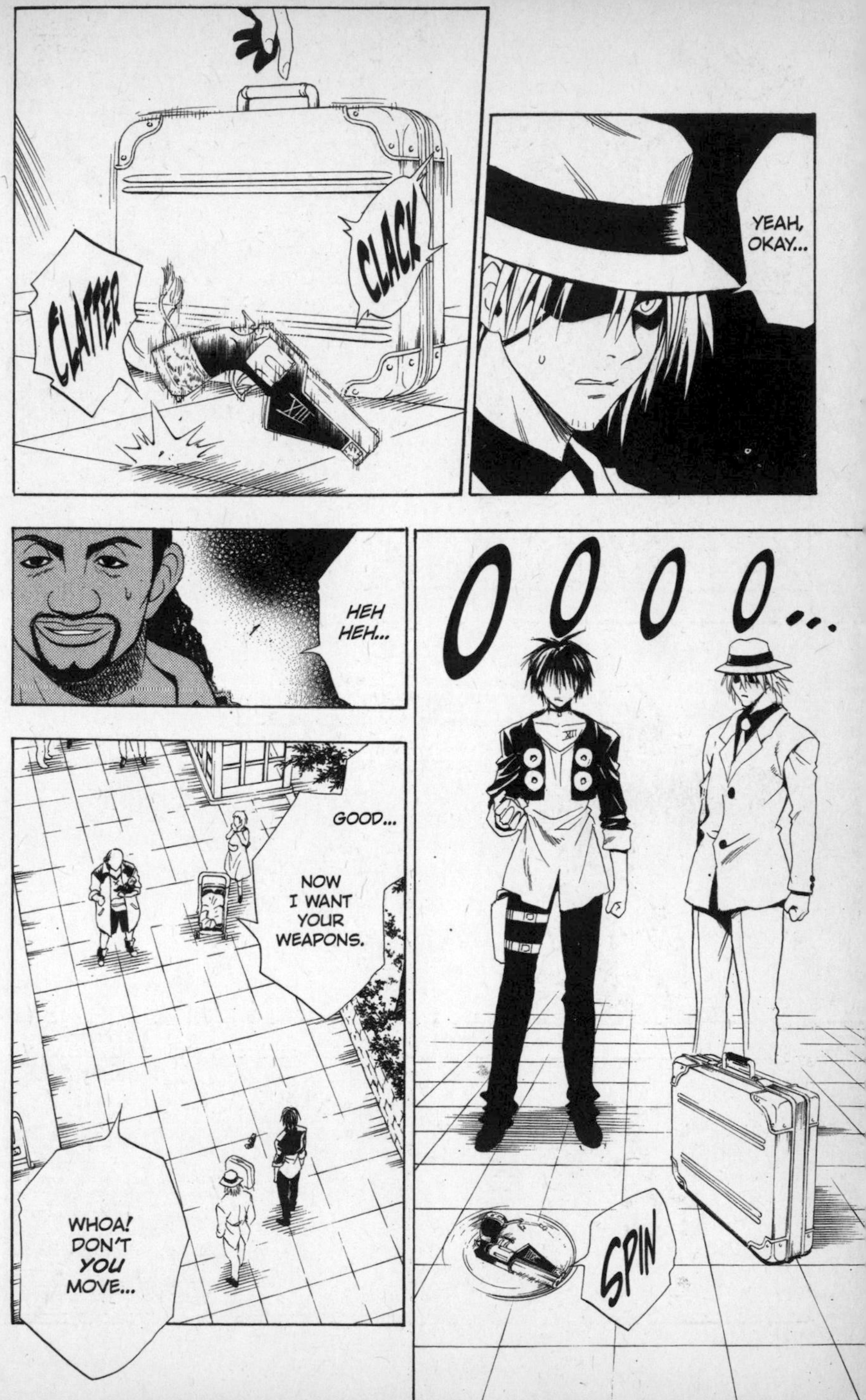

YEAH, OKAY...
CLACK
CLATTER
OOOO...
SPIN
HEH HEH...
GOOD...
NOW I WANT YOUR WEAPONS.
WHOA! DON'T YOU MOVE...

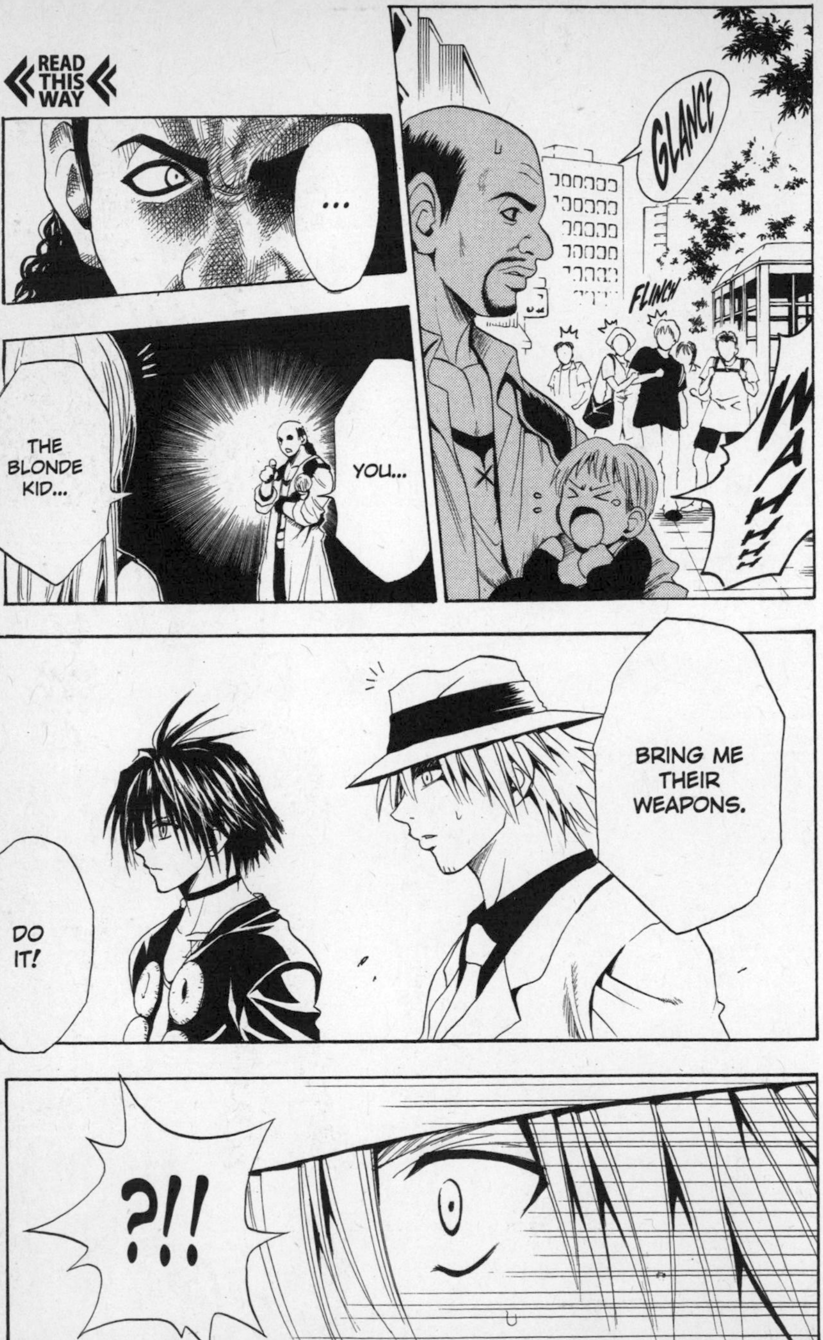
READ THIS WAY
GLANCE
FLINCH
WAAHHH
...
YOU...
THE BLONDE KID...
BRING ME THEIR WEAPONS.
DO IT!
?!!

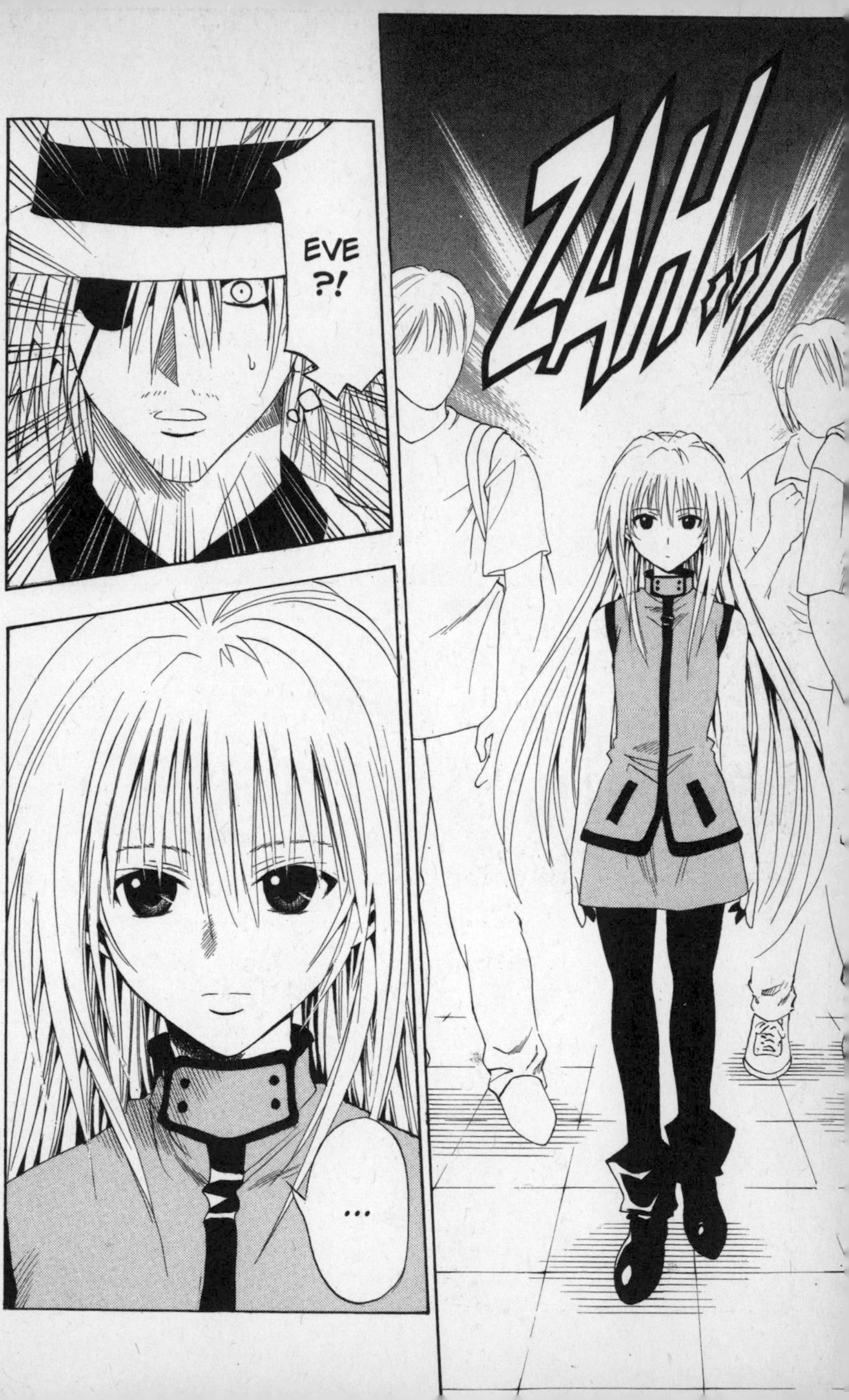
ZAH
EVE ?!
...

READ THIS WAY

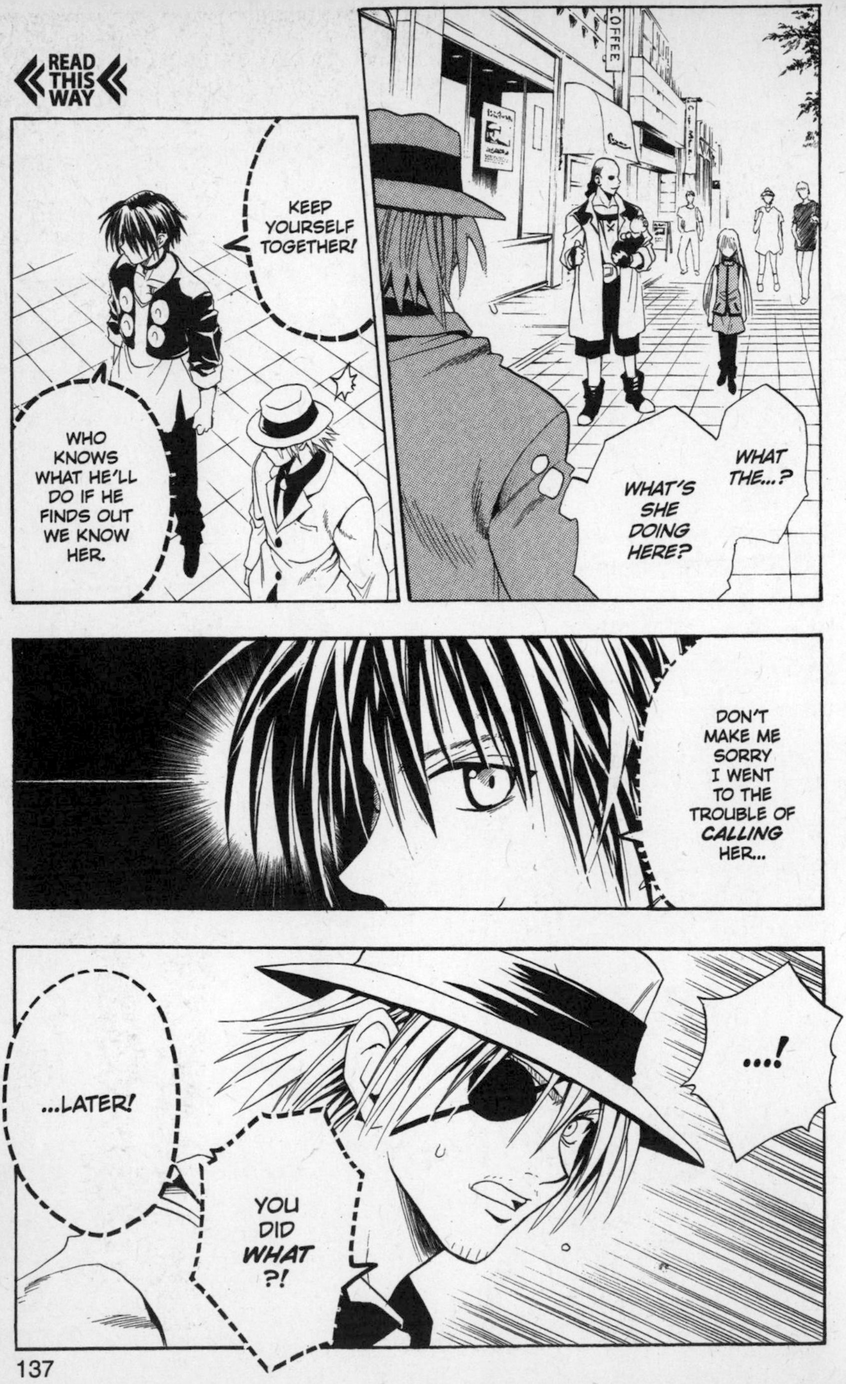

WHAT THE...?
WHAT'S SHE DOING HERE?
KEEP YOURSELF TOGETHER!
WHO KNOWS WHAT HE'LL DO IF HE FINDS OUT WE KNOW HER.
DON'T MAKE ME SORRY I WENT TO THE TROUBLE OF *CALLING* HER...
...!
YOU DID *WHAT*?!
...LATER!

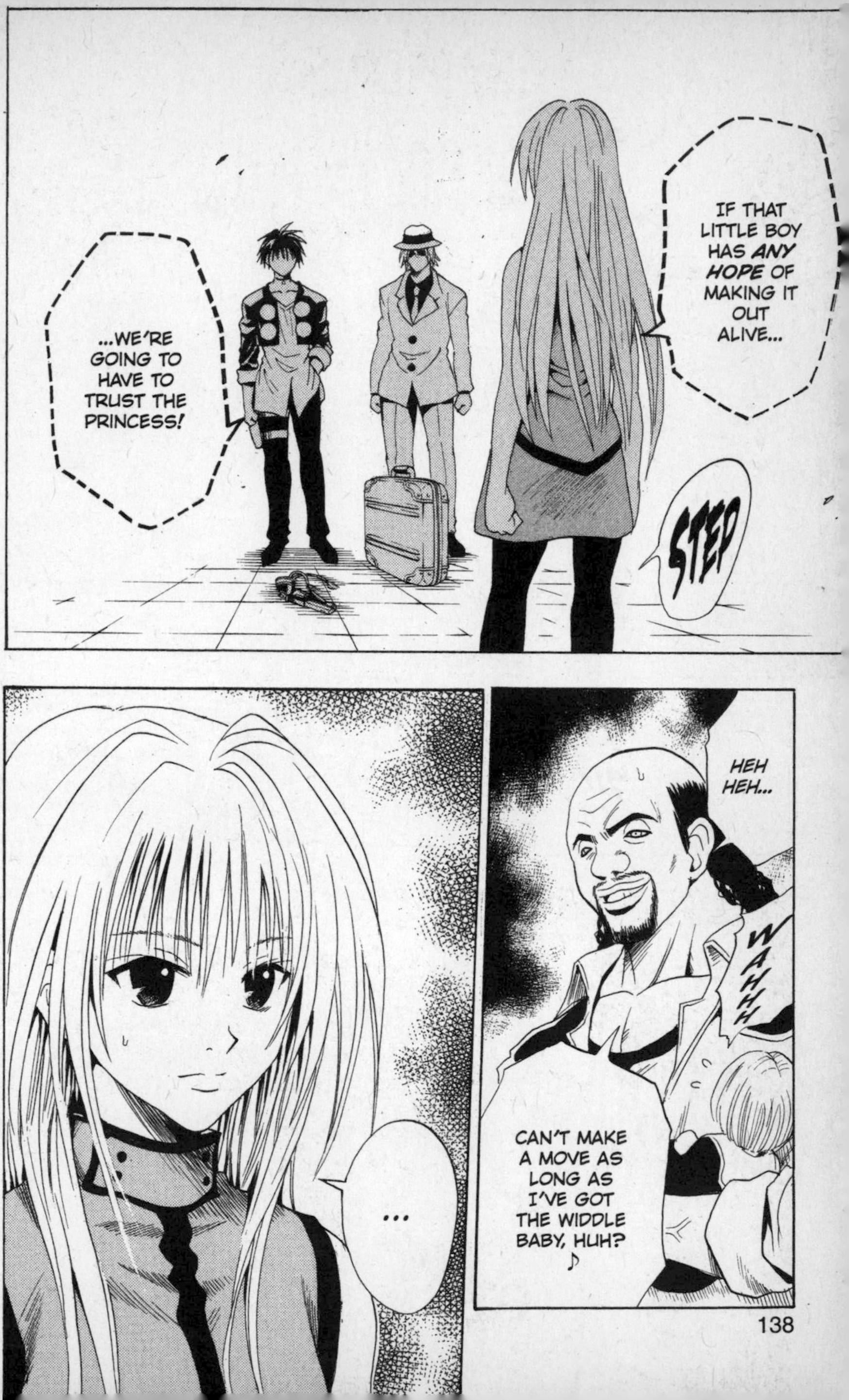
IF THAT LITTLE BOY HAS *ANY HOPE* OF MAKING IT OUT ALIVE...
...WE'RE GOING TO HAVE TO TRUST THE PRINCESS!
STEP
HEH HEH...
WAHHH
CAN'T MAKE A MOVE AS LONG AS I'VE GOT THE WIDDLE BABY, HUH? ♪
...

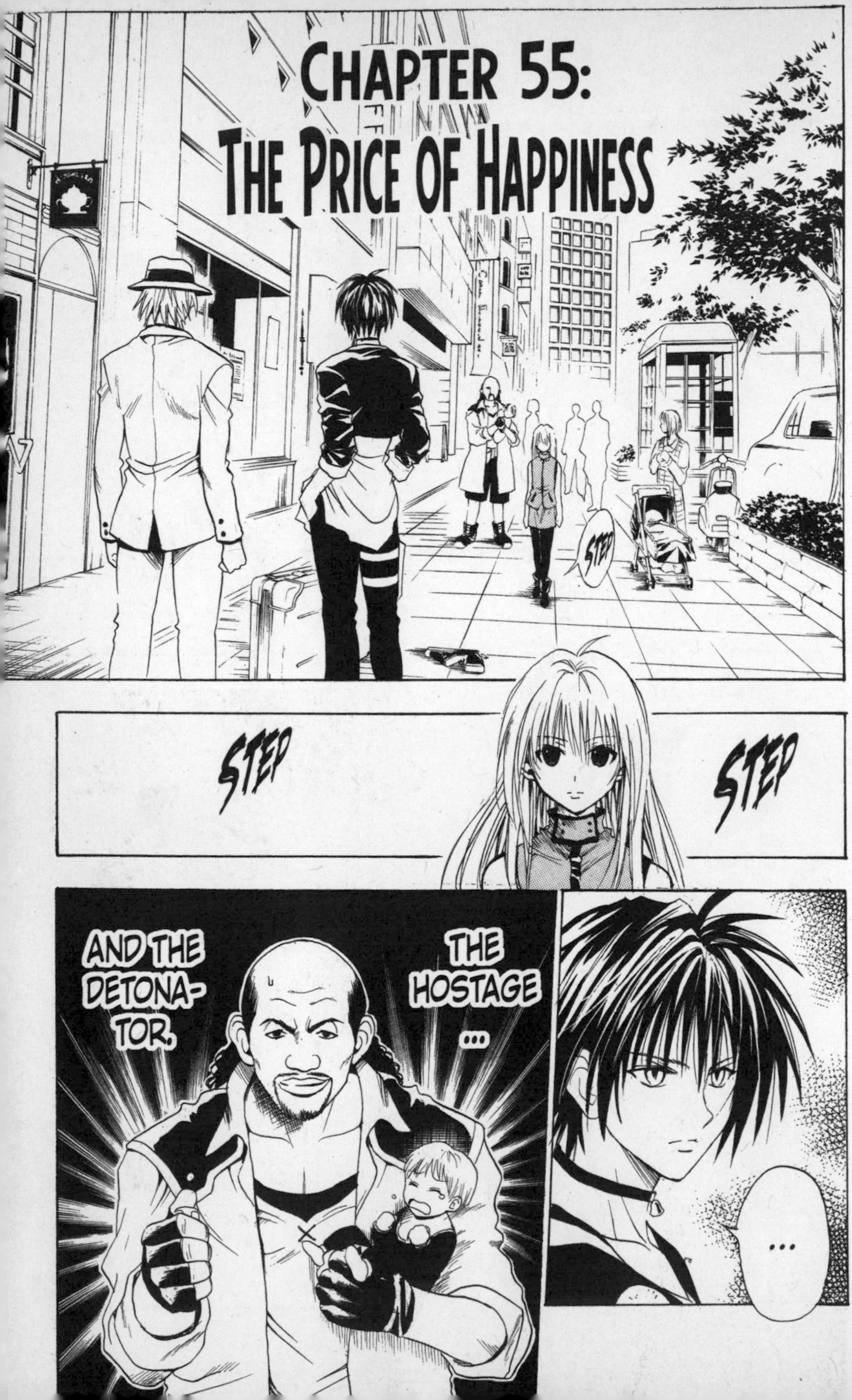
Chapter 55:
The Price of Happiness
STEP
STEP
STEP
...
THE HOSTAGE ...
AND THE DETONA-TOR.

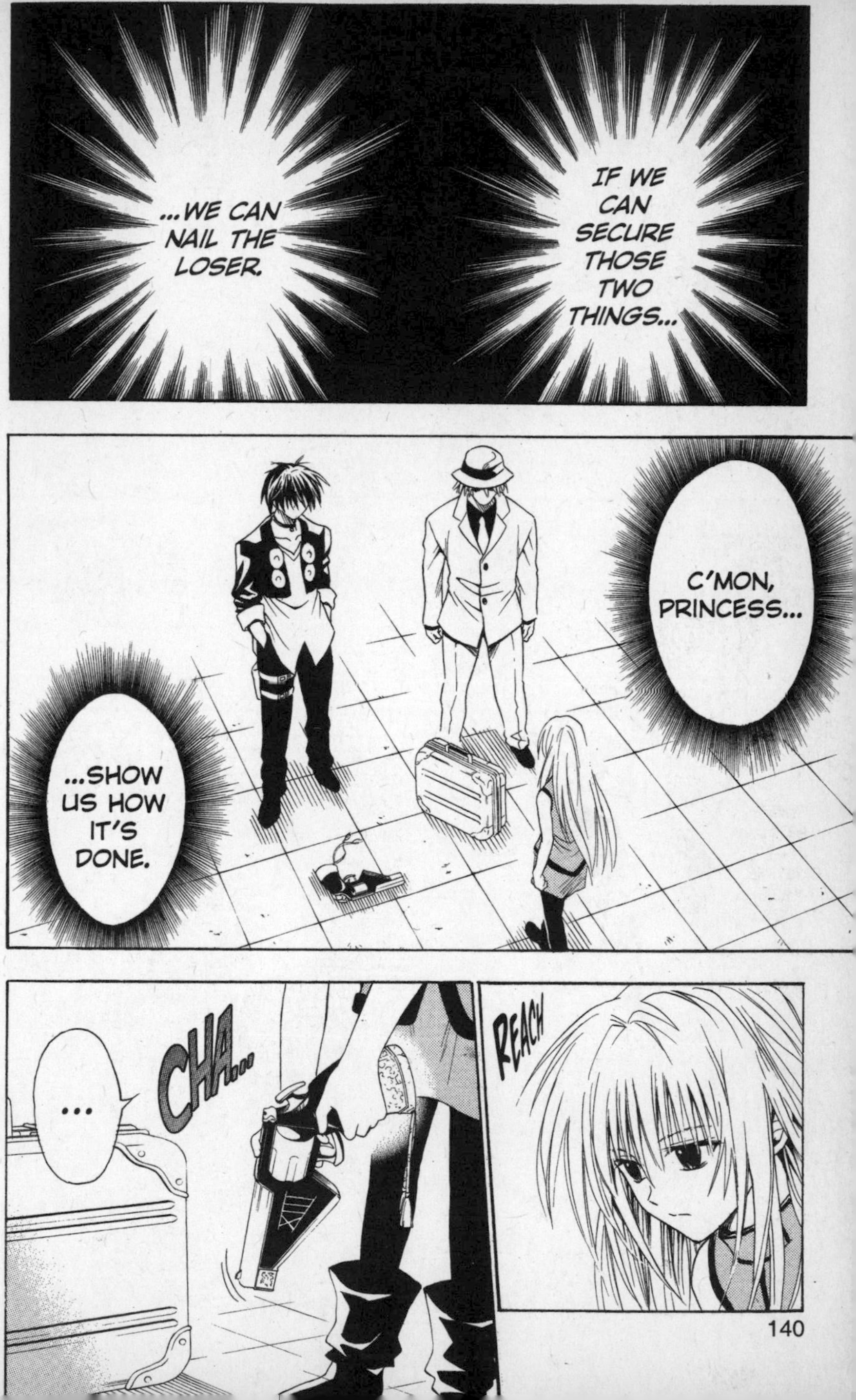
IF WE CAN SECURE THOSE TWO THINGS...
...WE CAN NAIL THE LOSER.
C'MON, PRINCESS...
...SHOW US HOW IT'S DONE.
REACH
CHA...
...

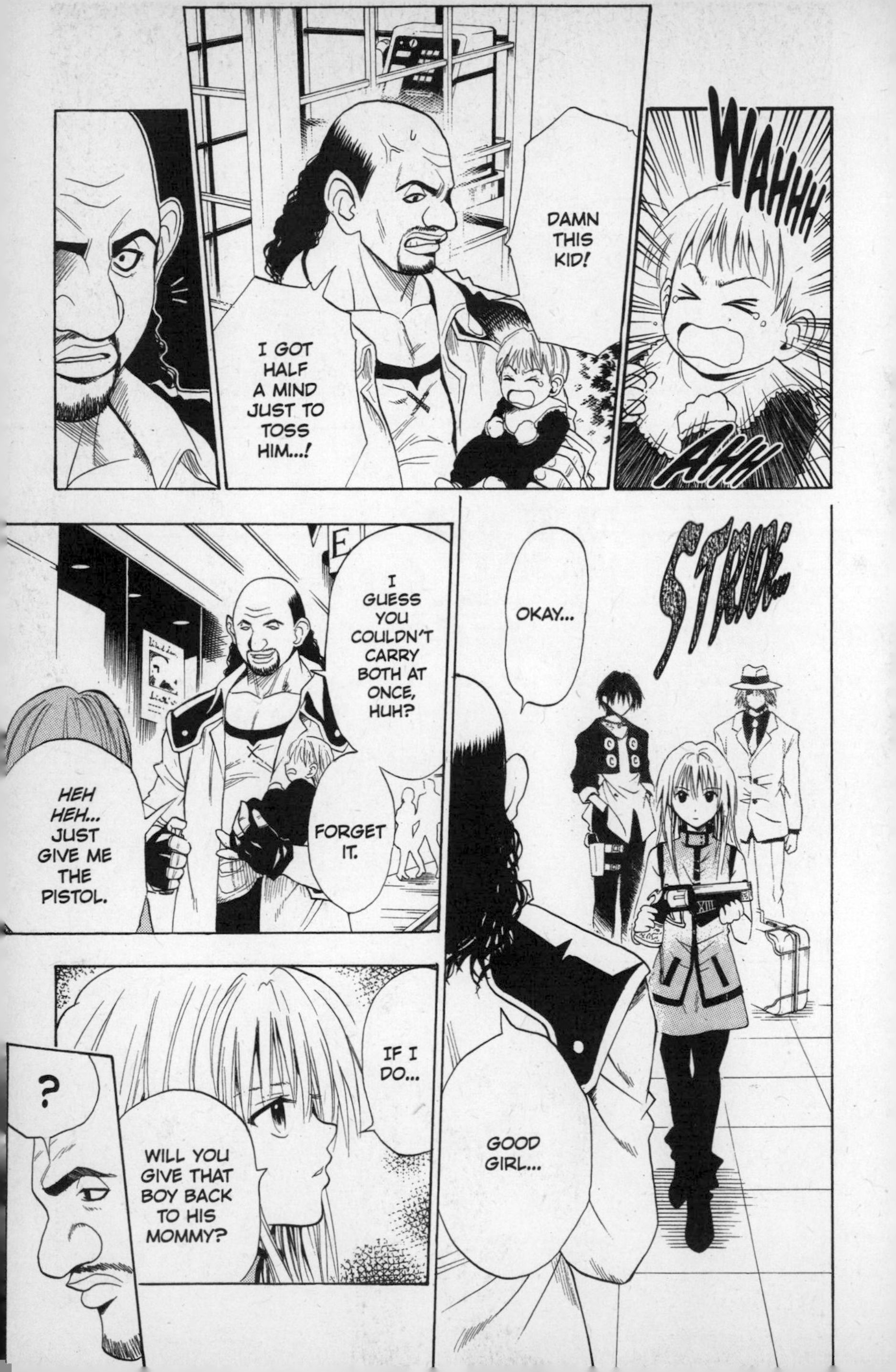
WAHHH
AHH
DAMN THIS KID!
I GOT HALF A MIND JUST TO TOSS HIM...!
STRIDE...
OKAY...
GOOD GIRL...
I GUESS YOU COULDN'T CARRY BOTH AT ONCE, HUH?
FORGET IT.
HEH HEH... JUST GIVE ME THE PISTOL.
IF I DO...
WILL YOU GIVE THAT BOY BACK TO HIS MOMMY?
?

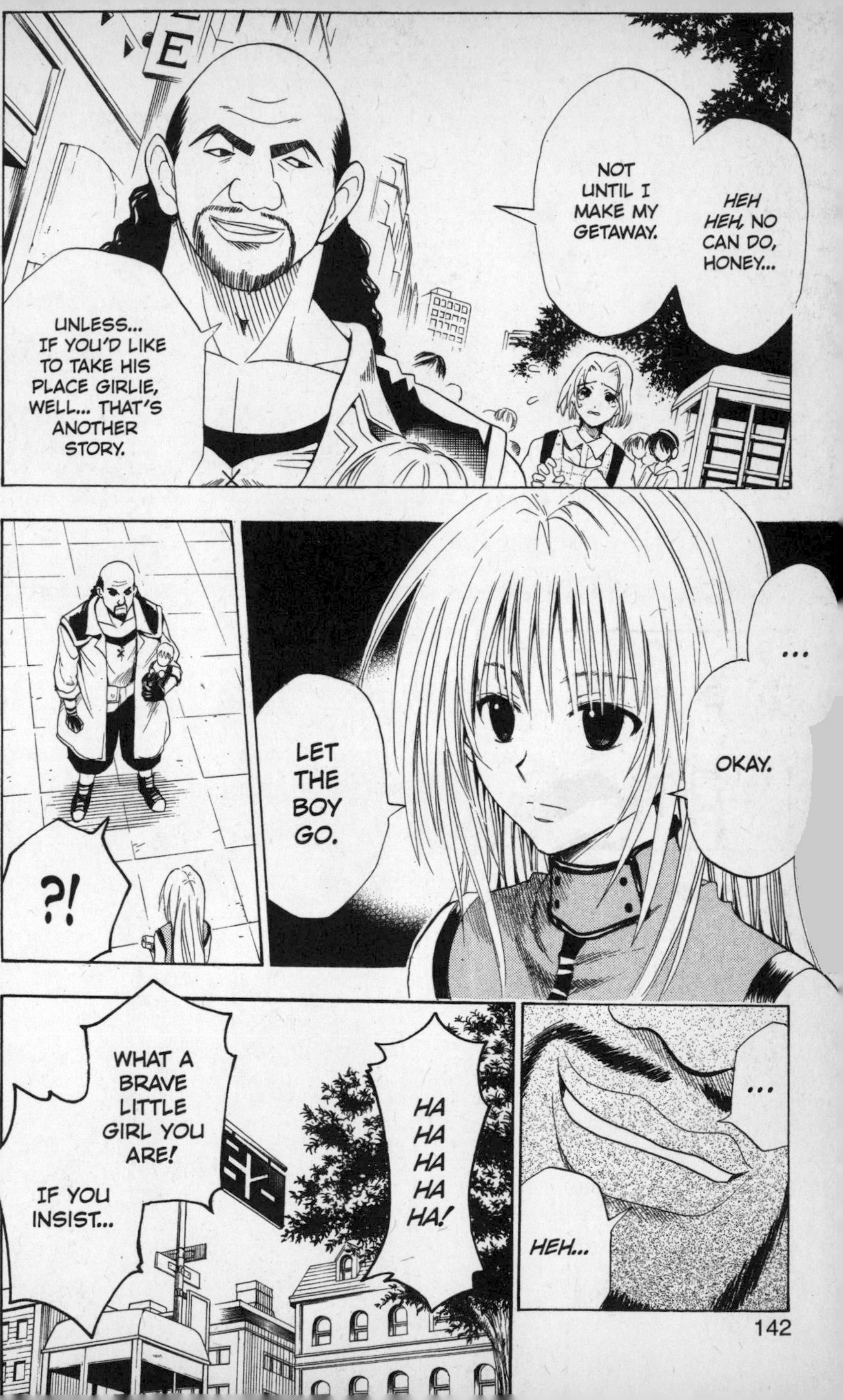
HEH HEH, NO CAN DO, HONEY...
NOT UNTIL I MAKE MY GETAWAY.
UNLESS... IF YOU'D LIKE TO TAKE HIS PLACE GIRLIE, WELL... THAT'S ANOTHER STORY.
...
OKAY.
LET THE BOY GO.
?!
...
HEH...
HA HA HA HA HA!
WHAT A BRAVE LITTLE GIRL YOU ARE!
IF YOU INSIST...

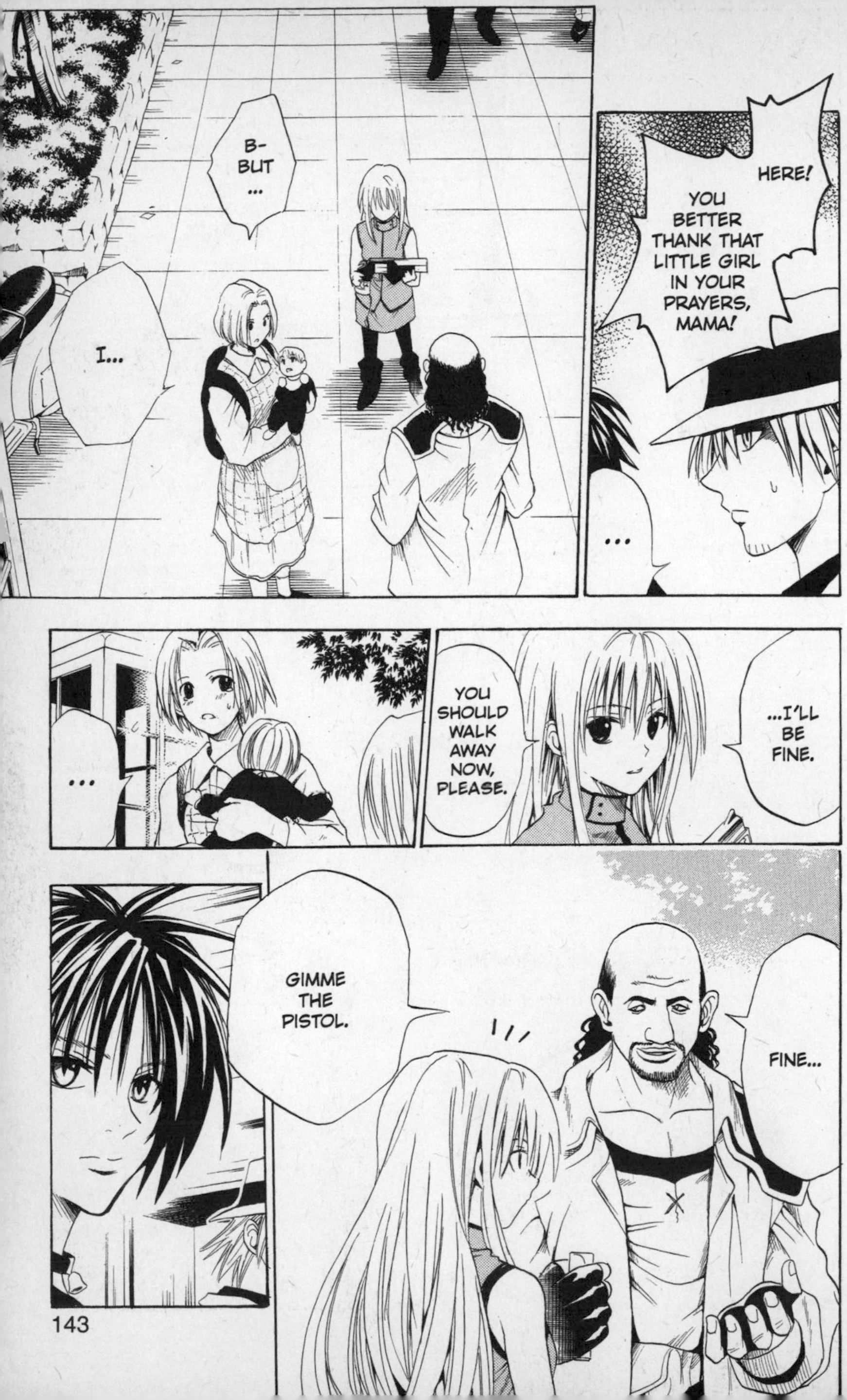
HERE!
YOU BETTER THANK THAT LITTLE GIRL IN YOUR PRAYERS, MAMA!
...
B-BUT...
I...
...I'LL BE FINE.
YOU SHOULD WALK AWAY NOW, PLEASE.
...
FINE...
GIMME THE PISTOL.

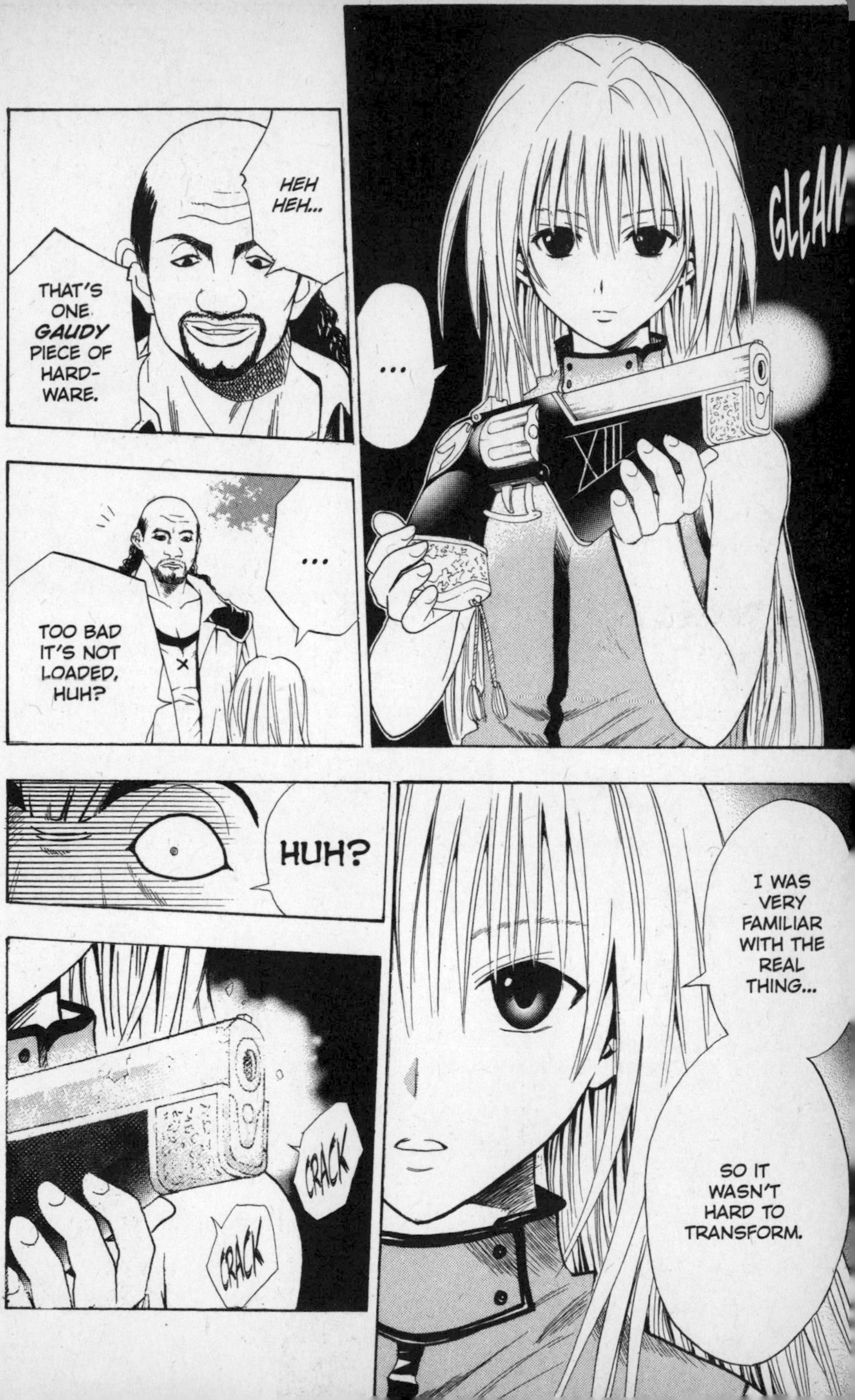
GLEAM
...
HEH HEH...
THAT'S ONE *GAUDY* PIECE OF HARD-WARE.
...
TOO BAD IT'S NOT LOADED, HUH?
I WAS VERY FAMILIAR WITH THE REAL THING...
SO IT WASN'T HARD TO TRANSFORM.
HUH?
CRACK
CRACK

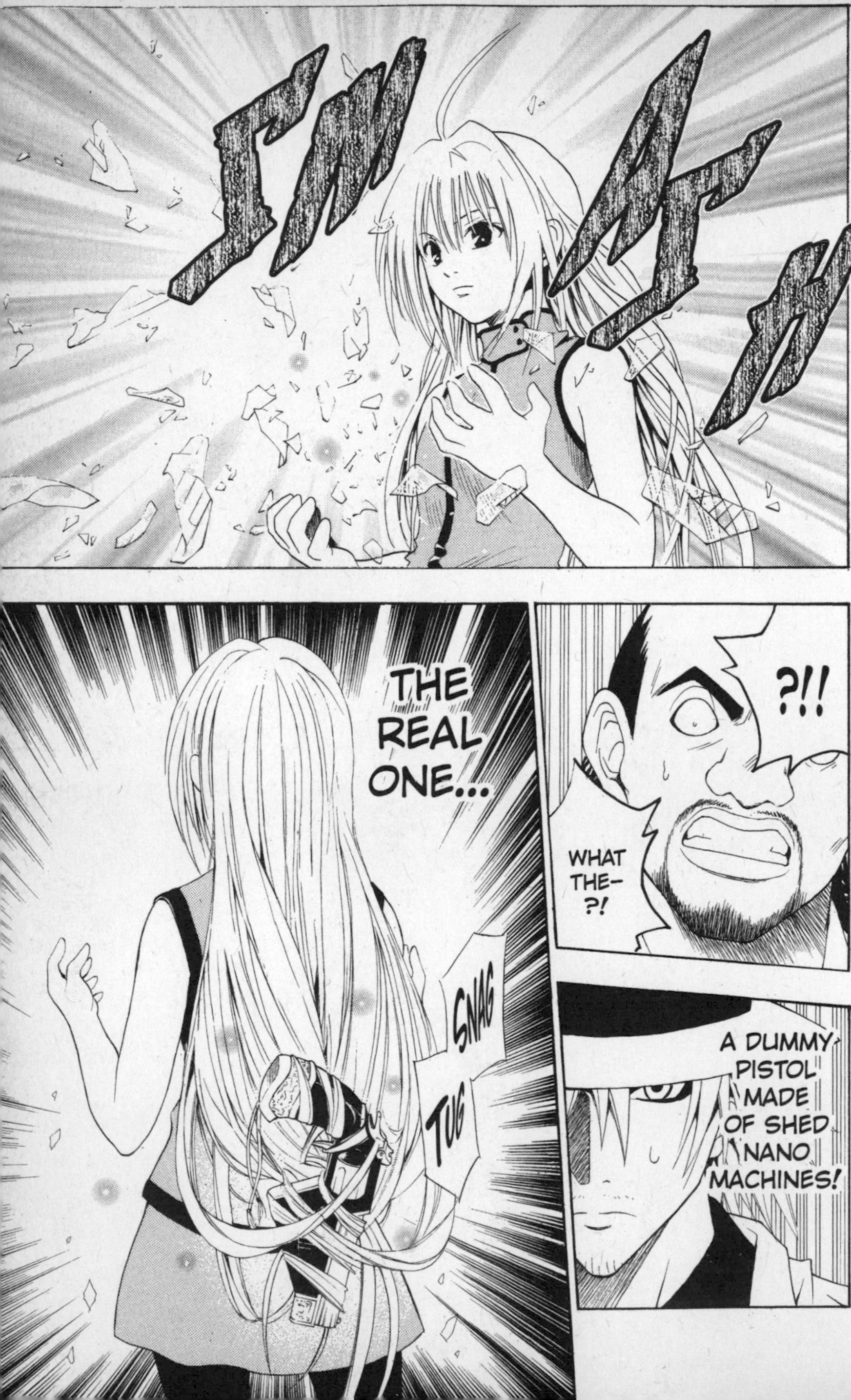
SMASH
?!!
WHAT THE-?!
A DUMMY PISTOL MADE OF SHED NANO MACHINES!
THE REAL ONE...
SNAG
TUG

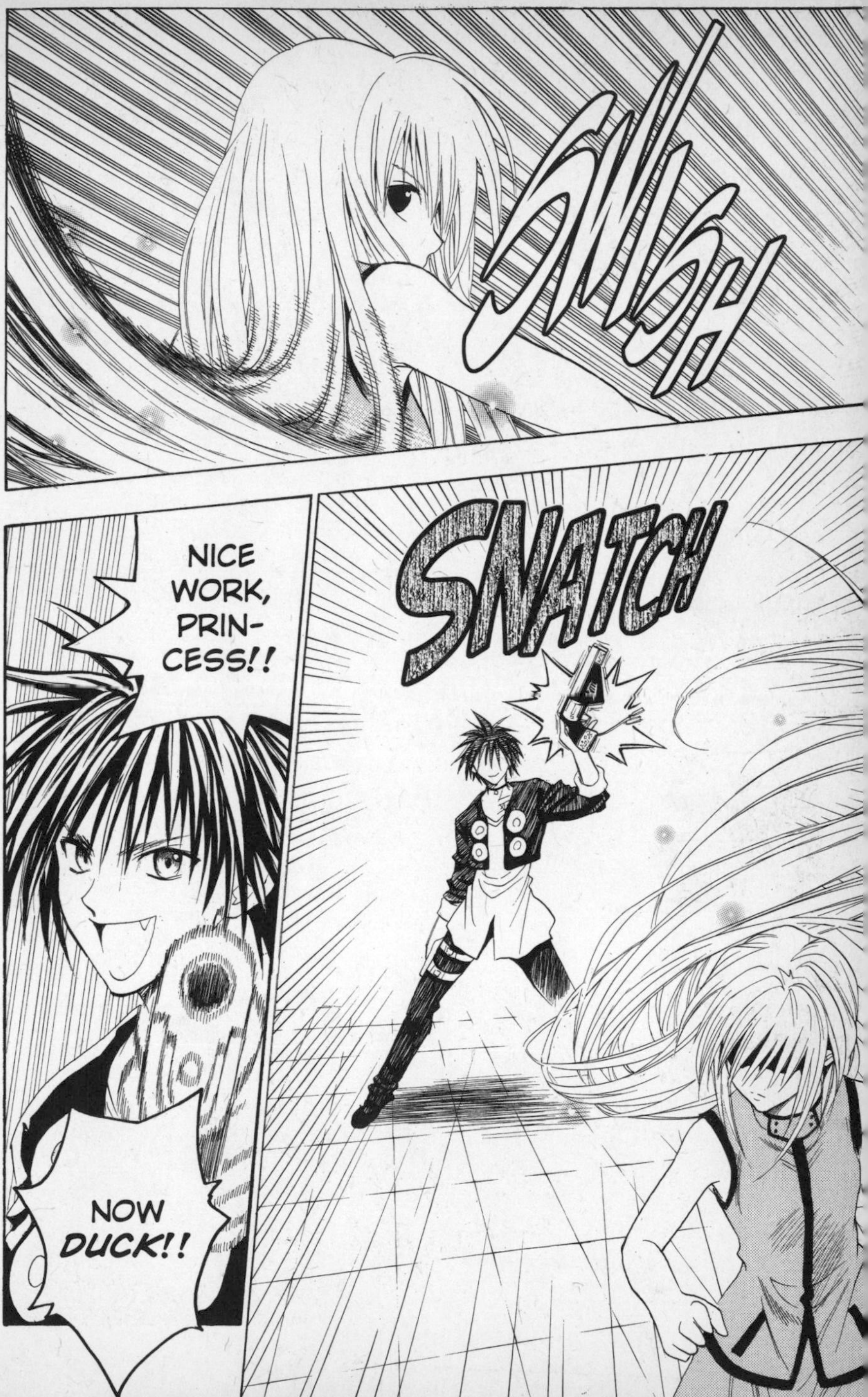
SWISH
SNATCH
NICE WORK, PRIN-CESS!!
NOW DUCK!!

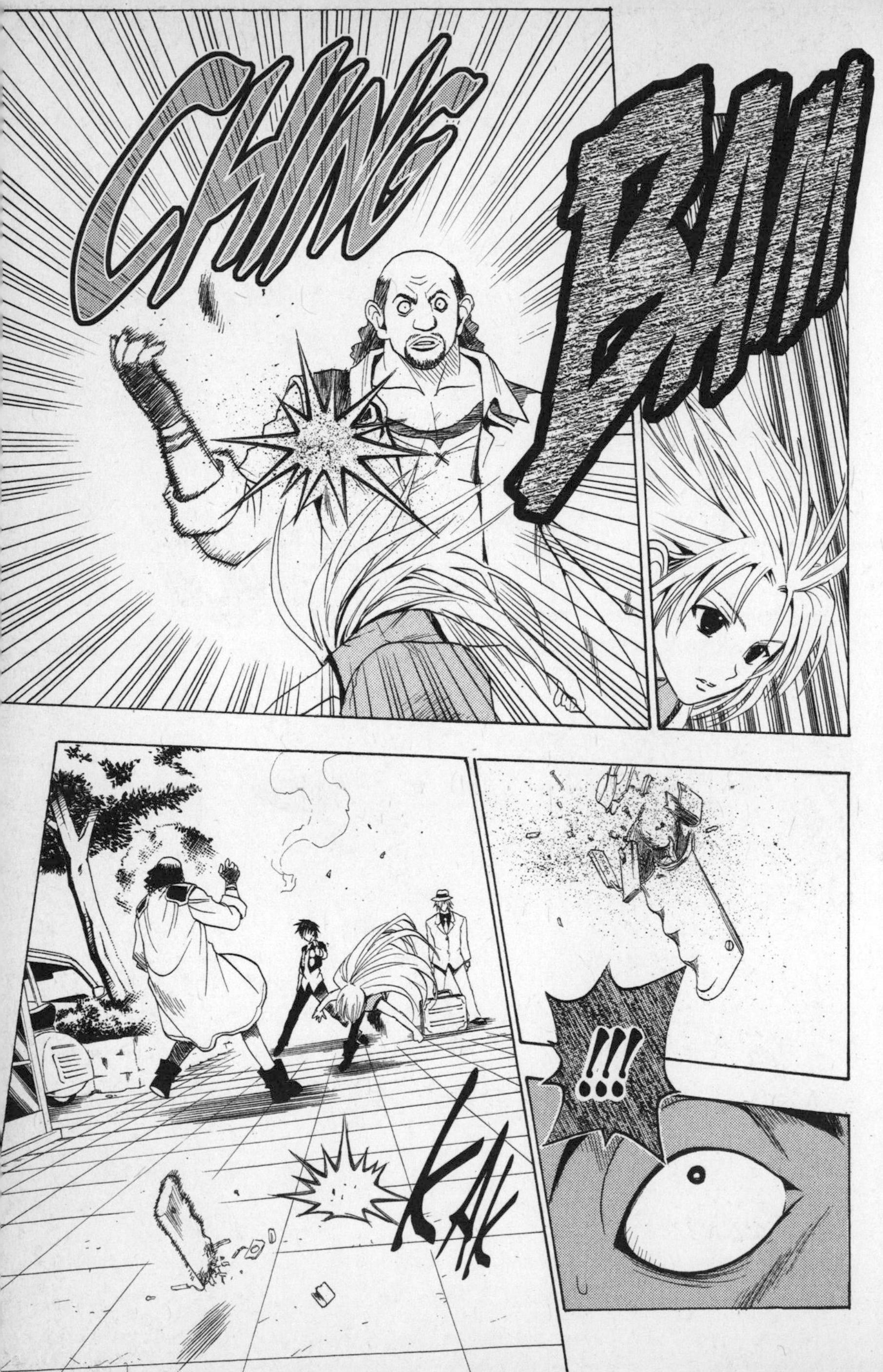
CHING
!!!
KAK

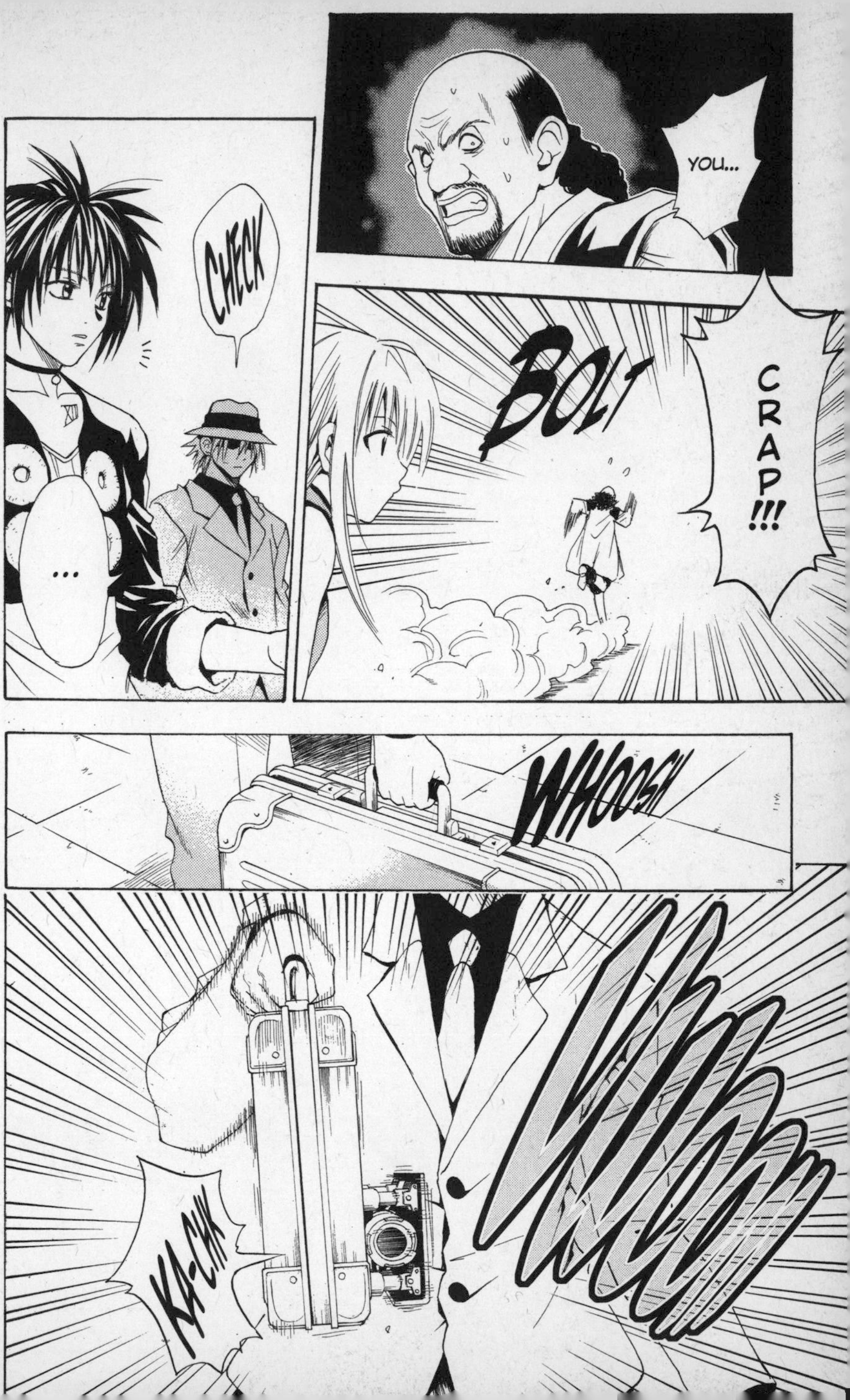
YOU...
CRAP!!!
BOLT
CHECK
...
WHOOSH
KA-CHK

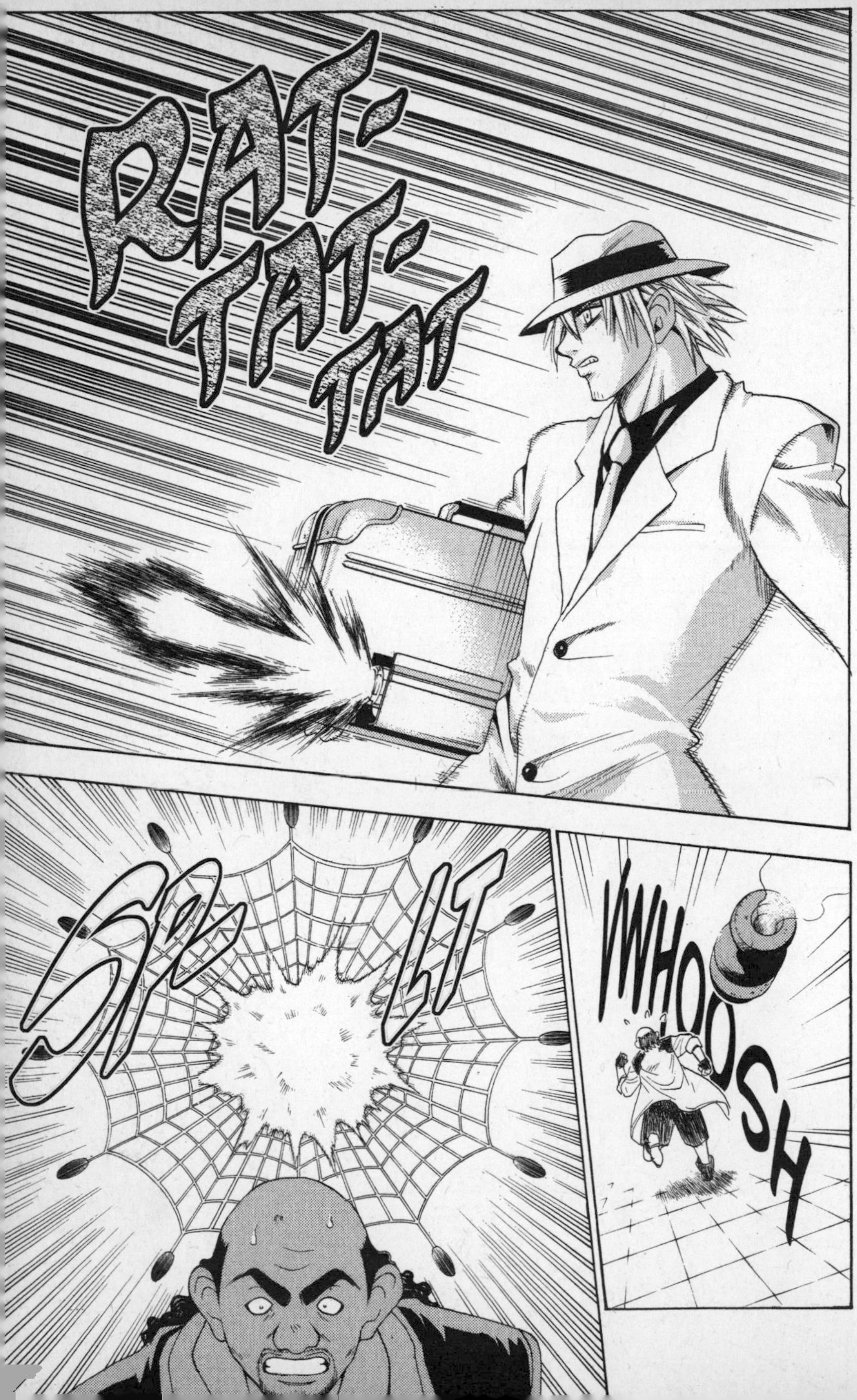
RAT-TAT-TAT
VWHOOSH
SPLIT

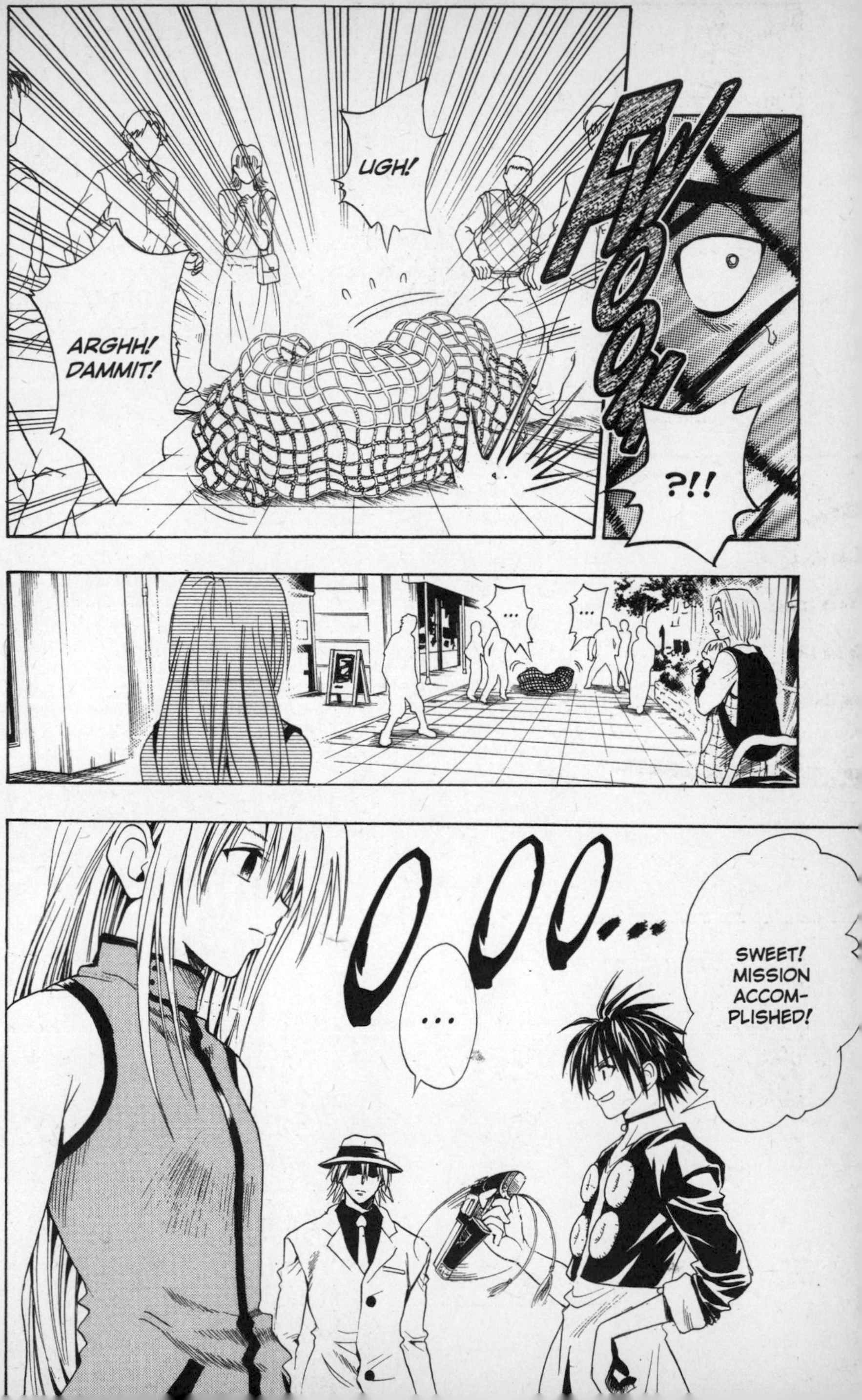
?!!
UGH!
ARGHH! DAMMIT!
...
...
SWEET! MISSION ACCOM-PLISHED!
O, OO...
...

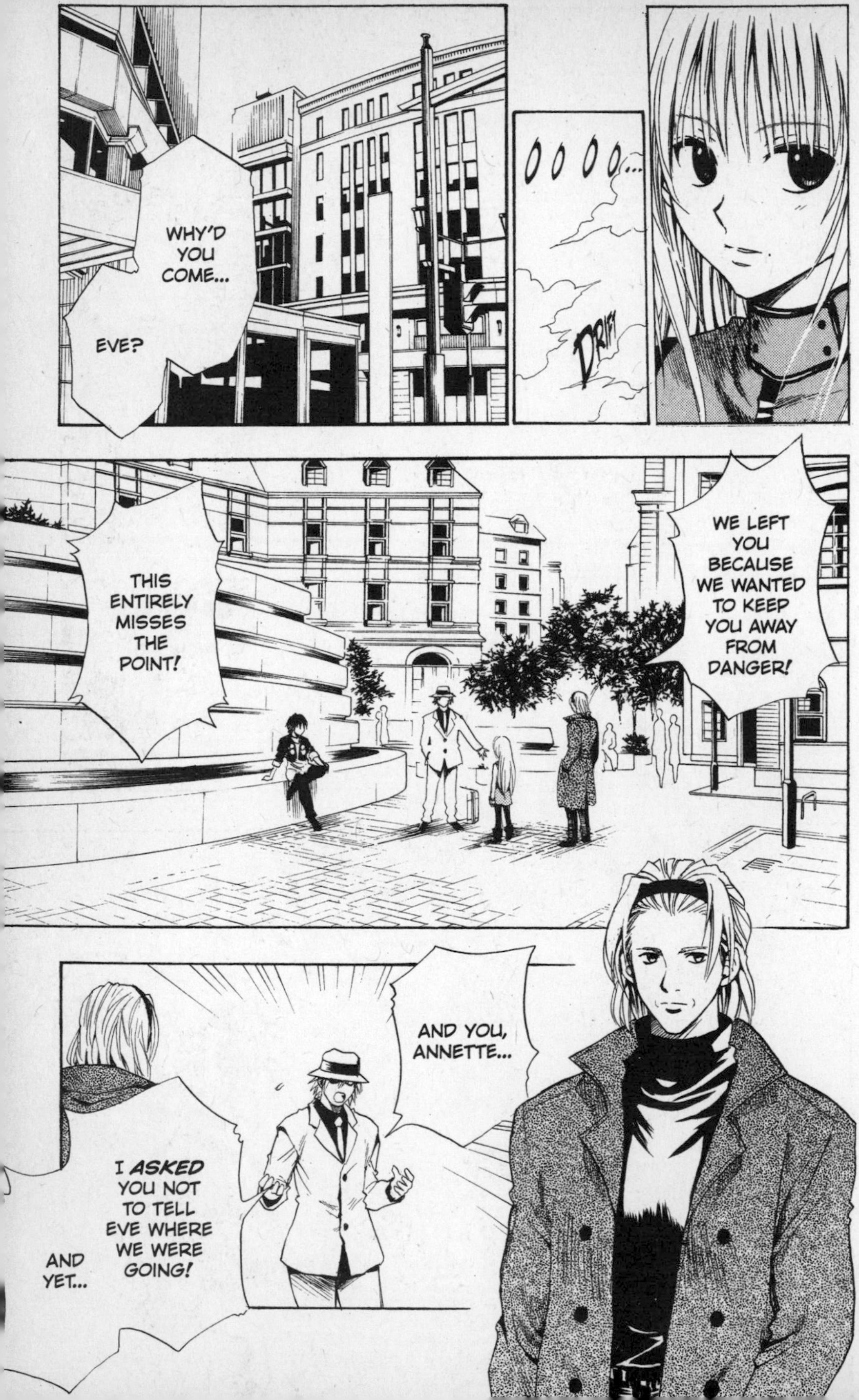
O O O O...
DRIFT
WHY'D YOU COME...
EVE?
WE LEFT YOU BECAUSE WE WANTED TO KEEP YOU AWAY FROM DANGER!
THIS ENTIRELY MISSES THE POINT!
AND YOU, ANNETTE...
I *ASKED* YOU NOT TO TELL EVE WHERE WE WERE GOING!
AND YET...

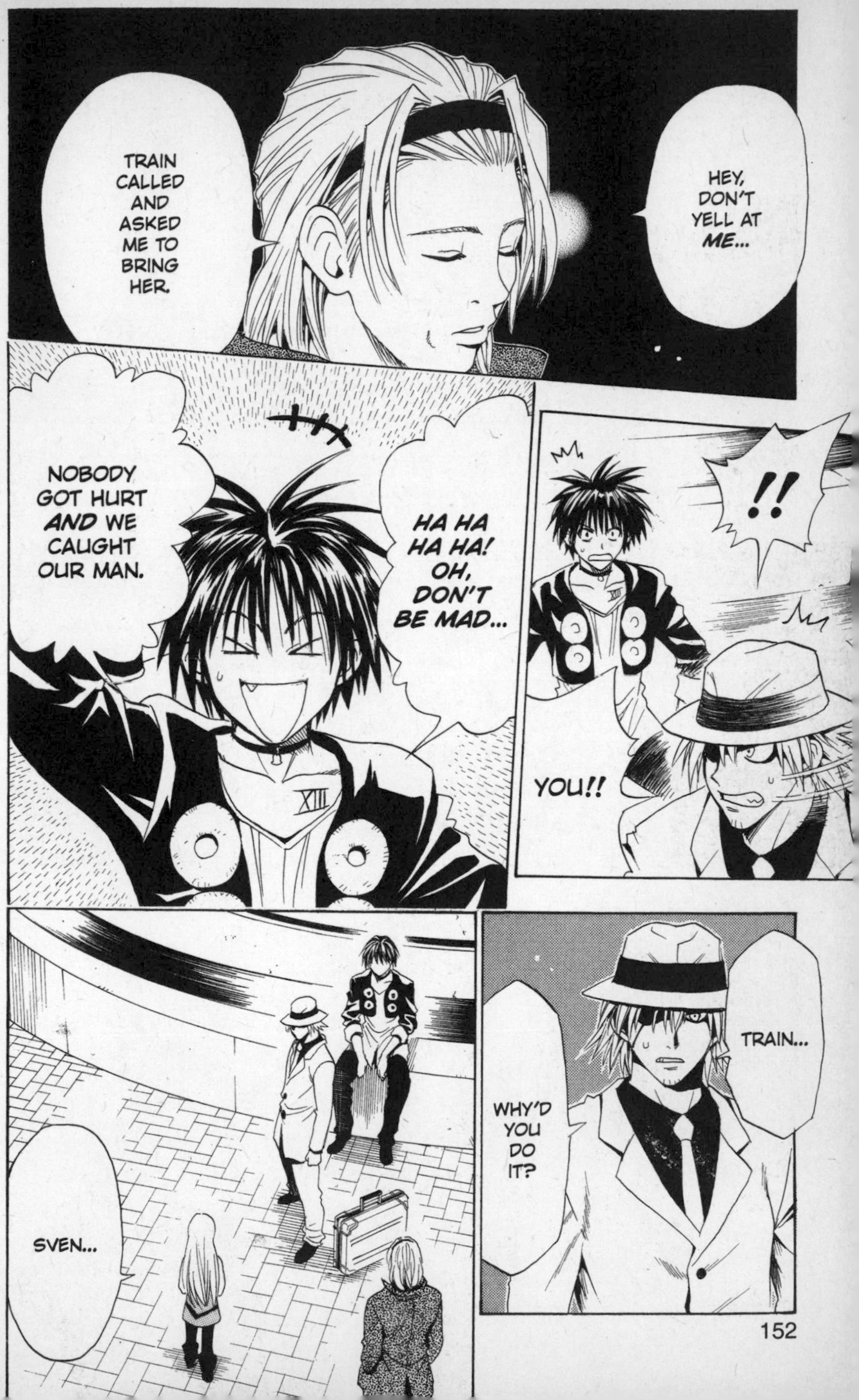
HEY, DON'T YELL AT *ME*...
TRAIN CALLED AND ASKED ME TO BRING HER.
!!
YOU!!
HA HA HA HA! OH, DON'T BE MAD...
NOBODY GOT HURT *AND* WE CAUGHT OUR MAN.
TRAIN...
WHY'D YOU DO IT?
SVEN...

READ THIS WAY

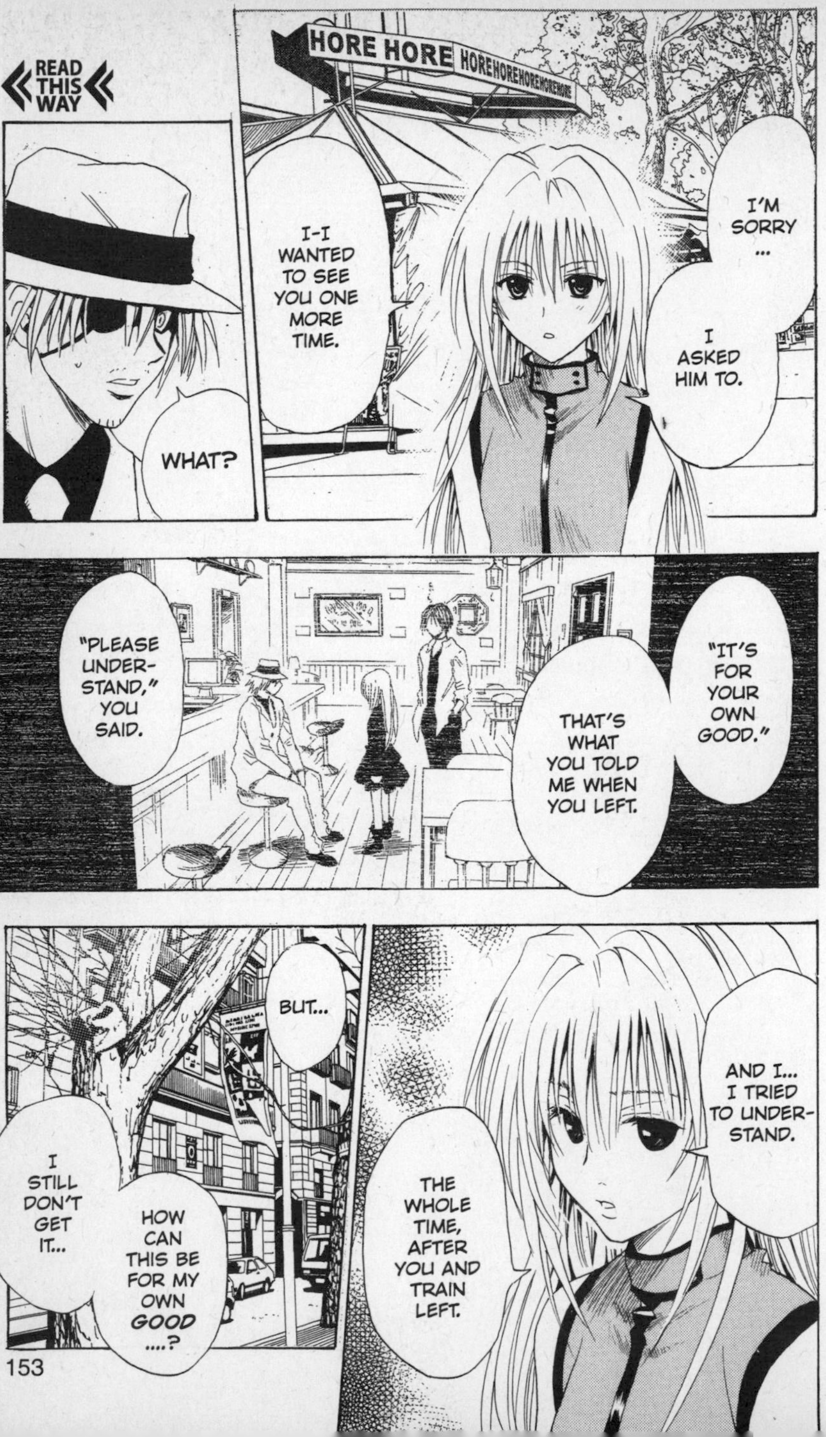
HORE HORE
I'M SORRY ...
I ASKED HIM TO.
I-I WANTED TO SEE YOU ONE MORE TIME.
WHAT?
"IT'S FOR YOUR OWN GOOD."
THAT'S WHAT YOU TOLD ME WHEN YOU LEFT.
"PLEASE UNDER-STAND," YOU SAID.
AND I... I TRIED TO UNDER-STAND.
THE WHOLE TIME, AFTER YOU AND TRAIN LEFT.
BUT...
I STILL DON'T GET IT...
HOW CAN THIS BE FOR MY OWN GOOD ....?

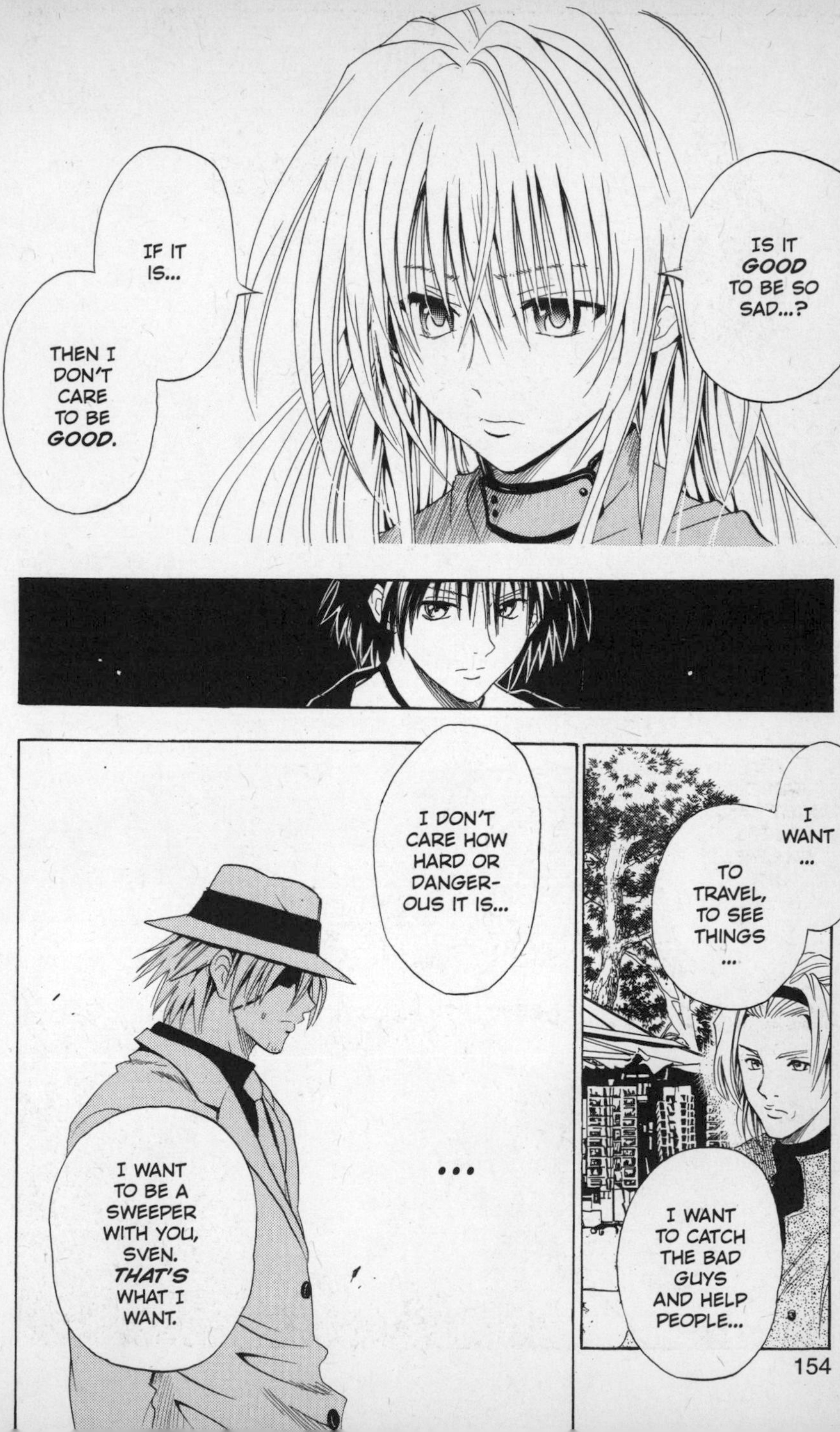
IS IT *GOOD* TO BE SO SAD...?
IF IT IS...
THEN I DON'T CARE TO BE *GOOD*.
I WANT ... TO TRAVEL, TO SEE THINGS ...
I WANT TO CATCH THE BAD GUYS AND HELP PEOPLE...
I DON'T CARE HOW HARD OR DANGEROUS IT IS...
...
I WANT TO BE A SWEEPER WITH YOU, SVEN. *THAT'S* WHAT I WANT.

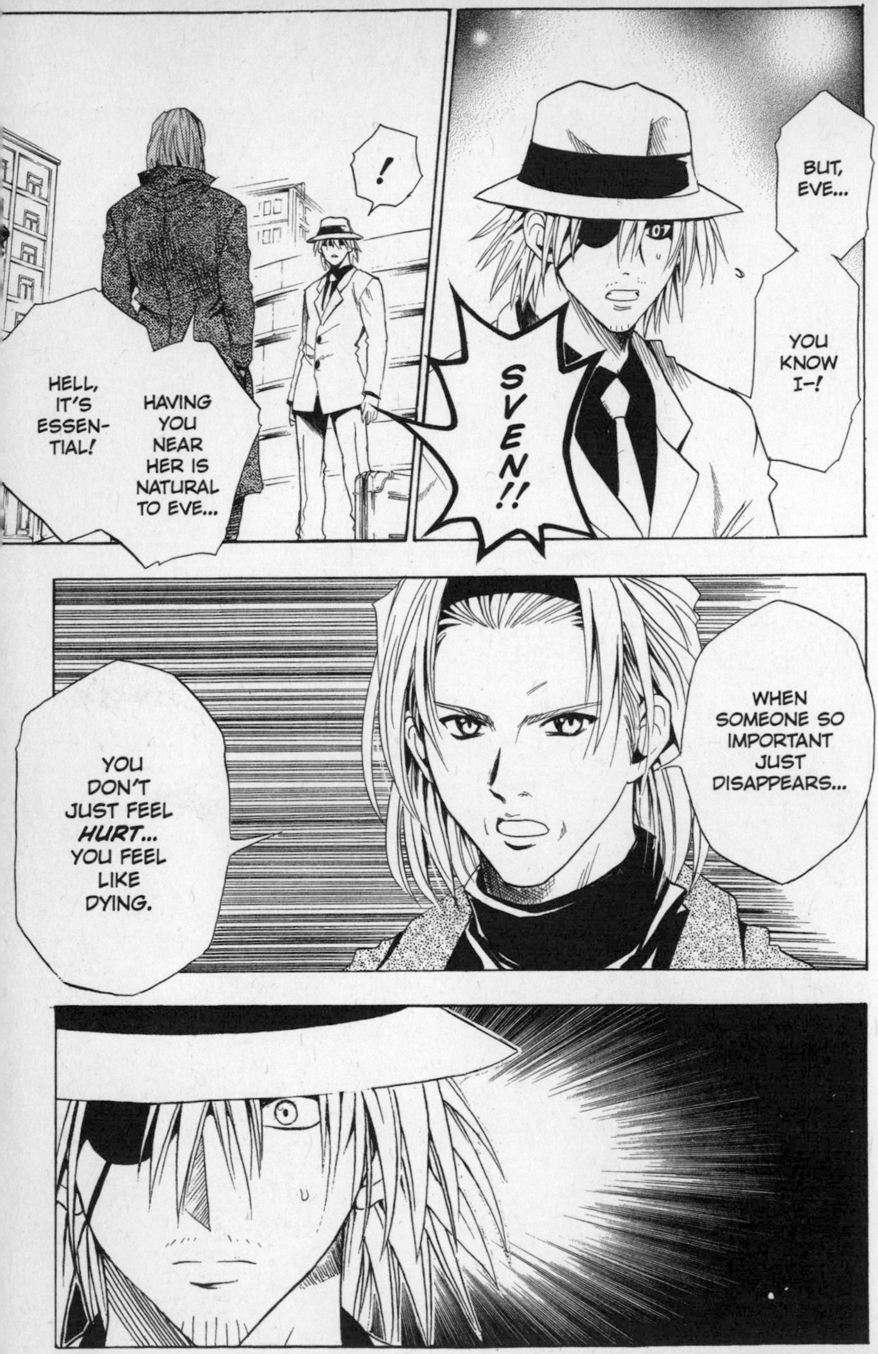
BUT, EVE...
YOU KNOW I-!
SVEN!!
!
HAVING YOU NEAR HER IS NATURAL TO EVE...
HELL, IT'S ESSEN-TIAL!
WHEN SOMEONE SO IMPORTANT JUST DISAPPEARS...
YOU DON'T JUST FEEL *HURT*... YOU FEEL LIKE DYING.

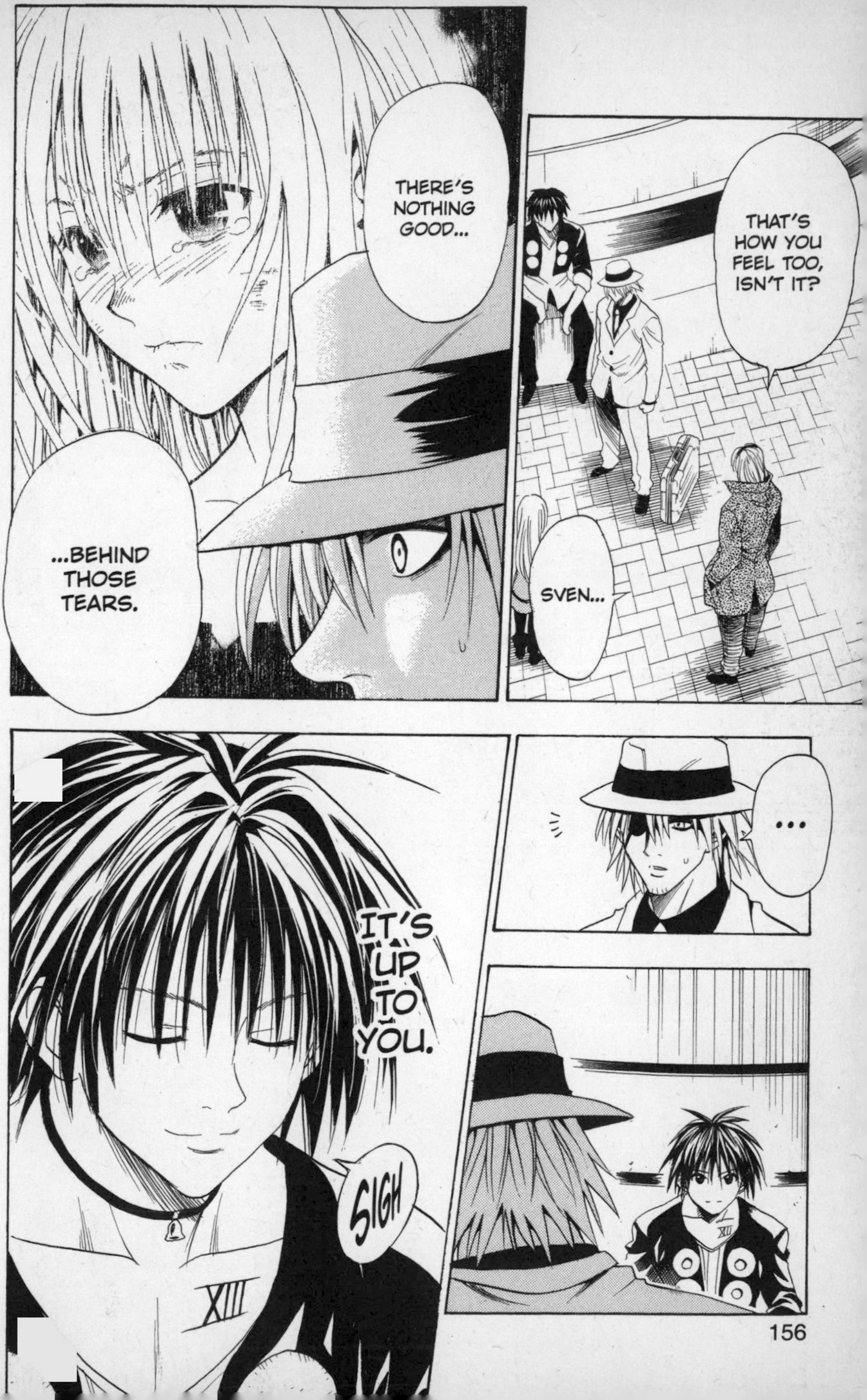
THAT'S HOW YOU FEEL TOO, ISN'T IT?
SVEN...
THERE'S NOTHING GOOD...
...BEHIND THOSE TEARS.
...
IT'S UP TO YOU.
SIGH

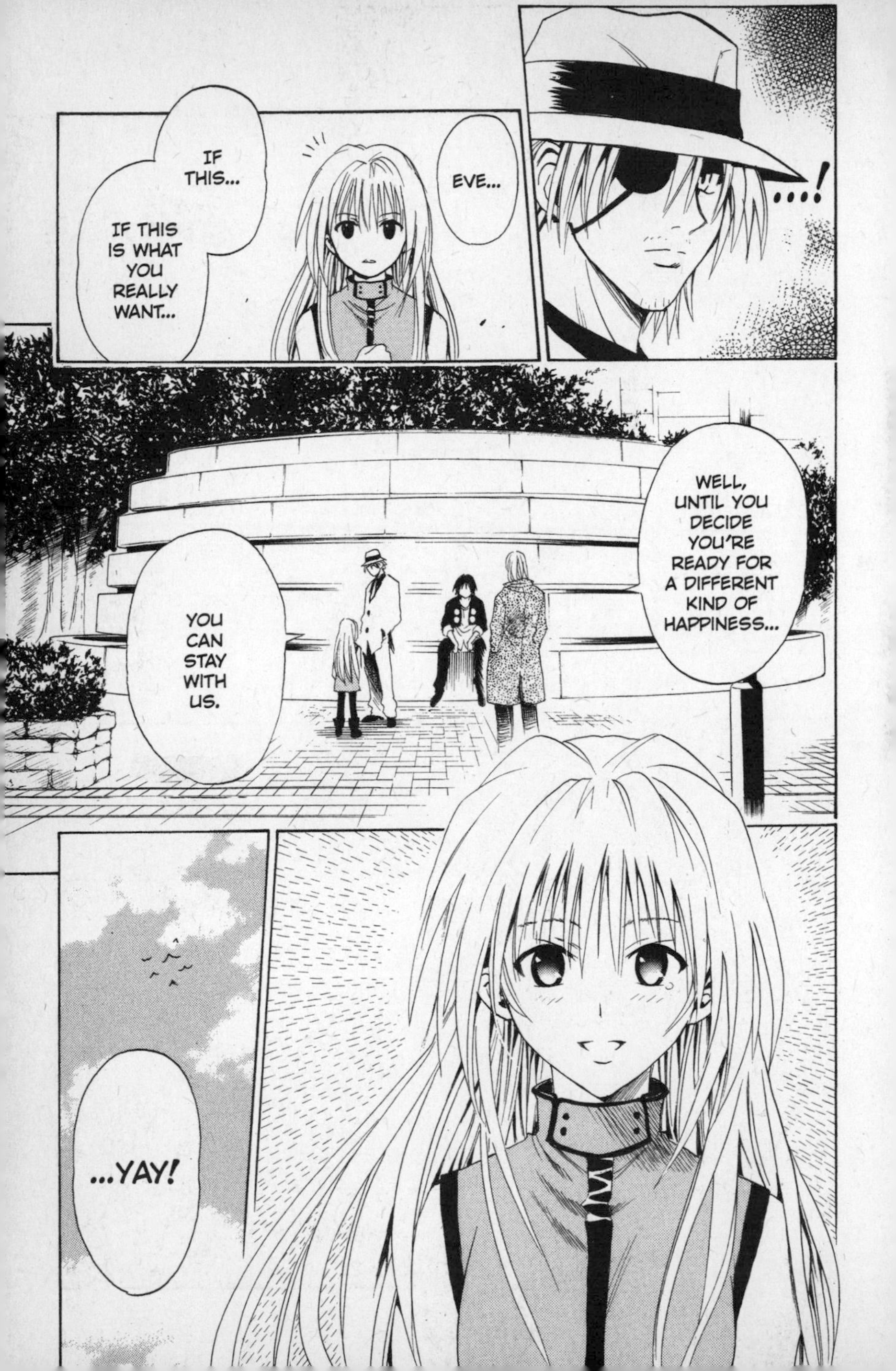
...!
EVE...
IF THIS...
IF THIS IS WHAT YOU REALLY WANT...
WELL, UNTIL YOU DECIDE YOU'RE READY FOR A DIFFERENT KIND OF HAPPINESS...
YOU CAN STAY WITH US.
...YAY!

SKETCHES: PART 1

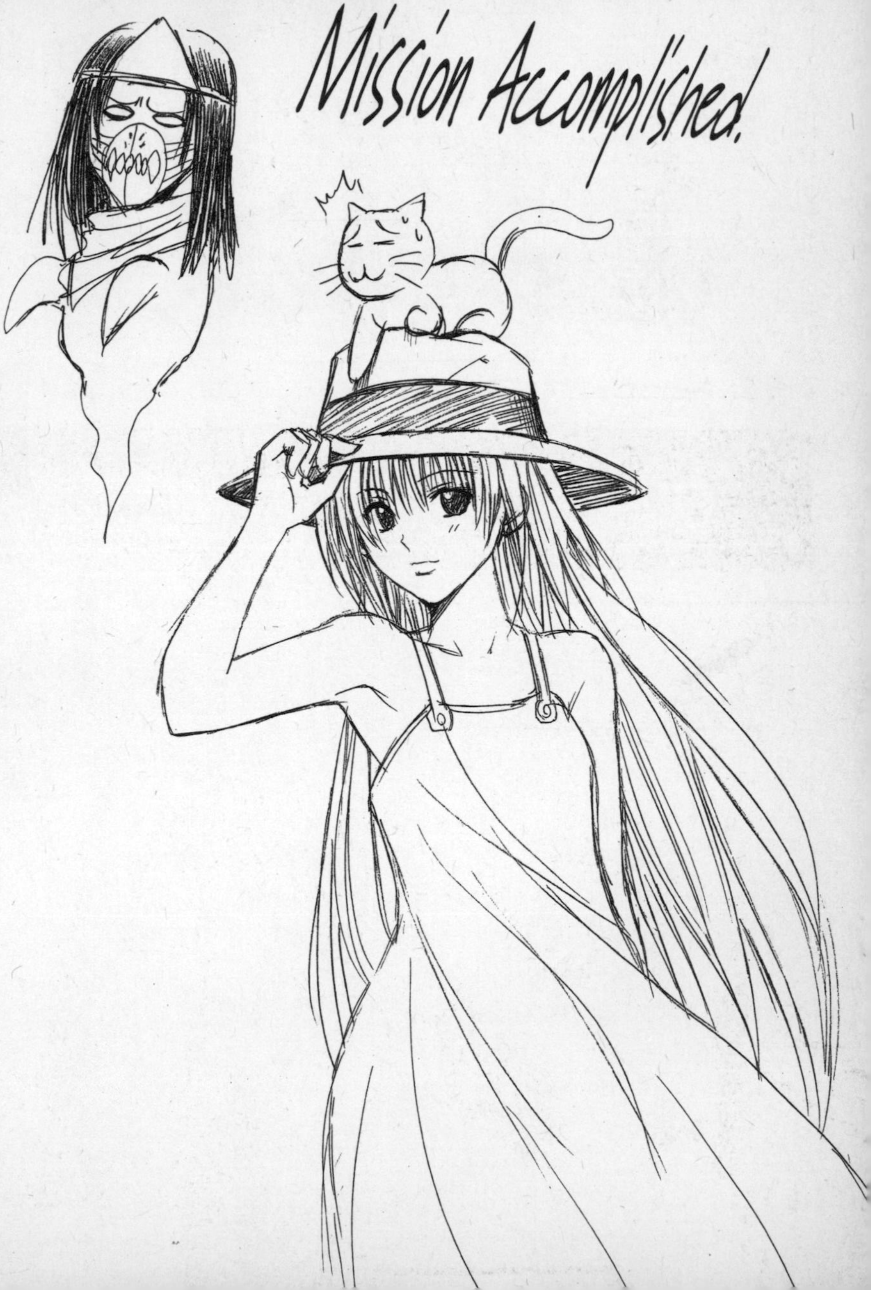
Mission Accomplished.

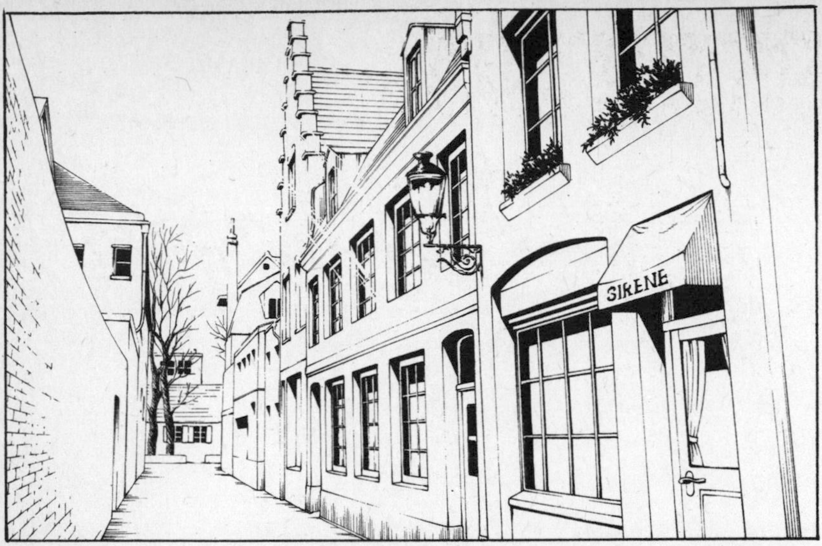
SIRENE

Chapter 56: Punishment

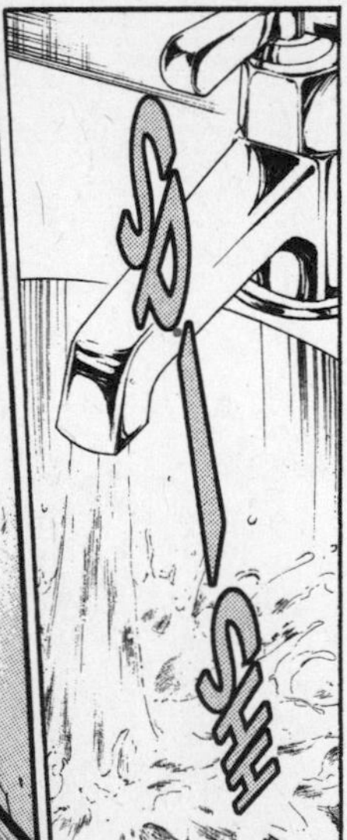
SP— —SHH

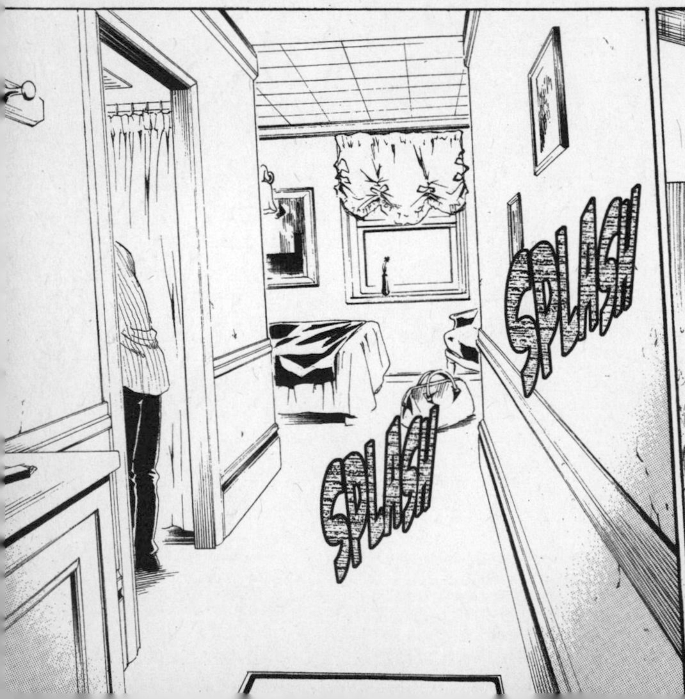
SPLASH
SPLASH

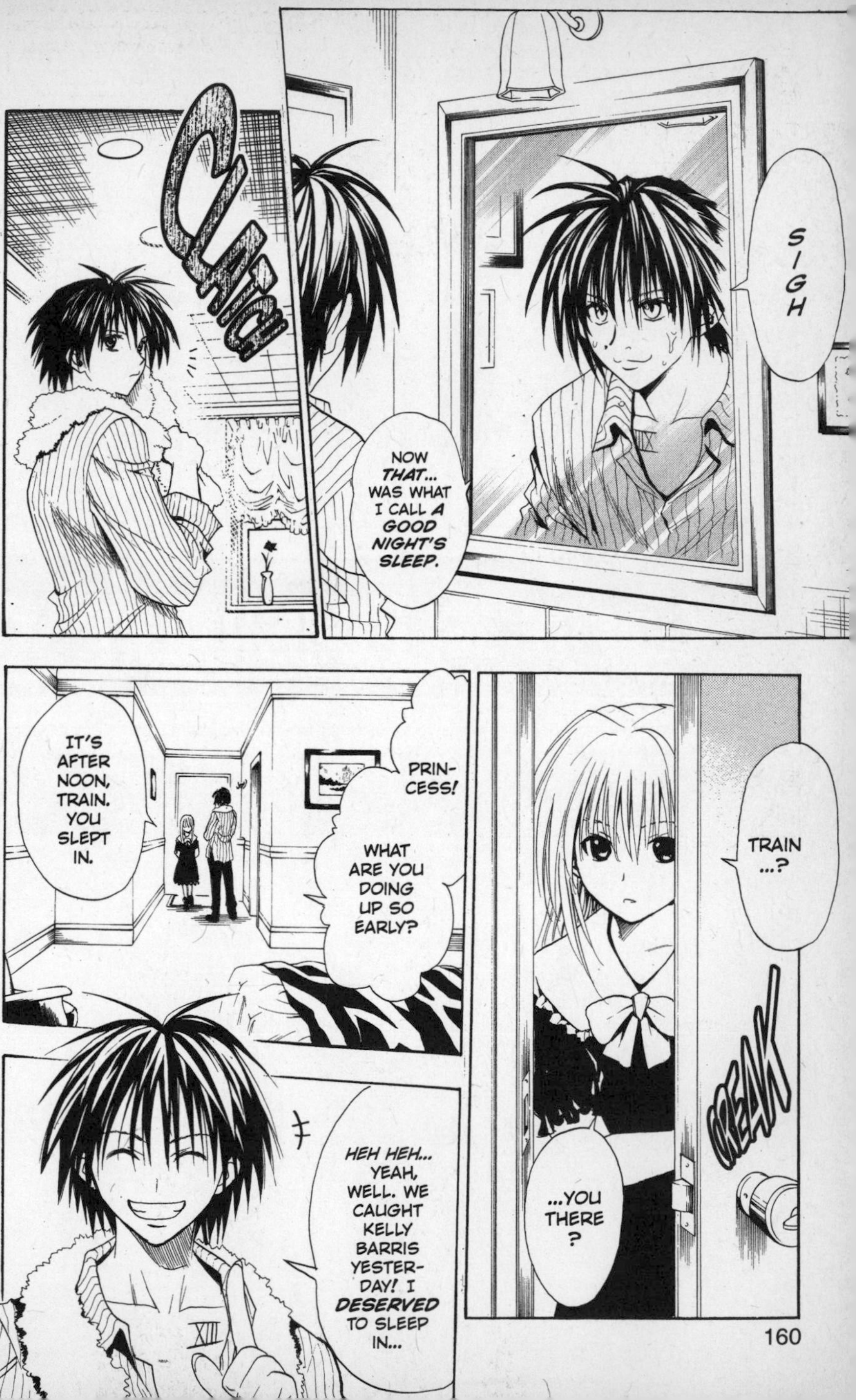
SIGH
NOW THAT... WAS WHAT I CALL A GOOD NIGHT'S SLEEP.
CLATCH
TRAIN ...?
...YOU THERE?
CREAK
PRIN-CESS!
WHAT ARE YOU DOING UP SO EARLY?
IT'S AFTER NOON, TRAIN. YOU SLEPT IN.
HEH HEH... YEAH, WELL. WE CAUGHT KELLY BARRIS YESTER-DAY! I DESERVED TO SLEEP IN...

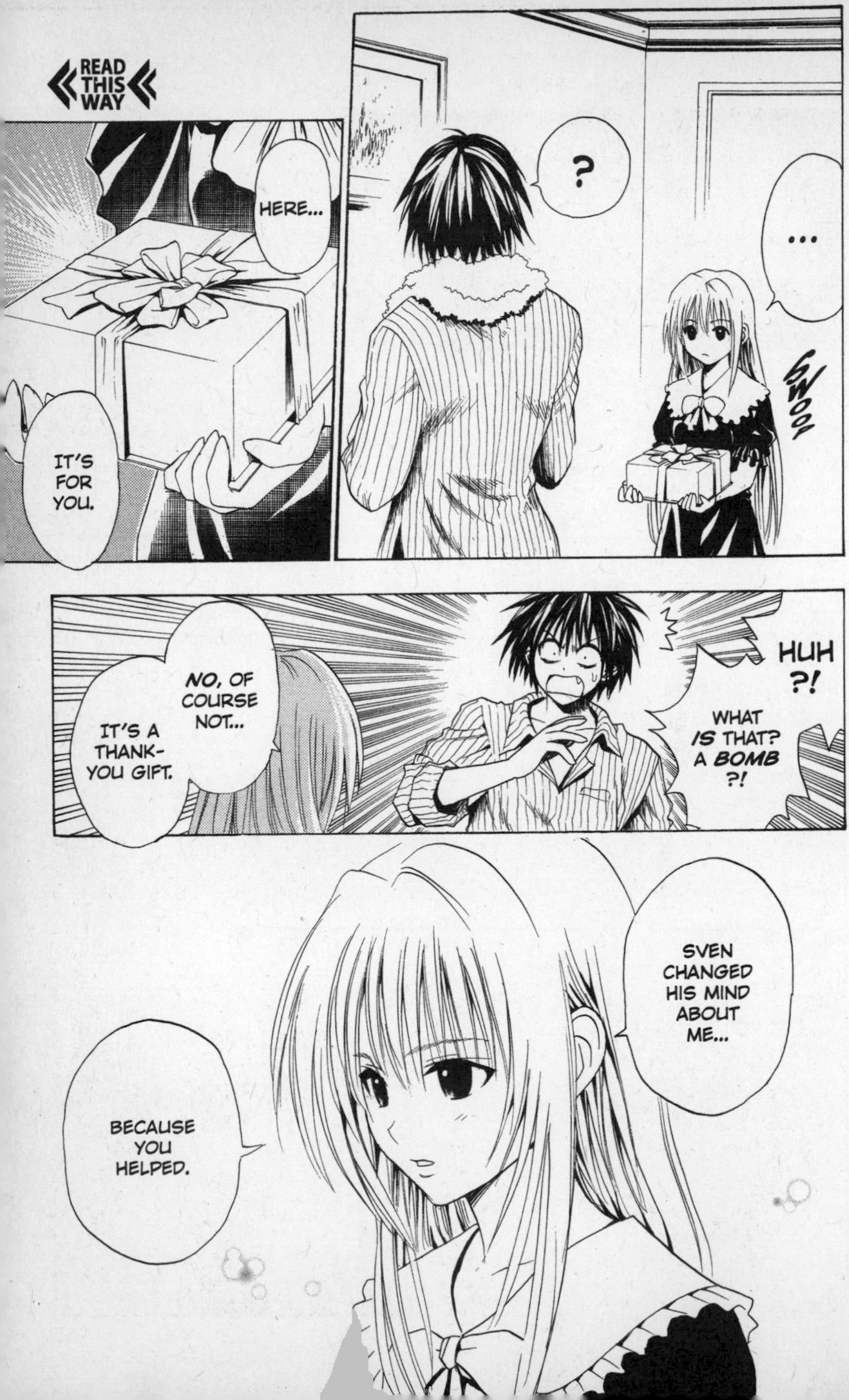
READ THIS WAY
...
?
HERE...
IT'S FOR YOU.
HUH?!
WHAT *IS* THAT? A *BOMB*?!
NO, OF COURSE NOT...
IT'S A THANK-YOU GIFT.
SVEN CHANGED HIS MIND ABOUT ME...
BECAUSE YOU HELPED.

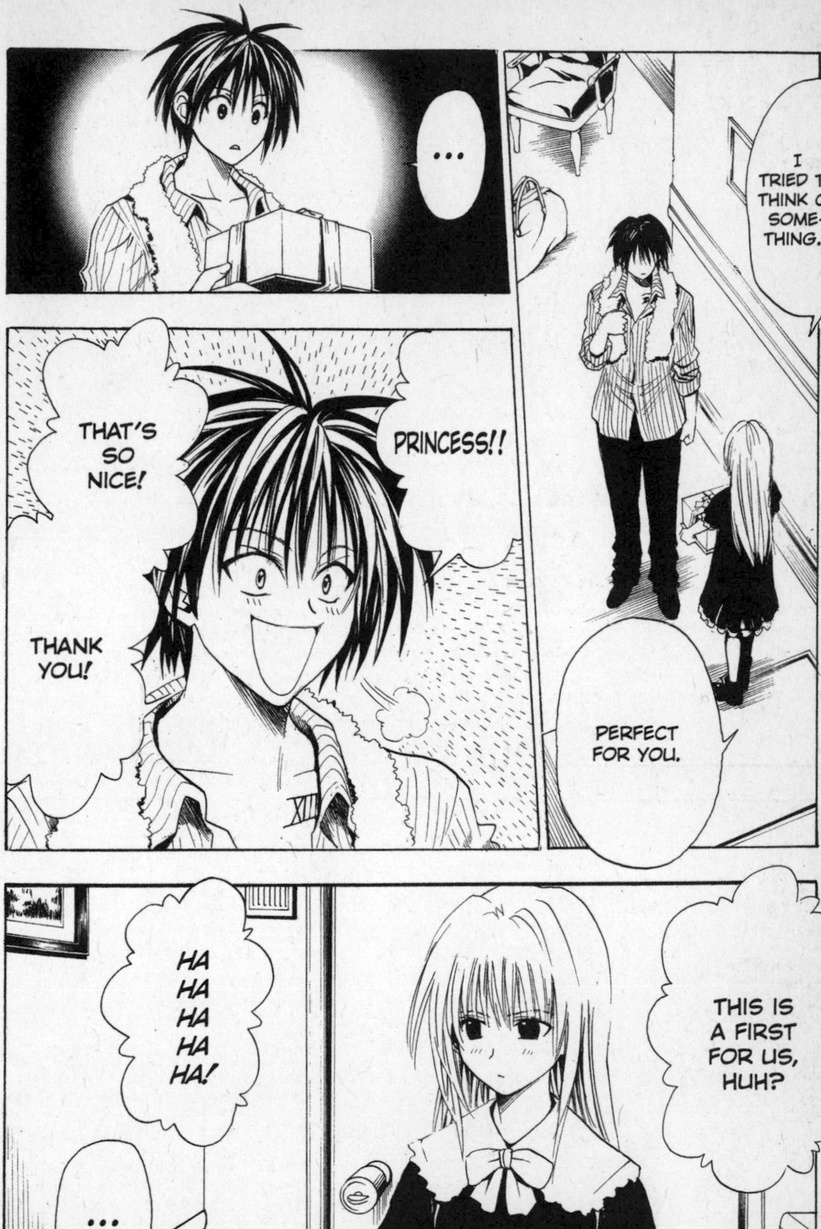
I TRIED TO THINK OF SOME-THING...
PERFECT FOR YOU.
...
PRINCESS!!
THAT'S SO NICE!
THANK YOU!
THIS IS A FIRST FOR US, HUH?
HA HA HA HA HA!
...

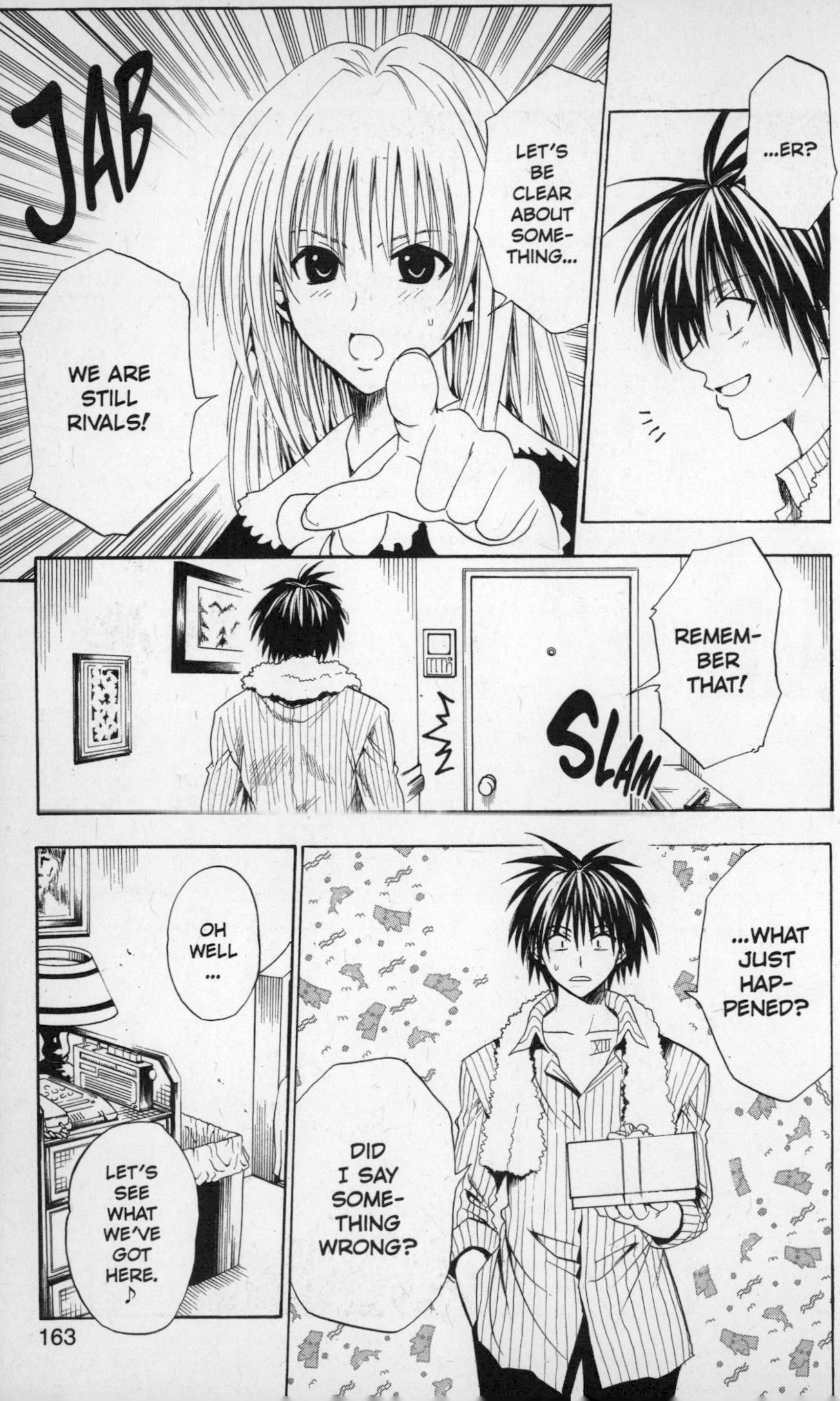
...ER?
LET'S BE CLEAR ABOUT SOME-THING...
JAB
WE ARE STILL RIVALS!
REMEM-BER THAT!
SLAM
...WHAT JUST HAP-PENED?
DID I SAY SOME-THING WRONG?
OH WELL ...
LET'S SEE WHAT WE'VE GOT HERE. ♪

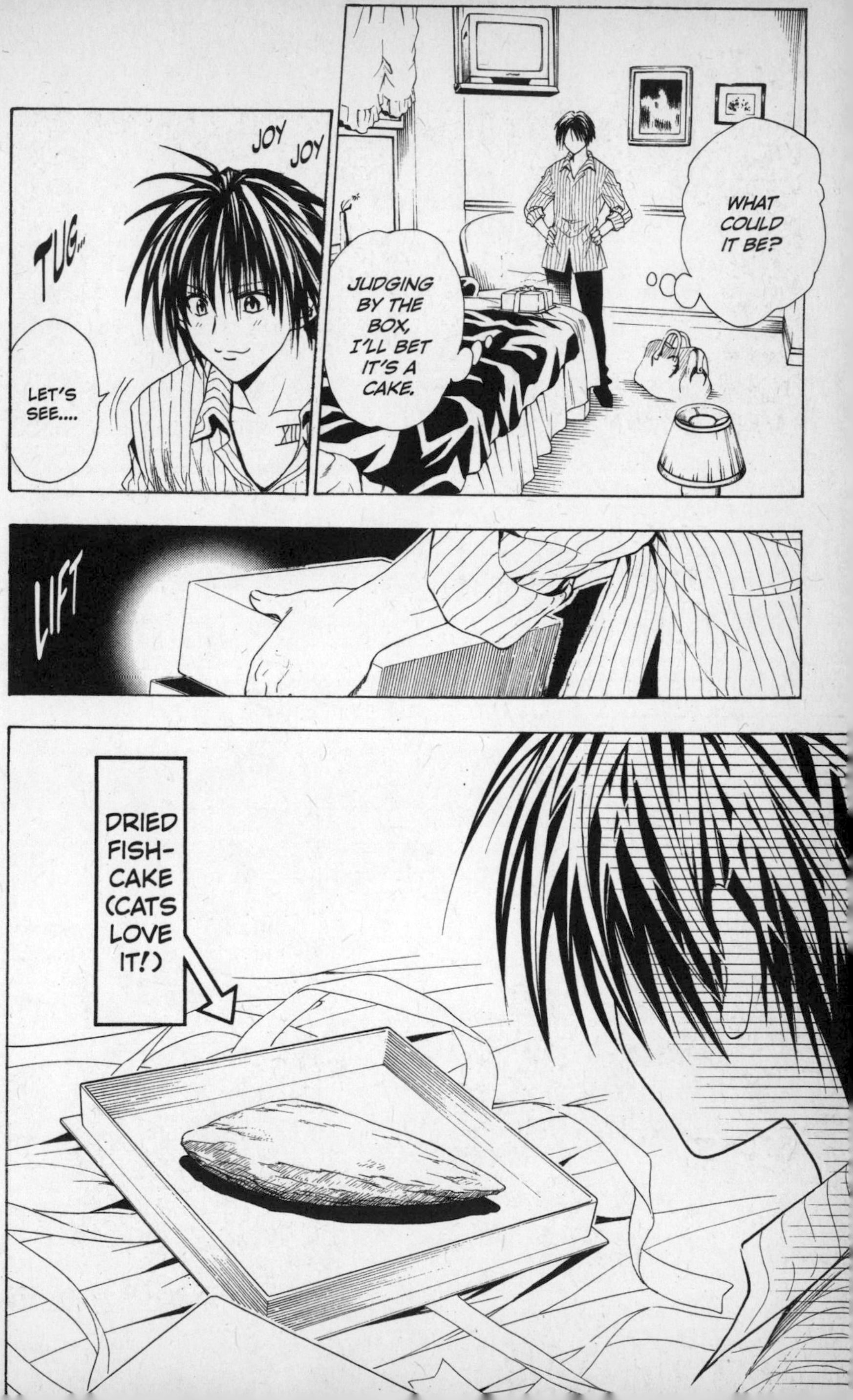
WHAT COULD IT BE?
JUDGING BY THE BOX, I'LL BET IT'S A CAKE.
JOY JOY
TUG...
LET'S SEE....
LIFT
DRIED FISH-CAKE (CATS LOVE IT!)

READ THIS WAY

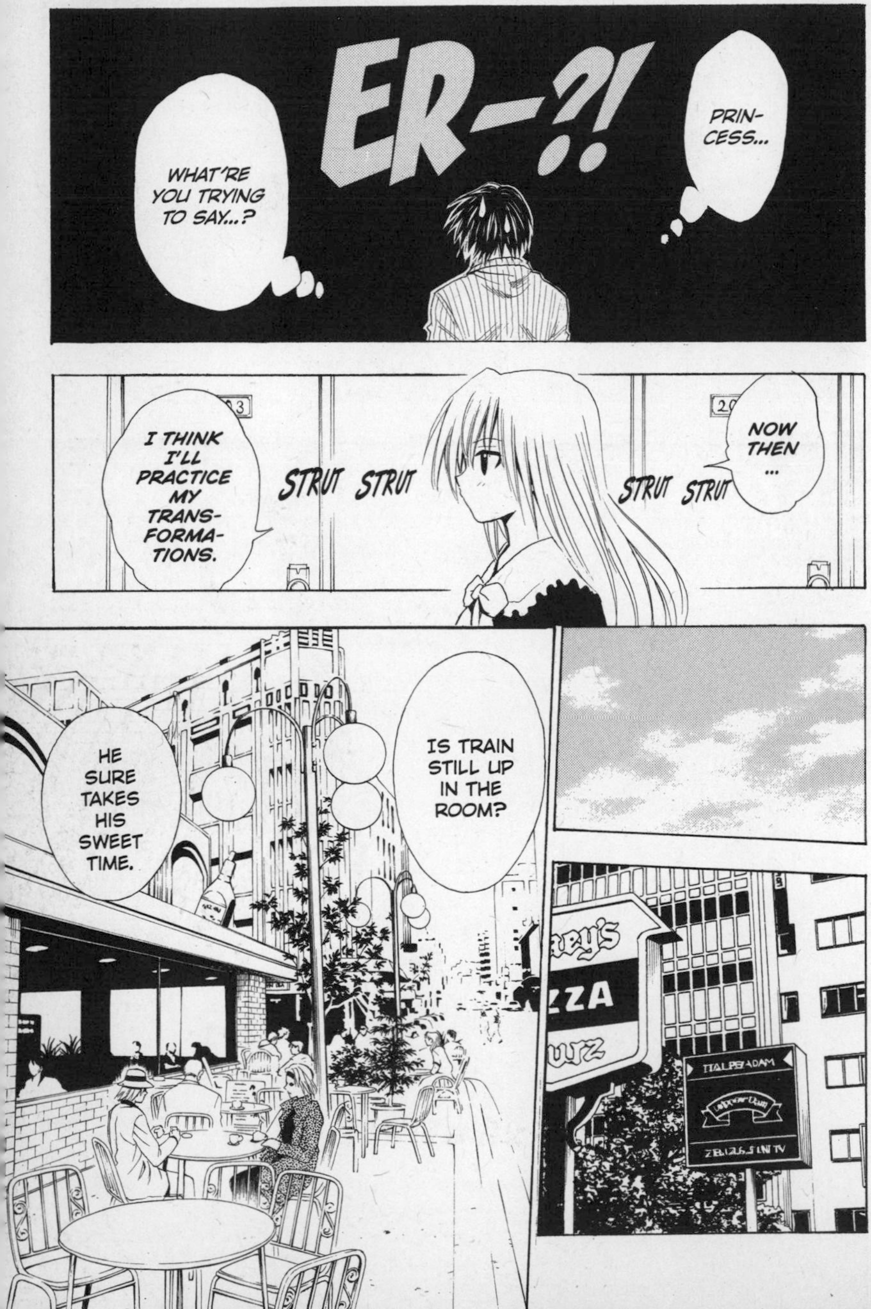
PRIN-CESS...
ER-?!
WHAT'RE YOU TRYING TO SAY...?
NOW THEN ...
STRUT STRUT
STRUT STRUT
I THINK I'LL PRACTICE MY TRANS-FORMA-TIONS.
ZZA
IS TRAIN STILL UP IN THE ROOM?
HE SURE TAKES HIS SWEET TIME.

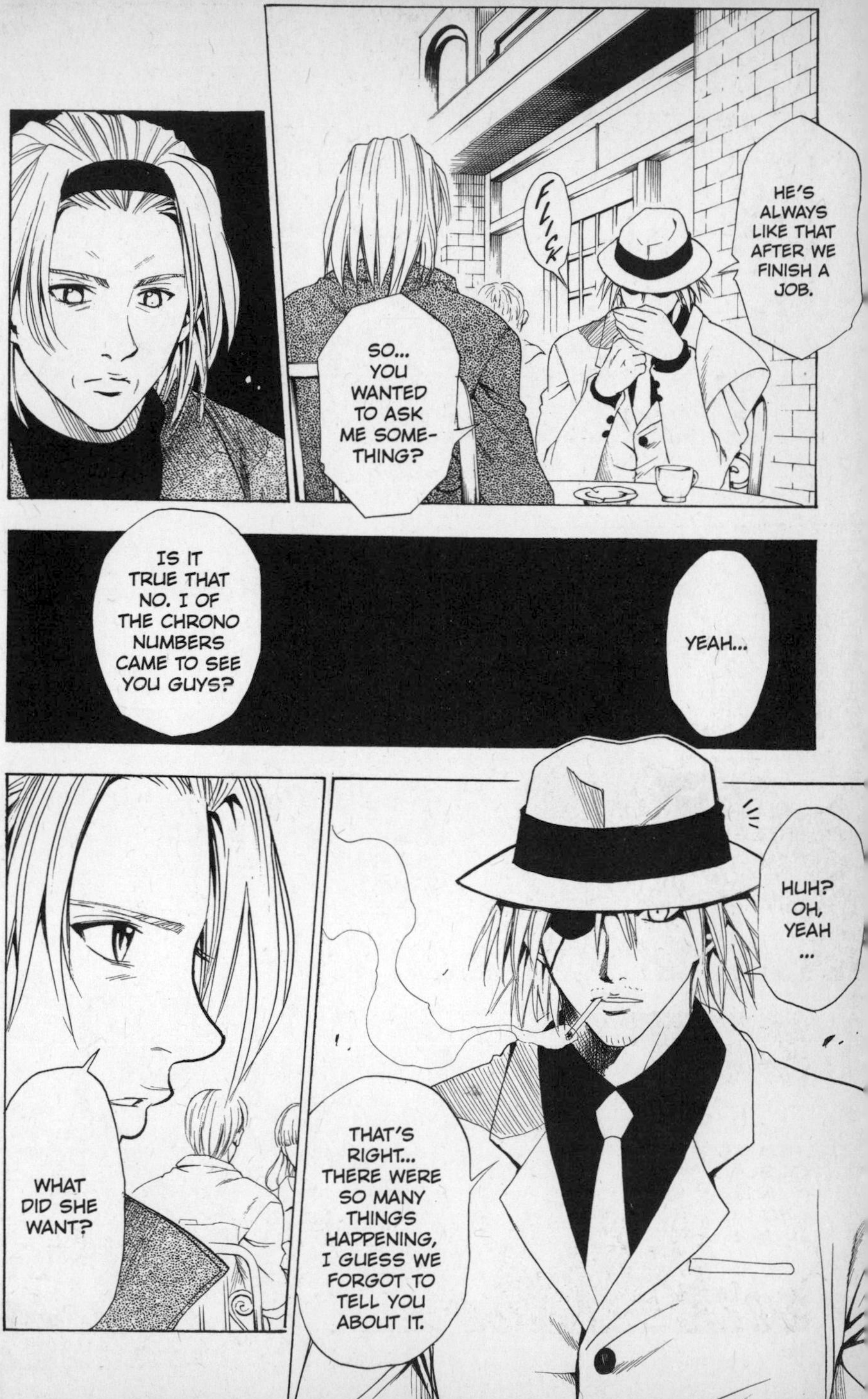
HE'S ALWAYS LIKE THAT AFTER WE FINISH A JOB.
FLICK
SO... YOU WANTED TO ASK ME SOME-THING?
IS IT TRUE THAT NO. I OF THE CHRONO NUMBERS CAME TO SEE YOU GUYS?
YEAH...
HUH? OH, YEAH ...
THAT'S RIGHT... THERE WERE SO MANY THINGS HAPPENING, I GUESS WE FORGOT TO TELL YOU ABOUT IT.
WHAT DID SHE WANT?

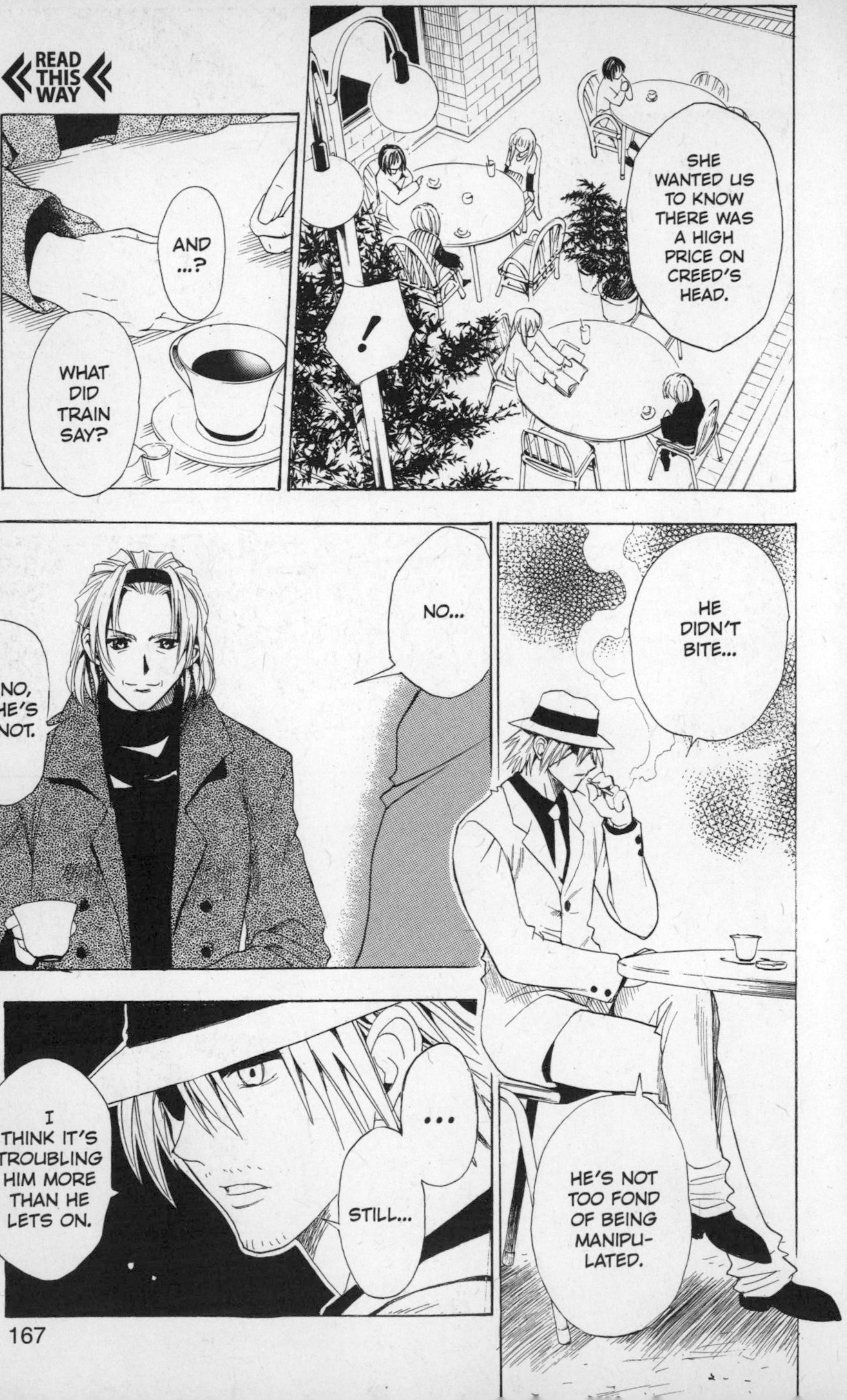
READ THIS WAY
SHE WANTED US TO KNOW THERE WAS A HIGH PRICE ON CREED'S HEAD.
!
AND ...?
WHAT DID TRAIN SAY?
HE DIDN'T BITE...
NO...
NO, HE'S NOT.
HE'S NOT TOO FOND OF BEING MANIPU-LATED.
...
STILL...
I THINK IT'S TROUBLING HIM MORE THAN HE LETS ON.

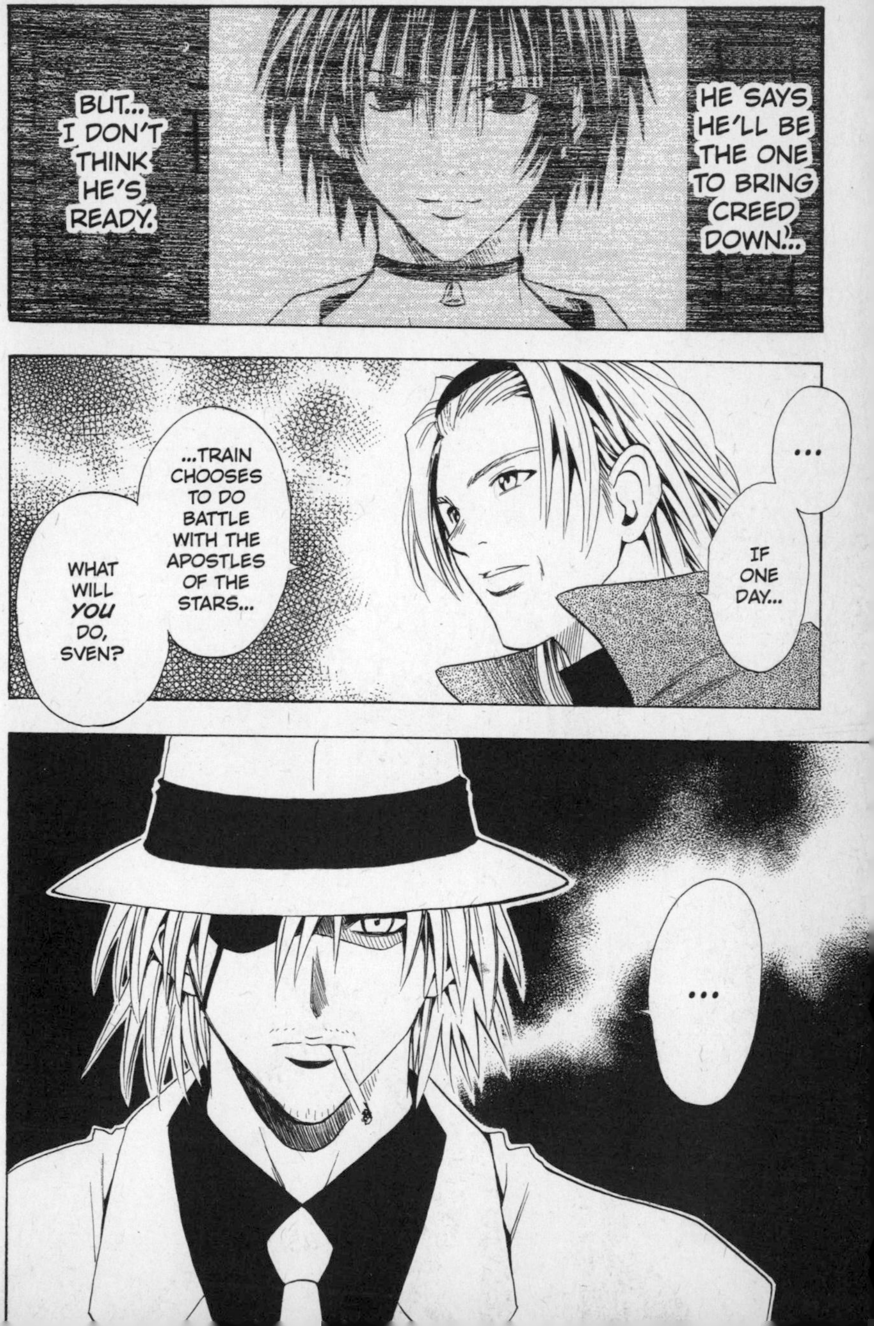
HE SAYS HE'LL BE THE ONE TO BRING CREED DOWN...
BUT... I DON'T THINK HE'S READY.
...
IF ONE DAY...
...TRAIN CHOOSES TO DO BATTLE WITH THE APOSTLES OF THE STARS...
WHAT WILL YOU DO, SVEN?
...

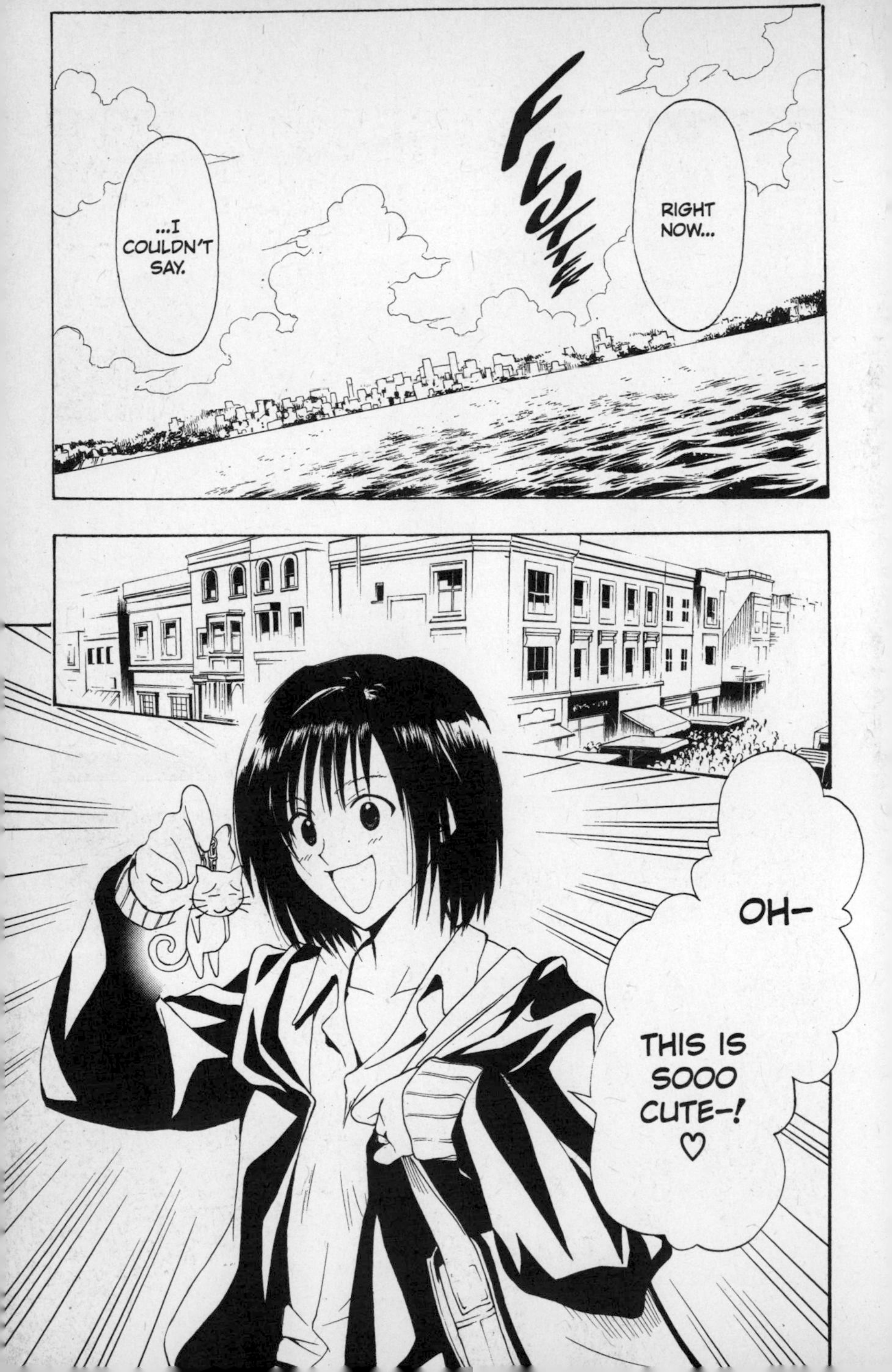
RIGHT NOW...
FWSHHH
...I COULDN'T SAY.
OH-
THIS IS SOOO CUTE-! ♡

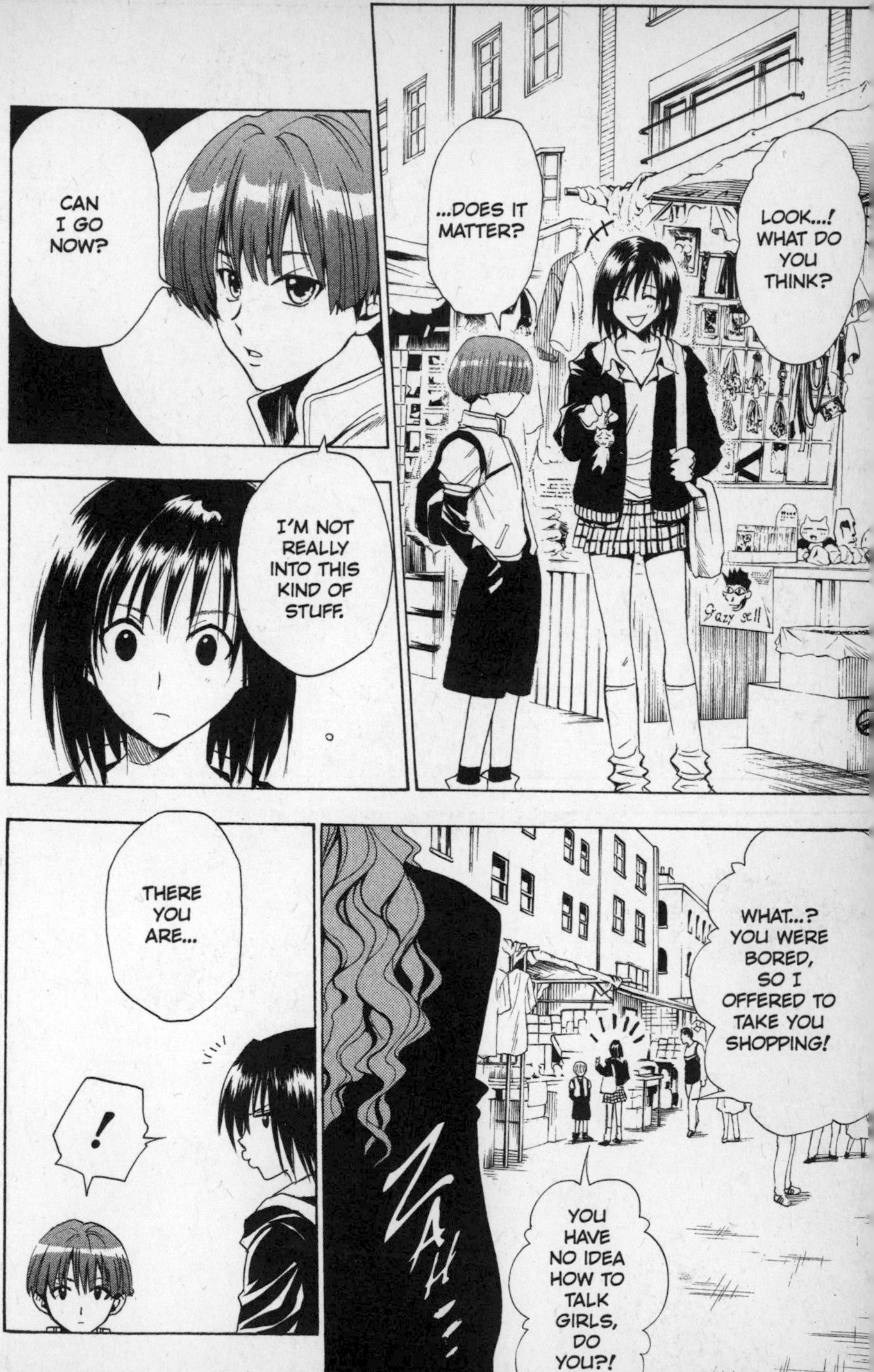
LOOK...! WHAT DO YOU THINK?
...DOES IT MATTER?
CAN I GO NOW?
I'M NOT REALLY INTO THIS KIND OF STUFF.
WHAT...? YOU WERE BORED, SO I OFFERED TO TAKE YOU SHOPPING!
YOU HAVE NO IDEA HOW TO TALK GIRLS, DO YOU?!
NAH...
THERE YOU ARE...
!

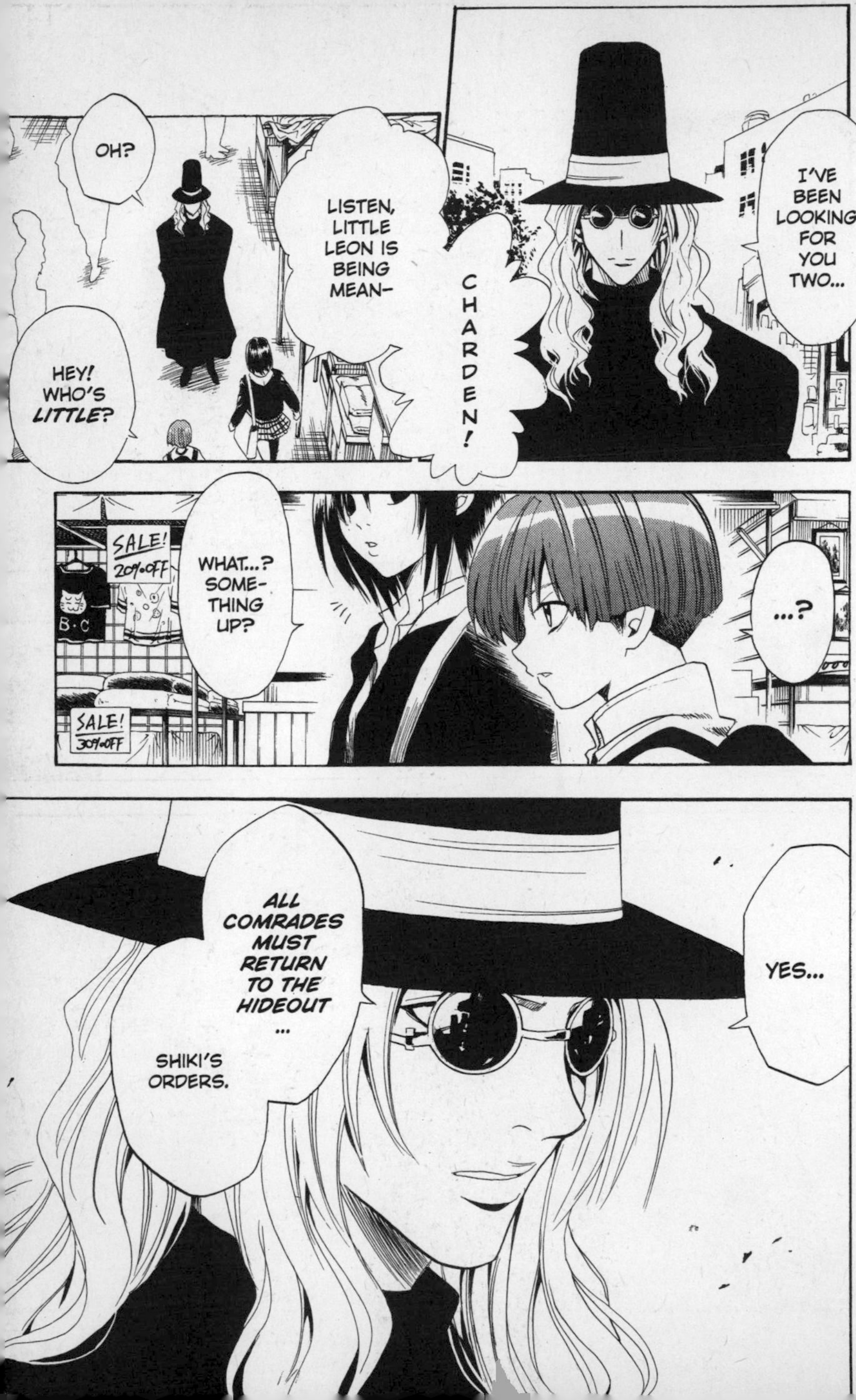
I'VE BEEN LOOKING FOR YOU TWO...
CHARDEN!
LISTEN, LITTLE LEON IS BEING MEAN-
OH?
HEY! WHO'S *LITTLE*?
...?
WHAT...? SOME-THING UP?
SALE! 20% OFF
SALE! 30% OFF
YES...
ALL COMRADES MUST RETURN TO THE HIDEOUT...
SHIKI'S ORDERS.

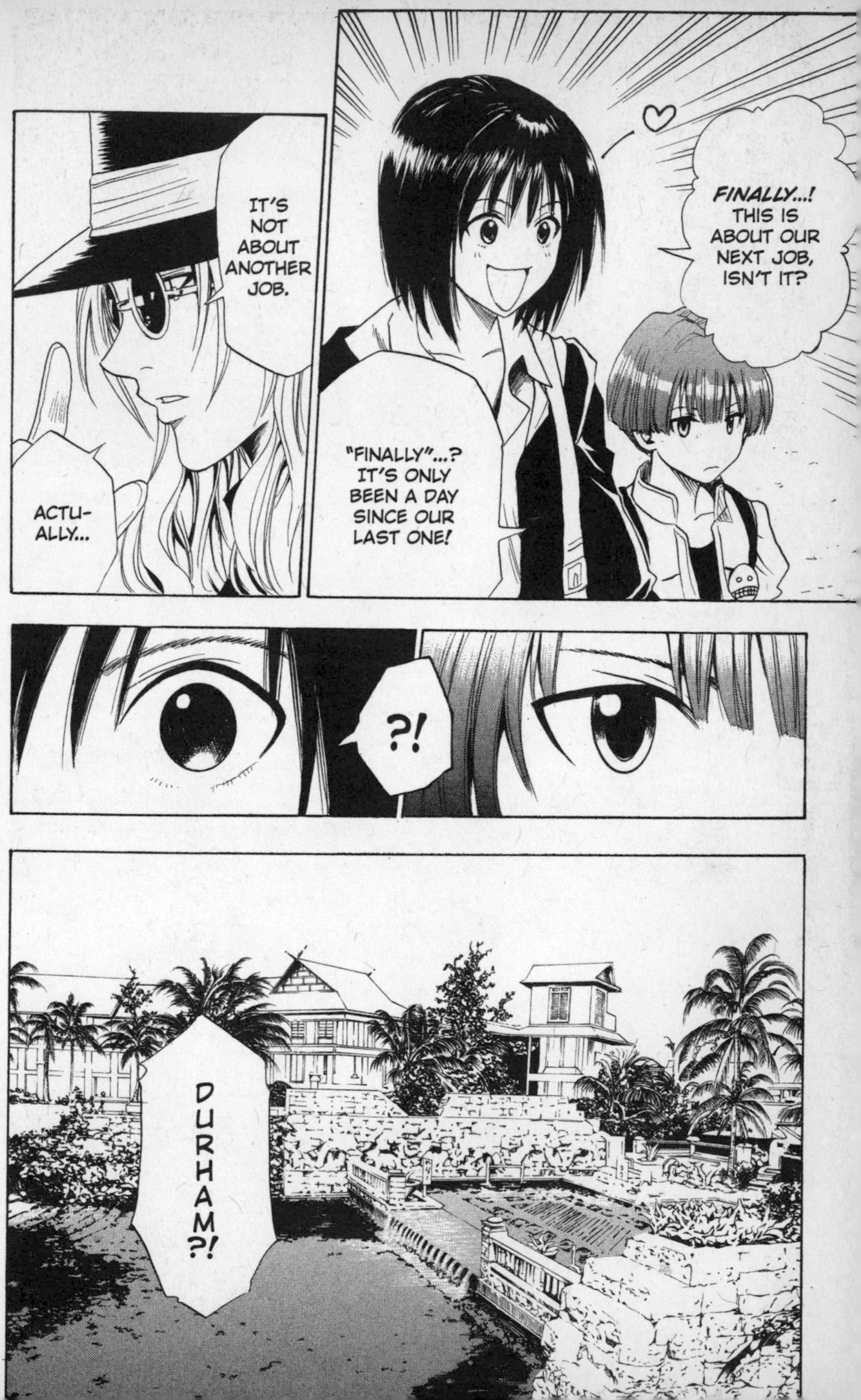
FINALLY...! THIS IS ABOUT OUR NEXT JOB, ISN'T IT?
"FINALLY"...? IT'S ONLY BEEN A DAY SINCE OUR LAST ONE!
IT'S NOT ABOUT ANOTHER JOB.
ACTU-ALLY...
?!
DURHAM?!

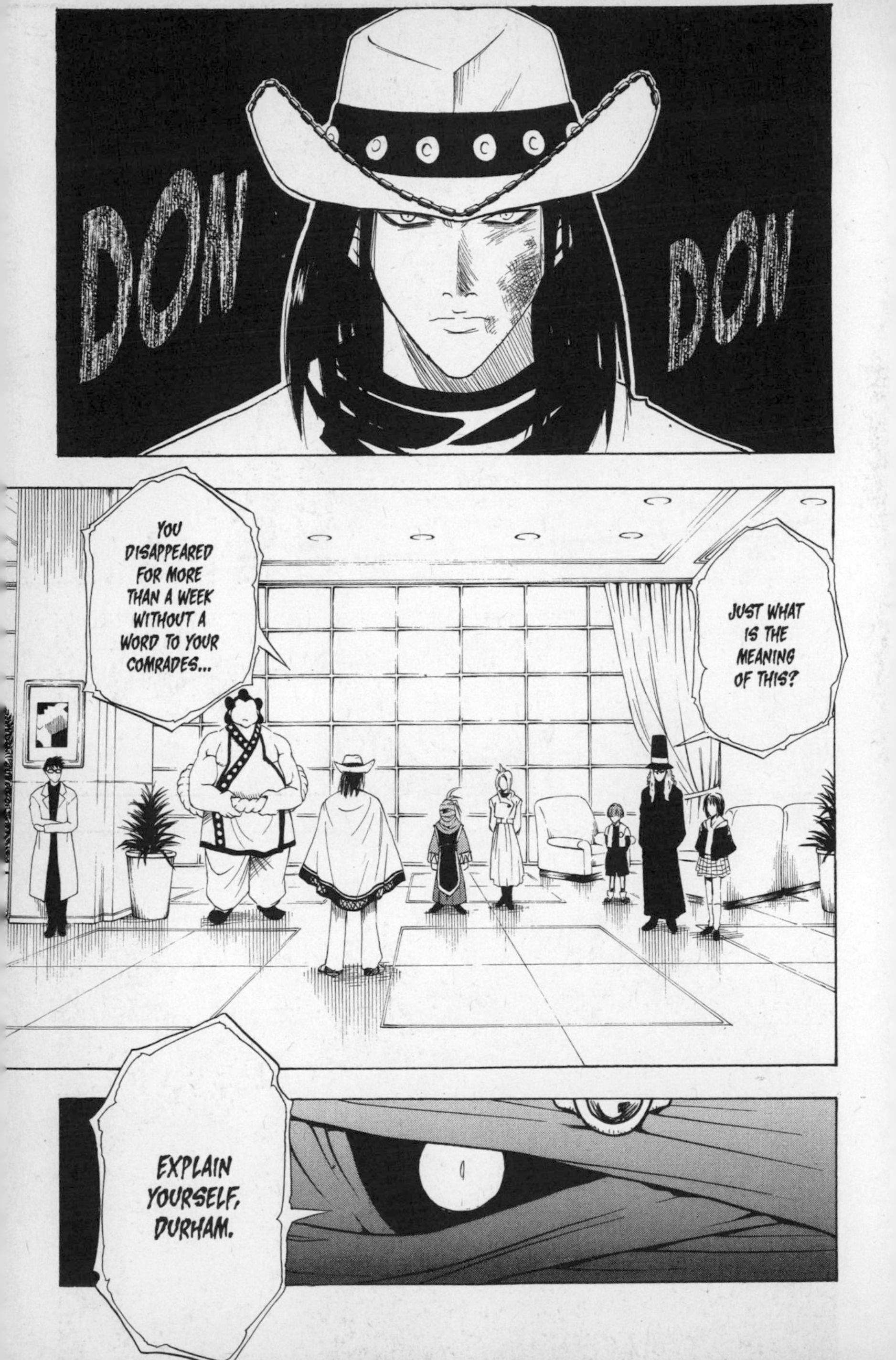
DON
DON
YOU DISAPPEARED FOR MORE THAN A WEEK WITHOUT A WORD TO YOUR COMRADES...
JUST WHAT IS THE MEANING OF THIS?
EXPLAIN YOURSELF, DURHAM.

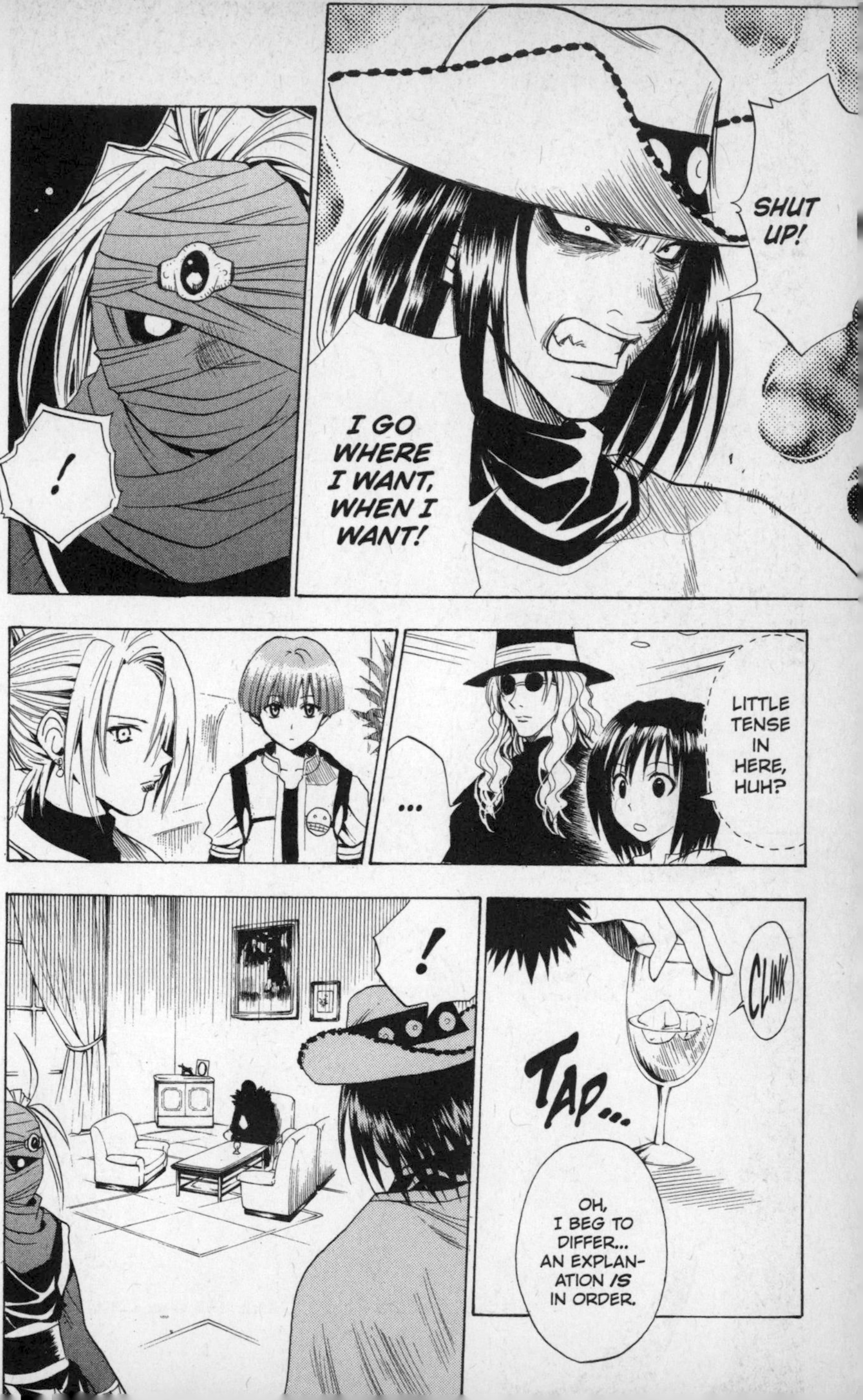
SHUT UP!
I GO WHERE I WANT, WHEN I WANT!
!
LITTLE TENSE IN HERE, HUH?
...
CLINK
TAP...
OH, I BEG TO DIFFER... AN EXPLANATION *IS* IN ORDER.
!

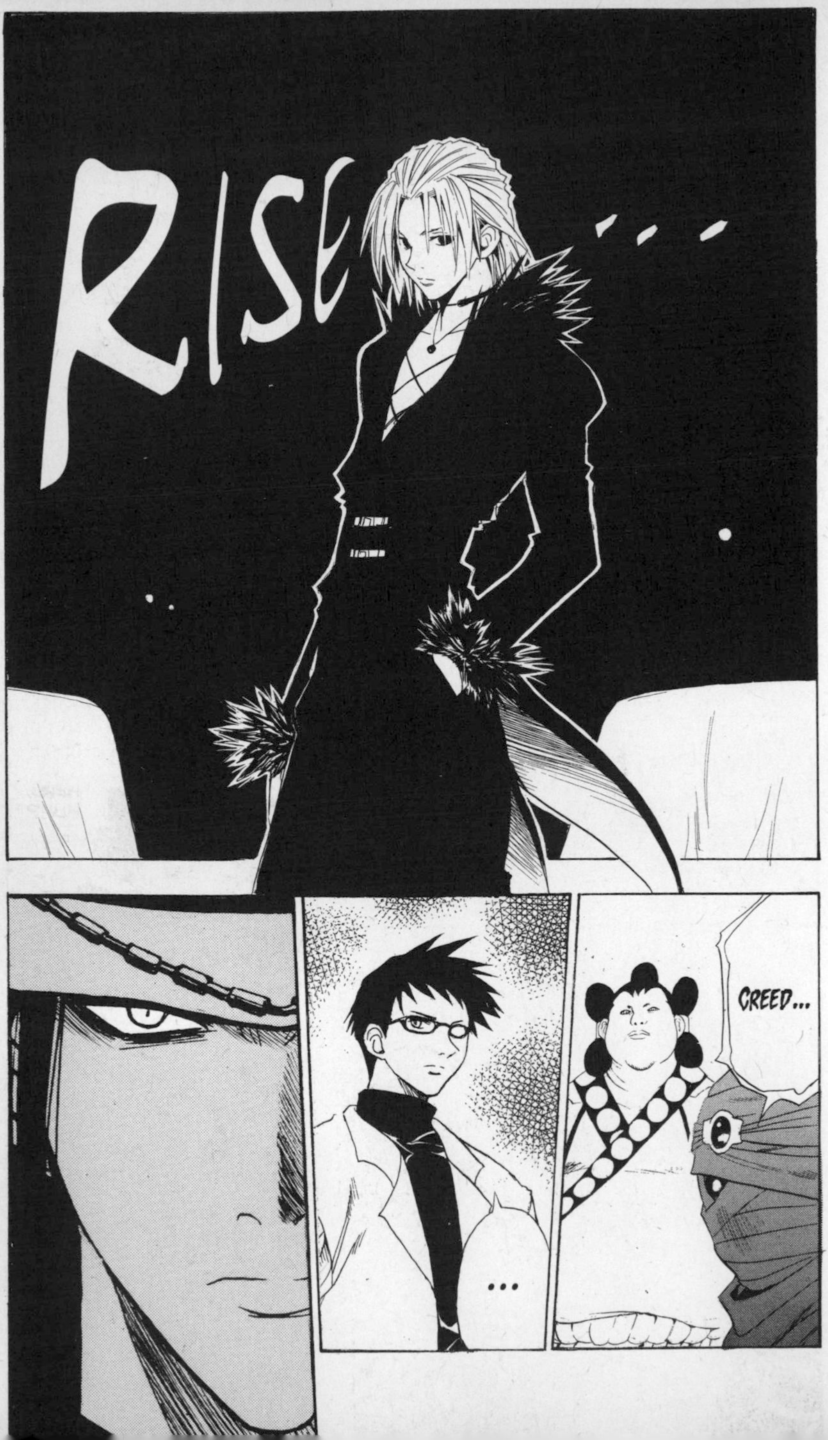
RISE...
CREED...
...

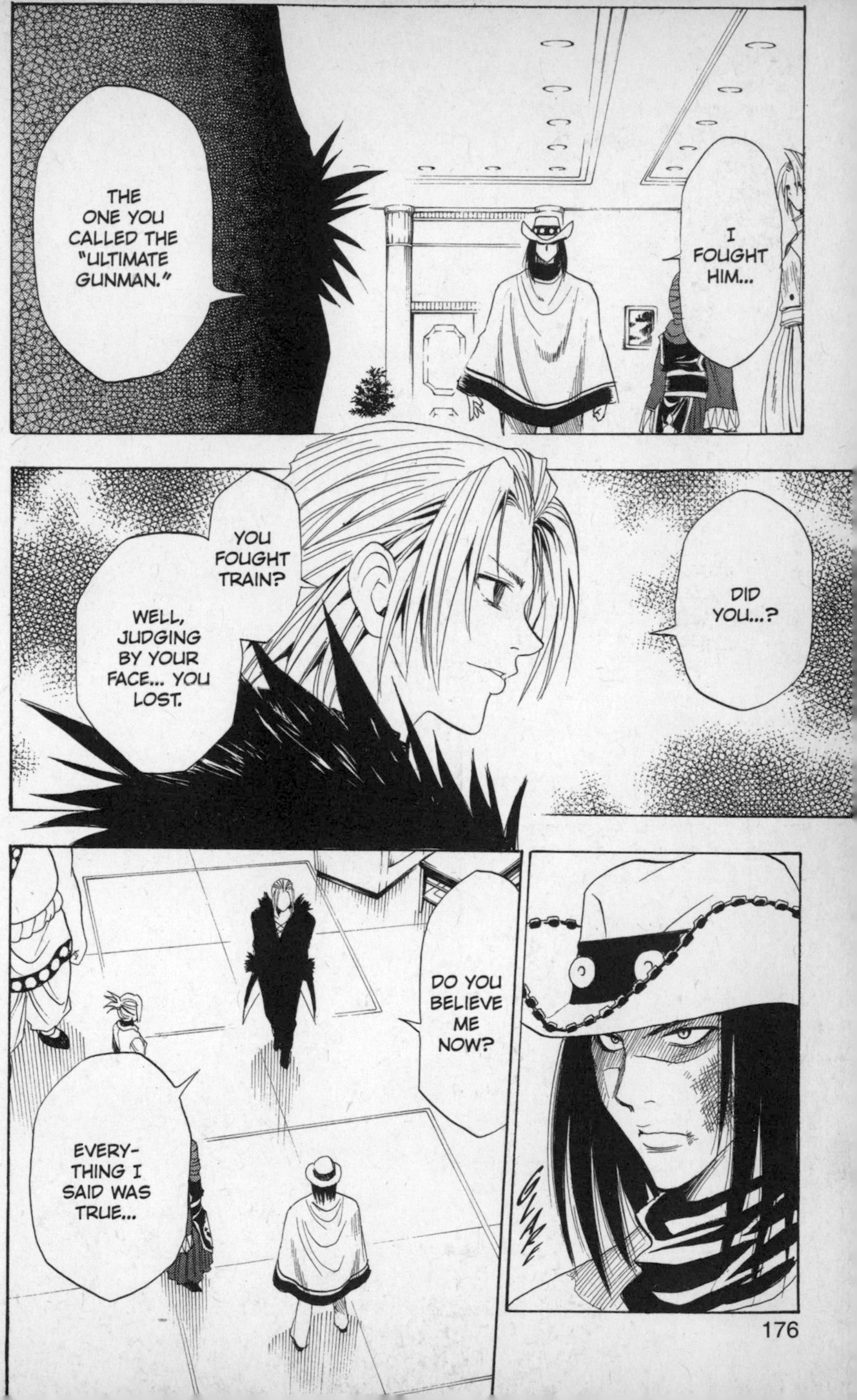
I FOUGHT HIM...
THE ONE YOU CALLED THE "ULTIMATE GUNMAN."
DID YOU...?
YOU FOUGHT TRAIN?
WELL, JUDGING BY YOUR FACE... YOU LOST.
DO YOU BELIEVE ME NOW?
EVERY-THING I SAID WAS TRUE...

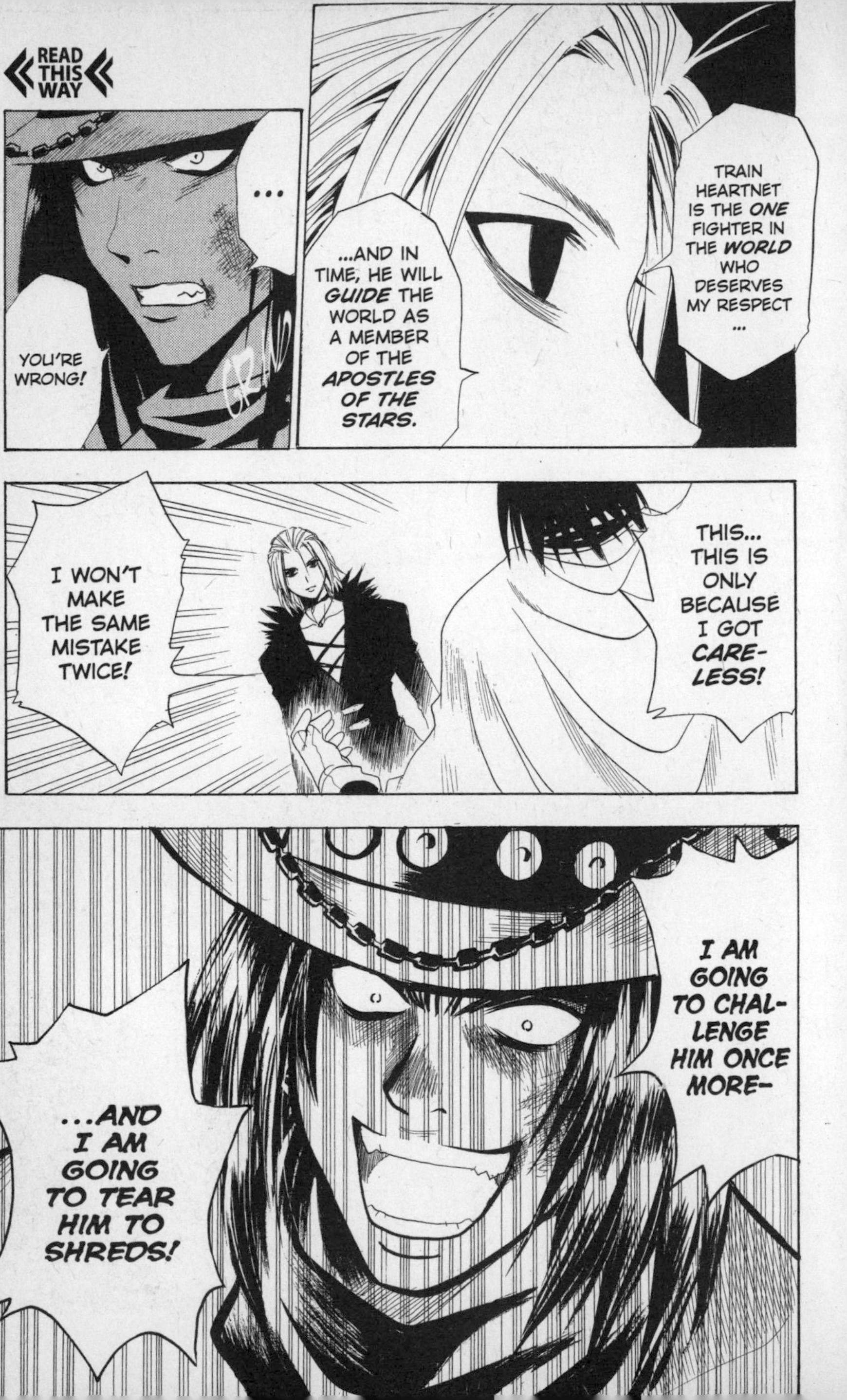
READ THIS WAY
TRAIN HEARTNET IS THE *ONE* FIGHTER IN THE *WORLD* WHO DESERVES MY RESPECT ...
...AND IN TIME, HE WILL *GUIDE* THE WORLD AS A MEMBER OF THE *APOSTLES OF THE STARS.*
...
YOU'RE WRONG!
GRIND
THIS... THIS IS ONLY BECAUSE I GOT *CARE-LESS!*
I WON'T MAKE THE SAME MISTAKE TWICE!
I AM GOING TO CHAL-LENGE HIM ONCE MORE-
...AND I AM GOING TO TEAR HIM TO SHREDS!

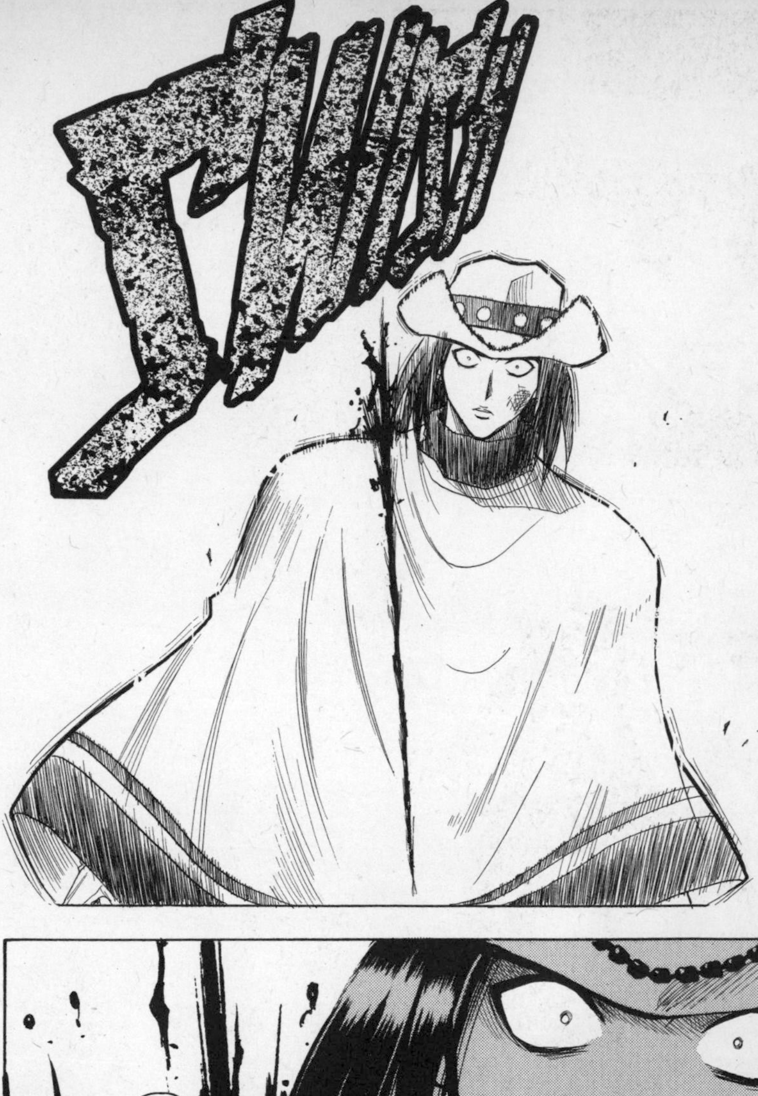

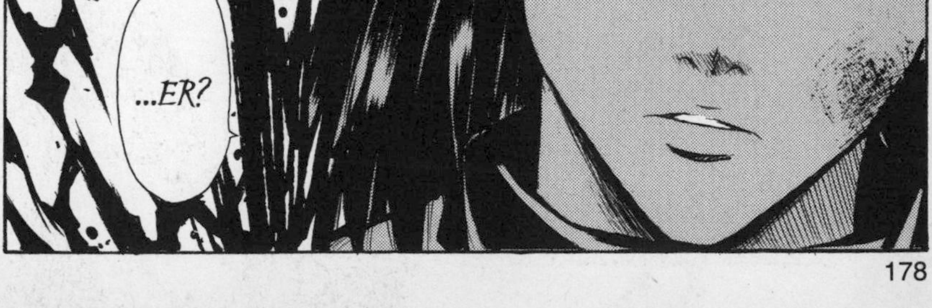
...ER?

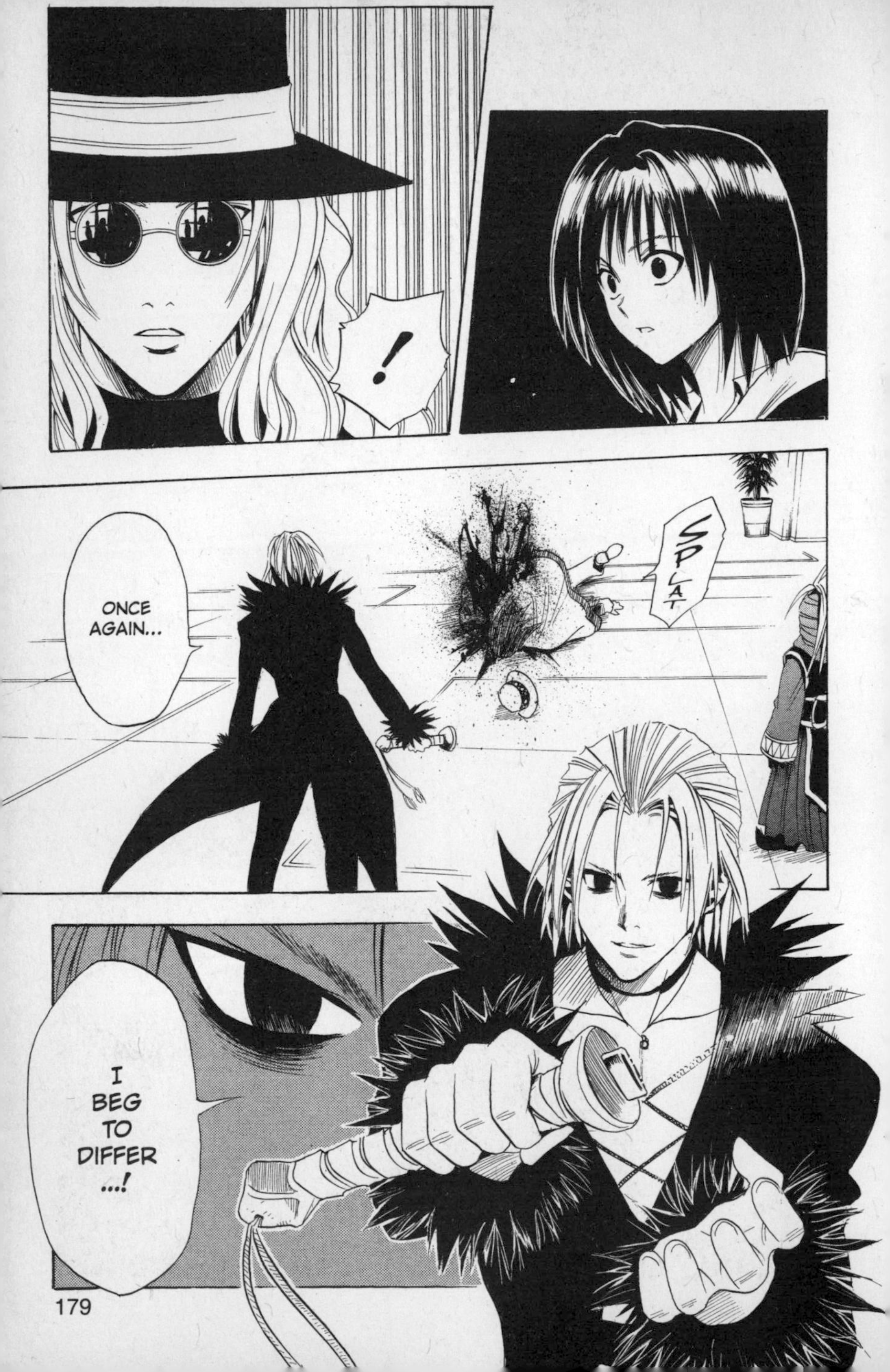
!
SPLAT
ONCE AGAIN...
I BEG TO DIFFER...!

Sketches: Part 2

I was trying to sketch a truly awful face and this is what I came up with...

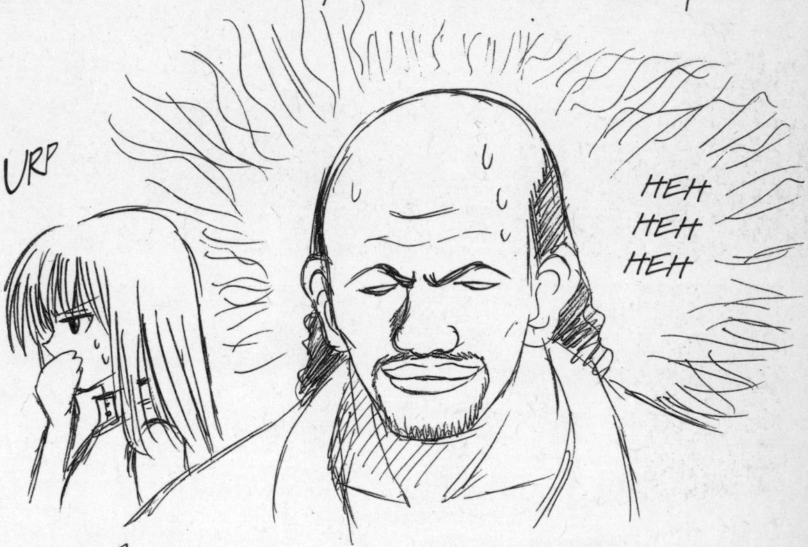
HEH
HEH
HEH
URP

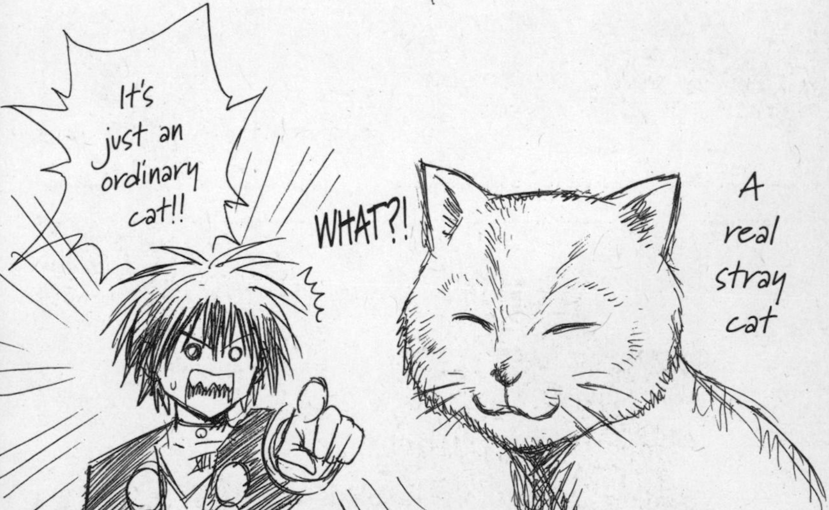
A real stray cat
WHAT?!
It's just an ordinary cat!!

Chapter 57: Charden's Doubts

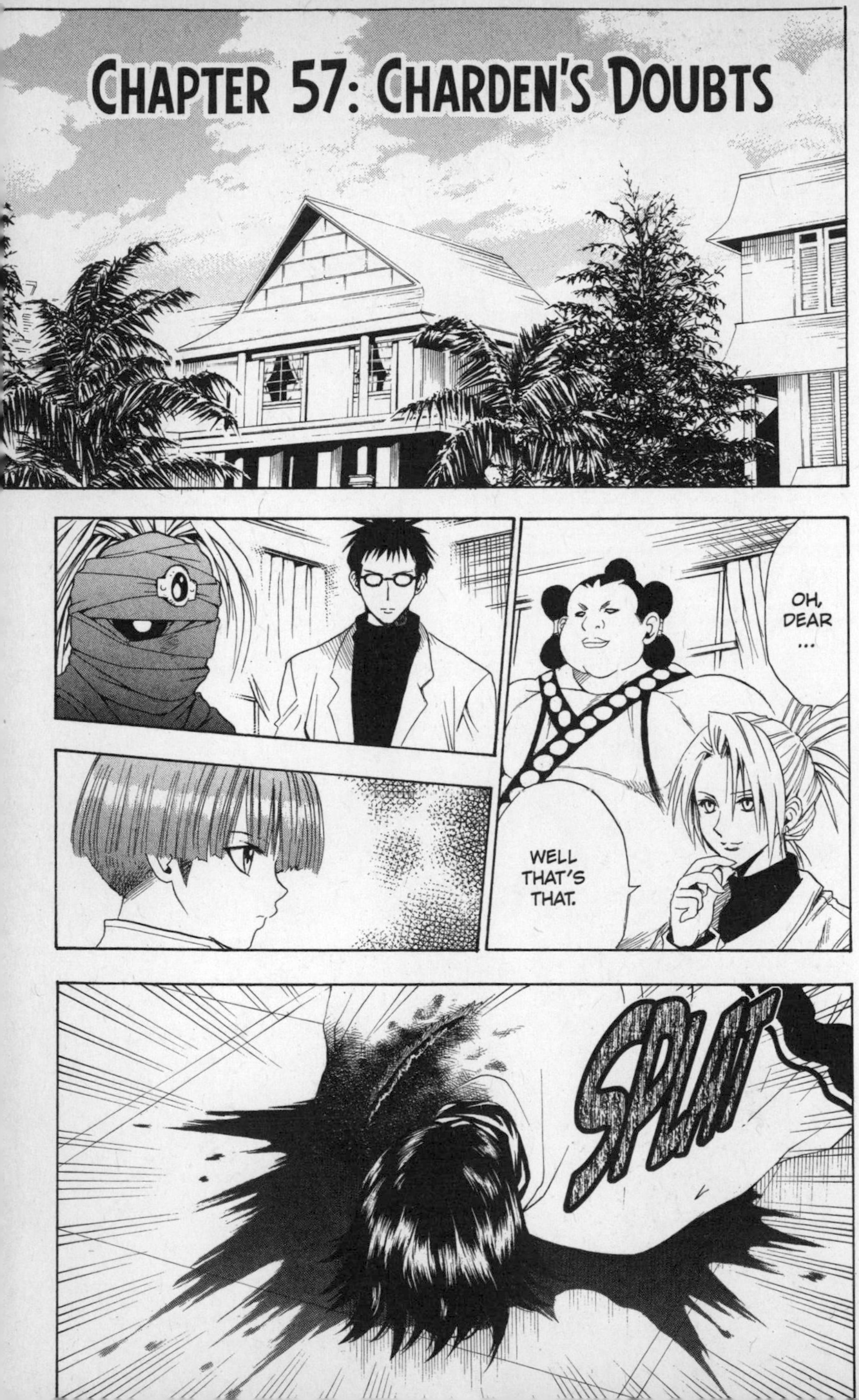
OH, DEAR ...
WELL THAT'S THAT.
SPLAT

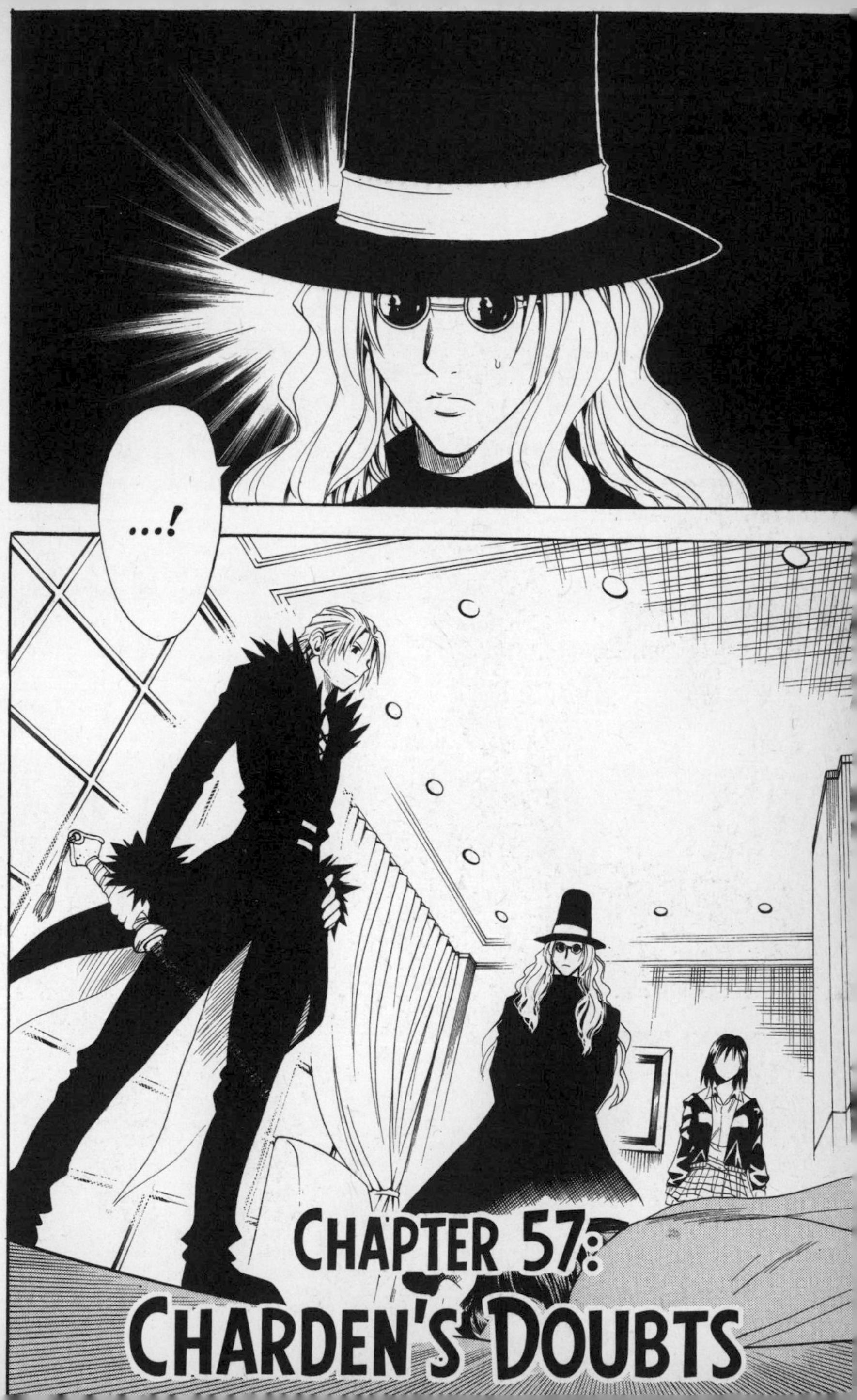
...!

Chapter 57: Charden's Doubts

READ THIS WAY

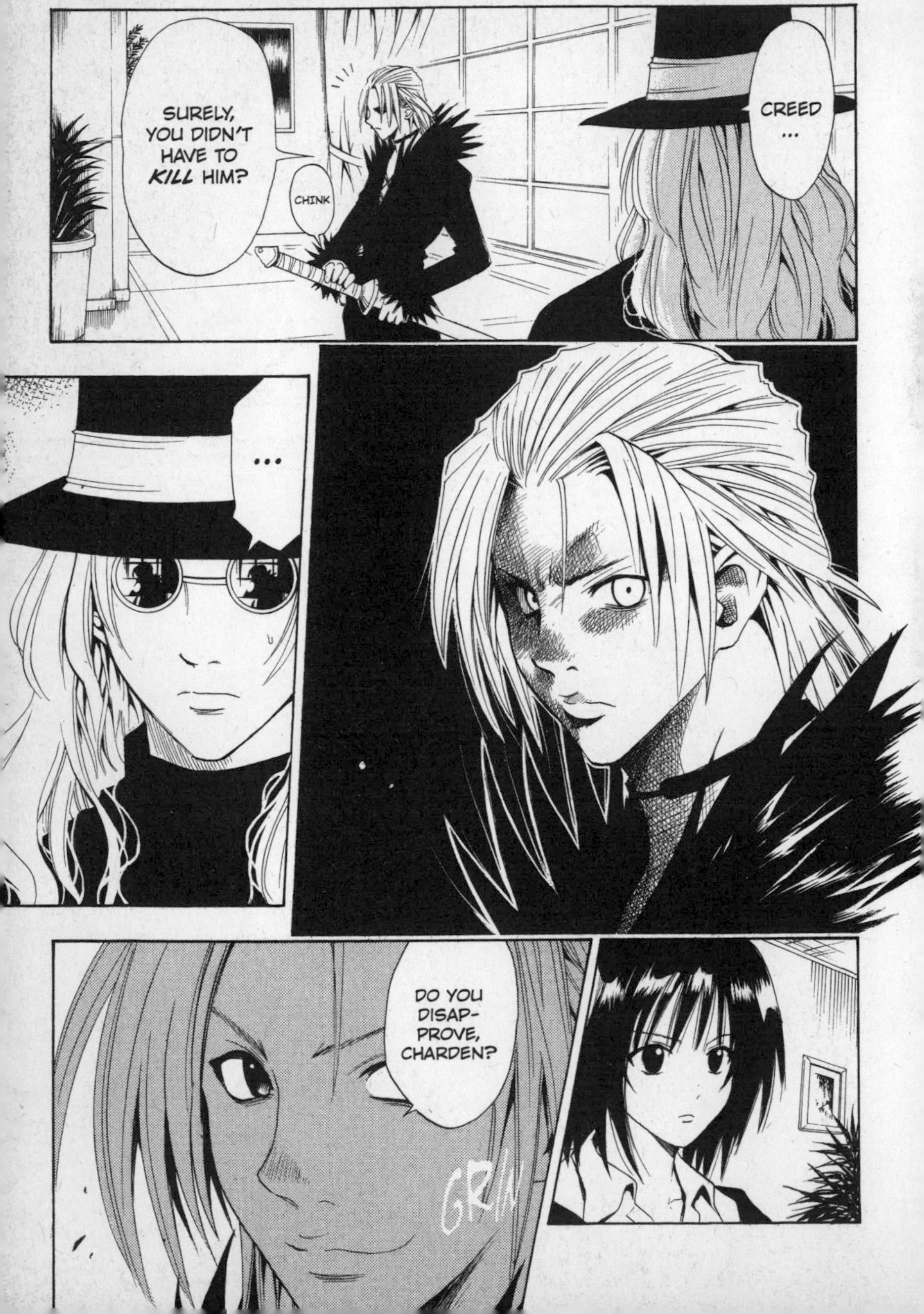
CREED ...
SURELY, YOU DIDN'T HAVE TO *KILL* HIM?
CHINK
...
DO YOU DISAP-PROVE, CHARDEN?
GRIN

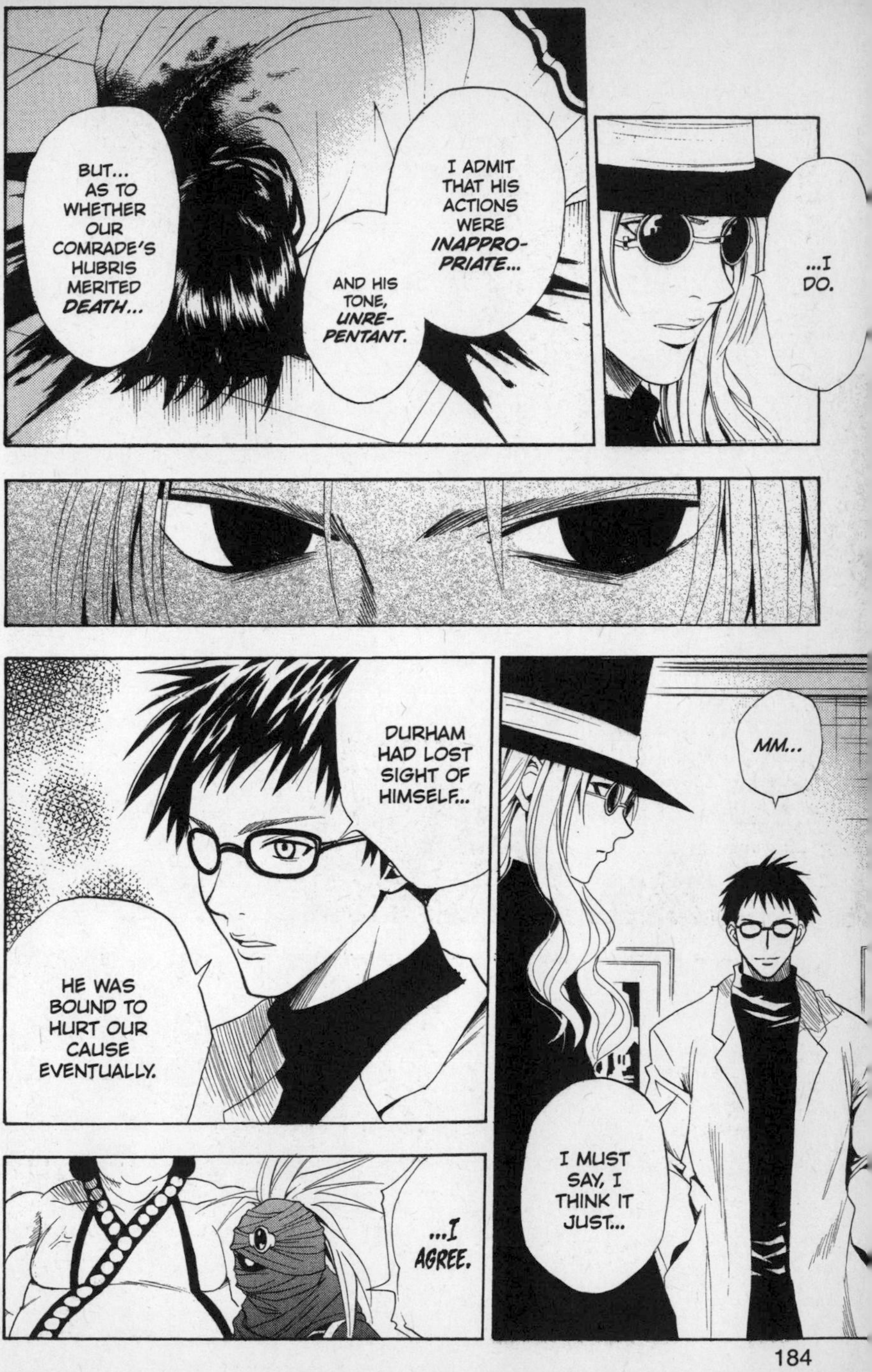
...I DO.
I ADMIT THAT HIS ACTIONS WERE INAPPROPRIATE...
AND HIS TONE, UNREPENTANT.
BUT... AS TO WHETHER OUR COMRADE'S HUBRIS MERITED DEATH...
MM...
I MUST SAY, I THINK IT JUST...
DURHAM HAD LOST SIGHT OF HIMSELF...
HE WAS BOUND TO HURT OUR CAUSE EVENTUALLY.
...I AGREE.

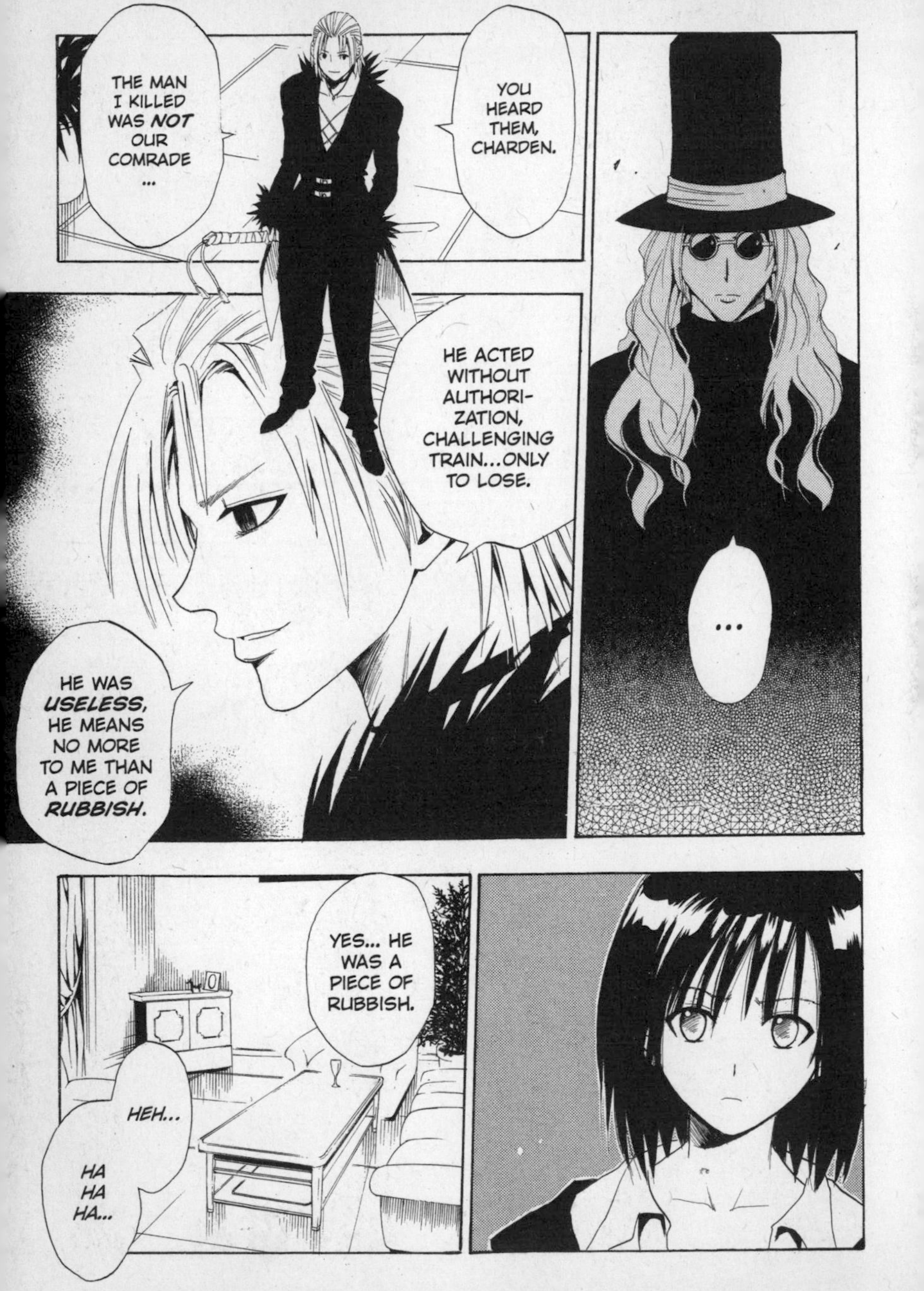
...
YOU HEARD THEM, CHARDEN.
THE MAN I KILLED WAS ***NOT*** OUR COMRADE ...
HE ACTED WITHOUT AUTHORI-ZATION, CHALLENGING TRAIN...ONLY TO LOSE.
HE WAS ***USELESS,*** HE MEANS NO MORE TO ME THAN A PIECE OF ***RUBBISH.***
YES... HE WAS A PIECE OF RUBBISH.
HEH...
HA HA HA...

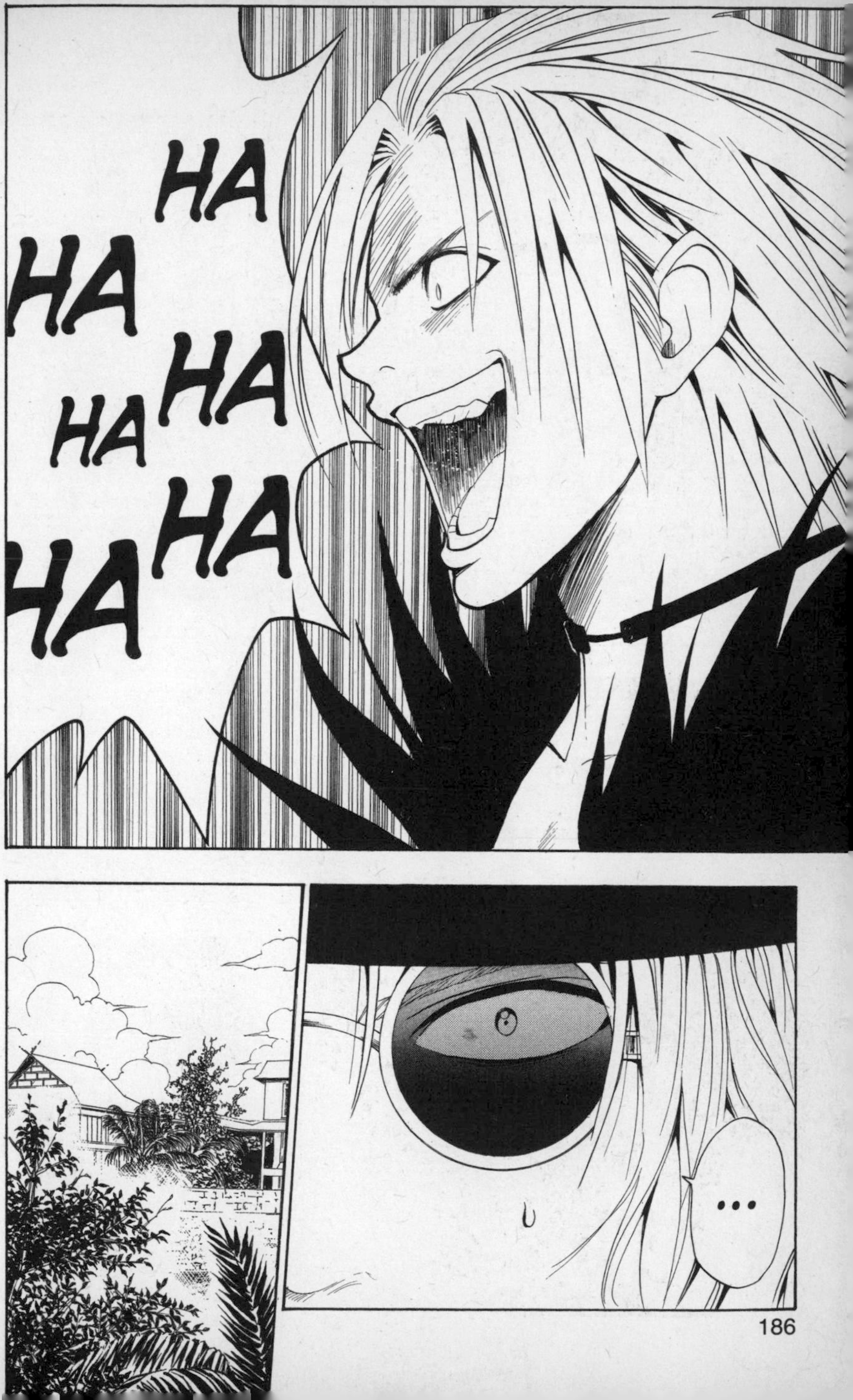
HA HA HA HA HA HA
...

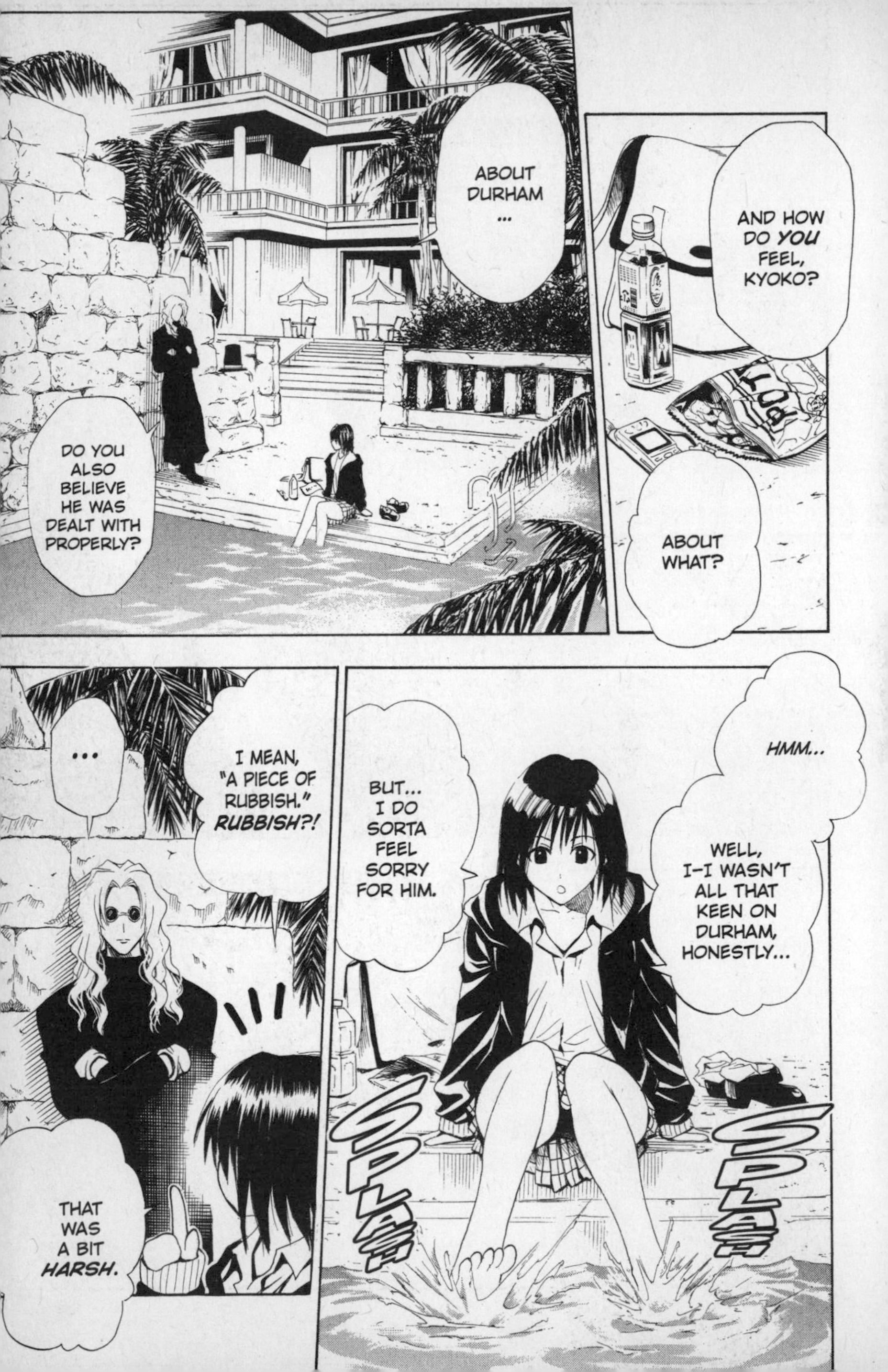
AND HOW DO YOU FEEL, KYOKO?
ABOUT WHAT?
ABOUT DURHAM ...
DO YOU ALSO BELIEVE HE WAS DEALT WITH PROPERLY?
HMM...
WELL, I-I WASN'T ALL THAT KEEN ON DURHAM, HONESTLY...
BUT... I DO SORTA FEEL SORRY FOR HIM.
SPLASH
SPLASH
I MEAN, "A PIECE OF RUBBISH." RUBBISH?!
...
THAT WAS A BIT HARSH.

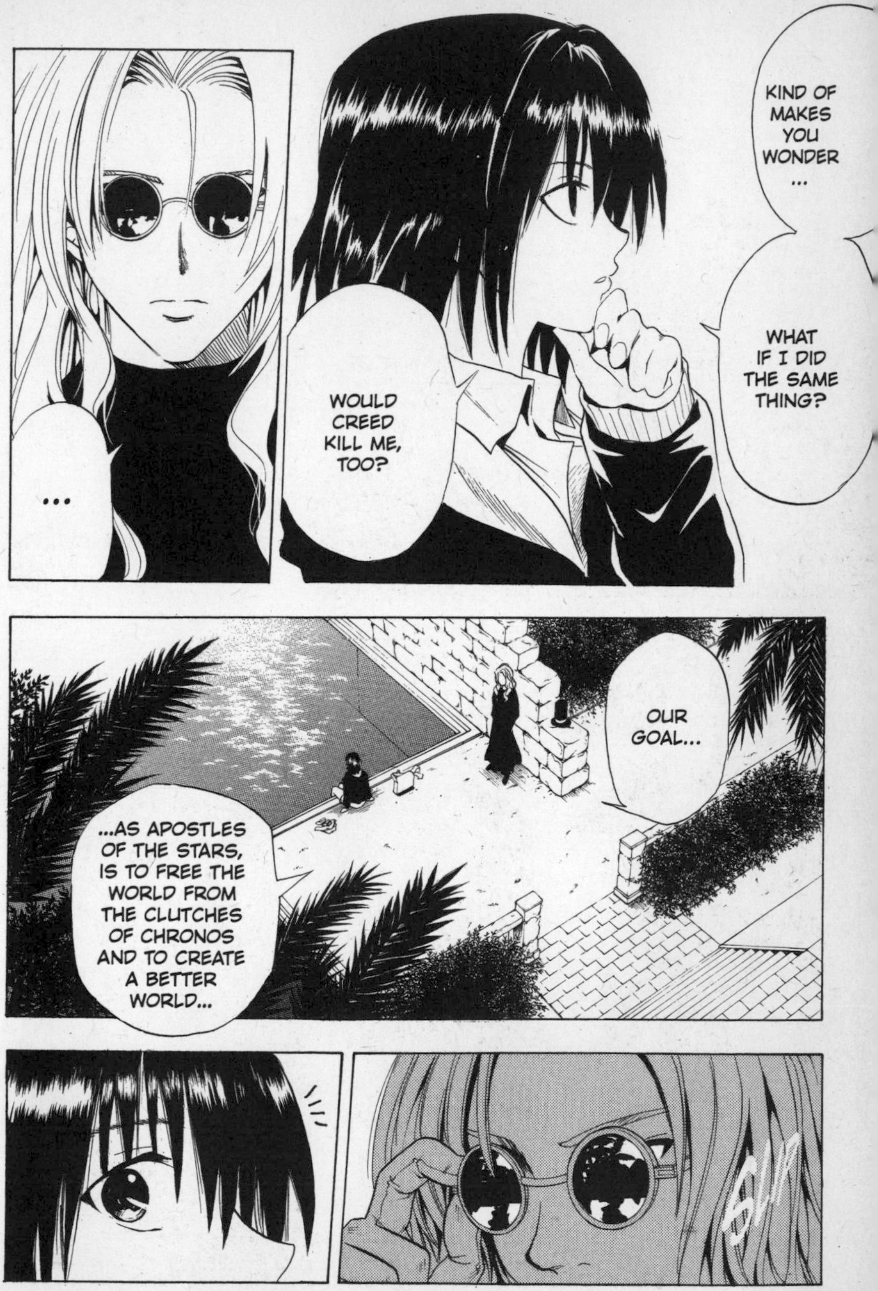
KIND OF MAKES YOU WONDER ...
WHAT IF I DID THE SAME THING?
WOULD CREED KILL ME, TOO?
...
OUR GOAL...
...AS APOSTLES OF THE STARS, IS TO FREE THE WORLD FROM THE CLUTCHES OF CHRONOS AND TO CREATE A BETTER WORLD...
SLIP

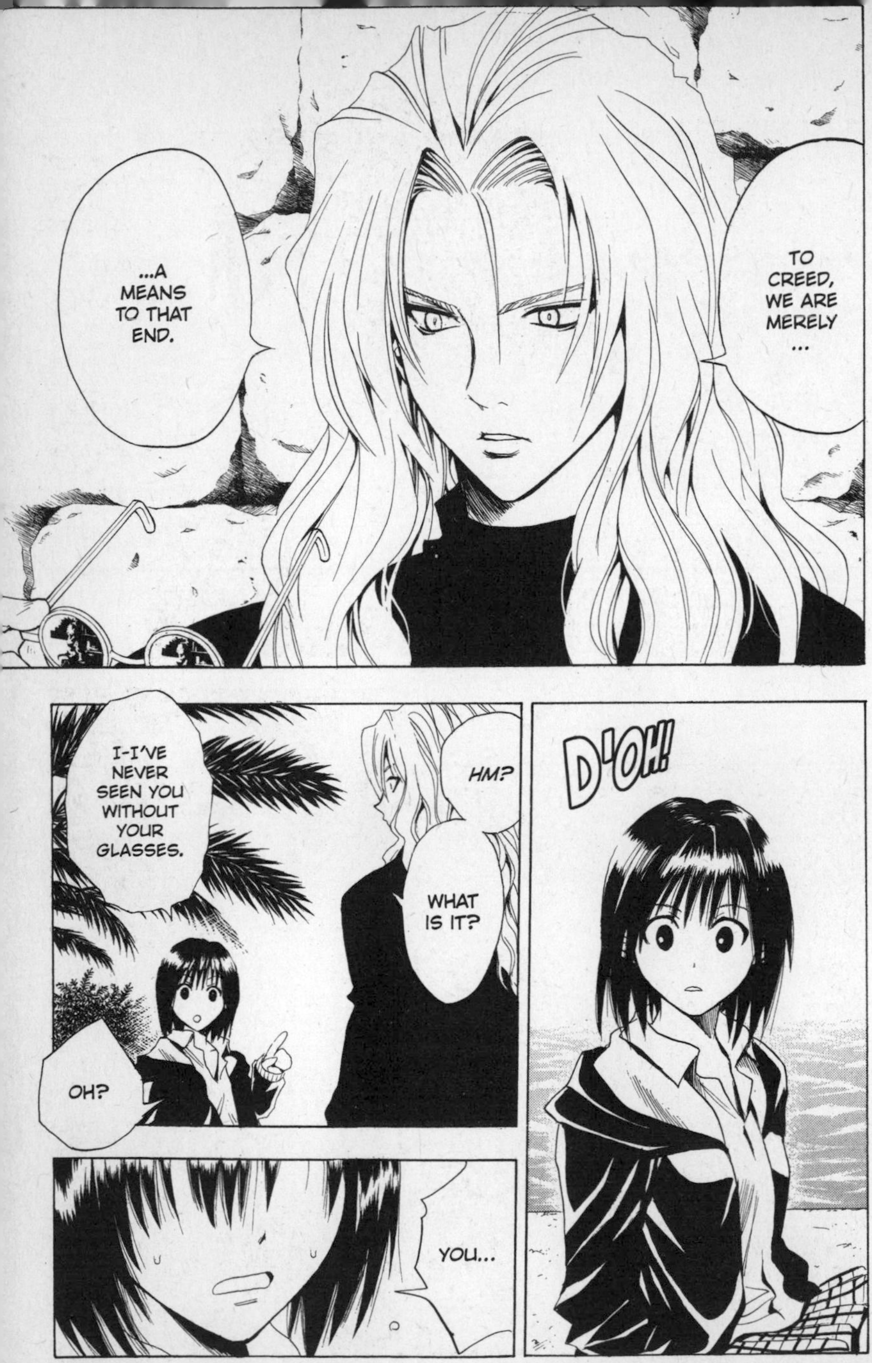
TO CREED, WE ARE MERELY ...
...A MEANS TO THAT END.
D'OH!
HM?
WHAT IS IT?
I-I'VE NEVER SEEN YOU WITHOUT YOUR GLASSES.
OH?
YOU...

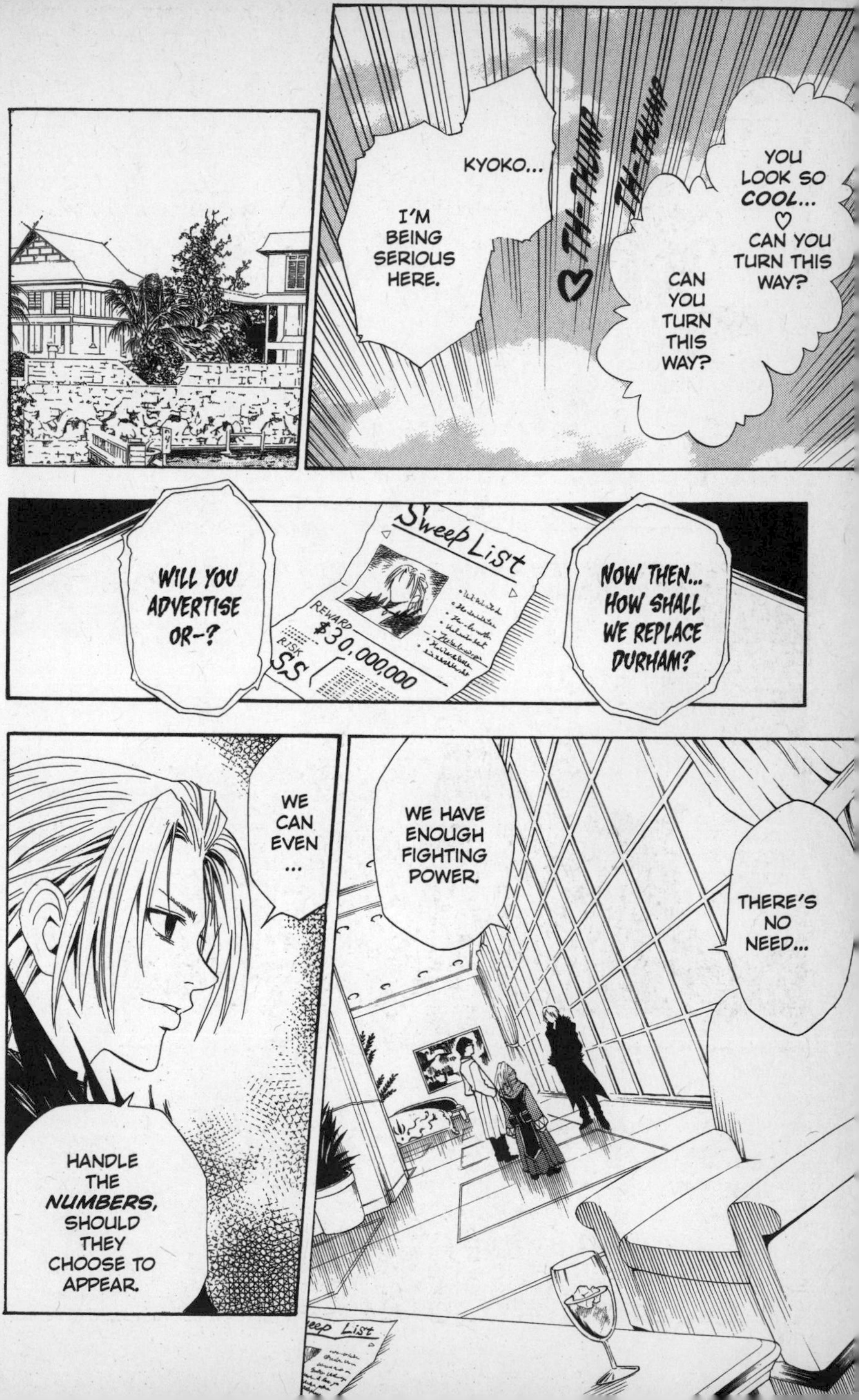
YOU LOOK SO COOL... ♡ CAN YOU TURN THIS WAY?
CAN YOU TURN THIS WAY?
♡ TH-THUMP TH-THUMP
KYOKO...
I'M BEING SERIOUS HERE.
NOW THEN... HOW SHALL WE REPLACE DURHAM?
Sweep List
REWARD $30,000,000
RISK SS
WILL YOU ADVERTISE OR-?
THERE'S NO NEED...
WE HAVE ENOUGH FIGHTING POWER.
WE CAN EVEN ...
HANDLE THE NUMBERS, SHOULD THEY CHOOSE TO APPEAR.

READ THIS WAY

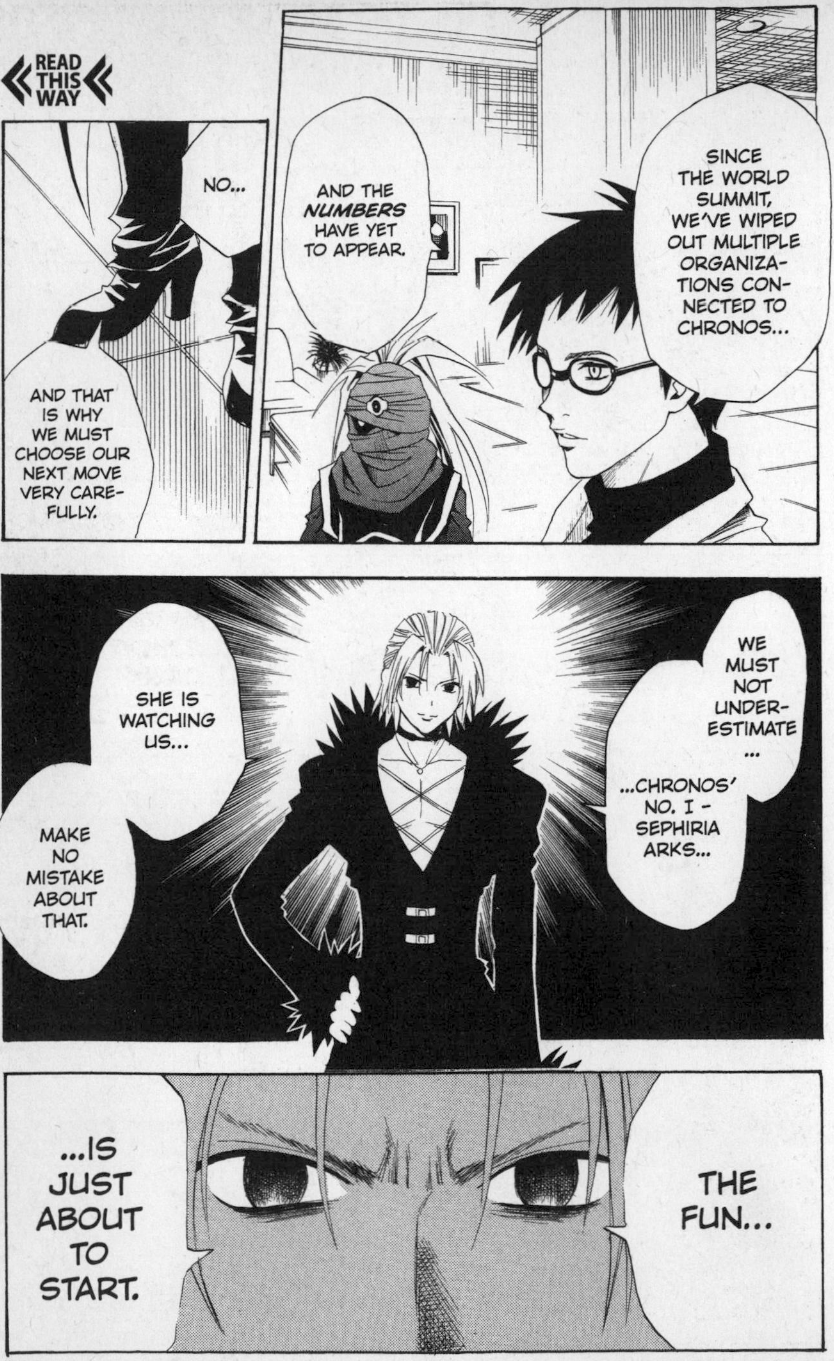
SINCE THE WORLD SUMMIT, WE'VE WIPED OUT MULTIPLE ORGANIZATIONS CONNECTED TO CHRONOS...
AND THE *NUMBERS* HAVE YET TO APPEAR.
NO...
AND THAT IS WHY WE MUST CHOOSE OUR NEXT MOVE VERY CAREFULLY.
WE MUST NOT UNDERESTIMATE...
...CHRONOS' NO. I - SEPHIRIA ARKS...
SHE IS WATCHING US...
MAKE NO MISTAKE ABOUT THAT.
THE FUN...
...IS JUST ABOUT TO START.

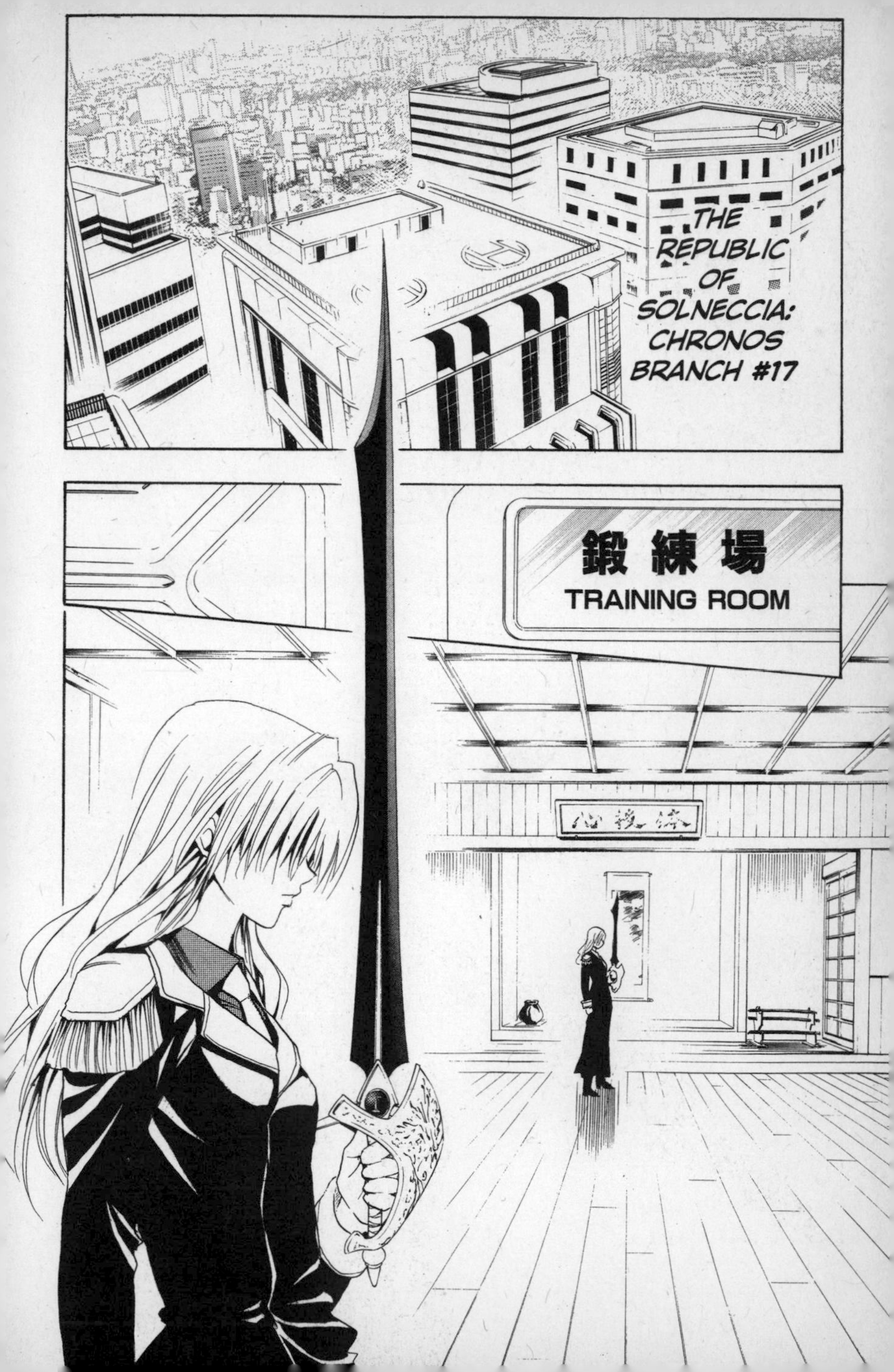
THE REPUBLIC OF SOLNECCIA: CHRONOS BRANCH #17
鍛練場
TRAINING ROOM

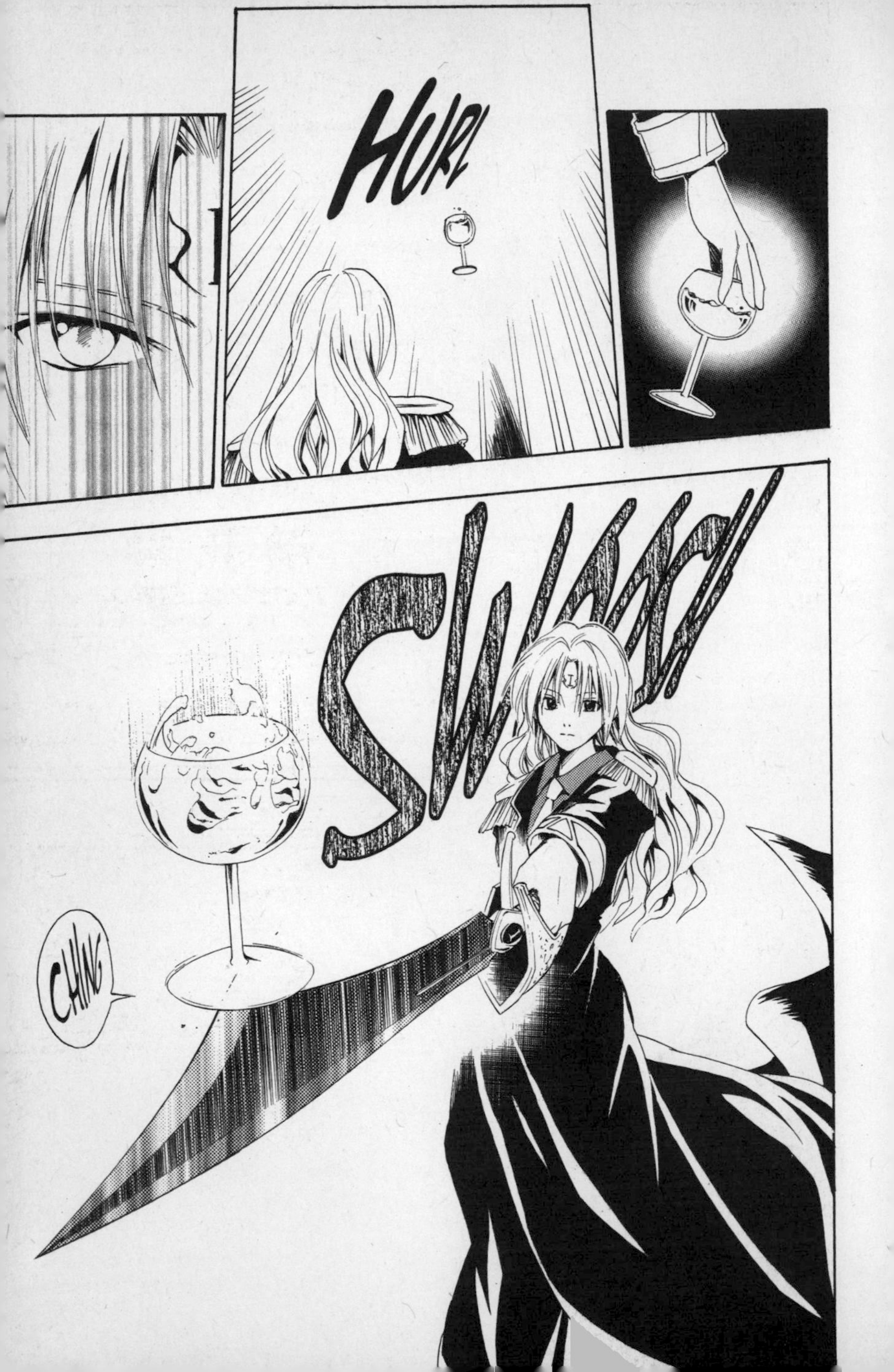
HURL
SWOOSH
CHING

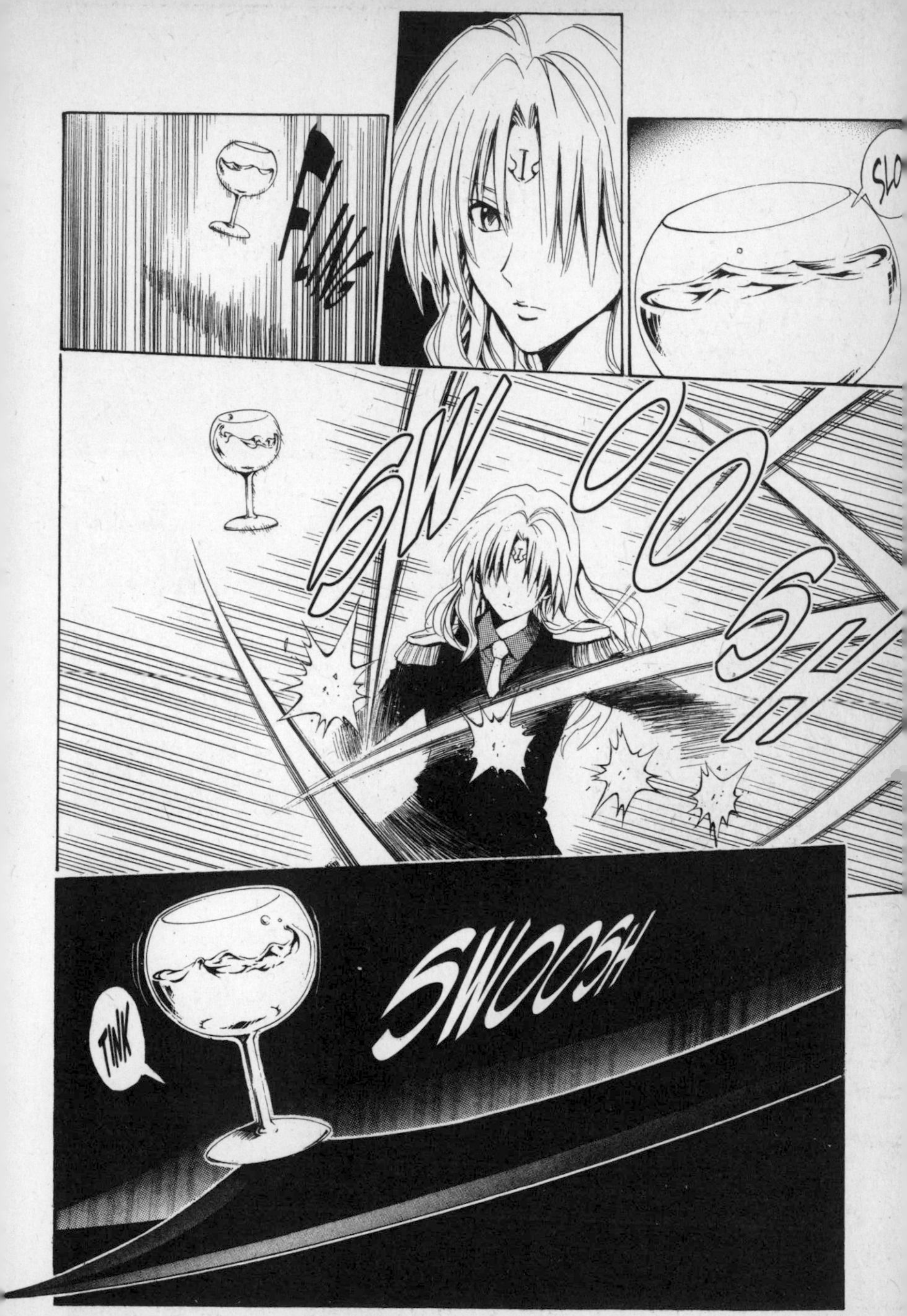
SLO
FLING
SWOOOSH
SWOOSH
TINK

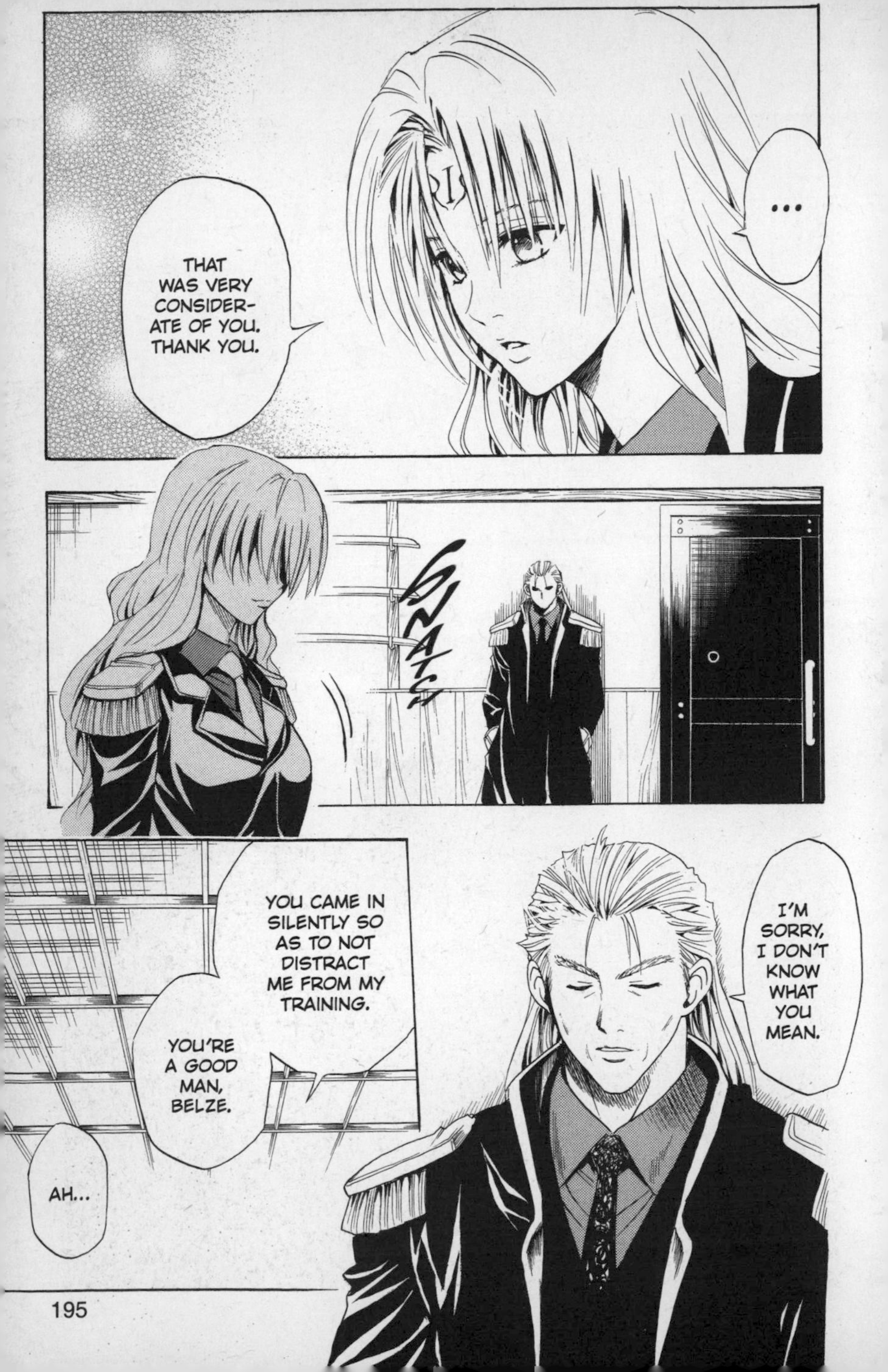
...
THAT WAS VERY CONSIDER-ATE OF YOU. THANK YOU.
SNATCH
I'M SORRY, I DON'T KNOW WHAT YOU MEAN.
YOU CAME IN SILENTLY SO AS TO NOT DISTRACT ME FROM MY TRAINING.
YOU'RE A GOOD MAN, BELZE.
AH...

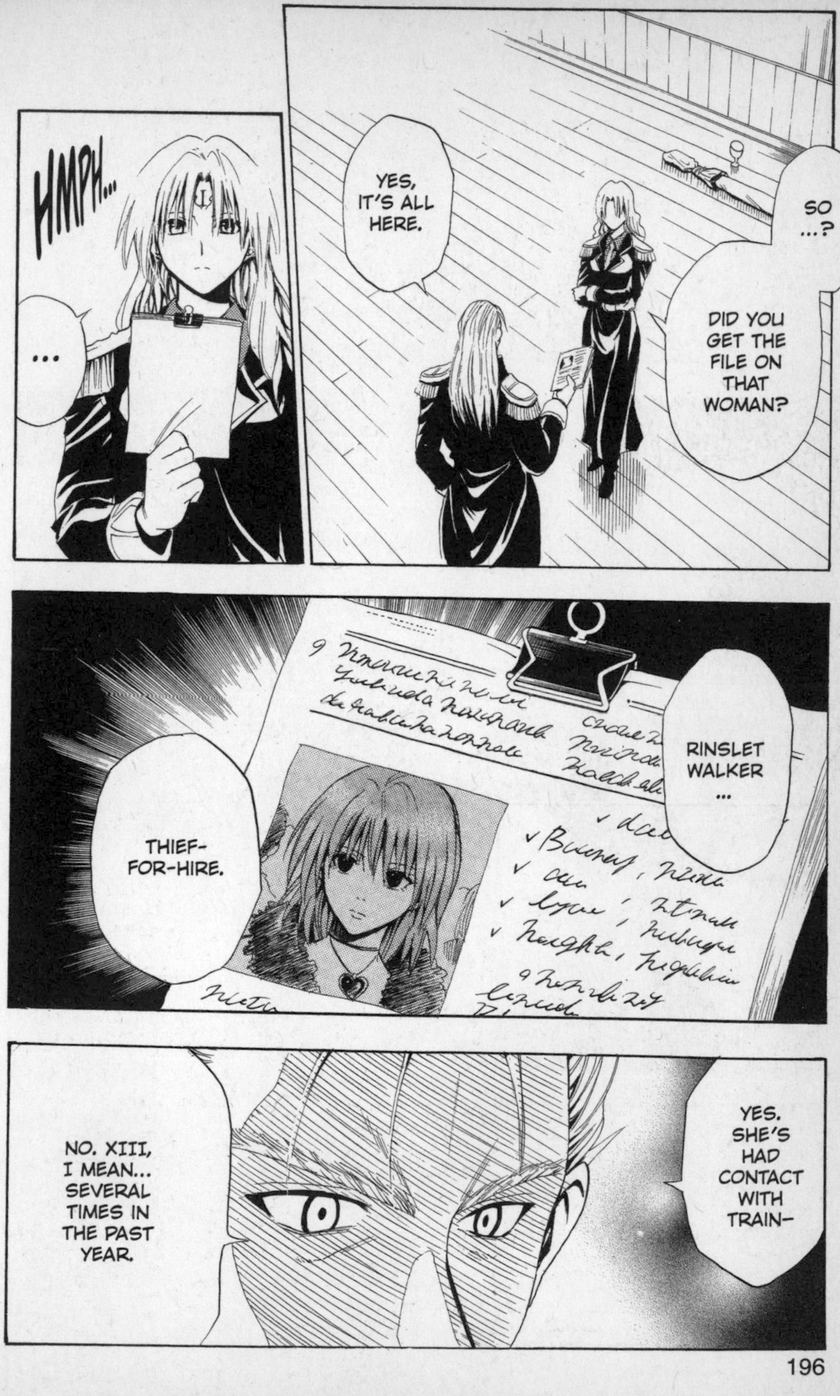
SO ...?
DID YOU GET THE FILE ON THAT WOMAN?
YES, IT'S ALL HERE.
HMPH...
...
RINSLET WALKER ...
THIEF-FOR-HIRE.
YES. SHE'S HAD CONTACT WITH TRAIN—
NO. XIII, I MEAN... SEVERAL TIMES IN THE PAST YEAR.

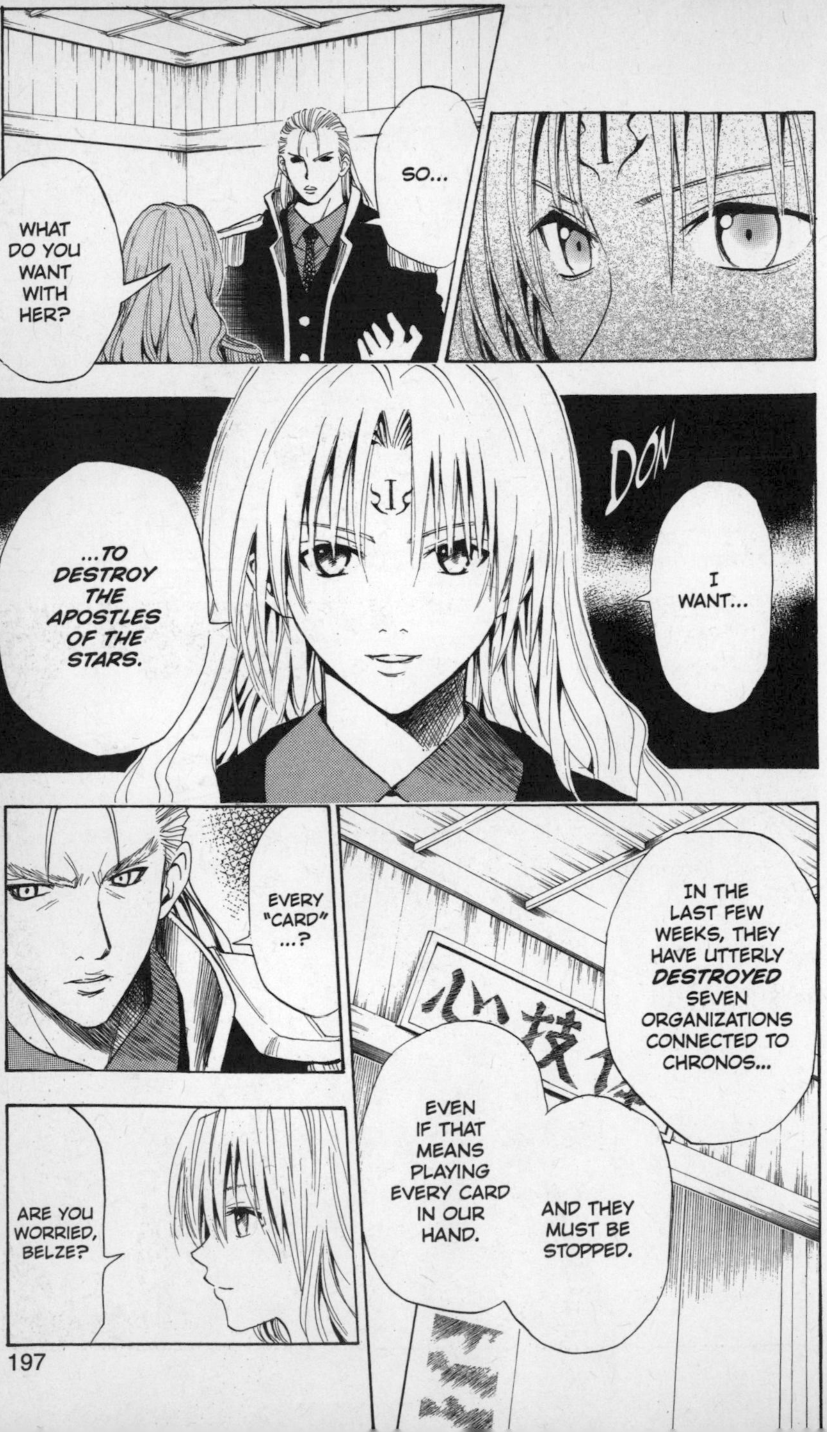
SO...
WHAT DO YOU WANT WITH HER?
DON
I WANT...
...TO DESTROY THE APOSTLES OF THE STARS.
IN THE LAST FEW WEEKS, THEY HAVE UTTERLY DESTROYED SEVEN ORGANIZATIONS CONNECTED TO CHRONOS...
AND THEY MUST BE STOPPED.
EVEN IF THAT MEANS PLAYING EVERY CARD IN OUR HAND.
EVERY "CARD" ...?
ARE YOU WORRIED, BELZE?

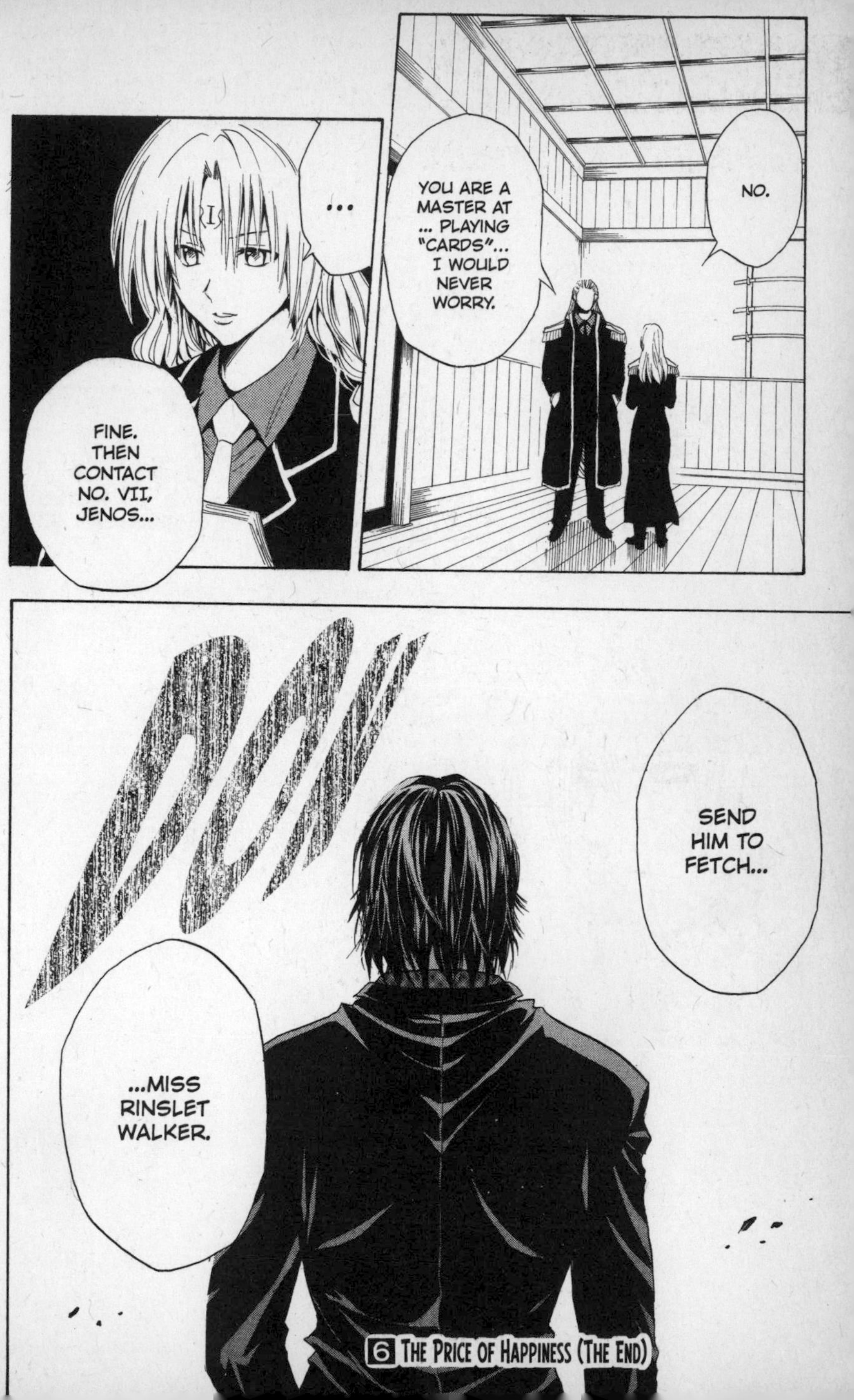
NO.
YOU ARE A MASTER AT ... PLAYING "CARDS"... I WOULD NEVER WORRY.
...
FINE. THEN CONTACT NO. VII, JENOS...
SEND HIM TO FETCH...
...MISS RINSLET WALKER.
6 THE PRICE OF HAPPINESS (THE END)

SKETCHES: NUMBER 3

◎ CHARDEN'S FACE: REVEALED!!

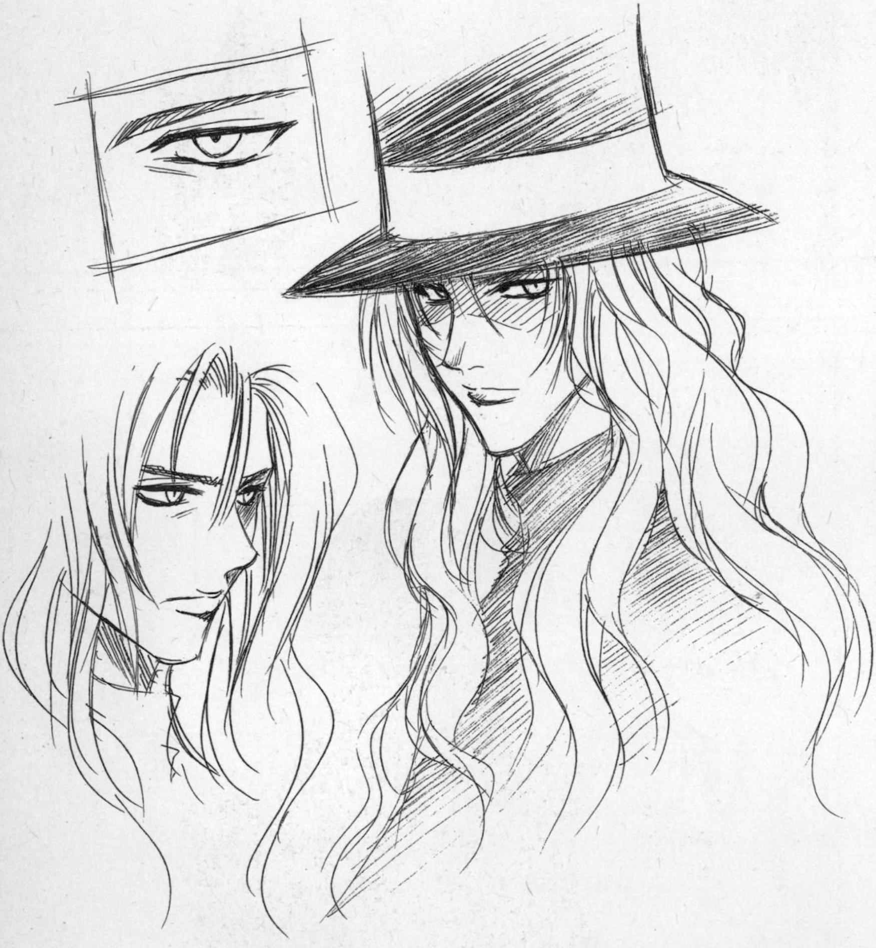

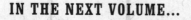

IN THE NEXT VOLUME...

On the wrong side of an eerie case of déjà vu, Train comes to the aid of a troubled boy seeking revenge for the death of his parents and is forced to confront his own vengeance-laden past. Meanwhile, Rinslet creates a shaky new relationship with a dangerous old enemy.

AVAILABLE MARCH 2007! ◄ ◄ ◄ ◄ ◄

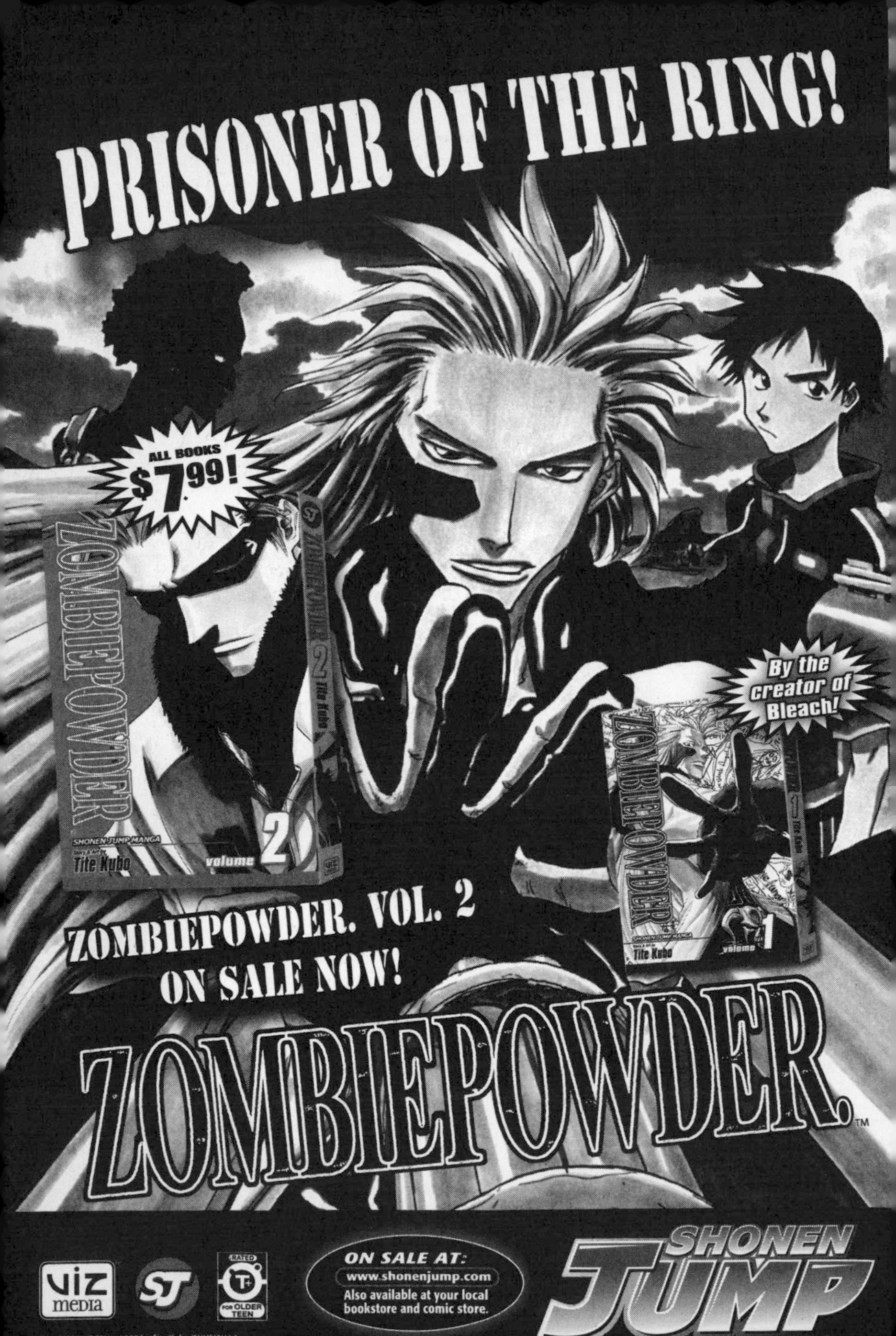

PRISONER OF THE RING!
ALL BOOKS $7.99!
ZOMBIEPOWDER. 2 Tite Kubo
SHONEN JUMP MANGA
Story & Art by Tite Kubo
volume 2
By the creator of Bleach!
ZOMBIEPOWDER. 1 Tite Kubo
SHONEN JUMP MANGA
Tite Kubo
volume 1
ZOMBIEPOWDER. VOL. 2
ON SALE NOW!
ZOMBIEPOWDER.™
viz media
SJ
RATED T+ FOR OLDER TEEN
ON SALE AT:
www.shonenjump.com
Also available at your local bookstore and comic store.
SHONEN JUMP

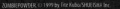

D.Gray-Man ™

Vol. 4
On sale Feb. 6!

Allen begins to probe the "Clan of Noah" mystery—the very reason he became an exorcist!

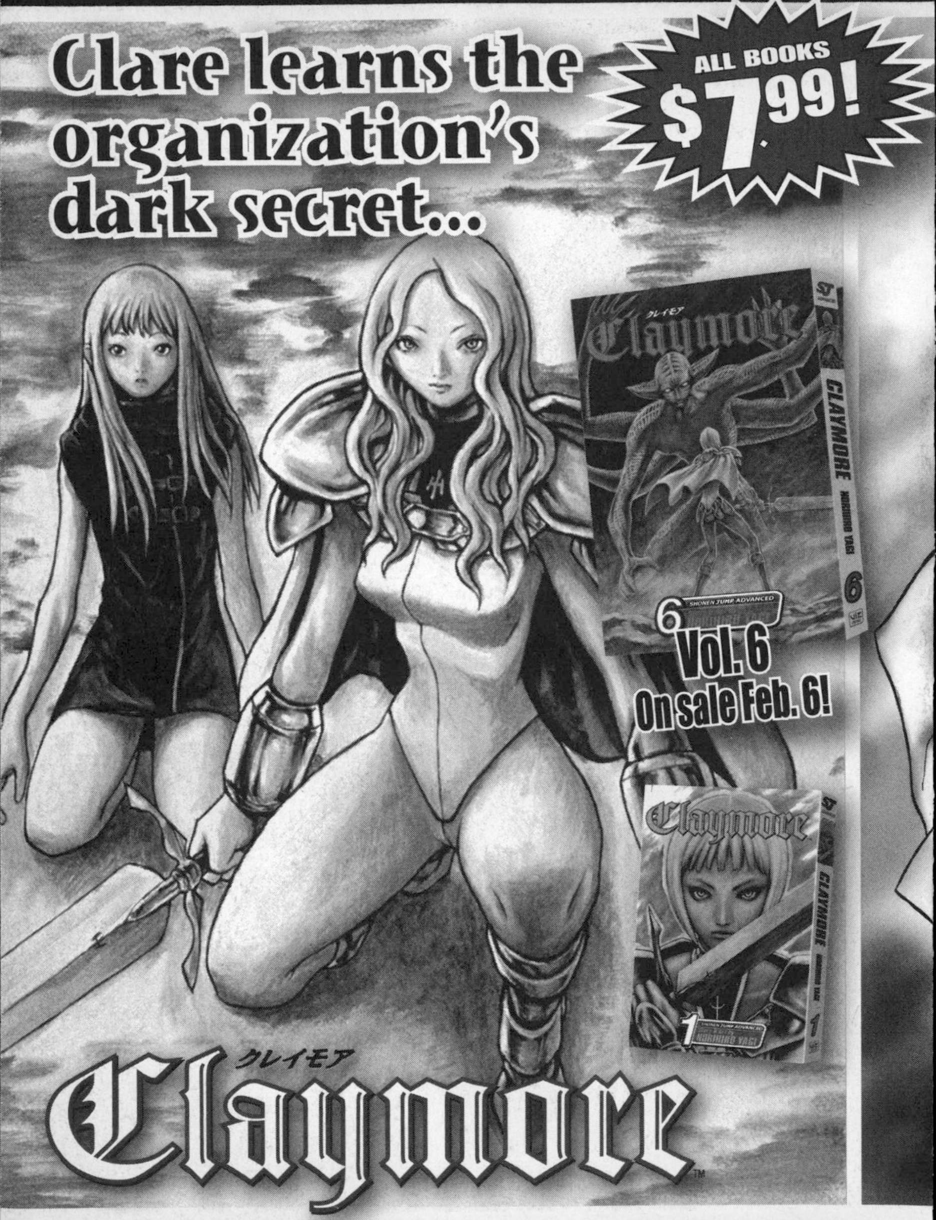
Clare learns the organization's dark secret...
ALL BOOKS $7.99!
Vol. 6
On sale Feb. 6!
クレイモア
Claymore™

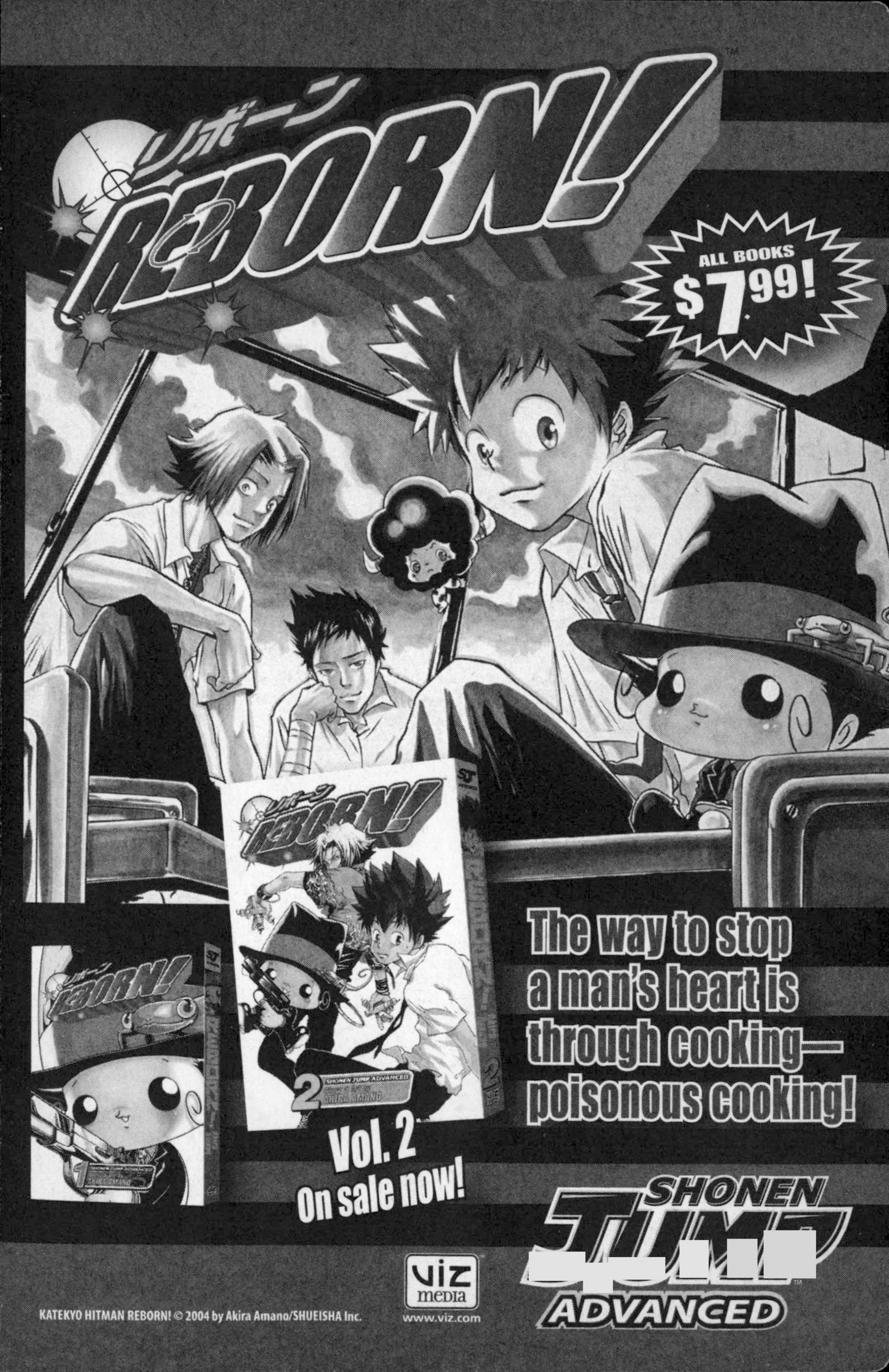

リボーン
REBORN!
ALL BOOKS $7.99!
The way to stop a man's heart is through cooking—poisonous cooking!
Vol. 2 On sale now!
SHONEN JUMP ADVANCED
viz media
www.viz.com
KATEKYO HITMAN REBORN! © 2004 by Akira Amano/SHUEISHA Inc.

Tell us what you think about SHONEN JUMP manga!

Our survey is now available online.
Go to: www.*SHONENJUMP*.com/*mangasurvey*

Help us make our product offering better!

THE REAL ACTION STARTS IN...

www.shonenjump.com
THE WORLD'S MOST POPULAR MANGA

ADVANCED

media

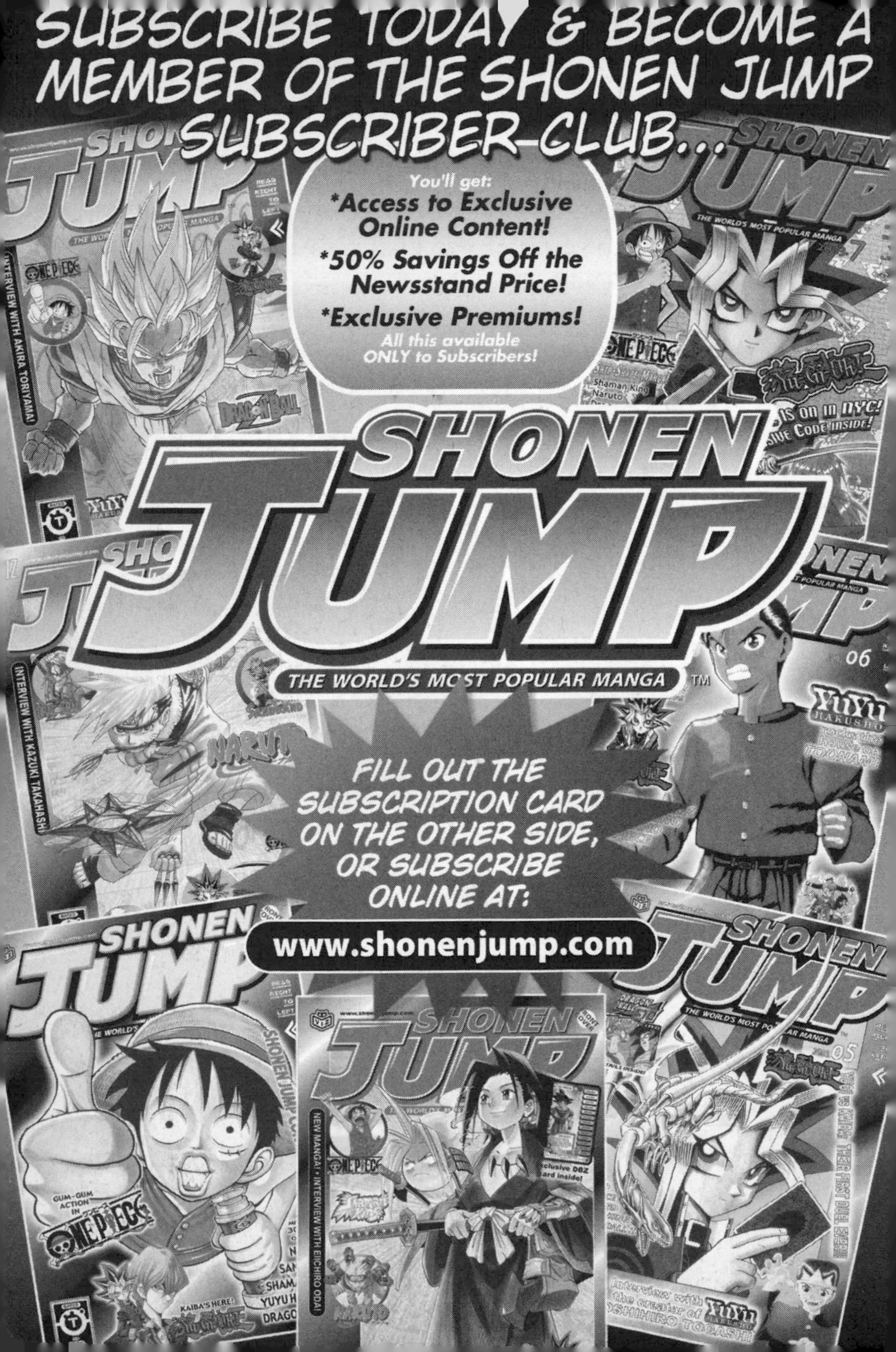
SUBSCRIBE TODAY & BECOME A MEMBER OF THE SHONEN JUMP SUBSCRIBER CLUB...
You'll get:
*Access to Exclusive Online Content!
*50% Savings Off the Newsstand Price!
*Exclusive Premiums!
All this available ONLY to Subscribers!
SHONEN JUMP
THE WORLD'S MOST POPULAR MANGA ™
FILL OUT THE SUBSCRIPTION CARD ON THE OTHER SIDE, OR SUBSCRIBE ONLINE AT:
www.shonenjump.com